TRA
Liter   on

INDIAN
SUBCONTINENT

EDITED BY
SIMON WEIGHTMAN

PASSPORT BOOKS
a division of *NTC Publishing Group*
Lincolnwood, Illinois USA

Published by Passport Books
a division of NTC Publishing Group
4255 West Touhy Avenue
Lincolnwood (Chicago), Illinois
60646-1975

ISBN 0-8442-8970-1
Library of Congress Catalog Card Number: on file

First published by In Print Publishing Ltd.

Typeset by MC Typeset
Printed by Bell & Bain, Glasgow
Front & back cover photos by Photo Network

Also available in the Traveller's Literary Companion series:
Africa
Japan
South-east Asia
South & Central America
Eastern & Central Europe

SERIES FOREWORD

This series of *Traveller's Literary Companions* is the series I have been looking for all my travelling life. Discovering new writers and new countries is one of the greatest pleasures we know, and these books will greatly increase the enjoyment of all who consult them. Each volume is packed with scholarly and entertaining historical, geographical, political and above all literary information. A country lives through its literature, and we have here an illustrated survey not only of a country's own writers, but also of the views of foreigners, explorers, tourists and exiles. The only problem I foresee is that each volume will bring about a compulsive desire to book a ticket on the next flight out.

The writers take us back in the past to each country's cultural origins, and bring us right up to the present with extracts from novels, poems and travel writings published in the 1980s and 1990s. The chapter introductions and the biographical information about the writers are invaluable, and will give any traveller an easy and immediate access to the past and present state of each nation. Conversation with hosts, colleagues or strangers on trains will be greatly assisted. An enormous amount of work has gone into the compiling and annotating of each volume, and the balance of fact and comment seems to me to be expertly judged.

Margaret Drabble

List of Maps

The Indian Sub-continent .... (x)
Pakistan and North-west India 39
Kipling's India 51
Central and North India 95
West India and Rajasthan 155
South India 213
North-east India and Bangladesh 265
Nepal 331
Sri Lanka 359

CONTENTS

Series Foreword: *Margaret Drabble* .... (iii)

List of Maps .... (iv)

Contributors .... (vi)

Using the *Companion* ....(viii)

Introduction: *Simon Weightman* .... (ix)

Classical Literature: *John D. Smith* 1

Pakistan and North-west India: *Christopher Shackle* 37

Central and North India: *Rupert Snell* 94

West India and Rajasthan: *Ian Raeside* 154

South India: *Geoffrey Holden* 212

North-east India and Bangladesh: *William Radice* 263

Nepal: *Michael Hutt* 329

Sri Lanka: *Christopher Reynolds* 358

Acknowledgments and Citations 404

Index 410

Contributors

Rachel Dwyer is Lecturer in Gujarati at the School of Oriental and African Studies (SOAS), University of London. Her PhD research was on the Gujarati lyrics of Dayaram and she is currently working on popular culture in India. She made additional contributions to several of the chapters.

Geoffrey Holden lives in the Netherlands. In addition to a collection of short stories inspired by the Parsi community in Bombay, he has also written extensively on the evolution of fictional identities in Portuguese Ceylon, a development of his doctoral thesis.

Michael Hutt is Senior Lecturer in Nepali at SOAS. His publications include *Himalayan Voices: An Introduction to Modern Nepali Literature* (1991), *Nepal: A Guide to the Art and Architecture of the Kathmandu Valley* (1994), *Nepal in the Nineties: Versions of the Past, Visions of the Future* (1993) and *Bhuttan: Perspectives on Conflict and Dissent (1994)*.

William Radice has a doctorate in Bengali literature from Oxford and is Lecturer in Bengali at SOAS. He is best known for his translations of Rabindranath Tagore's *Selected Poems* (1985) and *Selected Short Stories* (1994). He has also published *Teach Yourself Bengali* (1994) and five volumes of his own poetry.

Ian Raeside is former Senior Lecturer in Marathi and Gujarati at SOAS. His publications include *The Rough and the Smooth* (1966), *Wild Bapu of Garambi* (1969), *The Decade of Panipat (1751–61)* (1984) and *Gadyaraj: A Fourteenth Century Marathi Version of the Krsna Legend* (1988).

Christopher H.B. Reynolds is former Lecturer in Sinhalese at SOAS. He received an honorary doctorate from the University of Colombo in 1991. His publications include two anthologies of Sinhalese literature in translation, published for UNESCO in 1970 and 1987.

Christopher Shackle is Professor of Modern Languages of South Asia at SOAS. He has written many articles on Panjabi and Urdu literatures. He is co-author with D.J. Matthews and Shahrukh Husain of *Qasida Poetry in Islamic Asia and Africa* (1985) and co-editor with Stefan Sperl of *Qasida Poetry in Islamic Asia and Africa* (1996).

John D. Smith is Lecturer in Sanskrit at the University of Cambridge. He has written articles on Indian epic literature, including the Sanskrit *Mahabharata* and *Ramayana* and has also published *The Epic of Pabuji*. He is currently working on an abridged English translation of the *Mahabharata*.

Rupert Snell is Reader in Hindi at SOAS. His connection with India first developed through a fondness for Indian music. His research interests include the literature of the 16th and 17th centuries in the Braj Bhasa dialect; his publications on this subject include *The Hindi Classical Tradition: A Braj Bhasa Reader* (1991) and *The Eighty-Four Hymns of Hita Harivamsa* (1991). He is also co-author with Simon Weightman of *Teach Yourself Hindi* (1989).

Simon Weightman is Senior Lecturer in the religions of South Asia and head of the Department for the Study of Religions at SOAS. His special interests include Hindi, medieval literature, Hinduism and Sufism. He is the author of *Hinduism in the Village Setting* (1976) and co-author with Rupert Snell of *Teach Yourself Hindi* (1989) as well as of numerous journal articles.

Using the Companion

Each region of the sub-continent has its own chapter, subdivided into four distinct sections: (1) an introduction to the geography and cultural and political background; (2) a Booklist giving full publishing details of all the books mentioned in the introduction and extracted; (3) a selection of extracts; (4) biographical details and summaries of major works.

Extracts are ordered alphabetically by place and each is assigned a number to make it easy to locate from elsewhere in the chapter.

The **symbol** ◊ after an author's name indicates that there is a biographical entry in the chapter.

Bold type is used to highlight references to places.

There is a general **index of authors** at the end of the book.

INTRODUCTION

Simon Weightman

> The slow movement seems,
> somehow, to say much more /
> To watch the rarer birds, you
> have to go / Along deserted
> lanes and where the rivers
> flow / In silence near the
> source, or by a shore /
> Remote and thorny like the
> heart's dark floor.
> '*Poet, Lover, Birdwatcher*'
> *Nissim Ezekiel*

The purpose of this *Traveller's Literary Companion* is to introduce interested travellers to the Indian sub-continent, whether actual or armchair, to the rich and varied literatures that were born in and belong to the very places through which they will pass, so that their encounter will not be restricted to the visual and anecdotal, but will include, in some measure, a deeper contact with the spirit of the place. To someone coming to South Asia for the first time, perhaps the overwhelming impressions will be the geographical vastness of the sub-continent, the great diversity of its regions, but, above all, the unique blend of the ancient and the modern, of tradition and modernity, that characterizes almost every scene. Such impressions are not misleading, since these are the defining characteristics of almost all aspects of the culture of South Asia, whether religious, artistic or literary. In every domain there is a vast wealth of material, an enormously rich diversity, and the continuity of the traditional alongside modernity and change. In no field is this more apparent than in literature. Any introduction to South Asian literature must, therefore, first seek to establish the scale of its human and geographical extension, and then determine the nature of its historical depths.

Consider first the sheer human scale of the sub-continent; the population of its various countries at present totals over 800 million people. Furthermore, not only is this vast population spread over a huge geographical area, but it is in no sense homogeneous, displaying great ethnic, cultural, religious and linguistic diversity. Although there

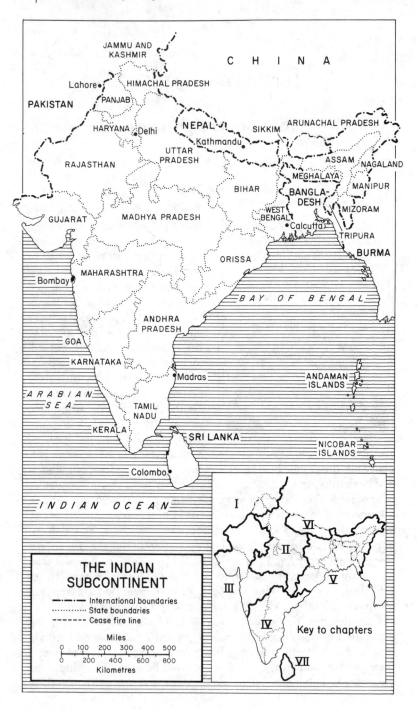

are 18 major regional languages, the number of dialects in which everyday conversation is conducted runs to several hundred. For the purposes of this guide, a division has been made into seven regions (see Map 1 on page x): **Pakistan and north-west India**, where the main regional languages are Urdu, Panjabi, Kashmiri and Sindhi; the **central and northern region**, incorporating Uttar Pradesh. Madhya Pradesh and Bihar, where the main languages are Hindi and Urdu; **western India**, incorporating Maharashtra, Gujerat and Rajasthan, where the main languages are Marathi, Gujarati and Rajasthani; the **south**, incorporating Karnataka, Andhra Pradesh, Tamil Nadu and Kerala, where the main languages are Kannada, Telegu, Tamil, and Malayalam; the **eastern region**, incorporating Bangladesh, Bengal, Orissa and Assam, where the main languages are Bengali, Oriya and Assamese; **Nepal**; where the main language is Nepali; and **Sri Lanka**, where the main languages are Sinhalese and Tamil. All of these languages except for the four southern ones are Indo-Aryan languages and belong to the great Indo-European family of languages. They are therefore related to English, French, German, etc albeit at some remove. The four southern languages, Tamil, Telegu, Kannada and Malayalam, belong to the Dravidian family of languages. There are, additionally, tribal languages, some with flourishing oral literatures, which belong to other language families, but these are beyond the scope of the present volume.

Having looked at the geographical and human scale of our subject, and the diversity of literary languages, there is now the historical dimension to consider. Literature as we know it begins in South Asia with the arrival of the Aryans in the north-west around the middle of the second millenium BC, that is 3 500 years ago. The Harrapan culture, which flourished in this region from about 2 300 to 1 700 BC and is primarily associated with the city sites of **Harrapa** and **Mohenjo Daro**, was probably already in decline. The script of this Indus valley culture remains undeciphered to this day. The Aryans brought with them the early Vedic religion, a sacrificial cult whose purpose lay in honouring the gods to win blessings of various kinds. The priestly class of Aryan society transmitted the sacrificial Vedic hymns orally with extraordinary accuracy, and amongst these hymns are some of considerable literary merit. The various Aryan tribes and clans gradually moved eastwards towards the Gangetic plain, taking with them the spoken dialects from which the modern Indo-Aryan languages were later to derive.[1]

---

[1]Historically Indo-Aryan is divided into three stages: Old Indo-Aryan, comprising Vedic and classical Sanskrit; Middle Indo-Aryan, comprising Pali, Prakrit and Apabhramsha; and New Indo-Aryan, comprising the medieval and then the modern forms of the

The eastward expansion of the Indo-Aryans led to the establishment of a number of independent kingdoms leading in turn to the first true empire, centred in what is now southern **Bihar**, which was established by Chandragupta Maurya whose rule began in 321 BC. The third Mauryan emperor was the great Ashoka who became a major patron of Buddhism. During his reign great efforts were made to propagate Buddhism and the Pali Buddhist cannon was codified in what is now modern **Patna**. A Hindu general wrested power from the last Mauryan emperor in 184 BC, but the dynasty he founded was ended by 72 BC. The following period was one of fragmentation, marked by incursions into the north-west by Greeks, Scythians and Iranians. Uncertain as the political picture was, Hinduism was certainly evolving, both by internal development, evidenced by a change of emphasis from a ritualistic religion to a faith offering a more personal relationship with a deity, and also by assimilation, as more local cults were brought into the developing mythologies of Vishnu and Shiva. In literature the two great Indian epics, the *Ramayana* (Classical Literature, Extract 15), which is held to have developed between 200 BC to 200 AD, and the *Mahabharata* (Classical Literature, Extract 11), whose beginnings were probably in the middle of the first millenium BC, but which was not finalized until about 400 AD, provide evidence of considerable religious and literary activity and growth throughout this period. Meanwhile, in the far south, in three small Tamil kingdoms, the foundations were being laid for what was to become a prolific and vigorous literature in Tamil.

The 'golden age' of Hindu civilization is generally considered to be the age of the Guptas, from 320 AD until the middle of the 7th century. It was during this period that Sanskrit literature reached its highest point with the Ujjain poet and dramatist Kalidasa (Classical Literature, Extracts 4, 8, 13), whose works, displaying freshness and vitality combined with polish and sophistication, place him amongst the world's finest writers. The story of Sanskrit literature is well told in the chapter 'Classical Literature'. Sanskrit literature is not only important and valuable in its own right, it also provided a rich source of

languages already given. Each stage is marked by changes in phonology, grammar and vocabulary, overall in the direction of simplification and greater 'speakability'. Languages were often used for literary purposes long after they ceased to be spoken. Sanskrit, for example, probably had ceased to be spoken by the middle of the first millenium BC, but it was used as the main literary vehicle for religious and literary works certainly until 1 000 AD, and to a lesser extent after that. In this way it functioned in the same way as Latin in medieval Europe. The Middle Indo-Aryan languages were used for specialized purposes; Prakrit was used by Hindus for popular speech in Sanskrit plays, and for popular lyric poetry, and by Jains for scripture, while Pali was the major literary vehicle for Buddhism. The Middle Indo-Aryan period is considered to be from about 500 BC until about 1 000 AD.

inspiration for later authors, certainly up to the middle of the 19th century.[2] While it is true that this highly cultivated and sophisticated literary culture showed a tendency towards artificiality and over-elaborateness after the middle of the first millenium AD, this certainly is not apparent in one of the most loved and widely influential works of Indian literature, the twelfth century *Gitagovinda* of Jayadeva (Classical Literature, Extract 9), of which it has been said: 'Jayadeva's verses nowhere praise unbodied joy; they are explicitly sensual, and celebrate the sensual joy of divine love. Through imagery, tone colour, and rhythm, Jayadeva interweaves levels of physical and metaphysical associations, and the cosmic energy of Krishna's love with Radha is condensed into a religious ecstasy'.[3]

Returning to history, the 9th century Arab conquest of **Sind** was a harbinger of what was to come. After a number of partial incursions, in 1192 Muhammad of Ghur won a decisive victory over the Rajput chieftain Prithviraja which was to mark the beginning of many centuries of Muslim dominion in India. The first major period of Muslim rule is the Delhi Sultanate (1192–1526) within which there were five separate dynasties: the first, named the Slave Kings (1206–1290), was founded by Qutb ud Din Aibak, a general and former Turkish slave who, on the death of Muhammad of Ghur in 1206, assumed the title of Sultan. The Slave Kings were followed by the Khaljis (1290–1320), the Tughluqs (1320–1388), the Sayyids (1414–1450) and the Lodis (1450–1526). The Sultanate expanded its dominion until about 1340 during the rule of Muhammad Tughluq, at which point it held sway over virtually the whole of the sub-continent except for a few pockets, mainly in the far south. Thereafter its influence contracted as regions revolted, and independent kingdoms, both Muslim and Hindu, were established. Independent Muslim kingdoms were founded in Bengal, Jaunpur, Gujarat and Kashmir, the most powerful being the Bahmani kingdom in the **Deccan** (1347–1512) which continued in the form of the five kingdoms of **Golkonda, Ahmadnagar, Berar, Bidar** and **Bijapur** until the first half of the 17th century. Independent Hindu kingdoms were established in **Orissa, Mewar, Assam** and **Nepal** with the most splendid being the Telegu

[2]One category of works that is not dealt with in this chapter but which also provided a rich source for later writers are the great compendiums of mythology called the *Puranas* which began to be produced during the Gupta age. One in particular, the *Bhagavata Purana*, which shows strong influences of Tamil devotional poetry and was probably finalized during the 9th or 10th century, was the major source for much of the devotional Krishnaite literature produced in such profusion in the later centuries.

[3]Barbara Stoller Miller, *Love Song of the Dark Lord*, Columbia University Press, New York, 1977, p 17. The first English translation was by Sir William Jones in 1792 which Goethe was familiar with through Dalberg's German rendering. One of the most loved English translations was Sir Edwin Arnold's *The Indian Song of Songs* (1875).

kingdom of **Vijayanagar** (1336–1646). By the death of the last Lodi
Sultan, Ibrahim, in 1526, the Sultanate of Delhi comprised only the
areas of the **Panjab** and modern **Uttar Pradesh** and **Bihar**.

The second major period of Muslim domination was the Mughal
empire (1526–1757). The founder of the empire was Babur (1526–
1530), a Chagatai Turk and descendant of Tamberlane who overthrew
Ibrahim Lodi in the battle of **Panipat** in 1526, having previously taken
Kabul and **Lahore**. By the time of his death four years later he had
subdued most of northern India. His son, Humayun (1530–1556),
however, was defeated by the Afghan chieftain Sher Shah in 1539 and
retreated to Persia to retrench, only recapturing **Lahore** and **Delhi** just
before his death in 1556. It was under Humayun's son Akbar (1556–
1605) that the Mughal empire really established its power and
dominion. He established Mughal authority over the whole of north,
west and central India, leaving only the Deccan in the hands of the
independent Muslim kingdoms. Akbar was followed as Emperor by
Jahangir (1605–1627), Shah Jahan (1627–1659), who had the Taj
Mahal built, and Aurangzeb (1659–1707). By the death of Aurangzeb
virtually the whole of India was under Mughal control, but the empire
was essentially too large to be sustainable, and its disintegration now
began with quarrels over the succession. The Deccan became independent in 1729; Avadh (Oudh) became virtually independent with a
magnificent new capital at Lucknow which drew luminaries and writers
from Delhi; **Bengal** fell to the British; the Jats became independent
around **Agra**; Afghans formed a state in **Rohilkhand** east of Delhi; and
the Sikhs were increasingly militant in the **Panjab**. In 1739 the Persian
Nadir Shah temporarily occupied **Delhi**, while in 1751 the Afghan
chieftain Ahmad Shah Abdali took **Kashmir**, and in 1757 looted
Delhi, being rewarded with the **Panjab**, **Sind**, **Sirhind** and **Kashmir**.
Only the Marathas, inspired by their former great leader Shivaji
(1627–1680), constituted any coherent force; they expanded northwards until in 1757 they too were defeated by Abdali at **Panipat**. It was
this state of confusion and weakness that provided the British with
their opportunity, but before the British period is considered it is
necessary to return to languages and literature.

Over the centuries, the Muslims brought to the sub-continent not
just a vigorous and compelling faith, but an entire evolving civilization.
This comprised law, theology, philosophy, science and mathematics,
medicine, art and architecture and a literary tradition, expressed
mainly in Arabic, Persian and Turkish, which was rich in works,
genres, themes and imagery, and which accorded high regard to men of
letters and learning. It could be said that literature was not a by-product
of Islamic civilization, but rather one of its most essential institutions.
Another institution of particular importance to the spread and develop-

ment of Islamic culture in the sub-continent, both spiritual and literary, was Sufism. Most of Indo-Muslim literature, certainly in the earlier period, was produced either by court-sponsored writers or by those supported by religious, particularly Sufi, institutions. The courts and the religious houses were not simply suppliers of patronage, however, they were the sources of inspiration for literature in all fields. Chronicles, histories and panegyrics, together with secular poetry and works in the various sciences were produced from the courts, while works of theology, philosophy, spiritual treatises and various genres of religious poetry such as lyrics and mystical romances were typically the products of the religious houses. Indo-Muslim literature is considerable both in quantity and quality; it was written in medieval times primarily in Persian, although some Arabic and Turkish literature was produced, and latterly in the New Indo-Aryan languages, to which we must now return.

It has been noted that Indo-Aryan underwent three stages of development: Old Indo-Aryan (Vedic and Sanskrit), Middle Indo-Aryan (the Prakrits, Pali and Apabhramsha), and New Indo-Aryan (Hindi, Bengali, Marathi, etc). The New Indo-Aryan languages emerged variously between 1 000 and 1 300 AD, although in most of the newly emerged languages there is little evidence of significant literary activity until the 14th and 15th centuries. How literature developed in each of the languages and regions is told in the following chapters but there are two generalities that should be mentioned. First, beginning from the 15th century in virtually all the new Indo-Aryan languages there was an outpouring of devotional poetry of varied inspiration that continued with undiminished vigour for over two centuries. Most of the finest works in these languages belong to this period, and, in contrast, the 18th century seems generally somewhat arid although there are, of course, exceptions. Second, classical Sanskrit had a pervasive influence on the development of these languages and literatures, supplying vocabulary, traditional themes and images, a preference for poetry over prose and increasingly a tendency towards the learned, the ornate and the artificial.

Mention should be made here of the emergence of Urdu. Urdu has as its basis the same grammatical structure (the dialect of Khari Boli) and much of the same vocabulary as modern spoken Hindi, but it developed as a literary vehicle for Muslim culture long before this dialect came to be used for literary purposes in Hindi which in medieval times had flourishing literatures in two other dialects, Braj Bhasa and Awadhi. While the Muslim authors in Delhi used Persian, from the middle of the 16th century Sufi writers in the Deccan and Gujarat began to produce religious works in Urdu which became increasingly Persianized. Only Persian metres were used in Urdu from 1580. With the conquest of Bijapur and Golkunda by Auranzeb, the centre of Urdu writing moved first to **Gujarat** (1680–1760), then to **Delhi** (1707–80) and finally to **Lucknow** (1780–1850) with the demise of the Mughal empire. The richness of Urdu literature makes it one of the most significant products of Indo-Muslim culture, although Muslims also contributed major works in many of the new Indo-Aryan languages.

Returning to history, the next period in the history of the Indian sub-continent is that of British expansion. Having been granted trading bases in the 17th century in **Calcutta**, **Madras** and **Bombay**, the British took advantage of the collapse of central authority to expand either by annexation or by treaty until they had almost total control over the sub-continent. There were several phases to this expansion: the annexation of **Bengal** after the battle of Plassey in 1757, the defeat of Avadh and the Mughal forces in 1764, the first Maratha war (1775–82), the defeat of **Mysore** in 1799 and the overthrow of **Hyderabad** in 1800, the second Maratha war (1803–05), the Gurkha wars (1814–16), the third Maratha war (1817–19), the conquest of **Sind** in 1843, and the Sikh wars (1845–49).

After the events of 1857–58, variously called 'The Mutiny', 'The First War of Independence' and 'The last gasp of the Mughal Empire', the British placed India under direct rule from London. No attempt can be made here to relate the events and processes that characterized the 100 years until India became independent in 1947 and Pakistan was born from partition. The introduction of the English language and Western culture, the coming of the printing press, the encouragement of prose, the spread of universities, libraries, schools and the emergence of a new middle class in cities, all had a direct impact on the literature of India. There were equally indirect results arising from reaction; the renaissance of Hinduism, the fostering of indigenous literatures, the birth of the Indian National Congress which brought Mahatma Gandhi to prominence, the re-foundation of the Muslim League by Jinnah which formulated the demand for a Muslim homeland in Pakistan, and the poetical restatement of Islam by Iqbal.

The consequences of all of this for the New Indo-Aryan and the Dravidian languages was a standardization and modernization in terms of grammatical usage and vocabulary, and, in the case of Hindi, the emergence of the Khari Boli dialect written in the Devanagari script as the main written form of Modern Standard Hindi. In literature, in many cases a modern literature had to be created totally *ab initio*. Until literacy, education and publishing were able to deliver a readership, individuals wrote often for themselves or a small circle of friends giving the early decades a patchy, random appearance across India as a whole, but it is possible to identify certain major periods or trends. The first phase was the initial awakening inspired by contact or conflict with the

West. This was followed by the phase of growth in national and moral consciousness inspired by Gandhi's leadership. A reactionary phase against moral austerity followed producing varieties of romanticism; in its turn to be followed in the 1930s by a literature of essentially Marxist inspiration. The next phase was characterized by experimentalism in both literary form and content. Independence brought a greater national awareness and hope, only to be followed by a disillusionment which gave birth to 'new writing' in almost every literature. The 'Modern Age' of Indian literature, which began around the middle of the 19th century, is now about 150 years old. This is very little in the 3 000 years of the sub-continent's literary history, but there has been an acceleration in the rate of progress and now each of the separate languages has been formed into a settled, established and mature cultural vehicle of considerable potential and most have already considerable literary achievements behind them.

Of course, one of the most culturally significant consequences of the British presence in India is the use of English, which is considered a curse by some, a blessing by others, but as both by most. India inspired non-Indian writers to produce a literature in English whose considerable proportions were not matched by its overall quality. Nevertheless, a handful of writers from Rudyard Kipling, through E.M. Forster to Paul Scott have produced works that are classics of their kind. Fine writers such as R.K. Narayan, and great orators like Jawaharlal Nehru, have added a valuable indigenous component to this literature in English which contains a number of classics such as Nirad Chaudhuri's *Autobiography of an Unknown Indian* (see 'East India and Bangladesh') which should certainly be read by any interested visitor to the sub-continent. In post-colonial times, and particularly in recent years, those who might be called both 'Midnight's children and grandchildren', some of whom were born, educated or lived outside the sub-continent and are, in most senses, bi-cultural, have established considerable literary reputations in English amongst cosmopolitan international audiences and won various literary awards. In poetry, one thinks of Nissim Ezekiel, for example, an extract from whom heads this introduction, while in prose there are Amitav Ghosh, Upamanyu Chatterjee and Vikram Seth from an ever-growing band of writers. In these cases the notion of a regional or national literature breaks down and they have perhaps to be regarded as contributing more to an evolving international literature that is only now coming to be.

This all too succinct survey of the languages, history and literatures of the sub-continent should enable the reader to contextualize the following chapters, each of which is written by a specialist who brings to it a lifetime's experience of teaching the languages and literatures of their particular region. With regard to the question of literature and location, the original draft of Christopher Shackle's chapter on Pakistan and North-west India included the following passage:

> A direct relationship between what is written and what can be seen exists, though, only in the most unimaginative guidebooks, whose simple purpose is merely to increase the appreciation of their users when they get to the sites described. Literature exists as an experience in its own right, and when it touches on places these are only one element in the central relationship between writer and reader. The place may be the apparent focus, but the wise reader will wish to know something of the nature of the lens through which the writer approaches it. Such lenses do not merely consist of the ways in which the writer's words are patterned by the literary traditions of his language and by the conventions of his time, for the outlook and the spirit which underlie these traditions and conventions also go into their making. It is the purpose of the following paragraphs to sketch for the reader some of the more obvious of these determinants as an introduction to the extracts themselves . . .

This understanding underlies the approach of all of the chapters.

All works of this genre face the same dilemma of having long extracts and losing authors, or including most of the notable authors and having short extracts. The literary richness of the sub-continent, its vast geographical coverage and its historical depth have all conspired to shorten the length of the extracts but nowhere, it is hoped, to the point where the reader is unable at least to sample the taste of what is on offer. After all, the ideal travelling companion is one who is informative, who shows the way, but who doesn't talk too much. The sub-continent itself will certainly provide the visitor with rich and fascinating experiences and it is our hope that this companion will enrich the experience further, taking the reader, as in Ezekiel's opening poem,

> 'To where the women slowly turn around,
> Not only flesh and bone but myths of light
> With darkness at the core, and sense is found
> By poets lost in crooked, restless flight,
> The deaf can hear, the blind recover sight.'

CLASSICAL LITERATURE

John D. Smith

> How can the poet's slender powers / Deal justly with so large a theme? / Why should I think that I can cross / An ocean in a coracle? . . . Yet, where the ancient poets cut / The gateway, I may enter in. / Where diamond pierced the way, a pearl / Is threaded by the softest thread.
>
> *Kalidasa, Raghuvamsa*

By the second half of the second millennium BC large tracts of north India were in the control of a people who spoke an Indo-European language – that is, one related to Greek, Latin, and the Slavonic, Germanic, and Celtic languages (among others) – and who referred to themselves as *arya*, a word meaning 'noble'. The 'Aryans' worshipped a pantheon of numerous gods, offering sacrifices to them and praising them in hymns. These hymns, which were primarily used within the highly elaborate sacrificial rituals, were composed by poet-seers (*rishis*), who were said to 'see' them in a form of divine inspiration; they were regarded as sacred and powerful, and great efforts were taken to ensure that they were correctly transmitted. At some stage writing entered the picture, but the priests in charge of this body of 'knowledge' (*Veda*) always favoured oral transmission. To this day, traditional scholars in India commit huge quantities of such ancient texts to memory.

VEDIC HYMNS

The early transmitters of the Vedic hymns did their job well, for although centuries of slow linguistic change meant that much of their content became gradually obscured, their form was preserved with remarkable accuracy. Recent scholarship, much of it Western, has succeeded in shedding light on many of the problems, and so it is that we can now read the earliest poetic outpourings of the ancient Aryan

1

people of India with a clearer understanding than has been possible at any time within the past 2000 years.

The largest and earliest of the Vedic hymn-collections is that contained in the *Rigveda Samhita* ◊, the oldest parts of which are generally thought to date from about 1200 BC. Naturally, the 1028 hymns brought together in this collection were not composed as literature in the narrowest sense of the term, since their purpose was to propitiate the gods in the context of the sacrificial ritual; nonetheless that same high purpose led the poets to seek appropriately exalted forms of expression, and many of the hymns are excellent poetry. They range in subject-matter from boisterous eulogies of the warrior-god Indra, victorious in battle against enemies both demonic and human, to subtle speculation on the nature of the universe and the manner of its creation; from prayers addressed to ambivalent gods such as Rudra, pleading for safety against divine ill-will, to exultant praise for the effects of the sacred intoxicant Soma.

Interspersed among the numerous hymns dealing with religious themes, there are also a number of more secular compositions; these would tend to stand out anyway because of their different subject-matter, but it also happens that among them are some of the most striking evocations of life in India at a very remote period. The hymn to the forest (Extract 5) reflects a time when the whole of the land was not yet tamed, when outside the safe inhabited areas (*grama*, a word that later came to mean merely 'village') lay fascinating but dangerous forest wilderness (*aranya*). The 'gambler's lament' (Extract 6) describes the desolation of the ruined gambler, a familiar figure in ancient Indian society. Poems such as these have a freshness and vitality that succeed in bridging the enormous chronological and cultural gap that separates the Vedic age from ourselves.

Later works in the Vedic corpus are not and make no claim to be in any sense 'literary': they consist of *samhitas*, collections for liturgical or domestic use, *brahmanas*, discussions of the significance of the ritual, and *aranyakas* and *upanishads*, works dealing with forms of mystical knowledge. In addition to these texts, which brought the Vedic age to an end sometime in the middle of the first millennium BC, other important subsidiary treatises were composed, among them one which was to have a lasting influence on the history of classical Indian literature. This was the grammar of Panini (6th century BC?), an exceedingly concise but also exceedingly well-executed description of the language of the day.

SANSKRIT

Panini's chief purpose in composing the grammar was evidently to help with the correct preservation and interpretation of the Vedas, whose linguistic peculiarities he deals with in detail; but his achievement went well beyond this. Not only did he establish scientific study of language in India at a level of sophistication higher than anything attempted in the West prior to this century; he also – intentionally or otherwise – produced a codified standard for the language. At about the same time, the name 'Sanskrit' (*samskrita*) began to be used for this language, meaning 'refined, polished', evidently to distinguish it from rougher vernaculars that were beginning to emerge. (By the 3rd century BC Sanskrit had evidently been replaced as an everyday spoken language by Middle Indo-Aryan dialects such as those used in the inscriptions of the emperor Ashoka.) 'Paninian Sanskrit' was to be the literary language par excellence of ancient India. Other later forms of speech came to be employed for specific purposes: the Buddhists, for example, used the Pali language for their earliest scriptural writings, and the Jains made similar use of Ardhamagadhi Prakrit, in both cases presumably on the grounds that Sanskrit was not known to the common people and was tainted by its close association with the religion of the brahmans. But for works of literature – including much later Buddhist and Jain literature – the Sanskrit language as described by Panini remained the preferred option.

MAHABHARATA AND RAMAYANA

The earliest works of Sanskrit (as opposed to Vedic) literature are not in fact composed in the Paninian form of the language, but in a more popular, less 'correct' form. These are the two great epics of classical India, the *Mahabharata* ◊ and the *Ramayana* ◊, which are not merely texts of major importance in their own right, but have also provided the subject-matter for many later works, both in Sanskrit and in later languages. The popularity of these two ancient stories shows no sign of waning, as witness the numerous recent adaptations which have been made of them into media as diverse as films, comic-books and long-running television serials.

The earlier of the two, the *Mahabharata* (Extract 11), dates back to a period of religious upheaval in India. During the 6th century BC, the orthodox brahamanical religion – the religion of the Vedas – came under challenge from reformist movements led by teachers putting forward heterodox opinions. Principal among these were Gautama, known as the Buddha, founder of the Buddhist religion, and Mahavira, founder of Jainism, both of whom were specifically opposed to the orthodox faith. It is evident that during the same period other forces were at work seeking to modify brahmanism from within. During the second half of the first millennium BC, new gods began to emerge and

Mahabarata

Note: Scene from the television adaptation. Arjuna kneels at the feet of Krishna on the battlefield of Kuru.

old gods to acquire new characteristics, as a gradual fusion occurred between brahmanism and elements of popular religion. The *Mahabharata* is a great martial epic, but it is clear that its purpose was not simply the entertainment of the Kshatriya (warrior) class; it served also as the medium through which the god Krishna was revealed to his (chiefly Kshatriya) worshippers, and no doubt its performance was intended to be pleasing to Krishna. Krishna was one of the 'new' gods of the period, though he was claimed as an incarnation of the 'old' god Vishnu – thus a god who had taken human flesh and walked among humankind, a new, powerful and highly influential concept.

The story of the *Mahabharata* concerns the tangled dynastic history of the descendants of the great Kshatriya ruler Bharata, which leads to rival claims to sovereignty by two sets of cousins, the heroic Pandavas and the villainous Kauravas; these in turn precipitate a catastrophic war. In true epic style, the narrative progresses inexorably, stage by stage, to its disastrous denouement, highlighting particular tense or ironic scenes on its way. So Kunti, the mother of the Pandavas, calls out to her sons to share equally whatever they have brought home, without looking up to see that it is a girl, and thus unwittingly commits the heroes of the epic to a joint polyandrous marriage. Later the same girl, Draupadi, is dragged in front of the royal assembly by the vile Duhshasana, who then attempts to strip her naked; but the more garments he pulls off her, the more materialize to protect her honour, and Duhshasana has to give up. Bhima, the wild man of the Pandava brothers, vows revenge on Duhshasana; subsequently, at the height of the great battle, he fulfils his vow by cutting open Duhshasana's chest and drinking his blood. All the violence, grief, and fated destruction are described in simple narrative verse (chiefly in the undemanding *anushtubh* or *shloka* metre; the effect is probably stronger than would have been the case if the bards who created the *Mahabharata* had used all the stylistic subtleties of later courtly poets.

In assimilating Krishna into their pantheon, the guardians of brahmanical orthodoxy had also to assimilate the *Mahabharata* into their religious literature. This proved to be a lengthy process, one that was not completed until about 400 AD; it involved the interpolation into the epic narrative of vast quantities of new material, both narrative and didactic, until the original bardic poem – which consisted of perhaps 3 000 stanzas – had swollen into an enormous 100 000 stanza encyclopaedia, and until its pessimistic viewpoint had been overlaid by assertions of divine benevolence and human duty. Chief of all the interpolated passages was the *Bhagavad-Gita*, an entire treatise setting out the new orthodoxy, addressed by the divine Krishna to the heroic Arjuna just before the start of the great battle.

The second of the great classical epics, the *Ramayana*, seems to have come into being during the approximate period 200 BC–200 AD. Unlike the *Mahabharata*, its claim to be the work of a single poet, Valmiki, is widely accepted by modern scholarship, although the first and last books are generally agreed to be by later hands. It shares with the *Mahabharata* the quality of a theophany: as the earlier epic reveals the divinity of Krishna, so Valmiki's great poem reveals the divinity of Rama, another 'new' god and another incarnation of Vishnu.

Certain key aspects of the narrative are also highly reminiscent of the

Bhagavad Gita

Note: Scene from the great battle of Kuru – Krishna acts as Arjuna's charioteer. It was before this battle that Khrishna addressed the *Bhagavad Gita* to Arjuna.

story of the *Mahabharata*: the kingly family split apart by a wrangle over who shall inherit the sovereignty; the heroes' long exile in the forest; the great battle between the forces of good and evil. Similar patterns of characterization are also evident, especially the contrast between senior and junior brothers among the heroes: like Yudhishthira, the eldest of the Pandavas, Rama is depicted as accepting fate and bowing to the gods' will, whilst his younger brother Lakshmana, like Yudhishthira's younger brother Bhima, is shown as an aggressive, impetuous battler for his own will against the dictates of fate.

The style of the *Ramayana* is also for the most part similar to that of the *Mahabharata*, but it does contain a number of passages – such as Lakshmana's description of winter (Extract 15) – suggesting that a less bardic/traditional, more poetic consciousness may have been at work in its composition. There are other indications of a new 'literary' aspiration in Valmiki's work too, principally his habit of ending chapters with a verse in a different, more ornate metre than the simple *shloka* used to carry the basic narrative. These are the first hints at the style that would be developed by the classical poets who would follow Valmiki, and who would consider him their first true ancestor – the *adikavi* or 'first poet' of Sanskrit literature.

Even Valmiki's putative date (c 200 BC) places him at a period when Sanskrit had already been replaced as a language of ordinary discourse

Ramilia festival

Note: The festival takes place on the first night of the Hindu Festival of Asvin (September/early October). The plays are based on the *Ramayana* – the effigy shown here is that of Ravana, the demon king of Lanka.

by various forms of Middle Indo-Aryan. In his case it was no doubt natural to continue to use the language that was traditional for epic verse. But it is a remarkable fact, and one with a marked influence on the course of the classical literature, that almost all of that literature was composed in what under normal circumstances would be considered a dead language. Panini's grammar had fixed the form of Sanskrit for all time; brahmanical religion continued to use it for both ritual and instruction; it was cultivated by the elites in and around the royal courts; but it was not the language of the common people, and the literature that came to be composed in it was not popular literature. Sanskrit literature – and Prakrit literature in the Sanskrit style – was meant for the enjoyment of the precious few.

There are two specific ways in which classical Sanskrit's unusual status – that of a language whose literary use began after its death as a mother-tongue – affected the nature of the literary tradition that employed it. The first is that, unlike the authors of earlier Vedic and epic verse, classical poets began to revel in the language's inbuilt capacity to form compound nouns and adjectives, building up longer and longer examples as time went by. A typical and by no means extreme instance occurs in Meghaduta ◊, where Kalidasa ◊, personifying the river Nirvindhya as a beautiful woman, describes it as *vichi-kshobha-stanita-vihaga-shreni-kanchi-gunayah*, 'having as her girdle-string a row of birds that were twittering because of the buffeting of her waves'.

The second such feature is that, unlike natural language, classical Sanskrit is rich in synonyms, and it became a part of the poet's task to use these to the full. It is, in fact, largely the language's ability to form compounds that permitted this development: authors who were unfettered by living usage were happy to build on the analogy of existing forms such as *vihaga*, 'sky-goer', for 'bird', producing endless variations on 'egg-born', 'born twice', 'winged creature', 'creature with a beak', and so forth. This allowed a certain richness of texture unavailable to poets in more normal languages, but it was bought at a cost: words which are truly synonymous do not differ even in their connotations (if any). Nuance was something which Sanskrit poets had to struggle for.

POST-EPIC LITERATURE

The earliest surviving post-epic literature is the work of the Buddhist author Ashvaghosha ◊, who lived in the first or early second century AD. Two narrative poems, the *Saundarananda* and the incomplete *Buddhacharita*, have come down to us, together with fragments of a play. It is evident that Ashvaghosha was much influenced by Valmiki, but his writing, unlike the *Ramayana*, strives deliberately for literary effect – the well-turned phrase, the striking metaphor, the play of assonance and alliteration.

Ashvaghosha's style does not, in fact, reach any high level of literary complexity, but it does clearly show the direction in which classical Indian poetry was moving. Unlike the apparently spontaneous verse-making of the Vedic and epic periods, writing now involved a conscious effort to express ideas in a specially arresting or clever manner, and formal works on poetic theory began to emerge in which the different ways of achieving this aim – sound-effects, figures of speech, and so forth – were analysed. Coupled with the liking for long compounds (and also in some cases for the use of deliberately unusual grammatical forms), this could lead to poetry which was technically brilliant but extremely difficult to read, and, in the case of narrative verse, to stories choked by descriptive passages in which the poet could display his skill. This tendency towards subtlety and complexity of expression at the expense of clarity and expressive force did not produce its most extreme manifestations until the second half of the first millennium AD, with the works of poets such as Bharavi ◊, Magha ◊, Bhatti ◊ and Shriharsha. It is nevertheless present even in the writings of the more 'moderate' poets who preceded these, and can sometimes lead to the impression that the poet is performing a technical exercise – one at which he happens to excel – rather than giving expression to any personal feeling. An anonymous stanza quoted (with apparent approval) by John Brough (see Booklist) puts it rather well:

> The poet's purpose is not just to say
> The moon is like the lady's face,
> But to express it in a different way,
> And with a certain grace.

Many Sanskrit poets said it in many ways, some of them with considerable grace; but it is always the same lady and the same moon, and any sense of personal involvement is rare. (Among the honourable exceptions are Bhartrihari ◊ and Bilhana ◊.)

Two centuries or so after Ashvaghosha, another Buddhist poet, Arya Shura ◊, assembled his *Jatakamala* ◊ or 'Garland of birth-stories' (Extract 12). This is a sequence of stories telling of previous incarnations of the Buddha, told in alternating verse and prose (a form that later became popular under the name *champu*). The prose passages are particularly interesting in that they give the first hint of a new 'high style', favouring long (but usually grammatically quite simple) sentences containing multi-member compounds; in the passage in Extract 12, for instance, the first Sanskrit sentence runs as far as the phrase 'snake spirits and demons', and many of the phrases it contains, such as 'where fish of all sorts swarm in shoals', 'where strong gales lash the waves in wild delight', and 'the foaming crests are like wreaths of white blossom', are in the original single compound words.

As well as poems composed in verse or prose or both (in the Sanskrit literary tradition prose and verse are thought of as two forms in which poetry may be written), there existed a tradition of drama. The earliest surviving Sanskrit plays are those of Bhasa ◊, who lived at about 300 AD, but fragments of earlier works exist, and it is possible that dramatic representation in India goes back to a very early date. Bhasa was a fairly prolific author – 13 of his plays are known – and a very varied one, both in length (from one act to six) and in subject-matter (sometimes mythical, sometimes secular). It is interesting that in his work the normal convention over use of language is already in place: high-class male characters speak Sanskrit, women and the lower orders Prakrit. In some respects Bhasa's plays seem a little unsophisticated in comparison with those of later dramatists, but it is quite clear that he was in his day master of a tradition that was already thoroughly well-established. His *Charudatta* is the basis of the slightly later *Mricchakatika* ◊, attributed to one King Shudraka, which is one of the best-loved plays of the classical period.

It is generally agreed that the finest classical author was Kalidasa ◊, who probably lived around 400 AD. Kalidasa was both a dramatist and a poet: his chief compositions were the three dramas *Malavikagnimitra*, *Vikramorvashiya* ◊ and *Shakuntala* ◊ (Extract 4), the 'court epics' (narrative poems on grand mythical themes, but in a style far more polished than that of the pre-classical epics) *Raghuvamsha* ◊ and *Kumarasambhava* ◊ (Extract 13), and the poem *Meghaduta* ◊ ('The cloud messenger', Extract 8). It is certainly true that his writings display an easy mastery over the refined classical Sanskrit style without lapsing into the massive over-elaborateness which many later authors indulged in, and he has a sharp eye for the telling detail, the striking comparison, the unexpected generalization. Three verses, all taken from the first act of *Shakuntala*, may give some impression of his skill as a poet. All are spoken by the king, the first on learning that the beautiful Shakuntala is the daughter of a heavenly nymph, the second on further learning that she is under no religious vow to remain unmarried, and the third on having to leave her to return to his royal duties (from Michael Coulson's translation, see Booklist).

> I can well believe it.
> How could such beauty have been born
> Of any mortal woman?
> The tremulous lightning-flash
> Does not spring upwards from the earth.

Give way to your longings, my heart:
All doubts are now at rest,
What you feared might be fire
Is a jewel to be touched.

My body moves onward,
But my unsteady mind runs back
Like the silk of a banner
Carried into the wind.

Poetry was not restricted to the court epic, or to stanzas interspersed among prose passages in plays or in *champu*-like compositions. Many free-standing short poems exist: Kalidasa's *Meghaduta* is a particularly good instance of a thematic link being used to hold together a sequence of chiefly descriptive verses (a cloud is told to follow a certain route, each stage of which is described in detail). But single-stanza compositions also exist in large numbers; in some cases they are preserved in anthologies (Extracts 10 and 14), in others the poet himself has collected his own work together under general subject headings. Both kinds of collections abound in fine poetry: the restrictions of the form seem to bring out the best in the poets, and there is generally little sign of the excesses to which the authors of later court epics were prone. Among the authors who specialized in this type of composition, Bhartrihari ◊, Amaru and Bilhana ◊ are perhaps worth special mention.

PROSE AND LATER WORKS

One last literary genre requires some comment. Prose narration had been known in India since the later Vedic period, but in general authors seem to have felt that verse was the only appropriate medium for their stories. Arya Shura's narratives, told largely in elegant prose, were an exception, but no further development in this direction occurred until the 7th century, when Dandin's ◊ lively collection of prose stories entitled *Dashakumaracharita* ◊ ('The deeds of the ten princes', Extract 3) appeared. Stylistically, Dandin took over where Shura had left off three centuries earlier, favouring relatively long but simple sentences full of compound words; higher degrees of elaboration were for him a special effect to be used only occasionally and for some special purpose. His successor Subandhu reversed the balance: his *Vasavadatta* is a tour-de-force of alliteration, plays on words, highly protracted sentences and so forth. Yet it has never received the critical praise afforded the third of the major prose authors of the seventh century, Bana ◊. Bana's two great works, the *Harshacharita* ◊ (Extract 7) and the *Kadambari*, which form the *ne plus ultra* of classical ornate prose, have generally won the admiration even of those who rather disapprove of the genre on principle. His style is thoroughly artificial and extremely difficult to read – yet he is a highly effective story-teller.

Later authors in the other major genres also turned increasingly towards excessively elaborate styles. The court epics of Bharavi ◊, Magha ◊, Bhatti ◊ and Shriharsha are far more sophisticated than those of Kalidasa, but they are also far less satisfactory as literature. Much the same could be said of the dramas of Bhavabhuti ◊ (Extract 2). By the end of the first millennium AD, the classical literary tradition was unhealthily far removed from its roots in popular culture and real life. The most successful works of this final period are arguably those which brought outside influences into the tradition – popular narrative, as with the *Hitopadesha* and *Kathasaritsagara*, or the rhythms and rhymes of vernacular devotionalism, as with Jayadeva's ◊ *Gitagovinda* ◊ (Extract 9). No end date can be given: literature continued to be written in Sanskrit throughout the medieval period, and the language is still in use today. But by the time Muslim rule had been established in North India the focus had moved away from Sanskrit, and the literary history of India from that point on is the history of literature in the vernacular languages of the sub-continent.

BOOKLIST

The following selection includes all titles which are extracted in this chapter as well as other relevant works. The editions cited are not necessarily the only ones available. The exact location of the extracts can be found in 'Acknowledgements and Citations' at the end of the volume. Extract numbers are highlighted in bold for ease of reference.

Brough, John, trans, *Poems from the Sanskrit*, Penguin, London, 1968. **Extract 13.**

Coulson, Michael, trans, *Three Sanskrit Plays*, Penguin, London, 1981. **Extracts 1, 2, 4.**

Cowell, E.B., Thomas, F.W., trans, *The Harsha-carita of Bana*, Motilal Banarsidass, Delhi, 1968. **Extract 7.**

Goldman, Robert P., ed, *The Ramayana of Valmiki: An Epic of Ancient India, Vol 3, Aranyakanda*, Sheldon I. Pollock, trans, Princeton University Press, Princeton, 1991. **Extract 15.**

Ingalls, Daniel H.H., trans, *An Anthology of Sanskrit Court Poetry: Vidyakara's 'Subhashitaratnakosha'*, Harvard University Press, Cambridge, Massachusetts, 1965. **Extracts 10, 14.**

Keith, A. Berriedale, *A History of Sanskrit Literature*, Oxford University Press, Oxford, 1963.

Keith, A. Berriedale, *The Sanskrit Drama*, Oxford University Press, Oxford, 1964.

Khoroche, Peter, trans, *Once the Buddha was a Monkey: Arya Shura's Jatakamala*, University of Chicago Press, Chicago and

London, 1989. **Extract 12.**

Miller, Barbara Stoler, trans, *Love Song of the Dark Lord: Jayadeva's Gitagovinda*, Columbia University Press, New York, 1977. **Extract 9.**

Nathan, Leonard, trans, *The Transport of Love: the Meghaduta of Kalidasa*, University of California Press, Berkeley, 1976. **Extract 8.**

O'Flaherty, Wendy Doniger, trans, *The Rig Veda: An Anthology*, Penguin, London, 1981. **Extract 6.**

Ryder, Arthur W., trans, *The Ten Princes*, Phoenix Books, University of Chicago Press, Chicago, 1960. **Extract 3.**

van Buitenen, J.A.B., trans, *The Mahabharata: 1. The Book of the Beginning, 2. The Book of the Assembly Hall, 3. The Book of the Forest*, Chicago University Press, Chicago, 1973, 1975, 1978. **Extracts 5 and 11.**

Extracts

Classical India is no more, but India remains. In choosing extracts from the classical literature I have deliberately concentrated on passages which describe aspects of India that have a timeless quality – times and seasons, typical scenes, vividly characterised people – in the hope that the contemporary reader may be able to recognize something of what the ancient author had in his mind's eye.

(1) AUTUMN

Vishakhadatta, *Mudrarakshasa*

In this extract from the play Mudrarakshasa, the emperor praises the Autumn season as a time when the world returns to normal after the excesses of the monsoon rains. From Michael Coulson, Three Sanskrit Plays (see Booklist).

How lovely the skies are in the rich splendour of autumn:

Now they are calm, with sandbanks of scattered cloud,
And strewn with flocks of softly-calling cranes.
At night they fill with stars like blossoming waterlilies:
The skies are like rivers flowing away into the distance.

The rains are gone, and autumn corrects the world,
Teaching the swollen waters their proper limits,
Making the rice bow down in its time of richness,
Drawing from peacocks like venom their fierce passion.

Though Ganga was swollen with rage at her faithless spouse,
Autumn has brought her back to her true self,
And like a go-between skilled in love's adventures
Has led her sweet and calm to her lord the Ocean.

(2) THE BURNING-GROUND

Bhavabhuti, *Malatimadhava*

> The hero Madhava, convinced that nothing short of supernatural aid will prevent him from losing his beloved Malati, visits the burning-ground to seek the aid of its frightful inhabitants, whom he aims to placate with an offering of flesh. Here he describes the scene. From Michael Coulson, Three Sanskrit Plays (see Booklist).

Oh, what ghastliness is here?

This starveling ghost, having ripped at the skin and feasted
On bloated, stinking cuts of shoulder, rump and rib,
Has removed eyes, tendons and guts, and with bared teeth
Sits quietly picking at the bones of the carcase on his lap.

And

From many a pyre where heat-sweating bones have cooked the marrow,
Goblins drag off the still smouldering corpses
And detaching from its joints a shank-bone with the meat
    slipping from it
Are gulping down the emerging streams of liquid.

[*With a laugh*] The goblins have evening diversions!

With guts for bracelets, and elegant flower-chains of hearts,
And women's lac-painted hands for red lotuses at their ears,
With thick blood for make-up, the demon women join their lovers
And drink in skull goblets the marrow wine.

[*Moving about and again calling out*]

Flesh not hallowed by the knife,
Taken from human limbs,
Without fraud I offer you –
Come and buy, come and buy.

(3) A Chance Meeting in Town
Dandin, *Dashakumaracharita*

*Dandin's Dashakumaracharita ('The adventures of ten princes')
contains a sequence of picaresque first-person narratives told in a
variable style, now ornate and sensuous, now racy. This extract
is of the latter variety, and Ryder's translation does it full justice.*

On the journey I came to a large market town, where business men
were raising a tremendous bombilation over a cockfight, so that I could
not repress a snicker as I joined them. And a certain Brahman who sat
near me, a gay old gentleman, quietly asked an explanation of my
merriment. 'How in the world,' said I, 'can men be such fatheads as to
match Crane, that cock in the western pen, against Cocoanut, the
rooster in the eastern pen? Cocoanut outclasses him.' 'Be still,' said the
wise old boy. 'Don't give these ninnies a tip,' and he handed me some
betel gum (camphor flavor) from his little box, filling in the intermis-
sion with spicy anecdotes. Then the two birds went at each other full
tilt, stab and counterstab, with wing-flapping and defiant cock-a-
doodling. And the poor cock from the western pen was beaten. The old
gentleman, delighted at backing a winner, made a friend of me in spite
of the disparity in age; gave me a bath, food, and other comforts in his
own house that day; and when I started next morning for Shravasti, he
set me on my road, turning back with the friendly farewell: 'Don't
forget me when your business is done.'

(4) Daybreak
Kalidasa, *Shakuntala*

*Act IV of this most celebrated of Sanskrit dramas opens at
Kanva's hermitage. A pupil of Kanva enters, freshly risen from
sleep. From Michael Coulson, Three Sanskrit Plays (see
Booklist).*

My revered teacher Kanva is back from his pilgrimage, and he has asked
me to look at the time. So I'll go outside and see how much is left of the
night. [*Walking about and looking*] Oh, it's already daybreak:

On one horizon the Lord of Plants[1] nears the western mountain,
On the other the Sun has sent the dawn to herald his arrival.
That one great light should fail as the other grows in splendour
Shows how inexorable is the wheel of this world's fortune.

With the moon vanished, that pond of once blossoming lilies
No longer gladdens my sight: its splendour fades into a memory.
But of course the sorrow of those left alone
By a loved one's departure is beyond measure grievous.

Over the jujube trees the early dawn is reddening the dew.
The peacock wakes, and quits his grassy perch on the cottage roof.
And from the altar's hoof-marked verge a deer gets up,
Rearing its hind end suddenly, as it stretches itself.

The same moon that towered above the heights of Meru, greatest of
   mountains,
And occupied Vishnu's mid realm, defeating darkness,
Now drops from the sky, its rays grown few and feeble:
No matter how great, too high will mean a fall.

[1] The moon.

(5) THE FOREST

Rigveda

The poet describes the mystery of the forest, conceived as a goddess simultaneously benevolent and dangerous. From van Buitenen's translation (see Booklist).

Lady Forest, Lady Forest! you there who seem to disappear,
Why do you not ask for the village? Fear has not found you yet?
When the grasshopper chirps its reply to the call of the cricket,
Lady Forest exults like a king spreading terror with drummers,
Cows seem there to be grazing, a dwelling is seen perhaps –
Or is it the Forest Lady who seems to creak like a cart?
Someone is surely there calling his cow, someone's cutting up wood:
Spending the night at the Forest Lady's one thinks that someone has
   screamed.
Lady Forest does not kill unless somebody attacks her –
After eating the sweet fruit one later beds down as he pleases.
Anjana-scented and fragrant and yielding much fruit without ploughing –
She is the Lady Forest, the mother of game, whom I now have praised.

(6) THE GAMBLER'S LAMENT

Rigveda

Gambling figures prominently in early Indian literature, particularly the figure of the gambler who loses all (Yudhishthira and Nala in the Mahabharata are the two most prominent cases). In this hymn a ruined gambler addresses the nuts of the vibhidaka tree, which are used as dice (from O'Flaherty's translation).

The trembling hazelnut eardrops of the great tree, born in a hurricane, intoxicate me as they roll on the furrowed board. The dice seem to me like a drink of Soma[1] from Mount Mujavant, keeping me awake and excited.

She did not quarrel with me or get angry; she was kind to my friends and to me. Because of a losing throw of the dice I have driven away a devoted wife.

My wife's mother hates me, and my wife pushes me away; the man in trouble finds no one with sympathy. They all say, 'I find a gambler as useless as an old horse that someone wants to sell.'

Other men fondle the wife of a man whose possessions have been coveted by the plundering dice. His father, mother, and brothers all say of him, 'We do not know him. Tie him up and take him away.'

When I swear, 'I will not play with them', I am left behind by my friends as they depart. But when the brown dice raise their voice as they are thrown down, I run at once to the rendezvous with them, like a woman to her lover.

The gambler goes to the meeting-hall, asking himself, 'Will I win?', and trembling with hope. But the dice cross him and counter his desire, giving the winning throws to his opponent.

The dice goad like hooks and prick like whips; they enslave, deceive, and torment. They give presents as children do,[2] striking back at the winners. They are coated with honey – an irresistible power over the gambler.

Their army, three bands of fifty, plays by rules as immutable as those of the god Savitri.[3] They do not bow even to the wrath of those whose power is terrifying; the king himself bows down before them.

Down they roll, and up they spring. Handless, they master him that has hands. Unearthly coals thrown down on the gaming board, though they are cold they burn out the heart.

The deserted wife of the gambler grieves, and the mother grieves for her son who wanders anywhere, nowhere. In debt and in need of money, frightened, he goes at night to the houses of other men.

It torments the gambler to see his wife the woman of other men, in their comfortable rooms. But he yoked the brown horses[4] in the early morning, and at evening he fell down by the fire, no longer a man.

[*To the dice:*] To the general of your great army, the first king of your band, to him I hold out my ten fingers and swear this to be the truth: 'I am holding back no money.'

This is what the noble Savitri shows me: 'Play no longer with the dice, but till your field; enjoy what you possess, and value it highly. There are your cattle, and there is your wife, O gambler.'

[*To the dice:*] Grant us your friendship; have pity on us. Do not bewitch us with the force of your terrible sorcery. Lay to rest your anger, your hatred. Let someone else fall into the trap of the brown dice.

[1] A divine intoxicating drink.
[2] That is, taking them back again.
[3] A solar deity believed to impel men to action.
[4] The dice.

(7) The Hot Season

Banabhatta, *Harshacharita*

This passage is about one quarter of Banabhatta's description of the horrors of the Indian Summer. The second part of it (from 'But as the season's childhood passed away' to the end), is, in typical Sanskrit ornate prose style, only the first third of a single huge sentence; what appear as sentences and clauses in the translation are in the original simply compound adjectives qualifying the word 'summer' near the end.

The women themselves slept away the day, grey with sandal-wood applications, like the night-lotuses unable to bear the sight of the sun; their eyes, heavy with sleep, could not bear the light of their jewels, far less the cruel sunshine. In the sultry season the moonlight nights grew less and less, like the rivers, which cheered by the diminishing distance the parted pairs of *chakravakas* on their banks.[1] The fierce heat of the sun made people long not only to drink water perfumed with the strong scent of the trumpet-flower, but even to drink up the very wind.

But as the season's childhood passed away and the sun's rays became hotter, the lakes grew dry, the streams sank lower, the waterfalls ebbed away, the din of the crickets increased, every thing was deafened by the continued cooing of the distressed doves. Then the other birds grew audacious, the wind swept away the refuse, the shrubs grew less dense, the ripe (red) clusters of the grislea tormentosa were licked by the young lions in their blind thirst for blood, the sides of the mountains were wet with the water spouted from the fainting elephant-herds, and the bees were dumb, as they lay in the dark patches of the dried ichor of the heat-distressed elephants. The season appeared with its borders painted red with the blushing *Mandara* flowers, while the splitting crystal rocks were marked by the horns of the buffaloes as they were bewildered in the doubt whether what they saw was a flowing stream of water, – the dry creepers rustled in the sultry heat, the scratching wild cocks were frightened at the straw-conflagrations in the heated dust, the porcupines took shelter in their holes, while the pools were dried down to their muddy bottoms which were discoloured by the fishes as they lay rolling on their backs, disturbed by the troops of ospreys hovering in the *arjuna* trees on the banks; and the world lighted its forest conflagrations like a solemn lustration ceremony, and the nights fell into a consumption as the summer grew more mature.

[1]The chakravaka bird is believed to pine away during the night in separation from its mate.

(8) A JOURNEY BY AIR

Kalidasa, *Meghaduta*

Kalidasa's Meghaduta ('The cloud messenger') is one of the best-loved poems in Sanskrit. It tells of a certain yaksha – a semi-divine being – who has had the misfortune to displease his master and is suffering a year of banishment in consequence. Seeing a cloud pass by, he implores it to carry a message to his loved one far away. The route the cloud is to take is described in elegant, ornate stanzas, of which the following are typical.

I foresee, friend, that though you want to hurry
my message, there will be pause after pause
on each peak that blossoms with fragrant kakubhas,
and though peacocks, eyes moist with gladness,
make you welcome, their cries risen to meet you, I pray
you somehow find the will to move quickly on.

When you come to rest in the Dasharna country,
garden hedges will be white with ketaka flowers
opening at their tips, and the sacred trees
of its towns will clamor with crows building their nests,
its borders dark with ripened rose apples,
and geese will tarry there for days.

When you've come to the royal city, Vidisha, famous
everywhere, you'll get the whole fruit

of your thirsting desire, for you'll drink the savory water
of the Vetravati, whose tide ripples
like bent brows in a face made lovely frowning
at your soft thunder along her banks.

You should pause for a rest on the low peak called Nichais
where the kadambas will spring to full blossom
at your touch, like thrilled hair prickling with delight.
Its stone caves exhale the perfume
that bought women use for their loving, so the peak
accuses the wild young men of the town.

Rested now, go on, lightly shedding
fresh water on the masses of jasmine raised
on the banks of the woodland stream, touching a sweet moment
with your shade the faces of girls harvesting flowers,
who bruise the lotuses hung at their ears
each time they brush the sweat from their cheeks.

Though it takes you off your northward course,
don't neglect the view of the roofs
of Ujjayini's white mansions. If you aren't delighted
here in the women's eyes – their darting
sidelong looks startled by the glitter
of your cleft lightning – why, you have been cheated.

(9) KRISHNA THE DIVINE LOVER

Jayadeva, *Gitagovinda*

*Krishna is in some ways the most human of the great gods of
Hinduism: he is worshipped as a naughty child, as a devious
statesman, and – above all – as a young lover. Jayadeva's
Gitagovinda, composed in the east of India during the latter part
of the 12th century AD, celebrates his love-sports with the
cowherd girls of Braj, and above all with his favourite Radha,
using metres new to Sanskrit and, most strikingly, rhyme. Here
Krishna ('Mura's foe', 'Balarama's fickle brother', 'Hari',
'Madhu's foe') makes love to Radha: the erotic love between
man and woman is used as a metaphor for the divine love
between god and devotee.*

Her rapt face shows the passion her lips feel kissing him;
With deer musk he draws the form of a stag on the moon.

In woods behind a sandbank on the Jumna river,
Mura's foe makes love in triumph now.

He lays an amaranth blossom in clouds of hair massed on her soft face –
A shimmer of lightning shines in the forest where Love goes hunting.
   In woods behind a sandbank on the Jumna river,
   Mura's foe makes love in triumph now.

He smears the domes of her swelling breasts with shining deer musk,
He makes star clusters with pearls and a moonmark with his nail.
   In woods behind a sandbank on the Jumna river,
   Mura's foe makes love in triumph now.

The dark sapphire bangle he slips over each lotus-petal hand
Encircles her arm's cool pale supple stalk like a swarm of bees.
   In woods behind a sandbank on the Jumna river,
   Mura's foe makes love in triumph now.

Her broad hips are a temple of passion holding Love's golden throne;
He lays a girdle of gemstones there to mark the gate of triumph.
   In woods behind a sandbank on the Jumna river,
   Mura's foe makes love in triumph now.

He applies a shining coat of lac to feet lying on his heart
Like tender shoots tipped with pearls to honor Lakshmi's place inside.
   In woods behind a sandbank on the Jumna river,
   Mura's foe makes love in triumph now.

While Balarama's fickle brother is delighting some pretty girl,
Why does barren disgust haunt my bower of branches, tell me friend?
   In woods behind a sandbank on the Jumna river,
   Mura's foe makes love in triumph now.

Jayadeva, king of poets, echoes Hari's merit in the mood of his song.
Let evil dark-age rhythms cease at the feet of Madhu's foe!
   In woods behind a sandbank on the Jumna river,
   Mura's foe makes love in triumph now.

(10) THE RAINY SEASON

Subhashitaratnakosha

Eight stanzas describing the monsoon, from an 11th century anthology of courtly Sanskrit poetry.

The peacock calls gently to his mate who tarries,
and glances once again toward the sky;
then, leaping from his stage, the earth,
making a parasol of his unfolded tail,
to the sound of thunder sweet as loud reverberations of a drum
he performs his joyful dance.

The clouds, torpid from the much water they have drunk,
let fall the rain in steady streams
till sleep comes to our eyes from the sound of downpour.
When men then sleeping in every house are silent,
the sound of frogs, swelling without rival,
turns night to uproar.

In the paddy field flooded with fresh water
where the frogs begin to croak
and where the prickly cane along the bank is whiter then heaped
    pearls,
the children, sticks in hand and smeared with mud,
run after the rising fish,
yelling 'chubhroo, chubhroo!'

A cloth of darkness inlaid with fireflies;
flashes of lightning;
the mighty cloud-mass guessed at from the roll of thunder;
a trumpeting of elephants;
an east wind scented by opening buds of *ketaki*,
and falling rain:
I know not how a man can bear the nights that hold all these,
when separated from his love.

As the downpour steadily increases, urging the mind to numbness,
its sound being swollen by the wild trumpeting of elephants in rut,
the sky methinks has put its head into its lap
and snoring with the thundering of rainclouds
closes the sun and moon, its eyes.

Happy is he who in the monsoon nights,
with pumpkin vines growing over the firm roof
of his thatched pavilion,
lies breast to breast with a lovely woman,
listening in her embrace
to the constant downpour of the rumbling clouds.

The cloud by miring the road has spoiled the red lac of her soles
and with his rain has washed the cosmetic from her cheek;
but for these sins he makes quick recompense:
his lightning shows the wanton lass
the path that leads her to her lover's house.

At night the clouds bring the sky within your grasp and shorten the
    horizon;
briefly they interrupt the thick low sound of rain with thunder;
then, opening their eyes of lightning and viewing all the world
as if to see if any spot of land is left undrowned,
they rain again.

(11) A Royal Assembly
at a Royal Court

Mahabharata

> King Drupada of the Panchala country has announced that he
> will give his daughter Krishnā, also known as Draupadi, in
> marriage to whatever man can perform a spectacular feat of
> archery with an almost unbendably hard bow. Now princes,
> brahmans and ordinary townspeople are flocking to attend the
> competition.

On an even and consecrated stretch of land northeast of the city there
stood in all its beauty an arena that was completely surrounded by
stands. Around it ran a wall and a moat, and it was embellished with
grand gateways. The arena was entirely shaded by a colorful awning.
The sounds of hundreds of musical instruments filled it, it was perfumed
with costly aloe scents, sprinkled with sandal water, and decorated with
festoons of flowers. The arena was girt by a belt of well-enclosed,
expertly built, high-rising pavilions that seemed to scratch the sky like
the peaks of Kailasa,[1] wrapped in gilded trellises and sparkling with
mosaics of precious stones, with steps that rose gently, and fine seats
that were shaded by canopies. Carpets, not of the rustic kind, covered

those multitudinous pavilions, and they were superbly scented with aloe and white like geese, casting their fragrance to the distance of a league. A hundred wide doors gave access to them, beautiful seats and couches were placed about, and their elements were wrought with many metals as are the peaks of Mount Himalaya. On the many stories of the pavilions all the kings were seated, rivaling one another with the adornment of their persons. The townspeople and country folk, who had come to content themselves with the spectacle of Krishnā, sat all about on their own rich platforms and stared at the lordly, lionlike kings who were sitting there, of mighty courage and prowess, perfumed with black aloe – gracious and brahminic princes, the protectors of their realms and beloved of all the world for their hallowed good deeds.

The Pandavas[2] took their seats with the brahmins and gazed upon the matchless wealth of the king of the Panchalas. For many days the audience grew while it was heaped with largess of jewels and entertained by actors and dancers. On the sixteenth day, when there was a lovely crowd, Draupadi appeared, freshly bathed, in new clothes. Carrying the champion's goblet, which was made of gold and finely wrought, she descended into the arena . . . The priest of the Somakas, a pure brahmin who was learned in the spells, strewed sacred grass around and made an oblation of butter in the fire in the proper fashion. After having satisfied the fire and the brahmins, and having blessed the day, he stopped the music all around. When silence fell, Dhrishtadyumna strode to the middle of the arena and spoke in a thundering voice these polished and most meaningful words:

> 'Hear ye, all kings who are gathered here!
> Mark bow and target, and mark these arrows.
> You must hit the mark with these five arrows
> By shooting through this hole in the wheel.

> 'Whoever of lineage, beauty and might
> Accomplishes this most difficult feat,
> To him shall go my sister Krishnā
> To be his wife, and I say sooth!'

[1] A mythical mountain, believed to be the dwelling-place of the god Shiva.
[2] The heroes of the epic narrative.

(12) A Sea Voyage

Arya Shura, *Jatakamala*

Descriptions of the sea are not common in classical Indian writings. Though the sea is often used as a metaphor for greatness, all-inclusiveness, etc., relatively few authors would ever actually have seen it. The Buddhist Arya Shura seems to have been an exception. Here he describes the start of a voyage by a company of merchants.

In due course they took to the open sea where fish of all sorts swarm in shoals, where strong gales lash the waves in wild delight and the waters roar in fury. Above, the foaming crests are like wreaths of white blossom – while below, the ocean floor, encrusted with many kinds of gems, is forever changing. But in those unfathomable depths also lie the forbidding underworld haunts of snake spirits and demons. The coastline vanished as they ventured out into mid-ocean. All around them stretched the fathomless waters, deep sapphire blue. It was as though the sky had melted under the scorching rays of the sun.

Evening drew on, and the sun's ball of fire burned less fiercely. They were far out at sea when, suddenly, a vast and terrifying cataclysm burst upon them. From one moment to the next the sea grew wild: the whole mass of water became turbulent and groaned horribly at the buffeting of the violent wind. Shattered waves hurled sheets of spray. Whole tracts of water were tossed in the air by this hurricane and whirled about with frightening swiftness. The ocean took on a savage aspect, as does the earth at doomsday, when the mountains tremble. Dark clouds, with bright streaks of lightning like the flickering tongues of many-headed snakes, obscured the sun's path, and continual thunderclaps echoed menacingly. The sun gradually dipped toward the horizon, its fine mesh of rays blotted out by dense cloud, and darkness, unleashed by close of day, became palpable, enveloping all. As the stinging showers of rain lashed the encircling waves, the ocean heaved in rage, and the ship, as though in fear, shuddered horribly, filling the mariners' hearts with dismay. Each of them reacted according to temperament: some were panic-stricken and stood speechless and despairing, others kept calm and busily took countermeasures, while others were absorbed in praying to their guardian spirits.

(13) SPRING

Kalidasa, *Kumarasambhava*

The Kumarasambhava ('Origin of the war-god') is a 'court epic', a long poem in ornate style by Kalidasa, generally reckoned the finest exponent of the genre. Here he describes the arrival of Spring, season of love.

And then within these mountain-forest reaches,
Skilled to distract saints' thoughts from heaven above
The young awakening Spring now yawns and stretches,
Belov'd companion of the god of love.

. . .

Piyala-blossom clusters shed their pollen
In smoke-clouds; and the deer, bewildered, blind,
Through forest-glades where rustling leaves had fallen,
Made rash by springtime, coursed against the wind.

The cuckoo's song, hoarsened to gentle cooing,
When food of mango-sprouts tightened his throat,
Became the voice of Love, to work the undoing
Of maids cold-hearted, by its magic note.

The fairy-women, with their winter faces
Devoid of lipstick, saw their colour fade,
While with the Spring the rising sweat left traces,
Smearing the beauty-marks so carefully made.

(14) SUNSET

Subhashitaratnakosha

Five stanzas describing sunset from an 11th century anthology of courtly Sanskrit poetry

The sky wears undulating flight of birds
scattered about like strands of hair disheveled;
without her bright cosmetic of the sunset, pitiful,
her beauty hidden in the dark silk cloak of night,
she no more furnishes our eyes delight
as she mourns her lord the sun.

The cows come home, the birds are cooing in the trees,
the goblin women turn to household tasks,
and here is Nandin;[1] making sure the evening rites be done,
he rubs the drums in preparation for his master's dance.

The darkness wears the guise of rising smoke
and the sky is filled with opening stars for sparks
as the sun descends into the sunset fire.
As his loves, the lotuses, bow down in grief,
lamenting with the cry of struggling bees,
the goddess of the day turns west and joins him in his death.

Moths begin their fatal flight
into the slender flame;
bees, made blind by perfume,
wait in the closing bud;
the dancing-girls are putting on their paint
as one may guess from here
by the jingling of their bracelets
as they bend their graceful arms.

The sun runs swiftly west,
his light reduced, easy to look at
and red as a China rose.
The birds flit happily,
having gathered their food abroad,
now in the tops of their nesting trees.

[1] The god Shiva's bull.

(15) WINTER

Valmiki, *Ramayana*

Rama, his wife Sita, and his brother Lakshmana are in exile in the forest. The cold season has arrived, and Lakshmana describes its beauties.

The world crackles with frost and the earth is bedecked with a garland of crops; water is uninviting, and instead fire, the bearer of oblations, is what appeals most. Now is the time for pious men to worship the ancestral spirits and gods with offerings of first fruits, whereupon they are freed from sin. The countryfolk have all they desire; their cows give milk more richly than ever. And kings march forth on expedition with hopes of conquest. . . . Mist covers the fields and their stands of wheat and barley. How beautiful they look at sunrise, with the cranes and *krauncha* birds calling there. How beautiful the golden rice plants look. Their heads, the color of wild date palm blossoms, are so heavy with grain that the stalks are gently bowed. With its rays drawing near in a cloak of snow and frost, the sun, even at its zenith, resembles the moon. The morning sunshine is too weak even to be felt, but it grows pleasantly warm to the skin by noon. How beautifully it grows, a faint pale red upon the earth. How beautiful the floor of the forest appears, with the early morning sunlight playing upon it and the meadows slightly dampened by a fall of hoarfrost.

Biographies and plot summaries

Unlike many ancient cultures, which maintained detailed records of people, places and events, pre-Muslim India had no strong tradition of historiography (although it had a great fondness for quasi-historical legends). As a result, our present-day knowledge of early India is in many respects astonishingly vague: whole conferences have been devoted to attempts at settling important dates, such as those of the ruler Kanishka or Gautama the Buddha. This state of affairs applies equally to classical Indian literature: although there are exceptional cases where we have detailed and accurate information, it is more common to have to rely on approximate estimates of the probable date at which an author lived, and scholars do not always agree amongst themselves. The following 'biographies' are therefore in large part little more than best guesses.

ARYA SHURA. Shura was a Buddhist author (the 'Arya' is not strictly part of his name but a religious honorific akin to 'reverend') who probably lived in the 4th century AD, apparently in a courtly environment. His *Jatakamala* ('garland of birth-stories') consists of 34 *jatakas* ◊, most of them known also from the Pali collection, retold in Sanskrit in an elegant mixture of prose and verse (see Extract 12).

ASHVAGHOSHA. An early Sanskrit poet, author of two substantial narrative poems on Buddhist themes, the *Saundarananda* and the *Buddhacharita*. Ashvaghosha, who flourished around 100 AD, is said to have been a brahman who converted to Buddhism. He stands at the beginning of the Sanskrit poetic tradition, his style owing much to Valmiki's ◊ epic simplicity, but also anticipating later poets such as Kalidasa ◊ in variety of metre and complexity of figures of speech.

BANA, BANABHATTA. 7th-century author of two great prose narratives, the *Harshacharita* (◊, Extract 7) and the *Kadambari*. Unusually, Bana provides us with detailed information about himself in his works. He was a brahman who lived in the town of Pritikuta in the northeast; orphaned at the age of 14, he fell into dubious company and wandered far from home, but later settled down and became a protege of the great king Harsha, the subject of his *Harshacharita*. Bana's style is the ultimate in Sanskrit ornate prose: he revels in long, alliterative compound words and enormously protracted sentences.

BHARAVI. Sanskrit poet, traditionally ranked second only to Kalidasa; author of the *Kiratarjuniya* ◊. Bharavi probably flourished in the first half of the 6th century AD, but nothing is known for certain about him.

BHARTRIHARI. The likelihood is that Bhartrihari, despite attempts to identify him with a 7th-century grammarian of the same name, in fact lived about two centuries earlier; as usual, however, legend and speculation are our only sources of information. He was the author of the *Shatakatraya*, 'three centuries of verses': a hundred verses dealing with right conduct (*niti*), a hundred with love (*shringara*), and a hundred with renunciation (*vairagya*). Bhartrihari's poems have a personal quality unusual in Sanskrit, and reveal a man both captivated and disillusioned by the world of human affairs.

BHASA. The earliest Sanskrit dramatist whose work has survived (apart from fragments of a play by Ashvaghosha), Bhasa is thought to have lived about 300 AD. Of his 13 plays, several are based on episodes occurring in the two great epics (the *Mahabharata* ◊ and the *Ramayana* ◊),

while others are secular and romantic in character. His poetic style is simple but effective, and he was much imitated by later dramatists – indeed, Shudraka's *Mricchakatika* ◊ is a reworking of his *Charudatta*.

BHATTI. It is not possible to date Bhatti with any accuracy – all that can be said is that he probably lived sometime in the 6th or early 7th century AD – and equally nothing is known of his life. He was the author of the *Ravanavadha* ◊.

BHAVABHUTI. The dramatist Bhavabhuti was born into a scholarly brahmin family in south India early in the 8th century AD, and his works clearly reflect his learned background, for he favours an elaborate and high-flown style that contrasts sharply with that of his most eminent predecessor, Kalidasa (Extract 2). His three plays are the *Mahaviracharita*, 'The deeds of the great hero', a version of the story of Rama, *Malatimadhava* ◊, and the *Uttararamacharita*, 'The later deeds of Rama'.

BILHANA. The 11th century author Bilhana was a Kashmiri, but travelled widely in both north and south India. He has left two poetic works of very different character. One, the *Vikramankadevacharita*, is a long eulogistic history in honour of his patron King Vikramaditya, and is mainly interesting as being an early example of this type of composition. The other is entitled *Chaurisuratapanchashika*, 'Fifty verses on secret love', and is a charming exercise in remembrance of past happiness. All the verses are composed in the same metre (*Vasantatilaka*), and all begin with the words 'Even today' (*adyapi*).

DANDIN. The author of the *Dasha-kumaracharita* (◊, Extract 3), Dandin is also held by many to have written the treatise on poetics *Kavyadarsha*; others maintain that this must have been the work of a later writer of the same name. Nothing is known of his life; the most that can be said is that he probably lived early in the 7th century.

Dashakumaracharita. Dandin's *Dasha-kumaracharita* 'The deeds of the ten princes' (Extract 3) is the earliest surviving example of ornate Sanskrit prose: it is, or rather was intended to be, a collection of short stories, each consisting of a description by one of the ten princes of the adventures he experienced while searching for one of their number who had mysteriously disappeared. However, both the frame-story and the stories of the first two princes are missing (though versions of them were supplied by later writers). The tales are lively, full of vivid, often rather earthy characters; they are told in a prose style that succeeds for the most part in combining ornateness with readability. Dandin does occasionally splash out on a sequence of long compounds or an extraordinarily long sentence (the hallmarks of the style of Bana ◊), just as he sometimes introduces a deliberately overcomplicated element into the plot, but for the most part he is the most approachable of the Sanskrit 'novelists'.

Gitagovinda. A major work of Sanskrit poetry, Jayadeva's ◊ 12th century *Gitagovinda* ('Krishna (praised) in song') is both highly innovative and deeply appealing. It consists of sequences of verses in musical metres interspersed among passages in the more conventional 'syllabic' metres of Sanskrit verse, and it is clear that performance using both song and dance was the intention. The forms of the 'musical' verses no doubt reflect vernacular song-forms current in the Bengal of Jayadeva's time, but they are not translations into Sanskrit from other languages, as has sometimes been suggested – rather, they represent an attempt to enrich and refresh the Sanskrit tradition with lively new elements. Among the new elements is rhyme, here used as an essential feature of Sanskrit poetry for the first time. The poem describes Krishna and his love-affairs with the cowherd-girls of his native Braj, especially his favourite Radha. Unstated but underlying the entire composition is the idea that the sexual love between these two represents the divine love between Krishna and his devotees (Extract 9).

Harshacharita. Bana's ambitious prose narrative *Harshacharita* ('The deeds of Harsha') was composed as a tribute to his patron, the Harsha of the title (Extract 7). It is a long text in the most ornate Sanskrit style, full of alliterative language, multi-member compound words, and extraordinarily long sentences. After an introduction in verse Bana describes his own early life in detail (with the result that we know a great deal more about him than about most Sanskrit authors), and then tells the story of his arrival at Harsha's court. Then follows the birth and youth of Harsha himself, the death of his father, and his older brother's decision to renounce the throne, resulting in the sixteen-year-old Harsha becoming king. Disaster follows: the young king's sister is abducted, and his brother, battling against her captors, is killed by trickery. Harsha sets out with an army to avenge his brother and rescue his sister; he succeeds on both counts, and announces that he and his sister will become Buddhist mendicants.

Jatakas. 'Birth stories' of the Buddha, in which he tells of events that happened during his previous existences. The primary collection, over 500 in number, is in Pali, and consists mainly of prose narratives with interspersed verses; some, however, are told entirely in verse (including the great *Vessantarajataka*), and there also exist *jatakas* in Sanskrit, such as the *Jatakamala* of Arya Shura ◊.

JAYADEVA. Author of the *Gitagovinda* (◊, Extract 9), Jayadeva was one of five poets forming the 'five jewels' of the court of Lakshmanasena, who ruled in Bengal during the last quarter of the 12th century AD. We know nothing for certain about him save that he was the son of one Bhojadeva of Kindubilva; however, later legends describe him as an ardent disciple of Krishna, who received direct aid from the god in composing his masterpiece.

KALIDASA. Kalidasa is almost universally recognized as the finest poet of Sanskrit literature, and yet we know nothing about his life beyond the usual supply of later legends. Even his approximate date is uncertain: Western scholars, agreeing that he must have lived during the heyday of the great Gupta rulers of north India, have generally put him at about 400 AD, but even this tentative dating is uncertain. Whenever exactly he lived, he was able to adopt a relatively ornate style without becoming difficult for the sake of it – his poetry, though far more sophisticated than that of Valmiki or Ashvaghosha, lacks the sometimes excessive subtlety

and complexity of later writers such as Bharavi ◊ or Magha ◊. As a dramatist too he strikes a happy medium, and his *Shakuntala* (◊, Extract 4) is widely thought the finest Sanskrit play. His principal works are the three plays *Malavikagnimitra, Vikramorvashiya* ◊ and *Shakuntala* ◊, the two court epics *Raghuvamsha* ◊ and *Kumarasambhava* (◊, Extract 13) and the 'messenger poem' *Meghadua* (◊, Extract 8).

Kiratarjuniya. 'The story of Arjuna and the mountain-man' is a court epic by Bharavi ◊. It is based on the episode in the *Mahabharata* where Arjuna, chief warrior of the Pandava heroes, seeking the god Shiva in the mountains, encounters and fights a wild man there; he is defeated, whereupon the wild man reveals himself as Shiva and rewards Arjuna with the magic weapon he desires.

Kumarasambhava. Kalidasa's court epic 'Origin of the war-god' describes in eight cantos the events leading up to the birth of Kumara (= Skanda = Karttikeya), son of the god Shiva and his consort Parvati. The gods fear domination by the demon Taraka, and determine that their only hope is for Shiva, who is constantly engaged in meditation in his retreat in the mountains of Himalaya, to beget a warrior son on Parvati, Himalaya's daughter. Kama, the god of love, arrives to stir Shiva's heart into love for Parvati, but is destroyed by a blast of flame from Shiva's third eye. However, Parvati herself succeeds in winning Shiva over by practising severe austerities, and with her father's consent they are married. The poem ends with a long description of the divine couple's erotic pleasures; we are left to draw our own conclusion that the destroyer of the wicked Taraka will soon be born.

MAGHA. As usual, our knowledge of the poet Magha is minimal: we know the names of his father and grandfather, and we may know the name of the king in whose court that grandfather served as minister. A date of around 700 AD is generally agreed on. Magha knew the work of Bharavi ◊ and evidently tried to outdo him in poetic virtuosity: his only surviving poem, the court epic *Shishupalavadha* ◊ is clearly modelled on Bharavi's *Kiratarjuniya* ◊, which it seeks to excel in various ways.

Mahabharata. The *Mahabharata* ('The great (war) of the descendants of Bharata') is India's great epic tale (Extract 11). In barest outline, the story tells of a dynastic dispute between two sets of cousins, the wicked Kauravas and the virtuous Pandavas. The Kauravas cheat the Pandavas at gambling and send them into the wilderness for twelve years, but after the allotted period of exile the Pandavas return to claim their territory. War is clearly inevitable, and the divine Krishna, incarnation of the god Vishnu, agrees to help the Pandavas; at the start of hostilities he also addresses the doubts of the leading Pandava warrior, Arjuna, in the text known as the *Bhagavad-Gita*. The battle rages for eighteen days; finally the Pandavas triumph, but shortly afterwards most of their associates are slaughtered in a night-raid by the surviving Kauravas. The epic concludes with the Pandavas' journey to Heaven. The *Mahabharata* is an enormous poem (the traditional text consists of approximately 100 000 stanzas) which took many centuries to develop into the form in which we know it; along the way its character changed from that of an oral epic celebrating the deeds of heroes of the Kshatriya (warrior) class to that of a

religious narrative putting forward brahman (priestly) values. The earliest material contained in it probably dates from the middle of the first millennium BC, but additions continued to be made up until around 400 AD. Stylistically it is very simple and rather repetitive, but the unadorned style in fact allows the force of the narrative to come across more successfully than is the case with some of the highly literary court epics which followed it.

Malatimadhava. 'Malati and Madhava' (Extract 2) is the best-known play of Bhavabhuti ◊. It is a story of young lovers facing dreadful adversaries, and involves all sorts of melodramatic devices before everything finally turns out well. Bhavabhuti's language is complex and intricate, and it is certainly difficult to imagine that any audience of any period would have been able to follow it at a single hearing.

Meghaduta. Kalidasa's *Meghaduta* ('Cloud messenger') is a poem consisting of 110 stanzas in the stately *Mandakranta* metre, based around the conceit of using a monsoon cloud to carry a message on its journey northwards across India (Extract 8). The first five stanzas describe how a certain Yaksha (a semidivine being), who is undergoing a period of exile as punishment for a minor offence against his lord, sees a cloud and determines to use it to carry word to his beloved far away. The great bulk of the poem consists of the Yaksha's elegant description of the route the cloud will have to follow; finally, the message itself is stated, and the Yaksha bids the cloud farewell. The poem has always been a favourite work of Sanskrit literature, and led to a whole sub-genre of *dutakavya* or 'messenger poems'.

Mahabarata
Note: Krishna as portrayed in the television adaptation.

Mricchakatika. 'The little clay cart' is a play claiming to be by one King Shudraka, about whom we know nothing more than legend; scholars have generally agreed that it must have been composed at about the time of Kalidasa, that is, around 400 AD. As mysterious as the royal author is the work's relationship with the earlier play *Charudatta* by Bhasa ◊. This latter was not known until the early years of the present century, when an incomplete manuscript of it was found; it transpired that its four extant acts and the first four acts of the *Mricchakatika* were, by and large, the same. Whatever the case, the play is a triumph of the Sanskrit drama, with unusually rich characterization, a simple, forceful poetic style, and a satisfyingly complicated and 'dramatic' plot, culminating in the final act with the hero escaping execution for murder when the victim of his supposed crime appears on the scene.

Mudrarakshasa. 'Rakshasa and the ring' is the only complete extant play by Vishakhadatta, of whom we know practically nothing (Extract 1); estimates of his date vary even more wildly than usual, the 4th, 6th and 9th centuries AD all having their supporters. It is a most unusual work, falling into none of the conventional categories, for it deals with political intrigue: at its centre stands the implacable opposition between the minister Rakshasa and Canakya, the ancient Indian equivalent of Machiavelli who has caused the downfall of the dynasty Rakshasa serves. The plot is very complex, but also very well-turned; like the *Mricchakatika* ◊ it ends with a narrow escape from execution.

Raghuvamsha. Kalidasa's 'Dynasty of Raghu' is principally his version of the story of Rama, the incarnation of Vishnu whose epic struggle against the demon Ravana had earlier formed the subject of Valmiki's *Ramayana* ◊. But these events are sandwiched between an account of the deeds of Rama's various exalted predecessors in Raghu's dynasty and a sequence of the names of his successors. The work comes to a somewhat abrupt end in the nineteenth canto, and this has generally been taken to indicate that Kalidasa left it unfinished.

Ramayana. Like the *Mahabharata* ◊, the *Ramayana* (Extract 15) is a long epic narrative in verse: it is the story of the divine hero Rama, said to be an incarnation of the god Vishnu. Rama's father Dasharatha, king of Ayodhya, determines to install him as prince regent, but his jealous stepmother Kaikeyi insists that her own son Bharata is installed instead, and that Rama is exiled to the forest for fourteen years. Rama accepts his fate uncomplainingly, and sets out into the forest accompanied by his wife Sita and his younger brother Lakshmana. After many adventures, Sita is abducted by Ravana, the demon king of Lanka. Rama sends his friend the monkey-god Hanuman to locate her, and then launches an attack on Lanka; after a great battle he kills Ravana, rescues his wife, and returns to Ayodhya where, at last, he becomes king. The *Ramayana* was composed later than the earliest parts of the *Mahabharata*, probably during the period 200 BC–200 AD. It is said to be the work of the poet Valmiki, and, unlike the *Mahabharata*, one can believe that the bulk of it was indeed composed by a single poet (working with the model of the *Mahabharata* very much in mind). Modern scholars have, however, generally agreed that the first and last books of the epic are later additions by a different author or authors.

Ravanavadha. Bhatti's ◊ court epic 'The killing of Ravana' is often known simply as the *Bhattikavya* – Bhatti's poem'. The narrative is the story of Rama (see *Ramayana* above), and Bhatti tells it in a relatively simple style, but he also uses it as a vehicle for the illustration of rules of poetics and grammar. These are dealt with in sections; so, for instance, canto 10 is full of examples of para-nomasia, and canto 19 similarly full of optative and precative verbs.

Rigveda. The *Rigveda* (Extracts 5, 6) is the oldest *Veda* ◊: the earliest of the hymns which are collected in its *samhita* probably date back to around 1200 BC, and are in a form of language substantially different from later Sanskrit. The majority of the hymns are addressed to the various gods worshipped by the Aryans at this period: Indra the warrior and destroyer of drought; Agni the god of fire who carries men's sacrificial offerings to heaven; Varuna the all-seeing judge; gods of the Sun; and many others. Though composed with ritual purposes very much in mind, many of these hymns are also fine poetry.

Shakuntala. Generally agreed to be Kalidasa's finest play, *Shakuntala* tells of the love between the eponymous heroine and King Dushyanta. Shortly after their secret marriage, Shakuntala has the misfortune, in her love-distracted state, to be insufficiently polite to the hot-tempered sage Durvasas, who promptly curses her to remain unrecognized by her husband until she shows him the ring he gave her. But the ring is lost, and Shakuntala, now pregnant, is rejected by the king. Subsequently the missing ring is found, and Dushyanta realises what he has done, but it is now too late. Time passes; Dushyanta comes upon a boy playing roughly with a young lion, and feels himself strangely drawn towards him: the boy turns out to be his own son. Shakuntala and Dushyanta are reconciled, and general happiness prevails.

Shishupalavadha. A court epic by Magha ◊, 'The killing of Shishupala' tells the story of the episode from the *Mahabharata* in which Krishna, after long tolerating the misdeeds of the renegade king Shishupala, finally beheads him with his discus. Like Bharavi's ◊ *Kiratarjuniya* ◊ which it is clearly intended to emulate, the *Shishupalavadha* is a masterwork of technical poetic virtuosity.

VALMIKI. Reputed author of the *Ramayana* (◊, Extract 15), Valmiki is traditionally considered the *adikavi* or 'first poet' of Sanskrit. Certainly the *Ramayana* is a more unified composition than the earlier epic *Mahabharata* ◊, and it is widely accepted as being largely the work of a single author.

Veda. The Vedas are the earliest extant Indian literature. Composed in an ancient form of Sanskrit, they contain principally hymns and formulae for use in the great sacrificial rituals (collected into *samhitas*), interpretative treatises on the meaning and purpose of those rituals (*brahmanas*), and works of speculative theology (*aranyakas* and *upanishads*). The oldest part of the entire Vedic corpus is the *samhita* of the *Rigveda* ◊.

Vikramorvashiya. Drama by Kalidasa ◊. It tells the well-known story of the heavenly nymph Urvashi and the human king Pururavas. By the end of the third of the five acts, the two have fallen in love and overcome all obstacles to their happy union. Because of a curse, however, Urvashi is turned into a creeper, and Pururavas spends almost the whole of the fourth act desperately searching for her in the forest. Finally he regains her. The fifth and final act takes place after some elapse of time: Pururavas discovers tht he has a son by Urvashi, whom the latter has concealed from him. It transpires that she has done so because as soon as Pururavas sees the boy, she will have to leave him and return to heaven. However, the great god Indra intervenes to waive this sad requirement, and the play ends happily with the installation of the child as crown prince.

Pakistan and North-west India

Christopher Shackle

'Rose Cottage kiddhar hai?' Barbie asked Aziz.

Again making a gesture with his fully extended right arm he answered in English, 'There, on the other side of the big hill'.

She looked in that direction and saw how beyond the hill more distant ranges marched towards a mountainous horizon. Was that snow or sunlight on the farthest peak? She sighed, content to have seen such a vision of beauty even if it was not to be her luck to live out her days in constant sight of it.

Paul Scott, The Raj Quartet

While the blind man in the fable who managed to grasp the elephant's trunk was able to get no nearer to sensing what the great animal was like in its entirety than those others who touched its hide and its tail, he was surely the one lucky enough to have been granted both the most peculiar and the most interesting feeling experience. So too are the interlocking north-western regions of South Asia in many ways obviously, in others elusively, different from that common picture of 'India' which conveniently guides most Western readers' imaginations. Mostly contained since 1947 within the separate political entity of Pakistan, though with some natural overspill into adjacent areas of India, the northwest indeed has many aspects rather atypical of the subcontinent as a whole. Their special appeal has though not only given an individual colouring to local literatures, but has proved sufficiently powerful to excite memorable evocations from numerous outsiders also.

LAND

Effectively cut off from the sea by the inaccessible hills and sand dunes along most of its long coastline, much of the area consists of a barren mixture of mountains and deserts. The western regions, with their bitter winters, belong geographically to the central Asian plateau rather than to South Asia proper. The rocky hills of **Baluchistan** which cover so large a geographical proportion of the territory of Pakistan contain only a very small percentage of its population. The higher hills of the **North-West Frontier** proper on the Afghan border are hardly less barren, though the climate permits a denser population in the valleys, before the Hindu Kush gives way to the remote Himalayan peaks of the far north, more appealing to mountaineers than to most writers. Only in the valley of **Kashmir** is a romantic mountainous surrounding so combined with the comfort of a relatively accessible valley, particularly beautiful in spring and autumn, as to have encouraged lyrical descriptions in many languages.

Below the mountains lie the plains surrounding the Indus and its five great tributaries which give the **Panjab** its name (from the Persian *panj ab* 'five waters'). As one moves from the foothills and the broken plateau of the Pothohar around **Islamabad** south-eastwards past the historic capital of **Lahore**, the countryside with its villages ever more densely dotted among the fertile canal-fed fields becomes ever more South Asian in feel. The winters may be colder and the monsoon may come quite late, but this is unmistakeably a part of the endless Indo-Gangetic plain across which the **Grand Trunk Road** wends its way on to Delhi, eventually to Calcutta.

The modern appearance of the Panjab owes much to the massive extension of the canal system undertaken during the colonial period and further extended since. Historically, the now almost continuous patchwork of fields was more closely confined to the rivers themselves, with the less watered interriveraine areas being mostly scrubland capable only of supporting nomadic herdsmen. A remnant of this older landscape still survives in the south-western Panjab, where the canals have yet to make the deserts green. As one moves into Bahawalpur and Sind, the cultivated area follows the line of Indus with great deserts on either side, merging with the sands of Rajasthan in the east, and stretching to the equally empty wastes of Baluchistan on the west. The climate is famous above all for its heat, epitomized in stories told of the luckless inhabitants of Sibi on the Sind–Baluchistan border, who feel the need for overcoats in hell.

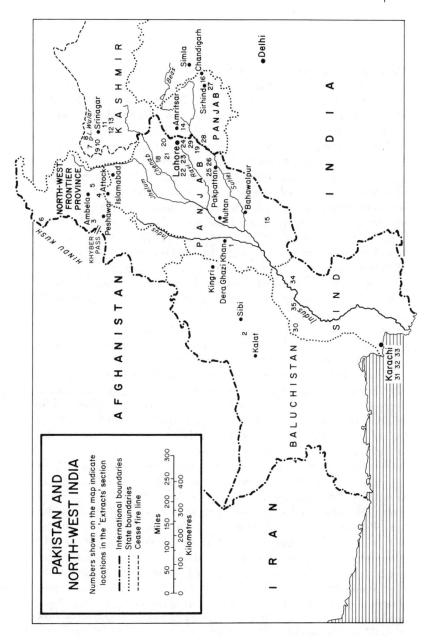

PAKISTAN AND
NORTH-WEST INDIA

Numbers shown on the map indicate
locations in the 'Extracts' section

—·—·— International boundaries
············· State boundaries
— — — Cease fire line

Miles
0   50   100   150   200   250   300
0   100   200   300   400
Kilometres

HISTORY

The prehistory of the region, attested by recent archaeological work in the Pothohar plateau, goes back further than that of any other part of South Asia. It is also the home of the oldest recorded South Asian civilization, the Indus Valley culture of Mohenjodaro and Harappa. But the region's excitement derives less from this antiquity than its shifting quality as a borderland.

This is, above all, frontier country, since it lies on the one land border of the sub-continent where the northern mountain chain permits access from west and central Asia. All the earlier civilizations of historic India indeed owe their formation to the successive movements of peoples through the **Khyber**, the **Bolan**, and the other great mountain passes. In the second millenium BC, this was the route followed by the Aryans whose language and religion were to fan out across the whole of northern India from their original settlements in the north-west, whose scenery is dimly to be discerned in the mythical settings of some of the Vedic hymns. From a similar direction came Alexander the Great in the abortive last thrust of his attempt at world conquest (327–25 BC). This foundered in the plains of the Indus, the Greek name for the great river whose Sanskrit name Sindhu yielded through Persian the blanket terms 'Hindu', 'Hindi' and 'Hindustan', just as 'India' itself comes to us through Greek.

Repeated further movements in subsequent centuries of peoples from the central Asian highlands added their mix to the local populations, whose high culture was seemingly never so closely intertwined with Hindu institutions as elsewhere at that period in South Asia, being rather linked with Buddhism, whose heritage is preserved in the graceful art of Gandhara or the romantic remains of Taxila.

The later history of the region is, however, chiefly tied to Islam. First introduced into **Sind** by an Arab invasion in 711 AD, Islam became the politically dominant creed of the north-west with the conquests of Sultan Mahmud of Ghazna in Afghanistan (1000–30), which led to the establishment of a Muslim kingdom in the Panjab for two centuries before the establishment of the Sultanate of Delhi reduced Lahore to the status of an important provincial capital only. This political establishment of Islam was accompanied by extensive conversions of the local inhabitants from Buddhism or Hinduism, largely as the fruit of the peaceable missionary work of the Sufi saints, the great Pirs whose magnificent tombs are still major focuses of devotion and pilgrimage throughout the region.

The final and most glorious phase of Muslim rule was inaugurated by Babur (ruled 1526–30) who followed the familiar path down the Khyber and across the Panjab on his way to Delhi and the establishment of the Mughal empire. His successors' authority was to run throughout the region as its semi-independent kingdoms were reduced to imperial provinces. Much of the finest architecture of the region dates from the Mughal period, especially in Lahore, developed as one of the premier cities of the empire, and in Kashmir, conquered under Akbar (ruled 1556–1605) and favoured by his successors as a summer retreat. Both **Lahore** and **Srinagar** have a **Shalimar Gardens**, equally redolent of this imperial past.

The Mughal period saw the foundation of the Sikhs in the Panjab as a distinct religious group. Although the teachings of their first Guru Nanak (1469–1539) were markedly pacific, the growth in the numbers and power of the Sikhs brought their leaders into increasing conflict with the emperors. By the early 18th century, the Sikhs in their still familiar distinctive uniform had been reorganized by their last Guru into a martial community actively rebelling against the Mughals, who were simultaneously facing other revolts throughout their overextended realms. Further Muslim invasions from Kabul ended the authority of the weakened Mughals throughout the north-west. From Kashmir to Sind, most of this huge borderland came once again largely to be ruled from Afghanistan, not from India. Only in the Panjab was a truly independent kingdom securely established in Lahore by the Sikh Maharaja Ranjit Singh (ruled 1799–1839), from whose lavish patronage derives the outward splendour of such famous Sikh buildings as the **Golden Temple** in **Amritsar**.

Throughout history, the north-west had been the first region of South Asia to be conquered by outside invaders. The British, however, came to it from the opposite direction, reaching its borders only some 50 years after their original annexation of Bengal. Sind was conquered from Bombay in 1843 in a short invasion led by Sir Charles Napier, as elegantly reported in his (sadly apocryphal) telegram *peccavi* 'I have sin(ne)d'. The two Anglo-Sikh wars (1845–49) against Ranjit Singh's formidably trained but now treacherously led armies made the Panjab a more expensive conquest, aided by the fateful sale of **Kashmir** with its large Muslim majority to the Hindu Maharaja who had been one of Ranjit Singh's chief lieutenants.

During the heyday of the British Raj, the Panjab was paternalistically favoured with a 'jewel in the crown' status. This derived in part from the loyalty of the newly conquered province during the Mutiny of 1857, leading to a new policy of recruiting for the Indian army almost exclusively from the Panjabis and Pathans, now deemed to be 'martial races' unlike the disloyal sepoys who had actually conquered most of India for the British. From its headquarters in **Rawalpindi**, the army's chief role was now to pacify the tribes of the frontier and secure it against the imagined threat of the Russian Bear. Ruled by administrators robustly free of the petty regulations in force in longer conquered provinces, the loyal yeomanry and feudal landlords of the Panjab were also favoured by the great extension of canal irrigation, making its wheatfields the breadbasket of an empire clothed from the cotton it grew for the Lancashire mills. Add to all this the Raj's summer capital of **Simla** in the Panjab hills, or those scenes of pig-sticking parties on delightfully crisp winter mornings sentimentally recalled in so many memoirs by retired Panjab officers, and some idea of that golden age can still be glimpsed.

Social and political realities are seldom amenable to such idealized pictures. However belatedly, the north-west became exposed to the new ideas of religious and cultural renewal and to the aspirations for political freedom earlier formulated in the distant metropolitan cities of India. Typically these first gripped the more educated Hindu minority who dominated urban life throughout the region, before spreading amongst the Muslims and, in the Panjab, the Sikhs. The splits which thus developed along religious lines became apparently irreconcilable as the date for independence approached under the shadow of the Muslim demand for Pakistan, catastrophically so as that date was vaingloriously advanced by the last viceroy.

The partition of 1947 was accompanied by truly unimaginable suffering. Perhaps a million people were killed, and many millions lost their homes as first the Muslim minority from the east and the Hindus and Sikhs from the west crossed the new Indo–Pakistan frontier which now divided the Panjab, then the Hindu minority were expelled from Sind, to be replaced by the Urdu-speaking Muslim *muhajir* refugees from north India who settled in Karachi and its other cities. While Pakistan thus came to have an almost entirely Muslim population, its relations with India were embittered from the outset by the Hindu ruler of **Kashmir** taking the largely Muslim population of most of his state into India.

Nor is there any denying the violence of much of the post-colonial history of the region. The period has seen three fruitless wars between Pakistan and India over Kashmir, and the recent sullen revolt of the Kashmiris following the alienation of the Sikhs from the Indian government after the storming of the Golden Temple in 1984, the rise of ethnic tensions in Pakistan which the periodic impositions of ruthless military authority have proved powerless to control, and the effects of the abortive Russian invasion and subsequent civil war in Afghanistan in causing yet another massive wave of immigration from the hills to the north-western plains.

Nevertheless, the landscapes of the region, still barely touched by industrialization outside the great Pakistani cities of Karachi and Lahore, are as lovely as ever. Still amply nourished by the rich waters of the Indus system, its agriculture is notably prosperous, and the dreadful poverty of too much of northern India is hardly to be seen. And, turning from the world of reality to that of imagination, the literary traditions of both the pre-colonial and the colonial past continue to be developed in a variety of languages, whose number is unusual even for the linguistically super-abundant sub-continent of South Asia.

LANGUAGES AND PEOPLE

Works in no less than nine languages have been drawn upon to provide the representative extracts which conclude this chapter. Six of these languages (Baluchi, Pashto, Kashmiri, Panjabi, Siraiki and Sindhi) are associated with the major ethnic groups and provincial units of the region, whose culture has been further subjected to the profound influence of three literary languages (Persian, Urdu and English).

The geographical division between the western hills and the Indus plains corresponds roughly to that between tribal speakers of languages of the Iranian family, and the settled populations speaking Indo–Aryan languages related to those of their eastern neighbours in India. There are two Iranian languages which extend into Pakistan. The scattered Baluch tribes of Baluchistan in south-west Pakistan and the neighbouring part of Iran speak Baluchi, an uncultivated country cousin of Persian, to which it is quite closely related. The far more numerous Pathans of the North-West Frontier, who still fiercely preserve one of the world's most vigorously masculine tribal societies in the wild hills straddling Pakistan and Afghanistan, speak Pashto. This belongs to a different branch of the Iranian family, and is very different in sound and basic vocabulary from its neighbours. Its heavy stress patterns and harsh clusters of consonants account for the popular description of Pashto sounding like someone talking with a mouth full of pebbles.

Kashmiri, by contrast, is given a honeyed quality by the unusual vowel harmonies and palatal consonants that make it sound like one of the gentler Slavonic languages. Although it is an Indo–Aryan language descended from Sanskrit, its long separate evolution from the languages of the plains means that it too is not immediately intelligible to plainsdwellers. Nor are the sharp-featured and slightly-built Kashmiris, forced to live by their wits by an environment which has historically been more lavish in the dispensation of visual beauty than of social justice, always easily understood or appreciated by their southern neighbours.

Few have much problem in understanding the Panjabis, famous for their loud manner, and the butt of much humour for the denseness which is supposed to accompany their striking aptitude for practical success at the expense of other groups consoling themselves with notions of their own greater sophistication. By far the most numerous of the region's peoples, Panjabis quickly established themselves as the dominant group in Pakistan, and even the prolonged tension which has recently afflicted Indian Panjab has been unable to destroy a society where the Sikhs and Hindus walk a lot taller than they do further down the Ganges. The bluff Panjabis might in fact be described as the Yorkshiremen or the Texans of India. The national tendency to throw their weight around is often thought to be reflected in their language, which is closely related to Hindi and Urdu, but sounds quite unlike them with its heavily stressed consonants, clipped vowels and dropped aitches.

The south-west Panjab along the middle Indus has a different character. Unlike the rather egalitarian society of peasant farmers and middle-sized landlords of the central and eastern districts lying across the five tributary rivers, this is historically feudal country, dominated by tribal chieftains and vast estates. The language of this area is Siraiki, only recently establishing itself as more than an aberrant dialect of Panjabi. Spoken along both banks of the middle Indus in all four provinces of Pakistan, its separate existence has yet to receive the all-important seal of political validation to match the general recognition of its sweet and courteous character.

Siraiki is in many ways a halfway house between Panjabi and Sindhi, with which it shares many common features, notably a set of 'implosive' consonants pronounced by drawing the breath in instead of out, an operation which sounds harder to do than it actually is, and which hardly does more to disturb its famous sweetness than provide a certain additional piquancy. The characteristics of language and society noted for Siraiki may be repeated with added force for Sind, where the sweetness of Sindhi has for some non-Sindhi ears an almost disagreeably 'niminy-piminy' quality and where traditions of brutal feudal exploitation that have for so long prevailed in this historically isolated province are only now being violently challenged.

Many of the region's writers have chosen not to write in any of these six, preferring the traditional South Asian solution to the problems created by an abundance of concurrent spoken languages through the cultivation of formal literary languages which could act as widely diffused standards, at least for those educated in their use.

In the classical period, as has been seen in the preceding chapter, it was Sanskrit which acted as just such a standard language among the educated Brahmans. When the Muslims conquered the region, Sanskrit was replaced outside orthodox Hindu circles by Persian, which had by then become established over Arabic (though written in the Arabic script and filled with Arabic loanwords) as the lingua franca of the eastern Islamic world. Intrinsically possessing the wonderful quality of being one of the easiest languages in the world to learn, Persian had the further advantage of being historically quite close to most of the local languages of the north-west. As a result of the long dominance of Persian as the chief cultural language of the region which lasted until after 1900, all six have been profoundly influenced by it in their vocabulary and syntax, and all are written in suitably adapted versions of the Perso–Arabic script, except for the special Gurmukhi script employed by Sikh writers in India for writing Panjabi.

Having already abandoned Persian in favour of English and Urdu for official and educational purposes in the northern provinces of India by the time they conquered the north-west, the British transferred this new system to the Panjab also. As elsewhere in the less metropolitan parts of South Asia, English was to be restricted as a natural language to the elite and the highly educated, although a much wider class was given an administratively necessary competence in bureaucratic formulae of the 'your immediate attention is kindly requested in this matter' type.

Urdu became much more profoundly implanted in the Panjab as a natural successor to Persian, itself of course a major influence on the earlier evolution of Urdu in northern India. Although later political agitation caused important groups of Hindus and Sikhs to turn against Urdu (in favour of Hindi and Panjabi respectively), its Islamic character ensured it a ready welcome among the Muslim majority in the colonial period, and its promotion as the national language of Pakistan after independence. Most Pakistani writers from the Panjab still prefer to write in Urdu, although its cultural dominance has come under increasing challenge from the regional languages in other provinces.

Pre-Modern Literatures

Persian was the preferred language of most of the region's tiny circles of literati throughout the eight centuries between the Muslim and the British conquests. Not then merely the 'Farsi' of Iran but one of the great international languages of Asia, Persian was the vehicle for an immense South Asian literature, ranging from the strictly Islamic to the purely secular. Only recently has Persian finally been dropped from local educational curricula, where it for so long formed a core subject, thus bringing to an end the long period during which Persian was not only itself the premier literary language of the region, but also acted as a continual influence upon literary expression in its other languages.

Poetry was always preferred for imaginative writing, but there is plenty of Indo–Persian prose as well. While many pompous court histories or austere Islamic treatises retain only a technical interest to scholars, there are some splendid books in Persian prose still amply worth reading as easier approaches than most of the poetry to the outlooks of the past. As tends still to be the case today, the most vivid pictures of local scenes come not from the over-familiar pens of local writers but from outsiders struck by their unusualness.

A classic illustration of this general rule is provided by the memoirs of the Mughal emperor Jahangir ◊ (ruled 1605–27). A gifted writer, though like most political autobiographers primarily concerned with self-justification, Jahangir had an undeniable eye for natural beauty. He makes for once appropriate and not too excessive use of the flowery conventions of Persian prose to record a general impression of **Kashmir**, one of the most favoured parts of his dominions (Extract 12). The passage is further embellished in the customary fashion with verses. This was an art that came to every gentleman, since his education would have entailed learning plenty of poetry by heart. In the highest social circles, the same education was also open to ladies, as shown by the wistful epitaph composed for herself by Jahangir's queen Nur Jahan (d 1646), which adorns her grave at the royal tomb-site at **Shahdara** across the river Ravi from **Lahore** (Extract 22).

It is in fact a good deal easier to write Persian verse than it is to translate it into English. Perhaps only Fitzgerald has ever quite managed to bring it off, in his versions of the *Rubaiyat*. Even by the time of Umar Khayyam (d 1123), contemporary with the first Muslim courts in **Lahore** (1050–1200), the essential characteristics of classical Persian poetry were already clearly constellated. These lie not only in the deceptive simplicity of its language and the neat elegance of its conceits (lending it a certain superficial similarity to the Augustan style in English), but also in its teasing equivocation between the sacred and the profane, relying on quite restricted sets of symbolic imagery, like the rose and the bulbul, the moth and the flame, or the morning breeze and the cup of wine. Linked to the scenery of Iran, this poetic vocabulary seldom allows the vivid depiction of South Asian scenes. The purpose of the poetry was, after all, less to accentuate regional differences than to bring all those who shared the high Muslim culture together. And though the elements of the poetry may be few, their supple manipulation for the expression of universals proved endlessly fertile in the generation of formal odes at court, the long rhymed narratives of love called *masnavi*, the romantic poems and quatrains respectively called *ghazal* and *rubai* for private enjoyment, or mystical hymns for musical performance at Sufi shrines.

Within the region, it is the last of these settings which has the greatest cultural and literary importance, given the central place of the great shrines in its spiritual life. The power of the Sufi orders derived from the charisma of the original saints and their successors around whose tombs the shrines were founded. In literature, this charisma is continually recorded in the tales included in the *malfuzat*, a peculiarly attractive genre of Indo–Persian prose summarizing the conversations of Sufi masters. If the saints were themselves poets, it may be expressed in often ecstatic poetry, either in Persian or in one of the local languages.

In the Panjab the greatest of the early saints was Shaikh Farid ◊, who settled by the river Sutlej at the site now called **Pakpatan** in what was then wilderness. The earliest picture of this Shaikh and his surroundings appears in the greatest of all books of *malfuzat*, the record compiled in the next generation (1309–22) of the conversations of his chief disciple Shaikh Nizamuddin Auliya, whose tomb is the greatest Muslim shrine in Delhi (Extract 25). To Shaikh Farid are also attributed a set of short couplets reckoned to be the oldest works of Panjabi/Siraiki literature, in which local scenery is used to illustrate moral and spiritual truths (Extract 26).

The same subordination of outer to inner reality runs throughout the magnificent hymns of Guru Nanak ◊, which far surpass the early Farid couplets in quantity and in imaginative sweep. One of the truly great and truly original religious poets of India, who always manages to linger just long enough in his passing descriptions of the physical world to fix his hearers in one form of reality before transporting them into the higher reality which lies just behind it, Nanak adapted seemingly almost every local genre of folk-poetry to develop the teachings which were to be formalized as Sikhism. One much loved example is his hymn on the folk-theme of the Twelve Months (Extract 21), from which the appropriate verse is sung in Sikh temples at the beginning of each month every year. None of Nanak's successors quite matches his originality and power. Although their hymns form a major part of the Sikh scriptures, the *Adi Granth* (1604), an increasing preference for Hindi over Panjabi symbolizes the gradual assimilation of Sikh literature to wearily familiar north Indian norms.

Other early literatures of the region are more sketchily preserved, but here and there contain some startlingly vivid evocations of local scenery. As always, the flavours of these evocations derive as much from genre and society as from setting. In all three respects, there is a total difference of flavour between the sweetly lyrical references to the flower-filled **gardens of Srinagar** by Habba Khotun ◊, the last queen of independent Kashmir (Extract 9) and the harshly heroic epithets of a Baluchi ballad grimly describing a fierce tribal war of the 16th century (Extract 2).

Predictably enough, the turbulent conflicts of the Frontier infuse much of Pashto literature with a similarly heroic spirit. The power of the greatest of all Pashto poets, Khushhal Khan Khatak ◊, derives however from a combination of this spirit with the sophisticated rhetoric of the Persian lyric. Khushhal Khan was himself an adept of Persian poetry, and his Pashto *ghazal*, looking wistfully towards the brave world of the hills beyond Peshawar from the Indian prison to which he had been consigned by the Mughal emperor Aurangzeb (d 1707), is a classic blend of the local and the high styles (Extract 4).

A similar blend underlies the great 18th century classics of Sindhi and Panjabi poetry, produced in the period following the collapse of Mughal authority in the Indus valley after the death of Aurangzeb. Critics are very fond of citing the analogy of Robert Burns in attempting to characterize Khushhal Khan or the Sufi poetry brought to its apogee in Sindhi by Shah Abdul Latif ◊ and in Panjabi by Bullhe Shah ◊. Like Burns, it is true, they have acquired the status of national poets in their respective regions most obviously through their prefer- ence for the vivid resources of local idiom over the bland sophistication of the chief literary language of the day. But just as Burns is a much subtler artist than the folksy Lowlander of sentimental imagination, so too in their very different cultural context do these poets embody the universal insights of islamic Sufism in local garb. Once again, the outer images are subordinate to the inner teachings in Bullhe Shah's reflections on the whiteness of cotton (Extract 19). The same sub- ordination underlies Shah Abdul Latif's picture of the terrors of the mighty river at night (Extract 35). Here, as so often in all these Sufi lyrics, an added cultural resonance is given by the setting of the scene within one of the great romantic legends of the Indus valley, the poet taking the part of the heroine usual in South Asian literary tradition who addresses herself to her divine Beloved.

These legends of Suhini and her lover Mehar, Hir and Ranjha, Sassi and Punnun, were also treated by other poets of the period in numerous full-length narratives, whose conventions owe quite as much to the formal Persian *masnavi* as to local bardic verse. One of these narratives, the *Hir* by Varis Shah ◊, is rightly reckoned to be quite the greatest classic of Panjabi literature, and desperately calls for adequate transla- tion in order to be more widely recognized as a true masterpiece in the world league. The richness of detail, the deft adaptation of Persian conventions, the exploitation of the full resources of Panjabi (including the crudities for which it is famous), above all the mix of tenderness with sardonic insight, can be barely glimpsed at best in our short extracts set on the river Chenab, known as the most romantic of the Five Rivers (Extract 18). It is easier to illustrate the still touching but much less concentrated quality of Hasham Shah ◊, Varis Shah's chief successor in the Panjabi narrative genre. In his well-known description of Sassi's desperate quest for her beloved, the conven- tions of the *masnavi* blur the directness in order to increase the pathos (Extract 30).

LITERATURES IN THE COLONIAL PERIOD

Since the British conquest of the north-west began only in the 1840s, this was one of the last regions of South Asia to feel the full impact of the new cultural and literary currents released by the impact of colonialism. Particularly in the culturally more isolated parts of the region, itself so distant from the distant cities of Calcutta and Bombay, traditional literary patterns long endured. By this time, much is naturally derivative. But in the secluded setting of the princely state of **Bahawalpur**, preserved by its ruler's convenient loyalty to the British during the conquest of the Sikhs, the last classic collection of Sufi poetry was produced in Siraiki by Khwaja Ghulam Farid ◊. His *malfuzat* often mention his deep love and knowledge of the vast deserts of Bahawalpur, the natural and magical setting for many of his most memorable and affecting lyrics (Extract 15).

The irruption of the colonial presence was more violently experienced in the western hills, where the tribes offered fierce resistance to pacification. Their reaction was customary enough, but now there were soon keen amateur folklorists to record some of the oral literature it generated. The British were of course very partial to those ballads which did them proud, like the one praising Sir Robert Sandeman (1835–92), the pacifier of Baluchistan (Extract 1). The same barren hill setting figures in the Pashto ballads of the period. A tougher nut to crack than the more organized Baluch tribes, the Pathans of the North-West Frontier preferred to celebrate the fierce triumphs of their nimble braves over the lumbering forces of the infidel 'Franks', the repeated theme of many contemporary ballads published with a certain glee in French from Paris (Extract 3).

The flush of conquest and subsequent glow of imperial achievement coloured the extensive literature on the region which appeared in English from the victorious side in the process of colonization. Like the Persian literature which had preceded it, much of this is now very dated and is to be taken only with very large doses of nostalgia. A few personalities still stand out from the early days, however, none more obstreperously than Sir Richard Burton ◊, later to achieve fame as one of the great Victorian explorers and notoriety for his supposed expertise in oriental sexuality. Burton began his career as a junior army officer working under Napier, the conqueror of Sind, but soon resigned his commission, partly because of the scandal attaching to his secret report on the homosexual brothels he had been able to penetrate through his mastery of languages and of disguise. His two-volume account of Sind is typically filled with much curious detail about this then very backward and remote area, equally typically expressing an arrogant superiority as remarkable as the bombastic style in which it is so suitably couched (Extract 31).

Like so many British writers on India, Burton hovers between literature and the more utilitarian genres of travelogue and ethnography. Many others hover perilously near the boundary between literature and kitsch in their attempts to capture something of the exotic world of the natives they romantically glimpsed from the cosy compounds of official bungalows. The glycerine is certainly amply smeared over the lens through which 'Laurence Hope' ◊, in real life the wife of an Indian army doctor, perceived the soft magic of Kashmir in a poem now evoking not so much memories of India as of those treacly mezzos or baritones of yesteryear performing it in another lady's well-known musical setting (Extract 10).

But the Raj would not have been the Raj without the one writer whose maverick genius was great enough to match its brief glory. This was, of course, Rudyard Kipling ◊. Kipling's brief Indian years (1882–89) were largely spent in the north-west, and many of his Indian writings are closely linked to the places of this region. **Lahore**, where he worked as a journalist, **Simla**, where he satirically observed British India at play in his early short stories, the cantonments of *Soldiers Three* and the *Barrack Room Ballads*, the **Frontier** and the **Grand Trunk Road** – all these were drawn into the British imagination through Kipling's cunning art. Among his prose writings, the strangely powerful appeal of his fantasy heroism (always only just one remove from the *Boy's Own Paper*), clothed in a mastery of the techniques of 19th-century narrative realism and a very sharp eye for physical feel, is most keenly experienced in *Kim* (1901), written long after his return to England (Extract 20). It is his poetry, however, that still stirs the blood of most readers. Kipling was the last great English ballad poet, and still no true Englishman can fail to be swept along by the surge of his galloping metres into the harsh Frontier hills where men are men (Extract 5).

Of course, the fastidious rightly detect a certain coarseness here, and may be allowed their point when it comes, for instance, to Kipling's doggerel Hindustani ('Hi! Slippy *hitherao*!/Water, get it! *Panee lao*,/You squidgy-nosed old idol Gunga Din.') It is interesting that similar objections were being levelled at this time by connoisseurs of Urdu poetry at the work of reformers forsaking the courtly conventions of Persian in favour of a more direct style based on English models. The pioneers of this 'natural' poetry were the circle of Urdu poets in **Lahore** in the 1870s inspired by their employer Colonel Holroyd, then Director of Public Education, to produce odes on 'Hope' or 'The Rainy Season', or heroic imitations of Victorian classics like Macaulay's *Horatius*.

The aspiration of many of these 'natural' poets was predictably more palpable than their achievement. But their example made possible the titanic art of Muhammad Iqbal ◊, which draws upon the resources of both east and west to create a heady vision of the unique potential of

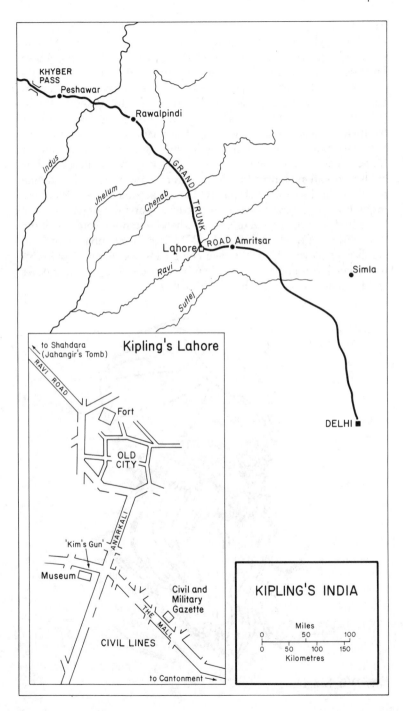

Islam for transforming the self and the world. Though often cloudy, this exalted vision was to provide one of the inspirations of the Muslim independence movement leading to the creation of Pakistan, where Iqbal is officially revered as the spiritual father of the nation. A Panjabi of Kashmiri descent, who spent most of his life practising law in Lahore, Iqbal wrote his theoretical works in English prose, his most powerful shorter poems in Urdu, and longer philosophical poems in the by then already antique medium of Persian. His poetry in both languages trumpets in a timbre sometimes strangely reminiscent of Kipling, but to infinitely more serious purpose. The landscape and its monuments are no longer seen as the natural outward symbols of divine reality, as in the earlier Sufi poetry, but are pressed into service as the inspiration for stern sermons on Islamic history and the present betrayal by its leaders of their glorious past, as when he stands before one of the great shrines of the Panjab (Extract 27). Or they are inflated into still grander employment as the launching-pads for heroic visions of regenerated Muslim destiny, as when he is stirred by the soaring peaks and foaming waters of **Kashmir** (Extract 8).

Bhai Vir Singh

A similarly spiritualized historicism pervades the equally copious oeuvre of Iqbal's long-lived contemporary Vir Singh ◊, revered by Sikhs for his double role as religious revivalist and pioneer of modern Panjabi poetry. His view of Indian history is naturally at odds with Iqbal's, but the lessons he draws from the ruins of the past are analogous in his contemplation of a well-known tourist landmark in Kashmir, the Hindu temple at **Avantipur** north of Srinagar (Extract 7).

Perhaps more familiar ground is reached with the next generation of writers, who grew up in the years when the long-drawn struggle for independence was well under way even in the sleepy cities and towns of the Panjab. Among the left-wing writers associated with the Progressive movement, religious revivalism was replaced by the secular appeal of communism, then at the height of its appeal as the colonial system was seen to be rapidly tottering towards its inevitable end. Too simplistic an ideal for the production of much truly memorable poetry, the social realism fostered by the movement found a more appropriate outlet in prose, where several fine writers, drawn from all three of the religious groups in the Panjab, produced important short stories in Urdu. Others chose English, notably Mulk Raj Anand ◊, whose characteristically Progressive approach may be seen in his richly biased evocation of **Amritsar**, written in wartime London NW1 (Extract 14).

LITERATURE SINCE 1947

The region was shattered by the Partition in 1947. Yet, at least in literature, the pieces which it left behind may be seen nearly half a century later to have come together in often unsuspected ways, as the splintered aftermath of colonialism gradually yields place to the one world of modern communications, and the literatures of the past become but examples of the literature of the present.

On the British side, the chief emotion aroused by the end of their Indian empire was regret. The last years of the colonial period have subsequently inspired quite a little sub-genre of their own in English. Some books deserve to be better known than they are, like the curious first-hand account of the often forgotten armed rebellion of a powerful Sindhi Pir's followers in the 1940s, later compiled from Sindhi sources by the British officer responsible for its suppression (Extract 34). Too many others are blurred by the fatal fuzziness of that nostalgia, still so cheaply exploited by profitable television series, but which is delightfully absent from the novels of Rumer Godden ◊, the superbly professional doyenne of the old Anglo–India. Few of the many who have tried have bettered the calm vividness of her picture of Kashmir (Extract 11).

Something of the same retrospective glow colours the perspective of that small group of locally born writers whose family background linked them to the British. This is nowhere more warmly applied than in the lovingly detailed family portraits by the blind Ved Mehta ◊, drawing on his amazingly clear childhood memories to fill a richly realized panorama of upper middle class Panjabi Hindu life from the turn of the century until independence (Extract 23).

For local writers who stayed in Pakistan or India, the feelings aroused by independence were perhaps both stronger and more mixed. For some, the freedom struggle was by no means concluded in 1947, least of all in Kashmir, where the continuing demand for popular representation inspired among others a vigorous renaissance of Kashmiri lyrical poetry. This was led by the Hindu poet Dina Nath Nadim ◊, who draws on the past to reveal a newly committed insider's view of the Valley (Extract 13).

For others, especially in the Panjab, the tragedy of Partition overlaid the triumph of independence, and formed the theme of many fine poems, novels and short stories in English, Urdu and Panjabi. Among the more accessible items of this literature are the English novels of the prolific Indian journalist Khushwant Singh ◊, one of which describes the trains which brought now the desperate living, now the murdered dead to their new countries across the new frontier (Extract 28). A still bleaker picture of the new border from the other side is sketched by the Pakistani writer Saadat Hasan Manto, driven by Partition from Progressivism to alcoholism, at the end of one of his most famous Urdu short stories (Extract 29).

While prose literature was by now firmly established locally, much of the finest Pakistani writing has continued to be in verse. Commonly agreed to be greatest Urdu poet of the post-Iqbal generation, Faiz Ahmad Faiz ◊ was another Progressive who came quickly into conflict with the repressive political system that soon came to control Pakistan. Many of his finest poems, employing an extraordinarily evocative mix of traditional and modern imagery to express their yearning for a better world, were the fruit of his enforced leisure as a political prisoner, as in his glimpse of Lahore from his incarceration in its **Mughal Fort** (Extract 24). Others were inspired by his travels as an internationally recognized journalist, as in his vision of the **Hindu Kush** from a plane (Extract 6), where in spite of the altitude his lyrical perspective stays closer to human feeling than the philosophical stratosphere into which Iqbal was so prone to soar. Other poets have a more caustic vision of reality, typified by the picture of the sprawling metropolis of Karachi given by Taufiq Rafat ◊, one of the tiny handful of Pakistani poets choosing to write in English (Extract 33).

Since the generals who have ruled Pakistan for so many years of its existence have generally been noted for their extreme suspicion of any literature which might conceivably be thought subversive, many younger Pakistani writers have been driven away from a commitment to changing society towards a more introspective cultivation of their art for its own sake. The detailed locales photographically conjured up by the preceding generation of social realists give way to a more shadowy world of often menacing anonymity in the Urdu stories of such Pakistani Panjabi writers as Mazhar ul Islam ◊. Though set in a nameless city, the ambience is nevertheless unmistakably Pakistani (Extract 17).

Contemporary novelists in English who have dealt with the region form such a very heterogeneous international group that it is impossible to characterize their work collectively. In *Shame* ◊, Salman Rushdie's controversial foray into Pakistan, a satirical picture of the feuds of feudal politicians is presented. The extracts given here from two London-based writers, for instance, could hardly be more different from this or from one another. In his often sinister tale of the more mysterious side of Karachi, the East African-raised Adam Zameenzad ◊ is detachedly humorous at the expense of the bizarre quality of seaside life in that disorienting city (Extract 32), while the Panjabi-born artist Balraj Khanna ◊ revels through the rueful persona of his hero in the ruder side of Panjabi life on the way to the new city of **Chandigarh** (Extract 16). Here we end, for once, with laughter.

POETIC GENRES

While English is the model for the short story and other modern prose genres in all languages, Persian patterns have been the main outside influence on poetic forms. The basic unit of Persian poetry is the end-stopped couplet with final rhyme, often with the first half-couplet also rhyming. Fitzgerald keeps the original rhyme-scene *aa ba* of the short *rubai* in his versions of Khayyam:

> Come, fill the Cup, and the fire of Spring
> Your Winter-garment of Repentance fling:
>   The Bird of Time has but a little way
> To flutter – and the bird is on the wing.

The rhyme-scheme of the most popular form, the more extended *ghazal*, is similarly *aa ba ca da ea* . . . , with the poet's pen-name included in the final verse. Most translators have to fall back on separately rhyming couplets in English (eg Extract 4). This simpler scheme *aa bb cc* . . . is, however, used only in Persian in the narrative *masnavi*. All these genres, together with the strict metres defined by quantitative patterns of long and short syllables (themselves partly borrowed from Arabic), were transferred directly into Urdu poetry, rather as if all English verse were to be composed in hexameters and other Latin metres.

Only after 1900 did the model of English free verse begin to encourage the development of more experimental forms in Urdu and the other languages. These are loosely called 'poem', or *nazm* in Urdu (eg Extract 24), *kavita* in Panjabi (eg Extract 7).

In the traditional poetic forms of the local languages of the region, metres tend to be quite simple and to be based on accent rather than quantity. Rhymes are however just as much of a problem for English translators, who have no convenient stores of grammatical endings to draw from. Each language has its own nomenclature and individual forms, but the genres are essentially of three main types. The shortest are individual couplets (eg Extract 26), formally resembling the Hindi *doha* and similarly typically used to express brief gnomic thoughts (see pp 106–108 for more on poetic genres). The medium-length lyrical genres are typically designed for singing, as short rhymed verses interspersed with a refrain. Examples include the secular *lol* lyric of Kashmiri (eg Extract 9) and the Sufi hymn called *kafi* in Panjabi (eg Extract 15). Longer narrative poems include irregularly rhymed ballads (eg Extract 1) and those more elaborately composed in rhyming stanzas (eg Extracts 18, 30).

BOOKLIST

The following selection includes all titles which are extracted in this chapter as well as other relevant works. The editions cited are not necessarily the only ones available. The exact location of the extracts can be found in 'Acknowledgements and Citations' at the end of the volume. Extract numbers are highlighted in bold for ease of reference.

Anand, Mulk Raj, *The Big Heart*, Hutchinson International Authors, London, 1945. **Extract 14**.

Abbas, Zainab Ghulam, *Folktales of Pakistan*, Pakistan Publications, Karachi, 1957.

Bakht, Baidar and Jaeger, K.G., eds and trans, *An Anthology of Modern Urdu Poetry*, Vol 1, Educational Publishing House, Delhi, 1984. **Extract 6**.

Beveridge, H., ed, *The Tūzuk-i-Jahāngīrī or Memoirs of Jahāngīr*, Rogers, A., trans, Low Price Publications, Delhi, 1989. **Extract 12**.

Bowen, J.C.E., *The Golden Pomegranate: A selection from the poetry of the Mughal Empire in India 1526–1858*, Thacker & Co, Bombay, 1957. **Extract 22**.

Burton, Richard F., *Scinde: or the Unhappy Valley*, Richard Bentley, London, 1851. **Extract 31**.

Caroe, Olaf, *The Pathans 550 BC – AD 1957*, Macmillan, London, 1958.

Cornell, L.L., *Kipling in India*, Macmillan, London, 1966.

Darmesteter, James, *Chants populaires des Afghans*, Paris, 1888–90. **Extract 3**.

Godden, Rumer, *Kingfishers Catch Fire*, Pan Books, London, 1966. **Extract 11**.

Halliday, Tony, ed, *Insight Guides: Pakistan*, APA Publications, Singapore, 1990.

Hasan, Mumtaz, ed, *The Adventures of Hir and Ranjha: A translation into English Prose by Charles Frederick Usborne from the Punjabi poem of Waris Shah*, Lion Art Press, Karachi, 1966.

Hasham Shah, *Sassi Punnun*, C. Shackle, trans, Vanguard Publications, Lahore, 1985. **Extract 30**.

Hashimi, Alamgir, ed, *Pakistani Literature: The Contemporary English Writers*, Gulmohar, Islamabad, 1987.

Hope, Laurence, *The Garden of Kama and other Love Lyrics from India*, William Heinemann, London, 1901. **Extract 10**.

Howell, Evelyn and Caroe, Olaf, trans, *The Poems of Khushhal Khan Khatak*, Pashto Academy, University of Peshawar, 1963. **Extract 4**.

Iqbal, Sir Muhammad, *Javid-nama*, Arberry, A.J., trans, George Allen & Unwin, London, 1966. **Extract 8**.

Jamal, Mahmood, ed and trans, *The Penguin Book of Modern Urdu Poetry*, Penguin Books, London, 1986.

Kachru, Braj B., *Kashmiri Literature*, Otto Harrassowitz, Wiesbaden, 1981.

Kaul, J.L., ed and trans, *Kashmiri Lyrics*, Rinemisray, Srinagar, 1945.

Khanna, Balraj, *Nation of Fools*, Penguin, London, 1985. **Extract 16**.

Kiernan, V.G., trans, *Poems by Faiz*, George Allen & Unwin, London, 1971. **Extract 24**.

Kiernan, V.G., trans, *Poems from Iqbal*, John Murray, London, 1955. **Extract 27**.

Kipling, Rudyard, *A Choice of Kipling's Verse*, T.S. Eliot, ed, Faber, London, 1941. **Extract 5**.

Kipling, Rudyard, *Kim* [1901], Macmillan, London, 1961. **Extract 20**.

Longworth Dames, M., *Popular Poetry of the Baloches*, Royal Asiatic Society, London, 1907. **Extracts 1 and 2**.

Lambrick, H.T., ed and trans, *The Terrorist*, Ernest Benn, London, 1972. **Extract 34**.

Matthews, D.J., Shackle, C. and Husain, Shahrukh, *Urdu Literature*, Urdu Markaz, London, 1985.

Mayne, Peter, *Saints of Sind*, John Murray, London, 1956.

Mazhar ul Islam, *Selected Stories*, Sang-e-Meel, Lahore, forthcoming. **Extract 17**.

Mehta, Ved, *Daddyji*, Secker & Warburg, London, 1972. **Extract 23**.

Naqvi, Tahira, *The Life and Works of Saadat Hassan Manto*, Vanguard Books, Lahore, 1985. **Extract 29**.

Quraeshi, S., *Legacy of the Indus: a Discovery of Pakistan*, Weatherhill, New York, 1974.

Rafat, Taufiq, trans, *Bullhe Shah: a Selection*, Vanguard Books, Lahore, 1982. **Extract 19**.

Rafat, Taufiq, *The Arrival of the Monsoon, Collected Poems 1947–78*, Vanguard Books, Lahore, 1985. **Extract 33**.

Raina, Trilokinath, ed and trans, *An Anthology of Modern Kashmiri Verse (1930–1960)*, Suresh Raina, Poona, 1972. **Extract 13**.

Riaz, Fahmida, *Pakistan: Literature and Society*, Patriot Publishers, New Delhi, 1986.

Schimmel, A., *Gabriel's Wing: A Study into the Religious Ideas of Sir*

Muhammad Iqbal, Brill, Leiden, 1963.

Scott, Paul, *The Raj Quartet* (*The Jewel in the Crown, The Day of the Scorpion, The Towers of Silence, A Division of the Spoils*), Pan, London, 1975. **Extract 36**.

Shackle, C., trans, *Fifty Poems of Khawaja Farid*, Bazm-e-Saqafat, Multan, 1983. **Extract 15**.

Sijzi, Amir Hasan, *Nizam ad Din Awliya* (*Morals for the Heart*) (*1309–22*), Bruce B. Lawrence, trans, Panlist Press, New York, 1992. **Extract 25**.

Singh, Harbans, *Bhai Vir Singh*, Sahitya Akademi, New Delhi, 1972.

Singh, Khushwant, *A History of the Sikhs*, 2 vols, OUP, New Delhi, 1977. **Extract 21**.

Singh, Khushwant, *Train to Pakistan*, Pearl Publications, Bombay, 1967. **Extract 28**.

Sinha, K.N., *Mulk Raj Anand*, Twayne Publishers, New York, 1972.

Sorley, H.T., *Shāh Abdul Latīf of Bhit: His Poetry, Life and Times*, Oxford University Press, Karachi, 1966. **Extract 35**.

Talib, G.S. and Singh, Harbans, ed, *Bhai Vir Singh, Poet of the Sikhs*, Motilal Banarsidass, New Delhi, 1976. **Extract 7**.

Taylor, David, ed, *World Bibliographical Series*, Vol 10, Pakistan, Clio Press, Oxford and Santa Barbara, 1990.

Zameenzad, Adam, *The Thirteenth House*, New Estate, London, 1987. **Extract 32**.

Extracts

(1) BALUCHISTAN:
FROM DERA GHAZI KHAN

A Siraiki ballad

From a ballad in honour of Sir Robert Sandeman (1835–92), the pacifier of Baluchistan. 'Garland of flowers' is the traditional epithet of Dera Ghazi Khan (dera phullan da sehra).

> On hearing of our ruler's coming
> Our souls were filled with heartfelt joy.
> The Frankish army pitched their camps
> The rebel strongholds to destroy.
> For bringing peace to this my land
> May Sandeman rewards enjoy!

His order read, at once in wrath
He called his army to his side.
'Up to the mountains come with me!
'From Dera Ghazi Khan I'll ride
'And from this flower-garland forth
'Across the plain through fair Syahaf
'Will fight full fierce at heart!' he cried.

(2) BALUCHISTAN: FROM SIBI TO KALAT

A Baluchi ballad

A prose version of part of one of the many traditional Baluchi ballads describing the ferocious tribal wars (c 1500) between the Lasharis and the Rinds, led to eventual destruction by the heroic Mir Chakur of Sibi.

When I fought with the thick-beards (the Rinds), the Rinds climbed up from below to the cold hill-skirts of Kalat. On the day when these words were spoken Chakur slaughtered a black cow; Chakur was filled with manly rage. He did not pass by the deep water of Jhal, nor did he saddle his mare Sangwath, nor did he bring his minstrel Gurgin with his tightly-stretched drums. Ha! Ha! what a victory was ours; we struck our foes a blow, and off went the chestnuts, like wild asses, with cup-shaped hoofs. Every mouthful in famous Sibi does Chakur carry off with livelong grief.

(3) FRONTIER: AMBELA

A Pashto ballad

The start of a ballad describing the fierce fighting at Qatal Gar ('The Killing Ground') during the Ambela campaign of 1863 between a British punitive expedition and the Pathans from Buner (Kipling's 'Bonair') summoned by the Wali of Swat as Ghazis or holy warriors against the Frankish infidels.

On the crest of Qatal Gar
How the Franks did suffer sore
Screaming, darkness filled their sight
As the Ghazis came to war.

On the crest of Qatal Gar
Lay the Franks encamped on high
Falcon-like, from far Buner
Those proud warriors drew nigh,
Scarlet-belted heroes who
Made their streams of bullets fly.

On the crest of Qatal Gar
How the Franks did suffer sore
Screaming, darkness filled their sight
As the Ghazis came to war.

(4) FRONTIER: ATTOCK

Khushhal Khan Khatak,
Home (From Captivity in Hindustan)

*This remarkable ghazal is an evocation of the beauties of the
poet's home in the hills.*

Now blessings on old Akoray! Believe me, he was wise
To make Surai his dwelling; no place with Surai vies,
Who fares on the royal highway, the road from Hindustan,
Must come to the Father of Rivers, ere he win to Khorassan,
Must cross by the Attock ferry, trembling the while with fear,
For Indus takes his tribute from pauper and prince and peer.
So shall he come to Surai, and if with a shower of rain,
Then shall he see life quicken over the verdant plain.
Stark and stern above Surai the peaks of Hodi tower,
Bur Surai looks to the northward over the vale of Peshawar.
Northward across the valley, where lesser streams unite –
Kalpani, Landai, Nilab, those waters of delight.
Swat and Tirah may be lovely, Hashtnagar may be fair,
But the sum of them all has nothing with Surai to compare.
Come then with your hooded falcons. Surai shall show you sport;
For the marches of Surai are teeming with game of every sort.
And Surai's sons shall go with you, ruddy are they and fair,
Merry-eyed, lithe and lissom, gallant and debonair.
God guard them all my kinsmen and keep them in good estate,
But I, Khushhal, am in exile. Who is stronger than Fate?
Yes, I, Khushhal, am an exile, and Oh but my heart is fain
To take the road for Surai and never leave it again.

(5) Frontier: The Hills

Rudyard Kipling, *The Ballad of East and West*

*The famous first line is only the start of a thundering ballad,
telling of the pursuit of a tribal horse-thief by an officer of the
Frontier Guides.*

Oh, East is East, and West is West, and never the twain shell meet,
Till Earth and Sky stand presently at God's great Judgment Seat;
But there is neither East nor West, Border, nor Breed, nor Birth,
When two strong men stand face to face, though they come from the ends
    of the earth.

Kamal is out with twenty men to raise the Border-side,
And he has lifted the Colonel's mare that is the Colonel's pride.
He has lifted her out of the stable-door between the dawn and the day,
And turned the calkins upon her feet, and ridden her far away.
Then up and spoke the Colonel's son that led a troop of the Guides:
'Is there never a man of all my men can say where Kamal hides?'
Then up and spoke Mahammed Khan, the son of the Ressaldar:
'If ye know the track of the morning-mist, ye know where his pickets
    are.
At dusk he harries the Abazai – at dawn he is into Bonair,
But he must go by Fort Bukloh to his own place to fare.
So if ye gallop to Fort Bukloh as fast as a bird can fly,
By the favour of God ye may cut him off ere he win to the Tongue of
    Jagai.
But if he be past the Tongue of Jagai, right swiftly turn ye then,
For the length and the breadth of that grisly plain is sown with Kamal's
    men.
There is rock to the left, and rock to the right, and low lean thorn
    between,
And ye may hear a breech-bolt snick where never a man is seen.'
The Colonel's son has taken horse, and a raw rough dun was he,
With the mouth of a bell and the heart of Hell and the head of a
    gallows-tree.
The Colonel's son to the Fort has won, they bid him stay to eat –
Who rides at the tail of a Border thief, he sits not long at his meat.
He's up and away from Fort Bukloh as fast as he can fly,
Till he was aware of his father's mare with Kamal upon her back,
And when he could spy the white of her eye, he made the pistol crack.
He has fired once, he has fired twice, but the whistling ball went wide.
'Ye shoot like a soldier', Kamal said, 'Show now if ye can ride!' . . .

(6) FRONTIER: HINDU KUSH

Faiz Ahmad Faiz, *Rendezvous*

Faiz provides the following note to this Urdu poem: 'On the flight from Moscow to Delhi, when the plane flies over the Hindu Kush mountains at 30,000 feet, around 3 to 4 a.m., the traveller can see at once night on one side, and dawn on the other.'

I have drunk the sun,
My breath comes quick,
And my thirst becomes intense.
From the land of light and fragrance
Morning has come down like the sun.
The crystal aircraft
High above the clouds
Glides swiftly,
On this side, all is night,
On the other, red sword of morning.
The sky is bathed in crimson,
Red stars shining in its glow,
The stars our playmates
And the moon our friend.
We fly surrounded by the song of life.
Every moment of our transitory voyage
Is eternal.
God, let our journey never end.

(7) KASHMIR: AVANTIPUR

Vir Singh, *Ruins at Avantipur*

A short Panjabi poem lamenting the destruction by Muslim iconoclasts in medieval times of the great ninth-century Hindu temples at Avantipur, north of Srinagar.

Avantipur is now
 Two temples' remains
A long gone culture's ruins
 Telling time's passing
Two witnesses to eyes
 Blinded by cataract
From recognizing art
 Bereft of the spirit.

Their breakers' sense of art
  Was by zeal confused
In pleasing others they
  Themselves became ill
That beauty's left these ruined
  Once-worshipped idols
Though idols we restore
  Who'll give the spirit life?

(8) KASHMIR: MOUNTAINS AND LAKE WULAR

Muhammad Iqbal, *Javed-nama*

After ascending through the spheres on the heavenly journey described in his Persian epic, the poet turns in despair from the spectacle of Islam in his native Panjab to be shown his ancestral homeland of Kashmir by Mulla Tahir Ghani (d 1669), a Kashmiri Persian poet, who first invokes the land of the Nehrus, then describes the turbulent river Jhelum as the symbol of the life force itself.

Who gave to India this yearning for freedom?
Who gave the quarry this passion to be the hunter?
Those scions of Brahmins, with vibrant hearts,
whose glowing cheeks put the red tulip to shame –
keen of eye, mature and strenuous in action
whose very glance puts Europe into commotion.
Their origin is from this protesting soil of ours,
the rising-place of these stars is our Kashmir.
If you suppose our earth is without a spark,
cast a glance for a moment within your heart;
whence comes all this ardour you possess,
whence come this breath of the breeze of spring?
It is from the selfsame wind's influence
that our mountains derive their colour and scent.

Do you not know what one day a wave
said to another wave in Lake Wular?
'How long shall we strike at each other in this sea?
Rise up, let us break together against the shore.
Our child, that is to say, yon ancient river
fills with its roar valley and mountains and meadow;
continually it smites the rocks on its path

until it uproots the fabric of the mountains.
That youth who seized cities, deserts and plains
took his nurture from the milk of a hundred mothers;
its majesty strikes terror into mortal hearts;
all this is from us, not from any other.
To live in the bounds of the shore is a sin;
our shore is but a stone in our path.
To accommodate oneself to the shore is eternal death,
even though you roll in the sea morning and evening;
life is to leap amidst mountain and desert –
happy is the wave that has transgressed the shore!'

(9) KASHMIR: SHALIMAR

Habba Khotun, *'For Him I Pick these Violets'*

A typically direct lyric by the poet-queen of Kashmir.

The sweat drops from my brow like pearls
I am his girl
For him I pick these violets.

In Shalimar I sit –
For him I fill these cups with wine.
For him I leap for joy –
My love will come to me.
For him these flower-wreaths I twine.
I am his girl
For him I pick these violets.

In Ishabar I sit –
For him I fill this glass with wine.
For him I braid my hair –
My love will come to me.
For him these flower-wreaths I twine.
I am his girl
For him I pick these violets.

(10) KASHMIR: SHALIMAR

Laurence Hope, *'Pale Hands I Loved'*

Made famous as an Edwardian drawing-room song in the setting by Amy Woodforde-Finden.

Kashmiri Song

Pale hands I loved beside the Shalimar,
  Where are you now? Who lies beneath your spell!
Whom do you lead on Rapture's roadway, far,
  before you agonise them in farewell?

Oh, pale dispensers of my Joys and Pains,
  Holding the doors of Heaven and Hell,
How the hot blood rushed wildly through the veins
  Beneath your touch, until you waved farewell.

Pale hands, pink tipped, like Lotus buds that float
  On those cool waters where we used to dwell,
I would have rather felt you round my throat
  Crushing out life; than waving me farewell!

(11) KASHMIR: SRINAGAR

Rumer Godden, *Kingfishers Catch Fire*

Through the thoughts of Sophie, newly arrived with her two children, the magic spell of (most of) Kashmir is sharply captured.

She and Teresa and Moo had come to Kashmir in the early summer. They had travelled up the old military road along the red gorges of the Jhelum river where boys threw bunches of flowers into the car. In spite of the flowers, Sophie wished she could have come by a more romantic way; by one of the caravan routes overland from China, through Manchuria and Sinkiang over the Himalayas or through Little Tibet, over the Zoji La pass with its great double glacier, or along the almost forgotten horse-path that came from Old Delhi, the path that the Mogul Emperor Jehangir used. 'But now tourists, not Emperors, come to Kashmir', said Sophie sadly. 'There are more cars than caravans.'

At first she had been bitterly disappointed; Srinagar the capital city, built on the Jhelum river like an Eastern Venice, was as surrounded by roads and cars and filling stations as any modern town; its suburbs were spread like Wimbledon or the suburbs of Capetown or Amsterdam. 'Suburbs *anywhere*,' wrote Sophie disgusted. It was crowded with tourists and the tourists had loud unbeautiful voices, cameras and radios, tartan rugs and picnic hampers. There was a plague of guides and touts, houseboat and tent agents, houseboat owners, taxi-boat man . . . 'and this is Kashmir!' wrote Sophie. 'The land of Lalla Rookh, the vale of paradise, the pearl of Hind!' She wished she had never come; then, one day, she took a little taxi-boat and was paddled down the Jhelum to the Old City, and away through crowded waterways, under wooden bridges by gardens and islands and villages till she came out on the Dāl Lake and, 'This is a beautiful, beautiful country', wrote Sophie. 'There is a quality in the beauty here that seals you.'

The vale, poets say, is set like a pearl between the mountains, a pearl of water and flowers; the water comes from the glaciers on the far snow peaks and runs through high alps and valleys where gentian and primula and edelweiss grow, through forests, down rapids till it falls to the vale floor and flows into its lakes and river and waterways.

The lakes are fringed with willows where the kingfishers live; the foot-hills are reflected in the water in green and pink and blue and white from the orchards and rice-fields and mulberry gardens and fields of flax. There are villages of tall, wooden-balconied houses standing in groves and orchards of chenar and walnut or fruit trees; the villages are scattered on islands in the lakes, or along the shores and foot-hills, with narrow humped-back bridges and built-up roads between them.

Sophie liked the people, the boatmen, the farmers, the shepherd boys, the pony-men, the Mohammedan merchants, the Hindu Pundits and their decorative women, even the poor women with their handsome faces and dirty clothes; everything she saw that summer, to her, was poetry.

(12) Kashmir: The Valley

Jahangir, *Tuzuk*

The Mughal emperor Jahangir devotes a few pages of his memoirs to the description of his beloved Kashmir.

If one were to take to praise Kashmir, whole books would have to be written. Accordingly a mere summary will be recorded.

Kashmir is a garden of eternal spring, or an iron fort to a palace of kings – a delightful flower-bed, and a heart-expanding heritage for dervishes. Its pleasant meads and enchanting cascades are beyond all description. There are running streams and fountains beyond count.

Wherever the eye reaches, there are verdure and running water. The red rose, the violet, and the narcissus grow of themselves; in the fields, there are all kinds of flowers and all sorts of sweet-scented herbs more than can be calculated. In the soul-enchanting spring the hills and plains are filled with blossoms; the gates, the walls, the courts, the roofs, are lighted up by the torches of banquet-adorning tulips. What shall we say of these things or of the wide meadows and the fragrant trefoil?

VERSE

'The garden-nymphs were brilliant,
Their cheeks shone like lamps;
There were fragrant buds on their stems,
Like dark amulets on the arms of the beloved,
The wakeful, ode-rehearsing nightingale
Whetted the desires of wine-drinkers;
At each fountain the duck dipped his beak
Like golden scissors cutting silk;
There were flower-carpets and fresh rosebuds,
The wind fanned the lamps of the roses,
The violet braided her locks,
The buds tied a knot in the heart.'

The finest inflorescence is that of the almond and the peach. Outside the hill-country the commencement of blossoming is the 1st Isfandār-muz (February 10). In the territory of Kashmir it is 1st Farwardīn (March 10), and in the city gardens it is the 9th and 10th of that month, and the end of their blooming joins on to the commencement of that of the blue jessamine. In attendance on my revered father I frequently went round the saffron fields and beheld the spectacle of the autumn. Thank God that on this occasion I beheld the beauties of the spring.

(13) KASHMIR: THE VALLEY
Dina Nath Nadim, *Our Motherland*

A Kashmiri poem on the beauties of the Valley and the inspiration of its great poetesses Habba Khotun and her predecessor Lal Ded (14th century).

Our motherland –

A flower
The lusty prime of spring
A bower in Shalamar
Ardour of young innocence
Excitement of new clothes
Lovers uniting after a quarrel
A lotus in full bloom
Memory of one's love

A habitat of flowers
Children's cheeks flushed with joy
Delightful greenery
The drunkenness of youth
First love

The light of one's eyes
Pure gold for one's daughter
Hope nearing fulfilment
Infant dawn
Joy of the peasant woman adopting a child
The wild abandon of youth

A lovely village
Peasant's siesta after hard toil
An evening on the Dal Lake
A green almond
A long absent uncle arriving from the village with a gift of apples
Sweetness flowing from mother's breasts

Softest wool
Garden conjured up by the embroiderer's needle
The cool feel of silk
A broad-bordered shawl
Youth carved on walnut wood
The vision of plenty

We are her sentinels
With the voice of Lal Ded ringing in our ears,
The fire of Habba Khotun glowing in our hearts,
And with new music we stand today –
With sweet songs that sing on the lips of the spring breeze!

(14) PANJAB: AMRITSAR

Mulk Raj Anand, *The Big Heart*

On Kucha Billimaran ('Cat-Killers' Alley'), the coppersmiths'
quarter in Amritsar.

It must be remembered, however, that Billimaran is not a blind alley.
Apart from the usual mouth, which even a *cul de sac* keeps open, it has
another, which makes it really like a two-headed snake. With one head
it looks towards the ancient market, where the beautiful copper, brass,
silver and bronze utensils made in the lane are sold by dealers called
kaseras, hence called Bazar Kaserian. With the other it wriggles out
towards the new Ironmongers' Bazar, where screws and bolts and nails
and locks are sold and which merges into the Booksellers' mart, the
cigarette shops and the post office replete with the spirit of modern
times.

And just as it has two openings into the outside world, so it has two
or three great neighbours. One of them, at the Bazar Kaserian end of
Billimaran, is the shrine of the Goddess Kali, mother as well as dread
destroyer who must always be appeased. Another, reached by way of
devious lanes, is the Golden Temple which was built three hundred
years ago by a Sikh saint with money donated by Akbar, the Great
Moghul, around the tank which gives to the whole city its name
Amritsar, Ocean of Nectar. Here the more skilled coppersmiths were
employed as hereditary artisans for some generations, embossing reliefs
of religious scenes on gold-washed brass and silver plates and making
the pinnacles which glisten on the top of the pure white marble. The
other neighbour is the Clock Tower, the monument which ushered in
the 'iron age', with the fancy weathercock on its steep needle which
talks to the sky and records the evanescent moods of the winds and the
spheres, and with its gigantic four-faced English clock from which the
families with the two- or three-storeyed houses in Billimaran can read
the movement of the two hands of the new god, Time.

One way or another, therefore, Billimaran has changed, outwardly
with the shadows which fall across it and in the inner life of its hovels
because the eyes of the old brass idols contemplate with their eternal

stares the European celluloid combs, the Pears soap, the bits of glassware, the rubber dolls, the electro-plated jewellery and the aluminium utensils strewn about.

(15) PANJAB: BAHAWALPUR DESERT

Khwaja Ghulam Farid, *The Rain-Clouds of July*

A Siraiki kafi, in which the poet describes the marvellous beauty of the Bahawalpur desert in the rainy season, when lovers long to meet.

> If you have pity, come, my love,
> To watch the rain-clouds of July.
>
> I sit to weep and watch the roads
> And let my raven fly.
>
> I seek the omens all night long:
> By day I cast my die.
>
> Without you, lord of Kech's land,
> How harsh a life have I.
>
> I wed you on the first of days –
> So why now me deny?
>
> The lonely dunes entrance my heart:
> I bid the town goodbye.
>
> That God has made Malhir to bloom
> This spring does testify.
>
> Now rivers from the pouring rain
> Flow in the desert dry.
>
> Blue, yellow, red, the rainbows glint
> Like fish-scales in the sky.
>
> The scarlet caper, bulrush white,
> The emerald alkali!
>
> Before each hut the pots are churned
> And sweet the cowbells cry.

The camels, cows, and goats, and sheep
In lines to graze pass by.

I'll doff these dirty clothes, Farid,
Should he to me draw nigh.

If you have pity, come my love,
To watch the rain-clouds of July.

(16) PANJAB: ON THE BUS
TO CHANDIGARH

Balraj Khanna, *'Nation of Fools'*

*In one of the many Salingeresque episodes of this story of modern
Chandigarh, Omi chances his arm on one of those typically
overcrowded buses which are the main means of transport in the
region today. As in much humorous English writing about South
Asia, there is a lot of play on translated local expressions besides
actual Panjabi words, like 'lucha badmash', weakly to be
translated 'dirty rascals'.*

Omi squeezed in next to a young village girl – and then an extraordinary thing happened. In spite of the tempest in his heart, Omi suddenly
became aware of her. His right elbow was in contact with her left breast
and it had taken him all that time to realise it. Omi sat up and looked
at his right. The girl was well built and a few years older than he. Next
to her sat a boy of Omi's age and Omi was sure he had seen him around
at the cinema. This had an inhibiting effect on Omi. But the girl
seemed unconcerned.

'What a day? A First in the morning, a brush-off in the afternoon,
and now this. What a day? God, you are quite extraordinary.'

Omi looked at the boy next to the girl, their eyes met and Omi
thought that he saw him smile faintly.

Omi thought of the last time he had made this journey and felt a
ripple of shame over his cheeks. A little later the girl raised her arm to
give more room to Omi's elbow. Omi thought of Satish and of what he
would advise under the circumstances. He smiled to himself as Satish's
advice flashed across his mind, and extended his left hand. The breast
was firm and round. The girl, like all village girls, did not wear a bra.

'What a day? A First in the morning, a brush-off in the afternoon
and now this.'

Omi discovered that there was an open vent in the kamiz shirt of the
village girl. Would she let him put his hand through it? Should he try?

It was an agonising decision. Time was passing – they were only a mile or two from the Chandigarh bus stand.

Omi tried. She let him. He caressed her beautifully shaped breast and was gone cock-a-doodle-do and ninety degrees. Then something else happened. Omi tried to reach the second breast. As he did so, his hand met another and the girl slapped Omi's face with one hand and that of the boy on her right with the other.

'What is going on here?' the conductor said.

'These lucha badmash bad men on my sides!' the girl said and started to cry loudly.

'I done nothing,' the other boy said quickly.

'You done something to the poor girl?' the conductor said to Omi, whacking him on the head before he could even open his mouth.

Omi was too confused to answer. The conductor slapped him on the head again, stopped the bus and put him outside in the blazing sun.

'You eat the white heat for the rest of the way home,' he shouted at Omi.

There was not even a tree in sight to rest under. The pink and cement-grey distant buildings of Chandigarh looked very distant indeed. They shimmered like a mirage in the June heat of the Punjab. The Kasauli mountain loomed on Omi's right, but home was far, far away, past several mirages that he saw as he cursed himself and Satish and the fifty-one laddus.

'If I don't die of sun-stroke, I will certainly die of cursing Satish.'

Omi wanted to cry. He couldn't, because he was laughing.

(17) Panjab: A City Hospital

Mazhar ul Islam,
'A Sweeper in the Whispers' Shadow'

A modern Urdu writer reveals an aspect of Pakistani life few tourists will wish to explore, deliberately suggesting the widespread alienation experienced under military rule through a humble Christian sweeper's glimpse of the other reality of an apparently well-equipped modern hospital.

At that moment Sadiq Masih saw a rat which had come creeping along the wall and was now standing a little way away from him. It lifted its face and looked at him, then suddenly turned to go back the same way it had come. He felt the rat was moving unusually slowly. It looked as if it wouldn't be able to run away if it suddenly had to. That is exactly what did happen when a nurse came from the same direction. Instead of taking itself off quickly, it crouched down by the wall. He realized it must be a rat from the hospital canteen, because the rats from the medical stores and the general wards weren't so lazy.

Besides, Sadiq Masih recognized that rat. He'd seen it two nights ago moving around the things on the counter in the canteen. As soon as it saw him, the rat had got into the box of leftover chapaties and started gnawing them. Of course there were rats everywhere in the hospital, but Sadiq Masih could tell which ward a rat belonged to by looking at its colouring and the way it moved. He was especially good at recognizing the rats which wandered about in dirty, smelly bathrooms with broken floors. When a patient killed bedbugs and flung them into the bathroom, the rats would polish them off in minutes.

(18) PANJAB: THE RIVER CHENAB

Varis Shah, *Hir*

Like many of the romances of the Indus valley, the setting of the Hir legends is the river Chenab, which occurs in many contexts in the poem by Varis Shah, often with a satirical colouring.

At dawn, when birds called travellers to reveille,
    And when the staffs to churn the milk were plied,
And folk arose and rushed to wash away
    All traces of the beds they'd occupied,
Did Ranjha to the river wend his way,
    To find the ferry on the other side,
Where, Varis, Luddan slumped and gross he saw,
    Like sacks of honey in a grocer's store.

Hir's boat on the Chenab is where the lovers first meet:

Hir screamed and raged and raised her switch to stun
    The mortal who had roused her fairy-wrath –
When Ranjha woke and said, 'O dearest one!',
    Hir laughed and sweetly plighted him her troth.

(19) PANJAB: COTTONFIELDS

Bullhe Shah, *'All cotton balls are white'*

In the refrain of this Panjabi kafi, the cotton-bolls which are so familiar a sight in the fields of the Panjab are used as a vivid symbol of the essential oneness of creation.

All cotton-bolls are white

Warp and woof, spindle and reel,
back and front, head and heel,
will end up in the one cloth
that will not last the night.

All cotton-bolls are white

Khaddar and muslin, coarse or fine,
dress for ploughman, groom, divine,
issue from the self-same loom
no matter what the guise.

All cotton-bolls are white

The bangles worn by girls, and rings
and bracelets and such adornings
are from the same silver beaten,
though hands are dark or light.

All cotton-bolls are white

(20) PANJAB: THE GRAND TRUNK ROAD

Rudyard Kipling, *Kim*

A truly classic piece of Kiplingese.

The lama never raised his eyes. He did not note the money-lender on his goose-rumped pony, hastening along to collect the cruel interest; nor the long-shouting, deep-voiced little mob – still in military formation – of native soldiers on leave, rejoicing to be rid of their breeches and puttees, and saying the most outrageous things to the most respectable women in sight. Even the seller of Ganges-water he did not see, and Kim expected that he would at least buy a bottle of that precious stuff. He looked steadily at the ground, and strode as steadily hour after hour, his soul busied elsewhere. But Kim was in the seventh heaven of joy. The Grand Trunk at this point was built on an embankment to build against water floods from the foothills, so that one walked, as it were, a little above the country, along a stately corridor, seeing all India spread out to left and right. It was beautiful to behold the many-yoked grain and cotton wagons crawling over the country roads; one could hear their axles, complaining a mile away, coming nearer, till with shouts and yells and bad words they climbed up the steep incline and plunged on to the hard main road, carter reviling carter. It was equally beautiful to watch the people, little clumps of red and blue and pink and white and saffron, turning aside to go to their own villages, dispersing and growing small by twos and threes across the level plain. Kim felt these things, though he could not give tongue to his feelings, and so contented himself with buying peeled sugar-cane and spitting the pitch generously about his path. From time to time the lama took snuff, and at last Kim could ensure the silence no longer.

'This is a good land – the land of the South!' said he. 'The air is good; the water is good. Eh?'

'And they are all bound upon the Wheel', said the lama. 'Bound from life after life. To none of these has the Way been shown.' He shook himself back to this world.

'And now we have walked a weary way,' said Kim, 'Surely we shall soon come to *parao* [a resting place]. Shall we stay there? Look, the sun is sloping.'

'Who will receive us this evening?'

'That is all one. The country is full of good folk. Besides', – he sunk his voice beneath a whisper, – 'we have money.'

The crowd thickened as they neared the resting-place which marked the end of their day's journey. A line of stalls selling very simple food and tobacco, a stack of firewood, a police-station, a well, a horse-trough, a few trees, and, under them, some trampled ground dotted with the black ashes of old fires, are all that mark a *parao* on the Grand Trunk; if you except the beggars and the crows – both hungry.

(21) PANJAB: THE HOT SEASON

Nanak, *Tukhari baramaha*

Although subordinated to a spiritual message, as so often in the poetry of Nanak, the images take on a vivid life of their own in their evocation of the burning summer heat of the Indian month of Asad (June–July).

In Asad the Sun scorches.
The sky is hot

The earth burns like an oven,
Waters give up their vapours.
It burns and scorches relentlessly in the month of Asad.

The Sun's chariot passes the noon's sky
The wife watches the shadow creep across the courtyard.
And the cicada calls from the glades.
The beloved seeks the cool of the evening.
If the comfort she seeks be in falsehood,
There will be sorrow in store for her.
If it be in truth,
Hers will be a life of joy.

(22) PANJAB: LAHORE

Nur Jahan, *'Epitaph'*

*Composed for her own tomb by the empress of Jahangir, herself
an accomplished poetess with the pen-name 'Makhfi'.*

Upon my grave when I shall die,
No lamp shall burn nor jasmin lie,
No candle with unsteady flame
Serve as reminder of my fame;
No bulbul, chanting overhead,
　　Shall tell the world that I am dead.

(23) PANJAB: LAHORE

Ved Mehta, *Daddyji*

*A wonderfully rich evocation of Lahore in the early years of the
20th century. The red-light district of the Hira Mandi is still
famous today for its dancing-girls.*

Ever since Daddyji could remember, he had been hearing about
Lahore. Lalaji had always said that the fortunes of the family would be
made there ('Aim your arrow at the sky'), and Bhaji Ganga Ram had
always talked about the city as the educational center of the world. As a
child, Daddyji would ask Manji to tell him about his grandfather's great
journey to Lahore, and she would say, 'I remember that when he came
back from there he had an entire cloth shop behind his saddle. All the
villagers gathered around him, and he said to them, "Touch! Touch!"
They had the hands of working people, but even they could tell that

the cloth from Lahore was softer than melted butter.' And now Daddyji had actually come to live in Lahore, the clamorous, clangorous city. Here there were whole streets of cobblers, weavers, and potters, and there was an entire bazaar for every imaginable trade – one for metalworkers, one for carpetmakers, one for dyers, one for cloth merchants, one for dry grocers, one for goldsmiths and silversmiths, one for confectioners, one for savory cooks. There was even a whole city-within-a-city, called Hira Mandi ('gem market'), which was dead and deserted by day but by night was glittering and alive with sound of music and laughter. Behind the bazaars and lanes were rabbit warrens of *mohallas*, or blocks of tenement houses, opening onto squares that were entered by still narrower *guillis*, and these *mohallas* and *guillis* contained more life and variety than could be found in any village. Bhaiji Ganga Ram, however, had taken lodgings in a new, open part of the city, where the British government officers and the Indians attached to the British establishment lived. These lodgings – three rooms and a kitchen, one flight up – were somewhat better than the ones in Multan. But what Daddyji liked most of all about them was a discovery he made within minutes of reaching them. Just outside the building was a curved pipe sticking up out of the ground, with a handle on top. When the handle was raised and lowered, water came gushing out of the mouth of the pipe, which was high enough to sit under. Daddyji had never seen anything like it, and the first thing he did in Lahore was to take a bath.

(24) PANJAB: LAHORE

Faiz Ahmad Faiz, *Oh City of Many Lights*

An Urdu poem expressing the poet's homesickness for Lahore, glimpsed from his imprisonment in the Fort.

Listless and wan, green patch by patch, noonday dries up;
Pale solitude with venomed tongue licks at these walls;
Far as the skyline, like a fog, an oozy tide
Of blockish misery swells and shrinks, heaves up and falls.

Beyond that fog the lights of my thronged city lie.
    O city of many lights! –
Who could make out what way from here your lights are? Dark
As a town's ramparts isolation hems me in,
And war-worn hope's faint soldiery droops on every side.

(25) PANJAB: PAKPATAN (SHRINE)

Amir Hasan Sijzi, *Favaid ul Fuad*

This record of conversations (malfuzat) of Shaikh Nizamuddin Auliya of Delhi contains numerous anecdotes of the holiness of his teacher Shaikh Farid al-Din (d 1266), who settled in the wilderness at Ajodhan (now Pakpatan), where his shrine is now one of the major centres of pilgrimage in the Panjab.

Then he began to speak about Shaykh al-Islam Farid al-Din – may God sanctify his dear and blessed secret! 'His was a different kind of work. Removing himself from the company of people, he preferred the isolation of uncultivated regions. He settled in Ajodhan. He opted for the bread of dervishes and other things that were available in that region. He was content, for instance, to have rough wood for his tooth brush. Despite his longing for solitude, there was no limit to the number of people who were forever visiting him.' . . .

Even as the master spoke, they brought in trays. Referring to this food and to the tablecloth they spread out for it, he told a story. 'Once there was a man named Muhammad. He came and sat down in the presence of Shaykh al-Islam Farid al-Din – may God bless his lofty secret! When they brought in a loaf of bread, they couldn't find a tablecloth or linen on which to set it. Shaykh Farid al-Din instructed them to put it on the ground. That Muhammad thought to himself, "How good it would be were there a cloth!" The Shaykh, with his index finger, drew a design on the ground and declared to that man: "O Muhammad, know that this is a tablecloth!" That Muhammad, added the master, 'was still a spiritual novice.'

(26) PANJAB: PAKPATAN

Shaikh Farid, *Couplets*

This world is also reflected, if less directly, in the early Panjabi/ Siraiki couplets (doha) believed to be by Farid, which refer to his ascetic practices or to the natural scenery of the region's deserts and rivers (C. Shackle, trans).

My bread is made of wood, and hunger is my salt,
Those eating buttered bread will suffer pain's assault.

Make your mind quite flat, without a dune or hill.
Then you need not ever feel the fires of hell.

Upon the brackish pond, the geese came to alight.
They dip their beaks but drink not, burning to take flight.

In pain the day is spent, in grief the night is passed.
'On the shoals', the sailor cries, 'the boat is now stuck fast.'

(27) PANJAB: SIRHIND

Muhammad Iqbal, *To the Panjab Pirs*

An Urdu poem inspired by the beautiful tomb at Sirhind of Shaikh Ahmad Sirhindi 'the Reformer' (1564–1624), whose proud independence from the Mughal emperor Jahangir is contrasted with the craven subservience of latter-day hereditary Pirs to the British Raj.

I stood by the Reformer's tomb; that dust
Whence here below an orient splendour breaks,
Dust before whose least speck stars hang their heads,
Dust shrouding that higher knower of things unknown
Who to Jehangir would not bend his neck,
Whose ardent breath fans every free heart's ardour,
Whom Allah sent in season to keep watch
In India on the treasure-house of Islam,
I craved the saints' gift, other-wordliness;
For my eyes saw, yet dimly. Answer came:
'Closed is the long roll of the saints; this Land
Of the Five Rivers stinks in good men's nostrils.
God's people have no portion in that country
Where lordly tassel sprouts from monkish cap;
That cap bred passionate faith, this tassel breeds
Passion for playing pander to Government.'

(28) PANJAB: TRAINS

Khushwant Singh, *Train to Pakistan*

Set in the summer of 1947, just after Partition, the story is located in the small village of Mano Majra, just inside the new Indian border, where the moneylender Ram Lal has been killed by dacoits.

There was a pause in the conversation. Iqbal slipped his feet into his sandals and stood up.

'I must take a walk. Which way do you suggest I should go?'

'Go in any direction you like. It is all the same open country. Go to the river. You will see the trains coming and going. If you cross the railroad track you will see the dark bungalow. Don't be too late. These are bad times and it is best to be indoors before dark. Besides, I have told the lambardar and Uncle Imam Baksh – he is mullah of the mosque – that you are here. They may be coming in to talk to you.'

'No, I won't be late.'

Iqbal stepped out of the gurdwara. There was no sign of activity now. The police had apparently finished investigating. Half a dozen constables lay sprawled on charpoys under the peepul tree. The door of Ram Lal's house was open. Some villagers sat on the floor of the courtyard. A woman wailed in a singsong which ended up in convulsions of crying in which other women joined. It was hot and still. The sun blazed on the mud walls.

Iqbal walked in the shade of the wall of the gurdwara. Children had relieved themselves all along it. Men had used it as a urinal. A mangy bitch lay on her side with a litter of eight skinny pups yapping and tugging at her sagging udders.

The lane ended abruptly at the village pond – a small patch of muddy water full of buffaloes with their heads sticking out.

A footpath skirted the pond and went along a dry water-course through the wheat fields towards the river. Iqbal went along the watercourse watching his steps carefully. He reached the riverside just as the express from Lahore came up on the bridge. He watched its progress through the criss-cross of steel. Like all the trains, it was full. From the roof, legs dangled down the sides on to the doors and windows. The doors and windows were jammed with heads and arms. There were people on buffers between the bogies. The two on the buffers on the tail end of the train were merrily kicking their legs and gesticulating. The train picked up speed after crossing the bridge. The engine driver started blowing the whistle and continued blowing till he had passed Mano Majra station. It was an expression of relief that they were out of Pakistan and into India.

(29) Panjab: Wagah

Saadat Hasan Manto, *Toba Tek Singh*

The Sikh lunatic Bishan Singh, snatched by the Partition from the Lahore asylum where he had long remembered only that he came from Toba Tek Singh, meets a tragic end at the Indo-Pakistan border post at Wagah between Lahore and Amritsar.

On an extremely cold day, lorries filled with Hindu and Sikh lunatics left the asylum in Lahore, accompanied by police and some higher officials. As Wagah, the superintendents from both sides met and, the initial formalities out of the way, the actual transfer began and continued all night.

Getting the lunatics out of the lorries and handing them over to the Indian officials proved to be an arduous task. Many of them refused to leave the lorries and those who did, ran about wildly, making it increasingly difficult for the guards and other officials to keep them under control; those who were naked tore off any clothing that was forced on them, many were swearing and cursing, one or two sang, some fought with each other, others cried or wailed. Confusion was rampant. The women were also a problem, and the cold weather made everyone's teeth chatter.

The majority of the lunatics was not in favour of the transfer because these people could not comprehend the reasons for being uprooted from one place to be thrown into another. One or two men, not completely mad, shouted, 'Pakistan zindabad!' and 'Pakistan murdabad!' This infuriated both the Muslims and the Sikhs, and altercations between them were avoided with great difficulty.

When Bishan Singh's turn came to cross the border, he asked the official who was entering his name on a register, 'Where is Toba Tek Singh? In Pakistan or in India?'

The official laughed. 'In Pakistan,' he said.

On hearing this, Bishan Singh leaped back and ran toward the remaining group of men who awaited their turn. The Pakistani soldiers caught him and tried to force him back to the check-point. He resisted strongly.

'Toba Tek Singh is here!' he yelled. 'Oper di, gur gur di, anx di, bay dhiana di, mung di daal di of Toba Tek Singh and Pakistan!'

The authorities attempted to reason with him. 'Look, Toba Tek Singh is in Hindustan now – and if it's not there yet, we'll send it there immediately.' But he was adamant and would not budge from the spot where he stood. When the guards threatened to use force, he installed himself in a place between the borders and stood there as if no power in the world could move him.

Because he was a harmless man, he was not coerced and allowed to remain in that place while the transfer continued.

Before the sun rose, a piercing cry emitted from Bishan Singh who had been quiet and unmoving all this time. Several officers and guards ran towards him; they saw that the man who, for fifteen years, had stood on his legs days and night, now lay on the ground, prostrate. Beyond a wired fence on one side of him was Hindustan and beyond a wired fence on the other side was Pakistan. In the middle, on a stretch of land which had no name, lay Toba Tek Singh.

(30) SIND: THE DESERT

Hasham Shah, *Sassi Punnan*

The high point of the classic Panjabi version of the tale of Sassi describes the agony of Sassi's journey from her home in Bhambhore across the desert of the Maru Thal in search of Punnun who had abandoned her while she slept.

At noontide then there fiercely blazed
    an incandescent heat.
From heaven blew a wind which brought
    the birds down from the skies.
A fiery river swiftly rose
    and swept across the Thal
Yet, Hasham, Sassi turns not back;
    for Punnun still she cries.

Her delicate and rose-soft feet
    made lovelier by henna,
To gain one glimpse of which her lover
    would willingly be slain,
Were roasted in the desert sand
    like barely in the oven.
But, Hasham, gaze on Sassi's faith
    unturned by toil or strain.

Her heart's afire, the Thal ablaze
    and parting burns her heart,
Her eyes console her lips a little
    while her tears still pour.
She steels and steels again her spirit
    but she is overcome,
Oh Hasham, in her suffering
    by thinking of Bhambhore.

'If I had known he'd leave me sleeping
   my eyes would not have closed.
'Now let me mingle with the sand-grains
   which here like jewels glint.'
Then in the glitter of the sands
   she thought she saw a sea.
Who else, oh Hasham, would in this
   of love discern a hint?

(31) SIND: KARACHI

Richard F. Burton, *Scinde: or the Unhappy Valley*

In his usual grandiloquent style, the famous explorer describes the appearance of Karachi soon after the British conquest of 1843, when it was still a small town surrounded by the desert.

How lovely are these oriental nights! – how especially lovely, contrasted with the most unlovely oriental day. The plain around us is nothing but an expanse of sand, broken into rises and falls by the furious winds, and scarcely affording thorns, salsolæ, and fire-plants, sufficient to feed a dozen goats and camels. Yet, somehow or other, the hour communicates a portion of its charms to this prospect. The heavy dew floats up from the sun-parched earth in almost transparent mists, that at once mellow, graduate, and diversify a landscape which the painful atmosphere during daytime lays out all in one place like a Chinese picture. The upper heights of the dome above us are of the deepest, purest, and most pellucid blue, melting away around its walls into the lightest azure; the moon sheds streams of silver liquid upon the nether world; there is harmony in the night gale, and an absence of every harsher sound that could disturb the spell which the majestic repose of Nature casts upon our spirits.

* * * * * *

Before we enter our bungalow, and "shut up" for the night, I must remark concerning what we have just seen, that Kurrachee, (the native town,) wants many an improvement, which perhaps old Time, the great Progressionist, has in store for it. To him we look for the clearing of the harbour, the drainage of the dirty backwater, and the proper management of the tidal incursions. He may please to remove the mountains of old rubbish which surround and are scattered through the native town; eventually he may clear away the crumbling hovels which received us, at the head of the Custom House Bunder, and occupy the space with an erection somewhat more dignified. Possibly he will be induced to see the pier properly finished, to macadamise the road that leads to the camp, to superintend the growth of a shady avenue or two, and to disperse about the environs a few large trees which may break the force of the fierce sea wind, attract a little rain, and create such a thing as shade. We trust implicitly in Time. Withal we wish that those who have the power of seizing him by the forelock would show a little more of the will to do so. The old gentleman wears a fashionable wig, curly enough in front, but close behind as a pointer's back; and we, his playthings, are always making darts at the wrong side.

(32) SIND: KARACHI

Adam Zameenzad, *The Thirteenth House*

Although its seafront has been totally transformed since Burton's time, many visitors are struck chiefly by the bizarre incongruities described in this recent novel.

Zahid had always thought of Sandspit as an island and had approached it from the sea. He was seeing it from a completely different angle today and it might as well have been his first visit. There was no point of reference. However he did remember unpretentious little cabins scattered all along the beach. Now the area had mostly been taken by newly-built structures, little and not so little, ugly and not so ugly. Some were simple and inexpensive while others must have cost a neat little sum and were probably considered very elegant by their owners. Apart from these the rest of the beach and the surrounding area was more or less unspoilt . . .

In spite of the holiday there weren't many people about on this part of the beach – just a couple of Pakistani families and a few foreigners. An outsized Begum of declining years was reclining in the porch of a big cottage built in a style combining the Roman, the Gothic, the Mogul and the Hindu, its exterior covered all over with bright orange, green, blue, yellow and white tiles. She was dressed in what looked like a wedding dress complete with jewellery. She was surrounded by other equally true-to-type members of her family, totally uninteresting or utterly fascinating depending on the dosage you had had of such specimens. Further down, some fresh-looking young men and girls were frolicking happily about – brothers and sisters, judging by their open, guilt-free expressions. They presented a strange contrast to another foursome, whose coy and furtive manner announced to the people of Pakistan that they were breathing the sea-air in sin, if only of holding hands.

(33) SIND: KARACHI

Taufiq Rafat, *Karachi*

For many Pakistanis from outside Sind, Karachi is something of a fascinating monster.

Karachi is the only city I know
where barbers solicit like whores, and papayas
are considered fruit. Sandwiched between
the desert and sea, it swells by reclamation,
and points to its belly shamelessly.
A windy instant burg, it lionises
artists whose chief merit is a big mouth.

(34) SIND: KINGRI

H.T. Lambrick, *The Terrorist*

Lambrick was the British officer in charge of operations in the 1940s against the Pir Pagaro of Kingri in north-east Sind, one of the most powerful Pirs of Sind, who mobilized his devoted Hurs against the British.

As Mohbat's relative I was able to go with him to the Estate openly by day, though the rule for Hurs coming from distant parts of Sind was to approach it by night from the river bank, where there is a big forest: Pir Saheb having provided boats for those crossing from the Larkana side. We walked out from Kingri along a road for a few miles, and at a turning came to a hedge of thorns, which, Mohbat told me, had been built in the last few months completely round the Estate, a distance of many miles, with only this one entrance on the north side, and another in the forest on the west. There was a guard post of Hurs here, who made their salaam to Mohbat, and we walked through. After nearly a mile we came to a much higher thorn hedge, which we had seen from a long distance against the dark green forest. Passing the guarded entrance, there was cleared ground inside for about two hundred paces, and then a second such enclosure: this too we entered. Mohbat pointed out yet another and still higher hedge further on, which he said contained the brushwood huts occupied by Pir Saheb and his family.

Ghazis were being enrolled not individually, but in batches, when a fair number of aspirants had gathered. Mohbat, who was from time to time called into the inner enclosure, told me that Pir Saheb would hold an enrolment the next morning, and all the recent arrivals who were camping simply under the trees, in other parts of the Estate, were being summoned. The ceremony only took place within the second enclosure, close to the gate of the inner one, where opposite to the guard room was a small platform, on which a green flag was flying. When we were all drawn up, about one hundred men, Pir Saheb came and stood on the platform. He was wearing a Seyd's green turban, and a khaki shirt and trousers, as at the times when I saw him out shooting. He was also girded with a sword and a pistol. We fell to our knees, but Pir Saheb ordered us to stand up and listen attentively to him.

(35) SIND: THE RIVER
Shah Abdul Latif, *Sur Suhini*

The romantic legend of Suhini reaches its climax as she prepares to cross the mighty river at night to meet her lover Mehar (here called Sahir 'Beloved') on the distant far bank.

The terror and the tumult rage within the flood
Where powerful crocodiles do congregate themselves
By thousands numbered, dreadful, and beyond all tale . . .

The terror and the tumult rage within the flood
Where monsters shelter and where brutes of prey do cry
And turn them hither thither. Ships in the abyss
Have been engulfed whole till not a trace of wreck
Nor any timber showed the catastrophe.
The whirling waters hold some power of dread: for ships
Depart thence and return not. Sahir, take thou them
Who have no skill of swimming, to that farther shore.

(36) TRAIN FROM DELHI TO PANJAB
Paul Scott, *A Division of the Spoils*

This extract from the final book of the Raj Quartet conveys both the intermitent nature of rail travel in the sub-continent and the violence of the Partition period.

The land now seems to be at peace. It requires some effort to see such a place as a background to any sudden or violent event. Perhaps there was no bloodshed, no murder on this stretch of line. But, as if remembering violence the train slows then draws to a stop. There is a clank under the carriage; cessation, immobility. The compartment – not airconditioned, one fan not working – grows warmer. Presently there comes the hollow sound of unevenly clunking goatbells and in a moment the straggling herd comes into view, driven by a lean man and naked urchin, in search of impoverished grazing. They go by without a glance, drugged by the heat and the singleness of their purpose. When they have gone there is silence but their passing has disturbed the atmosphere. The body of the victim could have fallen just here.

A few moments before, he is said to have gestured at the shuttered window of the compartment door on which strangers outside were banging and said 'It seems to be me they want', and then smiled at his shocked fellow passengers, as if he had recognized a brilliant and totally unexpected opportunity. In a flash he had unlocked the door and gone. Briefly, a turbaned head appeared, begging pardon for the inconvenience and then removed itself. The door banged to. One of the passengers stumbled across luggage and relocked it. After a moment he lowered the shutter and looked out. Those nearest him might have seen his horrified expression.

Just then the engine driver up ahead obeyed an instruction and the train glided forward. It was the smooth gliding motion away from a violent situation which one witness never forgot. 'Suddenly you had the feeling that the train, the wheels, the lines, weren't made of metal but of something greasy and evasive.'

Biographies and plot summaries

ANAND, Mulk Raj (b 1905–). Born in **Peshawar** and educated first in the Panjab then in London, where most of his prolific writing career has been based. *The Big Heart* (1945) is generally thought the finest of his many English novels (Extract 14), while his numerous other writings include a fascinating record of his early life (1985).

BULLHE SHAH (1680–1758). Panjabi Sufi poet (Extract 19). Drawing freely on local imagery and legends, his kafis are regarded as matchless examples of the genre. He is buried at **Kasur**, south of Lahore.

BURTON, Sir Richard Francis (1821–90). British writer and explorer. An exceptionally gifted linguist and master of disguise, his career as a young officer in India in the 1840s was followed by his explorations of Africa and Arabia, also a return to **Sind** in the 1870s (Extract 31). Nowadays best known for his translations of the *Arabian Nights* and Arabian erotica.

FAIZ, Faiz Ahmad (1911–84). Urdu poet (Extracts 6 and 24). Born in **Sialkot**, he became a lecturer in English, then after war service editor of a leading Pakistani English newspaper, interrupted by several years in prison for his communist sympathies. Awarded the Lenin Peace Prize in 1962, he later became Cultural Adviser to the Bhutto government in the 1970s, before the change of regime forced him into exile in Beirut, where he died.

FARID, Khwaja Ghulam (1845–1901). Hereditary Pir of the rulers of **Bahawalpur** state, whose Sufi lyrics are regarded as the classic works of Siraiki literature (Extract 15).

FARID, Shaikh (1175–1265). Revered throughout the Panjab as 'Baba Farid', the great saint buried at **Pakpatan**, to whom many miracles are attributed in the copious Persian hagiographic literature. Farid is named in the Sikh scriptures as the author of a hundred-odd Panjabi/Siraiki couplets.

GODDEN, Margaret Rumer (1907–). Novelist, children's writer and poet, who spent her childhood and early married life in India, the setting for several of her novels (Extract 11).

Rumer Godden

HABBA KHOTUN. Kashmiri lyrical poetess. Born a peasant girl called Zun ('Moon'), her beauty made her the bride of Yusuf Shah Chak (r 1578–86), the last king of independent Kashmir before its annexation by the Mughals.

HASHAM SHAH (1753–1823). Panjabi poet best known for his short narrative poems on the legend of Sassi and Punnun (Extract 30).

Hir. Legendary Panjabi heroine. The daughter of a chieftain of Jhang, whom she induces to employ her lover Ranjha as a herdsman. The scandal gets Hir married off, but Ranjha succeeds in regaining her by disguising himself as a yogi.

'HOPE, Laurence', pseudonym of Adela Florence Nicolson (née Cory) (1865–1904). Married to a Colonel in the Indian army, she killed herself after his death. Daring for their time, her passionate lyrics use the East as an exotic setting (Extract 10).

IQBAL, Sir Muhammad (1877–1938). Islamic philosopher, political thinker, Urdu and Persian poet. Born in **Sialkot** north of Lahore and trained in Germany and England, he practised law in Lahore while developing his ideas in numerous long Persian poems and Urdu lyrics (Extracts 8, 17). Knighted by the British for his political services, he is revered in Pakistan by such titles as 'Allama-i-Mashriq' ('Philosopher of the East'), and is buried in a prominent tomb opposite the **Lahore Fort**.

JAHANGIR (r 1605–27). Jahangir was the regnal title ('the World-Seizer') of the fourth Mughal emperor, author of the *Tuzuk* (1620), his Persian memoirs (Extract 12). A frequent visitor to Kashmir, he is buried in a magnificent tomb at **Shahdara** across the river Ravi from Lahore.

KHANNA, Balraj (1940–). Born in **Panjab** and educated at Panjab University, Chandigarh, he is now an established artist and lives in London (Extract 16).

KHATAK, Khushhal Khan (d 1689). Pashto and Persian poet. Chieftain of the Khatak tribe of Pathans, Khushhal Khan spent his later life in bitter conflict with the Mughal emperor Aurangzeb (r 1658–1707). See Extract 4.

KHUSHWANT SINGH (1915–). Sikh writer and journalist. Born near **Rawalpindi**, he was for many years editor of the *Illustrated Weekly of India*, and is the author of numerous novels, stories and essays in English, besides translations of Sikh and other Indian literature and studies of Sikh history (Extract 28).

Kim. Kipling's greatest Indian novel first published in 1901 (Extract 20). The young hero is first glimpsed playing on the great gun Zamzama outside the **Lahore Museum**. The son of an Irish soldier who is brought up as a native boy, Kim's search for his father is conducted in the company of a Tibetan lama in search of a mystical river. After numerous adventures, Kim is eventually taken up by a Colonel in the secret service and groomed for a career in the Great Game of espionage against Russian

Balraj Khanna

agents seeking to undermine the British empire in India.

KIPLING, Rudyard (1865–1936). Born in **Bombay** and sent after an idyllic childhood in India to England for an education which he hated. Returning in 1882 to **Lahore**, where his father was curator of the museum, he became a journalist on the *Civil and Military Gazette*, spending his summer leaves in **Simla**. Andrew Rutherford, ed, *Early verse by Rudyard Kipling* (1986) contains the uncollected poems of his Indian years, which saw the publication of *Departmental Ditties* (1886), and the volumes of short stories *Plain Tales from the Hills* (1888) and *Soldiers*

Three (1888). Having transferred from Lahore to **Allahabad** in 1887, Kipling left India for good in 1889. Most of his best loved Indian books date from the following years, including *Barrack-Room Ballads* (1892, Extract 5), *The Jungle Book* (1894), *The Second Jungle Book* (1895), and *Kim* (1901, Extract 20).

LAMBRICK, Hugh Trevor (1904–). Lambrick's long career as an administrator in **Sind** culminated in his being charged with the suppression of the Hur rebellion (1942–46), whose inside story from Sindhi sources is told in *The Terrorist* (1972, Extract 34).

Rudyard Kipling in Simla, c 1886

LATIF, Shah Abdul (1698–1752). Sindhi poet, whose *Risalo*, a collection of Sufi lyrics is universally reckoned the greatest work of Sindhi literature, and whose tomb at **Bhit** near Hyderabad is the focus of great devotion. See Extract 35.

MAZHAR UL ISLAM (b 1949). Prominent Urdu short story writer of the so-called 'Islamabad school' (Extract 17), well-known for his fondness for such fanciful titles as *The Man in the City of the Horses* (1983).

MEHTA, Ved (1934–). Long-time writer for the *New Yorker*, widely admired for the sensitive evocations of the old Panjab in the memoirs published as *Face to Face* (1957), *Daddyji* (1972, Extract 23), *Mamaji* (1979), *Vedi* (1982).

NANAK (1469–1539). The first Guru of the Sikhs, whose 974 magnificent hymns form the poetic and spiritual heart of the Sikh scriptures (Extract 21). His birthplace at **Nankana Sahib** south-west of Lahore is a major focus of Sikh pilgrimage in Pakistan.

NADIM, Dina Nath (b 1916). Kashmiri poet affiliated to the Progressive movement who is regarded as the most significant figure in the Kashmiri literature of the 1940s and 1950s.

NUR JAHAN (d 1646). Nur Jahan was the regnal title ('Light of the World') of the queen of the Mughal emperor Jahangir ◊, beside whom she is buried at **Lahore**. The daughter of a Persian soldier of fortune, her beauty secured her royal marriage in 1611,

thereafter Jahangir's deep love and great political influence (Extract 22).

RAFAT, Taufiq (1927–). Leading Pakistani English poet, who has also translated Bullhe Shah and other classics of his native Panjabi into English verse (Extract 33).

Sassi. Legendary Sindhi heroine. Princess of Bhambhore, Sassi is successfully wooed by Punnun, the young Baluch chief of Kech. When he is abducted by his jealous kinsmen, she follows his trail across the desert to her death.

SCOTT, Paul (1920–78). Scott served in the British Army from 1940 to 1946, mainly in India and Malaya. He turned to writing after a career as a literary agent. *The Raj Quartet* comprises *The Jewel in the Crown*; *The Day of the Scorpion*; *The Towers of Silence* and *A Division of the Spoils* (Extract 36). His other famous novel about India, *Staying On*, won the Booker Prize in 1977.

Shame. Salman Rushdie's 1983 novel, a very thinly disguised satire of the contemporary political and personal struggle between Zia ul Haq (d 1988) and Benazir Bhutto.

SIJZI, Amir Hasan (d 1336). Disciple of Shaikh Nizamuddin Auliya of Delhi (d 1325), whose conversations he recorded in the Persian *Favaid ul Fuad* (Extract 25), his major work besides his own Sufi Persian poetry.

Suhini. Sindhi name of the legendary Panjabi heroine Sohni. She used to cross the river Chenab using a pot as a float to meet her lover, the prince-turned-herdsman Mehar/Mahinval, but died when her jealous sister substituted an unfired pot.

VARIS SHAH. The greatest Panjabi poet, of whom nothing is known apart from his narrative masterpiece *Hir* (1766, Extract 18).

VIR SINGH (1876–1957). Sikh reformer and Panjabi poet, who spent most of his life as an enormously productive scholar and writer in **Amritsar** (Extract 7). Principally revered for his services to Sikh reformism, his literary reputation is chiefly based on the introspective Panjabi lyrics issued in several slim volumes from the 1920s until his death.

ZAMEENZAD, Adam. Brought up in East Africa and educated in Pakistan before settling in England, where his career as a novelist began with *The Thirteenth House* (1987, Extract 32) and achieved major recognition with *Cyrus* (1990).

CENTRAL AND NORTH INDIA

Rupert Snell

> Forget the pilgrim's path and tread / Vrindaban's arbour lanes / Where every step along the way / a pilgrimage contains.
> *Biharilal*

The verse which heads this section urges its 17th century audience to favour devotion to the deities Krishna and Radha in their north Indian domain of Vrindaban, relinquishing the long-ingrained habit of pilgrimage to the other sacred places of Hinduism which dot the map of our area. The poem indicates on the one hand the high place held by devotional religion in the life of north India; on the other it reminds us that in Hindu consciousness, India exists not only as a secular state but also as a sacred land whose spiritual topography includes countless pilgrimage places, excrescences of sanctity, which provide a focus for the religious life of the region. The traditional, pre-modern culture of north India, while often pan-Indian, has therefore special reference to such centres as the city of Varanasi, the sacred rivers Ganges and Yamuna, and the locations where incarnate deities such as Krishna and Rama spent their earthly lives.

This cultural map is enriched and made more complex by the overlay of successive cultures distinct from that of the Hindu majority. In particular the various Muslim dynasties which dominated northern India politically throughout so much of the medieval period have left a huge impress on the physical appearance of the human landscape, not only in architecture and the arts but in language, custom and way of life. European influence, especially during the two centuries of British ascendancy, had a cultural impact whose implications are still being played out today. India's characteristic gift for overlaying the new on the old has meant that the map of our northern area, so often the centre of the whole country's political and cultural life, is a palimpsest

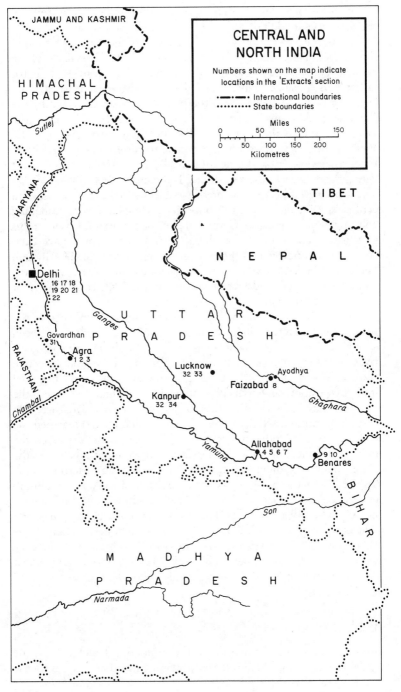

in which the older levels of inscription are still to be seen underlying the more recent additions.

Most of the area of northern India consists of the very flat terrain of the Ganges plain, which forms a trough between the Himalayas to the north and the Deccan plateau to the south. The **Ganges** itself (or rather 'herself', since 'Ganga' is a goddess in her own right) rises in the Himalayas and debouches onto the plains at **Hardwar**; joined by the **Yamuna** at **Allahabad**, and by a number of smaller tributaries, the Ganges eventually flows out to the Bay of Bengal through a huge delta system. The area through which this great river runs, known in ancient times as Aryavarta or 'the land of the Aryans', is amongst the most densely populated in the world, and is the crucible of Indian culture. The natural fertility of this area has declined over the last several centuries, bringing poverty to a once rich region; but modern canalling and irrigation has gone some way to reversing this trend. It is from this part of the subcontinent that the greatest Indian empires have been controlled politically; and the three major religions of ancient India – Hinduism, Buddhism and Jainism – also arose in this region, which continues to be regarded as the epicentre of India's sacred geography for the contemporary followers of these faiths.

Some features of northern India's dominating position, such as the national role given to its own modern language, Hindi, have been strongly objected to in recent times by the rightfully proud representatives of other regional traditions; but history shows that effective control over so vast an area as the subcontinent can best be managed from this position close to its geographical and cultural heart. Thus the city of **Delhi** has seen the rise and fall of numerous dynasties, and despite the various schismatic movements which have threatened the political union of India in recent years, Delhi remains very much the hub of the modern nation. The **Doab**, or interfluve between the Ganges and the Yamuna (compare the name 'Panjab', referring to the 'five rivers' of the north-west) is the location of some of Hinduism's most ancient and sacred centres. The ancient city of **Varanasi** or Benares, also called Kashi, has long encapsulated the philosophical and religious traditions of Hinduism. The Ganges, holiest of holy rivers (Extracts 14, 23), underscores the sanctity of Varanasi; its confluence with the Yamuna at Prayag is Hinduism's key pilgrimage site (Extract 7), an agglomeration of the sanctity which pervades the already sacred geography of India.

PEOPLE

In terms of ethnic composition, the region is dominated by the descendants of the Aryan settlers, now stratified according to the

Hindu system of class and caste. The Muslim population includes people having their origin in Afghanistan and other Islamic lands outside India, and those of Indian origin who have converted to Islam during the course of the centuries. Tribal populations, the so-called *adivasi* or 'aboriginal' peoples whose languages are amongst the oldest surviving on Indian soil, are of negligible numbers in Uttar Pradesh but form important minorities in **Bihar** and **Madhya Pradesh**.

Like most areas of the subcontinent, this region has a predominantly rural population, and a train journey through this great tract of land reminds one that for many millions of people, the rhythms of daily village life have changed little despite the technological advances so eagerly pursued by successive governments. But modern industrial cities such as **Delhi, Kanpur,** and **Bhopal** have grown rapidly during the present century, attracting the rural poor in considerable numbers. The *basti* or slum settlements which are such a commonplace sight in contemporary Indian cities show how false the dreams of urban riches can often prove to be.

HISTORY

The Aryan invaders, who had established themselves in north-western India c 1200 BC, gradually moved eastwards into the Gangetic plain during the centuries following. It was during this period that the basis of Brahmanical Hinduism became established, including on the one hand the social hierarchies of class and caste, and on the other the religious and philosophical speculations deriving from the Vedas. These matters are reflected in the text of the epic poem Mahabharata (Extract 11, Classical Literature), which was compiled from about 1000 BC, and whose narratives also reflect the warlike progress of the Aryan advance eastwards. The second great epic, Ramayana (Extract 15, Classical Literature), was composed at a similar or slightly later time, and with its interplay of spiritual and worldly themes is another source of information about life in northern India in the millenium BC.

This long and formative period in Indian history saw the emergence of various competing kingdoms, foremost of which were Magadha, in the eastern part of the Gangetic plain, and Kosala, which included the ancient capital of **Ayodhya** and the sacred city of Varanasi. Kosala was the home of the Buddha, born as the prince Siddhartha Gautama in about 563 BC, who revealed his teaching in a sermon given at **Sarnath**, near Kashi, after himself achieving enlightenment. The same century saw the birth of Mahavira, the founder of the Jain faith, near the modern city of Patna.

The Magadhan kingdom was massively expanded by the emperor Candragupta Maurya, who from about 321 BC began to consolidate his hold on what was to be the first great Indian empire. The throne of the imperial capital of Pataliputra (modern **Patna**) was inherited by Candragupta's son Bindusara and grandson Asoka. Asoka's embracing of Buddhism, whose non-violent teachings he promulgated through inscriptions on stone pillars, marked the end of a period of bloody territorial expansion; but by this time the Mauryan empire had in any case subjugated virtually the whole of the subcontinent except the Dravidian kingdoms of the extreme South.

There followed a period of disintegration as the central power of Mauryan rule waned. Various other dynasties came and went, none achieving the extent of the erstwhile empire. The next major power was the Gupta dynasty, which ruled the whole of the northern area (but not central or southern India) from the 4th century AD. The Gupta era was a golden age for philosophy, literature (including the dramas of Kalidasa), art and architecture, and for Brahmanical Hinduism. During this classical period were written the earliest of the Sanskrit texts called Puranas, great compilations of sacred legend, later to become the basis for popular devotionalism directed to one or other of the gods depicted in these Purana narratives. The Gupta dynasty lasted until the early 6th century, to be followed by a further period of disintegration with a variety of kingdoms being established throughout the region.

Muslim power in India

A succession of Muslim conquests was made by invaders from the north-west from the 10th century onwards. After the death of Muhammad of Ghur, who had defeated the Rajput chief Prithviraj, a dynasty was established by his Turkish slaves. They ruled firstly from Lahore, but in 1211 the king Iltutmish established **Delhi** as his capital. From the slave status of Iltutmish and many of the other generals and governors, this came to be called the 'Slave Dynasty'; but the kings also assumed the title of 'Sultan', from which this long-lived empire derives its name of 'the Delhi Sultanate'. The Sultanate was to endure for over 300 years, with successive Turko-Afghan dynasties occupying the seat of power; despite internal factionalism and the ever-present threat of Mongol invasions from the north-west, the empire reached its zenith under the rule of Alauddin Khalji (1296–1315). In 1398, Delhi was sacked by the armies of Timur (Tamerlane), a blow from which the Sultanate was never to recover; the following decades saw a repeat of the pattern of disintegration, with independent sultanates coming into being in a free-for-all of political power-hunting. The dynasties of Sayyids (1414–1451) and Lodis (1451–1526) could never regain the broad control of the Sultanate period, and were themselves to be outshone by the glorious empire of the Mughals which succeeded them.

The Mughal empire

Babur, a descendant of Timur's, defeated the last of the Lodi rulers at the battle of Panipat near Delhi in 1526. This decisive victory established the new dynasty in **Delhi** and **Agra**, and was quickly followed by other victories which further established the basis of Mughal rule. Babur's rule was as dramatic as it was brief, and by the time of his death in 1530 he held sway over much of northern India. His son Humayun, beset by threats to the integrity of this fragile new empire, failed adequately to consolidate it, and the period of his rule was characterized by a fluctuation of political and military fortunes. In 1555 Humayun fell to his death down the precipitous stone steps of his library in the Delhi fort, and was succeeded by his teenage son Akbar, destined to be one of the greatest of India's rulers and to usher in a period of unprecedented imperial splendour.

Akbar ruled for half a century. He steadily increased his territory, conquering especially a large part of the north-western region which had provided such ready access to invaders during the Sultanate period. But equally notable a feature of this reign was the stamp of Akbar's own personality: catholic and broad-minded by nature, he was actively interested in other faiths, and the spirit of his era was markedly more tolerant than others before and after. The hated tax on non-Muslims was abolished; many Rajput Hindus held positions of authority at the Agra court, and Portuguese Jesuits from Goa – among the first Europeans to establish a foothold in India – were also a common sight there. The arts flourished in the wealthy and relatively secure kingdom, in which military and revenue administration was greatly improved; and though Akbar's new capital of **Fatehpur Sikri**, near Agra, had to be abandoned because of its inadequate water supply, many other fine buildings, paintings and artefacts bear witness to an age of great artistic as well as military accomplishment.

In a pattern to be repeated more than once before the waning of the Mughal empire, Akbar was succeeded by a son who had earlier rebelled against him. The prince Salim came to the throne in 1605, inheriting an empire larger than any since the Gupta age (virtually the whole of India north of the river Godavari, apart from Gondwana); Akbar's legacy of political stability and imperial splendour enabled his son to assume the title Jahangir – 'seizer of the world'. Seizures and losses of territory continued throughout a reign in which Jahangir's own son Shah Jahan (builder of the Taj Mahal, see Extract 3), continued the tradition of rebellion against a reigning father. Shah Jahan succeeded Jahangir in 1627, and had to face new threats both from Uzbeks in the north-west, and from Marathas who were steadily extending their power from coastal Maharashtra into the Deccan.

While the instability of its border territories was a constant feature of the Mughal empire, its economic strength encouraged the development of major cities such as **Delhi**, **Agra** and **Lucknow** as important centres of trade. Such was the brilliance of the empire at its zenith that future generations of Muslim poets could only lament its passing, and a strong nostalgia pervades many of the later invocations of these cities (Extracts 20, 21, 22). But if the splendour of such cities reflected the glories of the empire, and of its increasingly militarized governing élite, this opulence was in stark contrast to the lives of the rural masses whose tax revenue ultimately funded the entire imperial machine. Furthermore, the policy of religious tolerance that Akbar had so carefully instituted gradually decayed during the reigns of his successors. The Hindu reaction against Mughal supremacy gathered strength throughout this period, provoked in part by the ever-higher land revenue demands imposed by the empire in a vain attempt to meet the cost of its never-ending military campaigns. Thus the empire at its period of greatest splendour contained the seeds of its own destruction. The policies of Aurangzeb, who reigned from 1658 to 1707, became stridently anti-Hindu in nature, with a large-scale reversal of the catholicity of his great-grandfather Akbar; a growing chorus of rebellion from within the Mughal territories was matched by a continuation of threats from outside, particularly in the form of the Marathas under their great leader Shivaji. At the death of Aurangzeb, the Mughal power – militarily overstretched and administratively losing effectiveness – was in steep decline.

The coming of the British

The various inheritors of the Mughal throne were unable to hold together the fabric of the great empire. The extent to which its political and military unity had been eroded was dramatically demonstrated in 1739 when Nadir Shah invaded India from Persia and sacked Delhi; and the establishment of new rival centres of power and culture in Awadh and other kingdoms in the second half of the 18th century are a more positive symptom of the same process.

Meanwhile, British trading interests in India were growing apace. Gradually eclipsing France and Holland as the premier European trading power in the subcontinent, the British East India Company became so powerful in eastern India that in 1765 Robert Clive was able to take over the revenue administration of Bengal. British interests were further advanced by a system of alliances, in which military protection was granted to independent kingdoms in return for the payment of a tribute to the British; and the Mughal 'emperors' ruling in Delhi were by now no more than figureheads operating under British control.

The expansion of British influence was dictated by a thirst for trade (much of it pursued by private individuals) and the need to protect it militarily. To some extent the British justified this expansionism by pointing to the licentious behaviour of Indian princes under whose rule a feudal élite enjoyed a lotus-eating aesthetic lifestyle (Extract 27) – a real-life fantasy world of court luxury, courtesans and cultural decadence which was to seize the imagination of many a later writer (Extract 34).

Indian reaction to the imperial advance, in which trade was a foot in the door for British territorial expansion, became vehement after Awadh was annexed in 1856; in the summer of the following year, a revolt amongst Indian soldiers at the garrison in **Meerut** began a widespread rebellion, long to be characterized by the British as 'the Indian Mutiny' but seen retrospectively by Indian eyes as the first move towards independence from British rule. This was a watershed in the history of the British in India, the tensions between ruler and ruled coming fully into the open; and the dramatic atmosphere of derring-do on the imperial side naturally made the Mutiny a favourite subject of much autobiographical and fictional writing (Extracts 24, 32). The rebellion was stamped out in the closing months of 1857, after the shedding of much Indian and British blood: but the results of the rebellion were to be long-lived, for in 1858 the East India Company was abolished, and its territories came under the direct control of the British sovereign.

The remainder of the century was characterized by a greater level of British intervention and paternalism in Indian affairs (Extract 8), as the Empire defined and justified its role increasingly in terms of the imposing of a civilizing influence on a 'backward' (and heathen) nation. The second half of the 19th century saw the establishment of many universities and schools in India, fostering the development of a middle class educated in English and acquainted with Western values. Both Hinduism and Islam reacted to the stimulus and challenge of new ideas by a restatement of their own ideologies, often in reformed mode: Dayanand Sarasvati's Arya Samaj sought to reaffirm the spiritual basis of Hinduism by clearing it of the mythological and ritualistic accretions of the middle ages, while Sir Sayyid Ahmad Khan propagated reformed Islam through the so-called Aligarh movement. The two organizations were instrumental in the promotion of the Hindi and Urdu languages respectively.

The introduction of Western ideas to India, or at least to the tiny élite which received Western-style education and a hand in the administration of the country, itself resulted in the birth of a sense of national identity; and developments such as the railways and the telegraph, while enabling the Raj to govern, also encouraged a greater sense of unity of political purpose amongst the people the Raj ruled. This unity led to the foundation in 1885 of the Indian National Congress, whose purpose in its early years was not to oust the British (under whose rule most Congress delegates had flourished) but rather to change the structures which limited Indians' participation in the running of their own country. Though the Congress sought to be widely representative of the Indian people, it was dominated by Hindu interests, and in 1906 the Muslim League was set up to represent Muslim interests.

A Royal Durbar was held at **Delhi** in 1911 as a grand fanfare to display the majesty of British rule. Meanwhile Delhi itself, so much closer than the old capital Calcutta to the hub of British territories, became the new centre of government for the Raj: once again north India's ancient capital found itself the hub of the political wheel. Both of these events were celebrated in the broad sweep of triumphal city architecture – a kind of British Fatehpur – designed by Lutyens as a fitting centre for the new capital. Even this imperial pomp and circumstance, however, could not hide the rumblings of discontent emerging from a unified front of Congress and the Muslim League, voicing a demand for some kind of self-government. The right to self-determination claimed by these organisations was an embarrassing echo of the principle on which the British were currently fighting the First World War, and was hardly to be ignored; although the Indian demands were not met in full, an increased Indian participation in government was conceded, and the possibility of some degree of eventual self-government within the Empire began to take hold in the imperial mind.

The following decades were dominated by the character and policies of Mahatma Gandhi. Although his 'non-cooperation' movement of the early 1920s failed in its attempt to achieve self-rule, his wider concept of the struggle towards independence confident not only in the moral rightness of the cause but also in the achievability of its aims through non-violent tactics, captured the imagination of a wider public than ever before. On the one hand, Gandhi's ideas were presented in terms of a religious symbolism that guaranteed a popular appeal, especially among the majority Hindu population; on the other, the more Westernized section of the population had by this time acquired all the necessary linguistic and political skills for a confident face-to-face confrontation with the Raj.

Independence and partition

The maintaining of common purpose amongst India's diverse communities continued to be a major problem to the freedom fighters, but even so this movement was to lead eventually to the granting of

Independence under the last viceroy, Louis Mountbatten. Anxieties about the prospect of being politically overwhelmed by the Hindu majority had led Muslims to call for a separate Muslim state, a demand spearheaded by Muhammad Ali Jinnah in the Pakistan Resolution of 1940. Independence came with great suddenness in 1947 with the partitioning of India into India and Pakistan; it was accompanied by widespread bloodshed as large numbers of Muslims and Hindus rushed to move respectively into and out of the new Muslim homeland carved out of the old united India.

Post-independence politics in India continued to be dominated by the Congress party, which was itself dominated for many years by members of the Nehru family. Jawaharlal Nehru, whose father Motilal had himself been a President of Congress in 1928, was the natural heir to Mahatma Gandhi as the leader of free India, though he differed from his mentor in urging the young country along a modernising path in keeping with his own cherished ideal of a secular socialism. When Gandhi fell into despondence at the vivisection of India, it was Nehru who, in a speech which marks one of the great turning-points in 20th century history, welcomed the birth of the new independent nation (Extract 17a); but the turbulence at the heart of that nation was demonstrated with horrible clarity just a few months later in 1948 when a Hindu fundamentalist organisation assassinated Gandhi in protest at his alleged appeasment of Muslim interests – leaving Nehru to resort once more to his oratory in broadcasting the news of the death of the 'Father of the Nation' (Extract 17b).

Whatever the vicissitudes of the Indian political scene over recent years, the democratic traditions of parliamentary government have been maintained almost without exception since Independence – a record which stands in marked contrast to the recent histories of other South Asian states. Only during the period of the 'Emergency' imposed by Nehru's daughter Indira Gandhi from 1975 to 1977, when the centre felt threatened by the turmoil of cessionist and other demands, was the democratic process suspended. But the spectre of 'communalism' is a constant reminder that the modern state is a fragile union of disparate communities, and the toll of those who have lost their lives in the resulting violence includes two prime ministers from the Nehru dynasty – Indira Gandhi and her son Rajiv – as well as the 'father of the nation', Mahatma Gandhi.

The age-old issues of community and caste, together with a tendency for political factions to be defined and dominated by the characters of the leaders, are at the heart of local and national political issues in India today. The long and tragic history of the political exploitation of communal divisions in India again found expression on 6 December 1992, when Hindu fundamentalists destroyed a mosque standing on a

Jawaharlal Nehru

site in Ayodhya, UP, believed to be the birthplace of the god Rama; but this history is rarely a straightforward one, and the apparently 'communal' motivations behind the widespread riots which followed that event were bound up in a mesh of naked political and commercial ambition.

LANGUAGE AND LITERATURE

Language and dialect

Like their great classical forebear Sanskrit, the modern languages of northern India belong to the Indo-European family and are thus ultimately related to European language such as English. India's famous linguistic diversity is as apparent in this northern area as anywhere, and the name 'Hindi' must be seen as an umbrella term covering a wide variety of dialects. In terms of literature, however, the situation is much simpler, since only a few dialects have developed major traditions of written literature.

Hindustani, Urdu and Hindi

The area in which Hindi and its closely related languages are spoken, stretching roughly from Delhi in the West to Bihar in the East, has a richly mixed culture: it is an area in which the Sanskritic civilization of Hinduism has flourished since ancient times, and yet which was politically dominated for several centuries by Muslim dynasties maintaining Persian and Turkish as their languages of high culture. Because of the historical and cultural importance of the Delhi region, the dialect called Khari Boli, whose widely-spoken colloquial form is called Hindustani, has served as a lingua franca all over northern India and beyond.

Two increasingly distinct linguistic and literary traditions stemmed from this shared 'Hindustani' speech. On the one hand is the Urdu branch, looking to Islamic civilization for its cultural roots, and thus adding a high proportion of Persian, Arabic and Turkish loanwords to the Hindustani base; on the other is the Hindi branch, whose cultural model and source of loanwords was Sanskrit. These very different cultural orientations of Urdu and Hindi, together with the fact that Urdu is written in the Persian script while Hindi is written in the Sanskrit or 'Devanagari' script, has meant that the two have tended to become increasingly polarized as 'Muslim' and 'Hindu' languages respectively. Thus while Hindi is the national language of modern India, Urdu, though having its origins in the environs of Delhi, is the national language of Pakistan as well as holding recognized status within India's family of languages.

Many people who classify themselves as speakers and readers of standard Hindi or Urdu, and who use one or other language in, say, their working lives, will use a different form of the language in their domestic context. Maithili (spoken in Bihar) and Bhojpuri (from the Varanasi area) are examples of Hindi dialects which are widely spoken domestically in the home, but whose speakers will frequently turn spontaneously to standard Khari Boli Hindi in more formal circumstances.

LITERATURE

The history of the literature of our area follows a pattern found all over northern India. Early origins in bardic and religious verse led to a flowering of devotional literature in the 15th and 16th centuries; Sanskrit texts such as the epics and the Puranas supplied the subject matter for much of the poetry, but there was also considerable influence from local folk traditions. Nearly all literature was in verse, and much of it was intended for singing or recitation; in many cases what we here call 'literature' was essentially an oral form, often influenced by folk song and other popular traditions. Court poetry in the late medieval period adopted many of the stock conventions and imagery of the devotional poets. The 19th century was a period of transition, during which Western literary conventions were gradually assimilated, heralding the advent of a truly 'modern' literature, defying categories of subject matter or style, in the present century.

Devotional poetry

The 'medieval' period of vernacular literatures came into its own in the 15th and 16th centuries. During this period, new forms of popular devotional Hinduism swept the region, spearheaded by cults based on the worship of such deities as Krishna and Rama. These two deities, whose iconography and mythology had gradually developed in the Sanskrit epics and Puranas, came to be worshipped as incarnate forms of the great god Visnu; temples housing images of these and related deities were built all over northern India, but particularly in those sites which the scriptures had named as being the 'actual' areas in which the incarnate deities had lived their human lives. Thus the area called **Braj**, between **Delhi** and **Agra**, described in the Bhagavata Purana as the place where Krishna spent his childhood, became an important centre of sectarian worship, and remains so to this day; fine temples such as those to be seen at Vrindaban were built to Krishna in his various aspects (as child-god; as precocious lover; as beloved of Radha). Similarly the town of **Ayodhya** in the eastern part of modern Uttar Pradesh came to be regarded as the birthplace and 'home-town' of Rama (now a flashpoint in the sad history of communal disharmony, as already noted); other locations throughout the country were also identified as places visited by Rama during the travels described in the Ramayana story.

These sacred sites were to become an important narrative focus for the praise-poems written in celebration of the deities who lived there; as places of pilgrimage the sites allow the devotee a way of mental access to a world beyond the material one, and for the poet they represent a symbolic metaphor on which to base his descriptions of *lila* or 'divine sport'. Some topographical features are regarded as intrinsically divine. The geographical settings of traditional poetry, however, are exploited for their symbolic value more than as 'landscape' in a Western sense, and the 'sense of place' so characteristic of Western genres is hardly to be found in this early literature: the dark-watered river **Yamuna** is beautiful because it is a metaphor for dark-skinned

Krishna, and the fish is beautiful because it reminds the poet of the gracefully tapering line of the heroine's eye.

These devotional or religious movements generated prolific amounts of literature. Braj Bhasa and Avadhi, the Hindi dialects spoken in Braj and Ayodhya respectively, became established as the most important literary dialects, and were adopted by poets from all over the linguistically diverse Hindi-speaking area. Much of the literature was composed and transmitted orally by 'singer-poets', and so the low levels of literacy in the region were never a major impediment to the widespread popular traditions of song and poetry. The genius of devotional poetry lies in its ability to blend sublime contemplation of the divine with a reassuringly homely idiom; God is abstract and aloof, but is also identifiable in the human form of incarnations.

One verse text of unrivalled stature is the *Ramcaritmanas*, 'The Holy Lake of Rama's Deeds' written by Tulsidas ◊, in 1574. This great Hindi version of the Ramayana story has held a special place in the affections of northern India for four centuries; its story of the noble king Rama, his affectionately dutiful wife Sita and an array of other divine and demonic characters, is a source of both spiritual sustenance and moral example, and countless people achieved a basic literacy expressly in order to read this one text. Tulsi's devotion to Rama is further reflected in his other works, especially his *Petition to Rama* (Extract 23) equally characterized by intense religious feeling and poetic artistry. Modern readers of this early poetry may rely quite heavily on modern Hindi commentaries to elucidate the now archaic language, and professional reciters will often add their own interpretative gloss to the original text.

Where Tulsi's Rama represents the lofty values of nobility and uprightness, the figure of Krishna described by poets such as Tulsi's earlier contemporary Surdas has an altogether more domestic aspect. Surdas was one of a group of poets, including also Chitsvami ◊ and Nanddas, whose verses extolled the sublime beauty of the child Krishna, whose feats included the lifting of Govardhan hill and numerous other miracles (Extract 31). The paradox of epiphany, in which the ineffable godhead is equated with the mischievous child-god, is at the heart of this literature; in a tone of bittersweet longing the poet tells of his desire to play with Krishna, to see him steal butter from the milkmaids, or to emulate the crow which steals the bread from Krishna's delicate hand.

Court poetry

The poetry described above belongs essentially to the temple and the devotee; but the genres taken up by poets of a more secular attitude, who enjoyed the patronage of the royal courts, were not so very different. The 17th century court poet Biharilal (◊, Extract 28), who lived under the patronage of Mirza Jai Singh at **Amber** near Jaipur in Rajasthan, but who wrote in the Braj dialect, is a case in point. In Biharilal's compositions it is hard to draw a line between the contexts of devotional verse (where divine love may be symbolized by romantic human love) and the poetry composed for the entertainment of those kings and princes whose palaces still stand as visible reminders of the secular opulence of courtly life. Thus Krishna and Radha, piously praised in devotional verse, became models for the distinctly worldly heroes and heroines of lyrical romances; and many set-piece conventions such as the 'descriptions of the seasons' deriving from folk poetry had a natural place in both genres. This genre of court poetry was an artificial splendour, like a costly ornament worn by one of its own heroines; a symptom of its artifice was that it was more concerned with its own elegant variations on idealised set-piece descriptions than with the broader sweep of human life.

An important survival of the traditional conventions and dialects of Hindi literature into modern times is to be found in the contemporary world of Indian music. The lyrics sung in the classical style called *khyal*, the predominant musical style found throughout the northern part of the subcontinent, frequently use a dialect, verse form and poetic idiom which would be quite familiar to the Hindi devotional poets of the 16th century. Indeed, devotional lyrics on such themes as the love of Krishna and Radha, or other religious themes, commonly form the basis of a modern performance, whether the singer be a Hindu or a Muslim. Perhaps in no other area of artistic life is the synthesis of Hindu and Muslim cultures so naturally maintained as it is in this world of classical music.

Persian and Urdu literature

Despite this example of synthesis in the musical sphere, there is of course a quite separate tradition of Islamic literature in the Indian sub-continent. Just as the contemporary Hindi speaker may look back with pride on several centuries of literary tradition, so too the contemporary Urdu speaker can contemplate a long list of poetic achievements stretching back to the days of the Mughal empire. Because Urdu literature derives its inspiration from the classics of the Persian tradition, whereas the Hindi poets look to Sanskrit as a model for their verse, Urdu and Hindi literatures have generally developed along quite separate lines (at least until the 19th century, when both fell under the influence of Western literary genres).

Islamic poetry of the pre-modern era was essentially a product of the court. Persian, the court language of the Delhi Sultanate, was maintained as a language of high culture throughout the period of Mughal rule, when it received the lavishly generous patronage so characteristic of the artistic life of that great empire. The Persian diaries and chronicles of the Mughal dynasty are themselves an important record and example of the cultural richness of their own period. Persian poetry also flourished in the independent Muslim kingdoms of the **Deccan**. Yet as the political and cultural dominance of Muslim rule became more and more firmly established, and the circle of poets grew to include many born on Indian soil and thus having no direct contact with the sources of Persian culture, there was an increasing tendency for Urdu to inherit the mantle of Persian as the language for verse composition. First in the Deccan kingdoms of Golkunda and Bijapur, Urdu began to be developed as a literary language in its own right, though with Persian and Turkish models never far from view; geographically divorced from the homeland of Urdu in the Delhi region, the so-called 'Dakani Urdu' and its poetry developed a particular style all of its own. Later, when the Deccan kingdoms had themselves become part of the Mughal empire, Urdu poetry began to be composed at the Delhi court also, eventually succeeding Persian as the prime literary vehicle.

Urdu verse reached new heights at the Delhi court in the late 18th century, by which time the Mughal empire was however in an advanced stage of fragmentation and decline. Though the political instability of this period was itself conducive to the writing of great literature, as Delhi poets reacted with sensitivity and satirical wit to their own changing fortunes, many were eventually driven to seek the relative security of the kingdom of Awadh ('Oudh'), whose capital, **Lucknow**, became the new focus of poetic and artistic creativity in the early 19th century. The Lucknow court, blissfully oblivious of the political upheavals taking place all around northern India as the British imperial machine drove inexorably onwards, tended towards the decadent in its artistic tastes; thus the poetry of this era was characterized by increasingly elaborate and fanciful confections, in which the style of expression was of far greater importance than substance or content.

19th century developments

During the 19th century, far-reaching changes in the fabric of urban Indian society were brought about by the European presence in the sub-continent; and these changes were followed by the emergence of new literary genres on Western models. Such factors as the development of a literate middle class, concern for social justice and reform, the birth of a sense of nationalism, and a reinforced sense of cultural self-confidence based on a renewed appreciation of India's own classical past all contributed to a need for a new literary 'voice' reflecting real social issues rather than the variously pious and decadently aesthetic concerns of the pre-modern period. These changes were helped not only by the spread of education through newly established schools and universities, but also by the arrival of printing presses, brought to India to propagate the Christian gospel and quickly adopted as a vehicle for India's own new literature. Thus while the increasingly dominant European culture challenged the very basis of Indian values and beliefs, it also, ironically, gave to India the technology and literary genres with which to defend itself.

The northern and central area was, during the 19th and early 20th centuries, some way behind Bengal in the establishment of this new literary voice. **Calcutta**, as a capital of British India until 1911, had always been the first city to encounter the Western world; the Bengali intellectual aristocracy was already becoming acquainted with Western ideas in the mid 19th century, while the Awadh court at Lucknow, for example, was still engrossed with the infamously hedonistic lifestyle of an essentially medieval kingdom. Thus when Hindi journalism began to take its first faltering steps, it followed the example of its Bengali cousin; and when Hindi writers took up the writing of fictional and essayistic prose, Bengali models (themselves often closely imitative of English conventions) stood them in good stead.

The 19th century was a period of transition for Hindi literature – the traditional literary dialects of Awadhi and Braj being gradually displaced by the lingua franca of Khari Boli – and most of the literary works of that period are of little more than historical interest; but Urdu literature, largely based on Khari Boli since its inception, can look back on the same century as part of an unbroken chronological heritage, and indeed as a golden age in which flourished some of its most illustrious writers. Greatest of these was Mirza Ghalib (◊, Extract 20), born in **Agra** in 1797, who wrote verse and prose in both Urdu and Persian, and whose colourful life included a spell as laureate to the court of Bahadur Shah Zafar, last of the Mughal emperors.

The 19th century saw a rapid growth of educational institutions such as Benares Hindu University, in which both Indian and Western values and cultural traditions were promulgated. The extent to which the British Raj should use its political power to spread Christianity among the Indian population was hotly debated for many decades; and though this question was never fully resolved, a less invidious machinery for the extension of Western cultural values was in any case to hand, in the teaching of English literature through the newly established academic system. Generations of Indian schoolchildren were consequently brought up on the classics of a Victorian literary library, works which were to be extremely influential in establishing the conventions of prose style for contemporary writers of Indian languages all over the country.

The 20th century: a new literary voice

As the rapid spread of journalism broadened the horizons of literature and made it available to a growing public, writers of such languages as Hindi and Urdu began to experiment with new genres such as the novel and the short story. The first examples were often quite crude, as one might expect of a fledgling literature; but the didacticism and high moral tone which was so much part of the Victorian outlook was readily transported to the Indian scene in the 19th and early 20th centuries, spawning numerous narrative accounts of Indian social life. A continuity of didactic purpose can be seen extending into the 1920s and 1930s, albeit with a new target in this later era when many writers became preoccupied with the 'Quit India' campaign and with nationalist and socialist ideologies. Writers such as the Urdu and Hindi novelist Premchand (◊, Extract 30) were much influenced by the political and social ideas of Mahatma Gandhi, whose vision of justice for all and of the sanctity of 'Mother India' informs much writing of this period. Genres of fiction, drama and poetry became increasingly well established in Hindi and Urdu, as well as in the other languages of the subcontinent; the short story, with its relatively modest demands on writers and readers alike, became a particularly popular genre. Many writers, especially Urdu lyricists, found a new source of patronage in the film industry, which grew from strength to strength in the 1930s and 1940s (Extract 12).

While it would be misleading to suggest that writers of any era were limited to particular set themes, it is true that a certain shift of emphasis was seen in much Indian writing after Independence in 1947. The optimism with which the struggle for Independence had been fought led to high hopes of a bright future after the last British ship left Bombay; but the realities of most people's lives remained substantially the same after the euphoria of what Nehru called India's 'tryst with destiny' (Extract 17). The up-beat and idealistic tone of pre-Independence writing proved to have been premature if not naïve, and much of the new writing in prose and poetry which emerged in the 1950s had an altogether darker tone and an increased interest in the psychological motivations underlying human behaviour. Satire, a well-established genre in Indian literature, found new targets in the individuals and institutions now holding the reins of power; and in adopting themes such as the alienation of the individual and the disintegration of the family unit, writers applied international literary trends to their own particular circumstances. Another literary fashion of the 1950s and 1960s was a kind of regionalism, which took the action or narrative to the hinterland of the Hindi-speaking region, painting local colour through the use of local dialect. The Hindi

The actress Rekha in the film Umrao Jaan
Note: Umrao Jaan is the film version of the Urdu novel *Umrao Jan Ada* (Extract 34).

novelist Phanisvarnath Renu (◊, Extract 11) was the best-known author of this style.

Literature, literacy and the cinema

Uttar Pradesh, though a cradle of Hindu and Islamic culture, has always been an area with a particularly low literacy rate: the figure of 41% in the 1991 census contrasts strongly with the 52% of the country as a whole. And whereas pre-modern literature and culture had primarily been disseminated through the oral tradition, modern literature on the Western model is essentially a 'literature' in the literal sense of something to be read, rather than as a performance text for public recitation or dramatic enactment. For this and other reasons it is important to bear in mind the ironic fact that 20th century literature in India, no matter how much it may agonize over and satirize issues of democracy, social reform and the grinding poverty of the rural poor, is written primarily by and for the literate élite of the urban middle classes (Extract 29). The vast majority of the Indian population lives in villages, has a lifestyle which has changed but slowly over the years, and continues to maintain, through legend and ritual, the folk traditions which have characterized India's cultural life for centuries.

A unifying factor between the urban middle classes and the rural majority is a universal fascination for the Bombay film, now increasingly watched on video rather than the big screen of the cinema hall. It would be almost impossible to overemphasize the influence of the cinema in modern India. Among the most popular films are the so-called 'mythologicals', which bring the personalities and deities of Hinduism vividly to life on the screen. The continuing use of classical narratives of this kind, and the evergreen popularity of such themes as sibling rivalry, separation and reunion, family honour, love and vengeance, are just two examples of the inherently conservative nature of popular Indian culture; to put it another way, the film world has inherited and maintained Indian narrative conventions which the more self-consciously artistic writers of modern literature have spurned in favour of a psychological attitude more in keeping with contemporary priorities.

Literature in English

Not all Indian literature is written in Indian languages. The general category of 'Indian literature in English' includes a wide range of types and genres, from the memoirs of British travellers and colonial administrators of centuries past, to the modern writing of those contemporary writers in India who choose, for various reasons, to write in English rather than a language such as Hindi or Urdu.

Much of the 'Anglo-Indian' writing of the 19th and earlier centuries, of course, enshrines attitudes which smack of the xenophobic, or which indulge in 'orientalist' exotica. Many volumes of Sahibs' and Memsahibs' memoirs, whether published as such or in lightly fictionalized form, were harmless enough, perhaps, in their mildly patronising tone; but at the other end of the spectrum there were authors who felt no compunction in writing a book with as brazenly judgemental a title as Beverley Nichols's *Verdict on India*. Much good, sensitive and informed writing is hidden away in the gazetteers and other reports which the Raj

Vikram Seth

commissioned so assiduously. Among the many novelists to adopt Indian settings, E.M. Forster is probably the best known; though *A Passage to India* (◊, Extract 14) is very much an account of the British experience of India, it does offer some unique insights into the country (and is by no means to be judged on the basis of David Lean's film version of the novel).

In marked contrast to the 'Anglo-Indian' writing of Forster and others is the rapidly expanding body of 'Indo-Anglian' literature, the product of contemporary English-speaking Indian authors. One of the most famous of such writers is Vikram Seth ◊, whose massive *A Suitable Boy* (Extract 13) was an international bestseller. Many such writers would feel uncomfortable with the implications of a category such as 'Indian literature', since they see themselves as belonging to a world tradition of writers of the English language. Their themes, styles, influences and attitudes are indeed far too diverse to allow any useful generalizations to be made; it is clear that the label 'Indian literature' now designates a diversity of material that not only stretches chronologically over several centuries, but also reaches in its points of reference well beyond the boundaries of the sub-continent.

BOOKLIST

The following selection includes all titles which are extracted in this chapter as well as other relevant works. The editions cited are not necessarily the only ones available. The exact location of the extracts can be found in 'Acknowledgements and Citations' at the end of the volume. Extract numbers are highlighted in bold for ease of reference.

Ackerley, J.R., *Hindoo Holiday: An Indian Journal*, Chatto & Windus, London, 1932. **Extract 15**.

Agyeya, *Signs and Silence*, the author and Leonard E. Nathans, trans, Simant Publications, Delhi, 1976. **Extract 26**.

'Ajneya', *Nilambari*, the author, trans, Clarion Books, Delhi, 1981. **Extract 26**.

Ali, Ahmed *Twilight in Delhi*, Oxford University Press, Bombay, 1966. **Extract 22**.

Banarsidas, *Half a Tale*, Mukund Lath, trans, Rajasthan Prakrit Bharati Sansthan, Jaipur, 1981. **Extract 1**.

Biharilal, *Bihari Ratnakar*, ed Jagannathdas 'Ratnakar', 5 ed, Granthkar, Varanasi, 1969. **Extract 28**.

Bowen, J.C.E. *The Golden Pomegranate: A Selection from the Poetry of the Mughal Empire in India 1526–1858*, Thacker & Co, Bombay, 1957. **Extract 2**.

Coppola, Carlo and M.H.K. Qureshi, 'A note on oral poems by Sahir Ludhianvi' in *Literature, East and West*, 10, 1966. **Extract 3**.

Desai, Anita *The Clear Light of Day*, Penguin Books in association with William Heinemann, London, 1980. **Extract 18**.

Farrell, J.G., *The Siege of Krishnapur*, Wiedenfeld and Nicholson, London, 1973. **Extract 24**.

Forster, E.M. *A Passage to India*, Penguin, Harmondsworth, 1967. **Extract 14**.

Hawley, J.S. and Juergensmeyer, M., *Songs of the Saints of India*, Oxford University Press, New York, 1988. **Extract 9**.

Jhabvala, R.P. *Heat and Dust*, Futura, London, 1976. **Extract 25**.

Mehrotra, A.K., *Middle Earth*, Oxford University Press, Delhi, 1984. **Extract 5**.

McGregor, R.S. *Hindi Literature from its Beginnings to the 19th Century*, Harrassowitz, Wiesbaden, 1984.

McGregor, R.S. *Hindi Literature of the 19th and early 20th Centuries*, Harrassowitz, Wiesbaden, 1980.

Naipaul, V.S. *India: A Million Mutinies Now*, Heinemann, London, 1990. **Extract 33**.

Nehru, Jawaharlal, *Jawaharlal Nehru's Speeches*, 3 vols, Government of India, 1949. **Extract 17**.

Newby, E. *Slowly Down the Ganges*, Picador, London, 1983. **Extract 7**.

Nirala, *Anamika*, Bharati Bhandar, Allahabad, 1963. **Extract 4**.

Premchand, *The Gift of a Cow*, G.C. Roadarmel, trans, Allen and Unwin, London, 1968. **Extract 30**.

Purchas, S., *Early Travels in India. First series, comprising 'Purchas's Pilgrimage' and 'The travels of Van Linschoten'*, R. Lepage, Calcutta, 1864. **Extract 10**.

Qamber, Akhtar, ed and trans, *The Last Mushai'irah of Delhi*, Orient Longman, New Delhi, 1979. **Extract 21**.

Renu, P.N., *The Third Vow and Other Stories*, Kathryn G. Hansen, trans, Chanakya Publications, Delhi, 1986. **Extract 11**.

Field-Marshal Lord Roberts of Kandahar, *Forty-one Years in India from Subaltern to Commander-in-chief*, 2 ed, Vol 1, Richard Bentley, London, 1897. **Extract 32**.

Russell, R. and Islam, Khurshidul,

Ghalib 1797–1869, Vol 1, Life and Letters, George Allen & Unwin, London, 1969. **Extract 20**.

Russell, R. and Islam, Khurshidul, *Three Mughal Poets*, Allen and Unwin, London, 1965/Penguin Books, India.

Rusva, Mirza, *The Courtesan of Lucknow: Umrao Jan Ada*, Khushwant Singh and M.A. Husaini, trans, Hind Pocket Books, Delhi. **Extract 34**.

Seth, Vikram, *A Suitable Boy*, Orion, London, 1993. **Extract 13**.

Shukla, S., *Thumri ki utpatti, vikas aur sailiya*, R. Snell, trans, Delhi University, Delhi, 1983. **Extract 27**.

Shukla, S. *Rag Darbari*, 2 ed, Rajkamal, Delhi, 1985. **Extract 29**.

Singh, Khushwant, *Delhi*, Penguin Books, Delhi, 1990. **Extract 16**.

Sleeman, W.H., *Sleeman in Oudh: An Abridgement of W.H. Sleeman's 'A Journey Through the Kingdom of Oude in 1849–50'*, P.D. Reeves, ed, Cambridge University Press, Cambridge, 1971. **Extract 8**.

Tulsi Das, *The Petition to Ram*, F.R. Allchin, trans, George Allen & Unwin, London, 1966. **Extract 23**.

Varma, M.A., *Pilgrimage to the Himalayas*, Radhika Prasad Srivastav and Lillian Srivastav, trans, Clarion Books, Delhi. **Extract 6**.

Wolpert, Stanley, *Nine Hours to Rama*, Hamish Hamilton, London, 1962. **Extract 19**.

Extracts

(1) AGRA

Banarsidas, *Half a Tale*

India's first real autobiographer, the Jain merchant and scholar Banarsidas, looks back in 1641 on a life of changing fortunes spent mainly in Benares, Jaunpur and Agra.

My story is now complete. I am fifty-five years of age, and I live in Agra with my wife in reasonably comfortable circumstances. I married thrice, and had two daughters and seven sons. But all my children died. And now my wife and I are alone like winter trees that have shed all their greenery, standing bare and denuded. Looking at it in the light of the absolute vision, you may declare that as a man takes unto himself, so he sheds. But can any man rooted in this world ever see things in such a light? A man feels enriched when he takes something unto himself and utterly lost when he is deprived of even a trifle.

I will now end. But before I do so, I would like to speak to you of my present good and bad attributes.

First, then, my good points. As a poet I am matchless in composing verses on spiritual themes, which I recite with great art and impact. I know Prakrit and Sanskrit and can intone these languages with faultless pronunciation. I also know many vernacular languages. In my use of language I am ever alive to nuances of words and meanings.

My temper is naturally forgiving. I am easily content, and not readily moved by worldly cares. I am sweet of tongue and good at mixing with people for I have great forbearance and shun harsh language. My intentions are unsullied; so the counsel I give usually proves helpful to others. I have no foul or vicious habits, and I do not run after other men's wives. I have a true, unwavering faith in Jainism, and a steadfast mind which remains unshaken in its determination. I am pure in heart and always strive for equanimity.

These are my various virtues, both small and big. None of them really touch supreme heights and none are quite without shortcomings.

Now for my bad points. I said I have little of anger, pride and cunning, yet my greed for money is great. A little gain makes me inordinately happy and a little loss plunges me into the depths of despair. I am indolent by nature and slow in my work, hardly ever wanting to stir out of my house.

I do not perform sacred religious rituals; I never utter the holy mantras, never sit for meditations (tapa) and never exercise self-restraint. Neither do I perform puja nor practise charity.

I am overfond of laughter, and love to poke fun at everything. I delight in playing the buffoon, indulging in these capers with great relish and gusto. I often utter things that should not be said without any sense of shame, revelling in narrating unutterable stories and escapades with much glee. I love to relate fictitious stories, often quite scanda-lous, and try to pass them off as true especially when I am in the midst of a large gathering. When I am in the mood for fun, nothing can restrain me from telling fanciful lies or untruths.

I sometimes break into a dance when I am alone. Yet I am also prone to sudden, irrational feelings of sheer dread.

Such is my temper. The good in my character alternates with the bad.

(2) AGRA/DELHI: TOMBS

Princess Jahanara (1614–1681), *Epitaph*

Written for herself by the favourite eldest daughter of Shah Jahan, supposedly while looking after him during his captivity in Agra by her brother Aurangzeb. Jahanara was buried in Delhi, near Nizamuddin. Taken from J.C.E. Bowen, The Golden Pomegranate (see Booklist).

The Green Grave of Princess Jahanara

When death at last arrives to set
  My prisoned body free
No vault shall claim my dust – but let
  The green grass cover me.

(3) AGRA: TAJ MAHAL

Sahir Ludhianvi, *Taj Mahal*

A progressive poet's harsh view of the famous building, said to have cost the then fabulous sum of forty million rupees.

To you, my love, the Taj is a symbol of love. Fine,
Fine too that you venerate this, the valley where it sits,
  But meet me somewhere else.

The poor visiting the royal assembly? Absurd.
What's the sense of lovers journeying on
That road which bears the prints of royalty's contempt?

Look at the emblems of arrogant majesty?
The backgrounds to this sign of love.
Do dead kings' tombs delight you?
If so, look into your own dark home.
In this world, countless people have loved.
Who says their passions weren't true?
They just couldn't afford a public display like this
Because they were paupers . . . like us.
These buildings and tombs, these abutments and forts
Are a despot's pillars of majesty,
Cancers upon the breast of earth, a chronic cancer
Which sapped the blood of our ancestors
Who, my love, must have loved too.
It was their art that shaped this exquisite form.
But their beloveds' tombs stand without name or fame;
Until today, no one even lit a candle for them.
This garden, this palace on the river's bank,
These carved doors and walls, this arch, this vault – what are they?
The mocking of the love of the poor
By an emperor propped up on his wealth.
    My love meet me somewhere else.

(4) ALLAHABAD

Nirala, *Breaking Stones*

This poem combines poetic diction with incisive social comment. The compassionate but hard-hitting poem is doubtless intended to stir the literati of Allahabad, whose 'mansions' were the crucible of modern Hindi writing. Translated by R. Snell.

She was breaking stones;
on the road in Allahabad I saw her –
she was breaking stones.

No shady tree
under which she sat, accepting;
dark of body, brimming youth bound,
eyes downward, mind on lover's deeds,
with the heavy hammer in her hand
she struck and struck again –
opposite: trees in rows, mansions, parapets.
The sun reached its height
of summer's heat

in raging day;
the wind rose scorching,
the earth like cotton burning,
the dust alive with sparks.
    Noon drew near –
    she was breaking stones.
She watched me watching once,
looked toward the house, shreds and tatters;
No-one to see,
looked back at me
as one who, beaten, does not cry;
a stirring strain
of some strung instrument I heard
not to hear again.
A moment later she trembled, graceful;
a drop of sweat rolled from her brow,
then turning to her work once more she seemed to say –
'I'm breaking stones'.

(5) ALLAHABAD

Arvind Krishna Mehrotra, 'The Roys'

The full poem, totalling about six times the length of these initial lines, steps further and further into a world of surreal images, but retains throughout the connection with the 'Civil Lines' area of the poet's hometown of Allahabad.

We've rented a flat in Ghosh Buildings, Albert Road,
And the Roys live across the street. Mr Roy,
General Merchant, dresses in white
Drill trousers, long-sleeved cotton shirts,
And looks like a friendly barn-owl.
His sons are in school with me. Ganesh,
The eldest, has a gleaming forehead,
A shelled-egg complexion, a small
Equilateral mouth; he belongs to a mystical
Group of philatelists. Together with Shaporjee,
The tallow-white Parsi next door, and Roger Dutt,
The school's aromatic geography teacher, he goes up
In a hot-air balloon and, on the leeward
Side of a Stanley Gibbons catalogue, comes down
Near a turret in Helvetia or Magyar,
Stamp-sized snowflake-like countries

Whose names dissolve like jujubes on my tongue.
We play french cricket, seven-tiles, I-spy, and Injuns.
Our tomahawks are butter knives, our crow
Feathers are real, and riding out from behind
Plaza Talkies we ambush the cowboys of Civil Lines.

(6) ALLAHABAD

Mahadevi Varma, *A Pilgrimage to the Himalayas, and Other Silhouettes from Memory*

Mahadevi Varma describes characters encountered during a life spent in the provincial town of Allahabad, one of the major centres of Hindi literature, set in the heartland of rural UP.

For more than a decade I have not changed my servant, milkman, washerman or tonga driver. If there can be any reason for such a change except death, it is known neither to them nor me.

Dhamrhi's mother has been washing my clothes since my student days. She had the misfortune to lose her children one after the other so, in order to fool the hostile stars, she put her newborn son in a cane winnowing basket and sold him to a neighbour for one dhamrhi. After the sixth day she bought him back for five dhamrhis, and to commemorate the sale and purchase she named him Dhamrhi Lal. You can attribute it to the folly of the creator or the strength of Dhamrhi – in any case he managed to avoid the valley of death. Dhamrhi is now grown up and married, but he still has not stopped his childish pranks. Sitting arrogantly in the courtyard of our house he will shout to Bhaktin who is working in the kitchen, 'Mother Bhaktin! I know how to drink tea, too. If you have brewed some for auntie, give me a cupful!'

(7) PRAYAG (ALLAHABAD)

Eric Newby, *Slowly Down the Ganges*

Eric Newby describes a scene at the Sangam, the confluence of the Ganges and Yamuna rivers at Prayag, the ancient city of Allahabad; each year in the month of Magh (January) a great fair is held at the sacred site (overlooked by a fort built by Akbar), where millions of Hindus bathe in the holy waters.

Eventually, we reached the Fort, and from the ramparts looked out over the sandbank which extended upstream for more than a mile from the confluence of the two rivers as far as the Izzot railway bridge. It was more like the camp of an army on the eve of a great action than a holy place. The sandbank was hidden from view by a blanket of low-lying fog and smoke which was illuminated by the flickering light of the camp fires, and the glare of kerosene lanterns. The long lines of electric lights on long poles which marked the way to the bathing areas were the only lights actually to rise above the fog; while overhead the stars looked down, pale and remote.

It was eerie, for apart from a few hundred pilgrims who were seeing the night through huddled against the wall of the fort, there was not a human being in sight. Only a muted and continuous roar from the sandbank and the encampments announced the fact that a million people were settling down for the night. A sound that was punctuated by the beating of gongs and drums, the ringing of bells, the rumbling of trains on the railway bridges and the noise of the loud-speakers which blared out injunction to this vast multitude on how it should comport itself the next day, on the morning of Makara Sankranti, when the sun and moon would be of equal degree.

(8) Awadh: Faizabad

W.H. Sleeman, *Diary of a Tour through Oude*

Sleeman's famous diary is a unique record of the circumstances of life in mid 19th century Awadh (Oudh, Oude), conducted shortly before the Mutiny of 1857. The passage describes one of the perils of cross-country travel in the days before rivers were bridged.

December 17, 1849. – Five miles to the left bank of the Ghaghra, whence we crossed over to Fyzabad, on platformed boats, prepared for the purpose by the Oude authorities. Our tents [were] in one of the large mango groves, which are numerous on the right bank of the river, but scanty on the opposite bank. [. . .] The morning was fine, the sky clear, and the ground covered with hoar frost. It was pleasing to see so large a camp, passing without noise, inconvenience or disorder of any kind in so large a river.

The platformed boats were numerous, and so were the peer-heads [sic] prepared on both sides, for the convenience of embarking and landing. Carriages, horses, palankeens, camels and troops, all passed without the slightest difficulty. The elephants were preparing to cross, some in boats and some by swimming, as might seem to them best. Some refuse to swim and others to enter boats, and some refuse to do either; but the fault is generally with their drivers. On the present occasion, two or three remained behind, one plunged into the stream from his boat, in the middle of the river with the driver on his back, and both disappeared for a time, but neither was hurt. Those that remained on the left bank got tired of their solitude, and were, at last, coaxed over, either in boats or in the water.

(9) BENARES

Ravidas, *Bani*

Ravidas, a low-caste chamar (leather-worker) of Benares, scorns the lofty Brahmins who dominate the religious and social life of his native city. Taken from Hawley and Juergensmeyer, see Booklist.

Oh well born of Benares, I too am born well known:
    my labour is with leather. But my heart can boast the Lord.
See how you honour the purest of the pure,
    water from the Ganges, which no saint will touch
If it has been made into intoxicating drink –
    liquor is liquor whatever its source;
And this toddy tree you consider impure
    since the sacred writings have branded it that way,
But see what writings are written on its leaves:
    the Bhagavata Purana you so greatly revere.
And I, born among those who carry carrion
    in daily rounds around Benares, am now
    the lowly one to whom the mighty Brahmins come
And lowly bow. Your name, says Ravidas,
    is the shelter of your slave.

(10) BENARES

Samuel Purchas, *Purchas's Pilgrimage*

Samuel Purchas describes a scene in Benares in the early 17th century. The deity 'Ada' is perhaps Adi Kesav, though the reference to 'claws' is puzzling; and the 'great place like a Well, with steps to goe downe' is perhaps Lolark Kund.

'Bannaras is a great Towne on Ganges, to which the Gentiles out of farre Countries come on pilgrimage. The men are shauen all but the crowne. Alongst the water side are many faire houses, in which stand images of euill fauour, made of stone, and wood, like Leopards, Lyons, Monkeys, Men, Women, Peacocks, and Deuils, with foure arms and hands, sitting closelegged, and holding somewhat in their hands. There are diuers old men, which on places of earth, made for that purpose, sit praying, and they giue the people (which by breake of day, and before, come out of the towne, to washe themselues in Ganges) three or four strawes which they take, and hold them between their fingers where they wash themselues: and some sit to marke them in the foreheads, and they haue in a cloth a little Rice, Barley, or Money, which they giue to these old men. After that, they goe to diuers of their images, and giue them of their sacrifices, those old men in the meanewhile praying, which maketh all holy. They haue one idoll called *Ada*, with foure hands and clawes. On certaine great carued stones also they powre Water, Rice, Wheat, &c. They haue a great place like a Well, with steps to goe downe, wherein the water standeth foule and stinketh, by reason of those many flowers, which they continually throw there into. Many people are alwayes therein, with imagination of pardon for their sinnes, because *God* (as they blaspheme) washed himself therein. They gather vp the Sand in the bottome, as a holy Relike. They pray not but in the water, and wash themselues ouer-head, lading vp water with both their hands, and turne themselues about, and then drinke a little of the water three times, after which they go to their gods in their houses.

(11) Bihar: Mithila

Phanishwar Nath Renu, *The Third Vow*

A leading figure in the 'regional' school of Hindi fiction describes the growing relationship between the cart-driver Hiraman, for whom India's big cities seem remote and inaccessible places, and the worldly dancer Hirabai.

Hirabai had appraised Hiraman and found him to be a genuine diamond. This sturdy dark-skinned villager, still young at forty, had no concerns in the world except his cart and his bullocks. At home his elder brother tended the fields and raised a family. Hiraman respected his sister-in-law more than his brother and was even a bit afraid of her. Hiraman had been married when he was a child. Before the marriage was consummated, his wife died. He couldn't even remember her face. As for a second marriage, there were many reasons against it. His sister-in-law insisted that Hiraman be married to a virgin, and a virgin meant a little six-year-old. No one observed the law against child marriages. But only parents in dire straits were willing to give a girl to a previously married man. Hiraman's sister-in-law had vowed that the girl must be a virgin, and even her husband couldn't overrule her. So now Hiraman had decided against marrying at all. Why borrow trouble? Anyway, a married man could hardly run a cart business. Even if he lost everything else, Hiraman would never give up his profession.

Hirabai had seen few people as guileless as Hiraman. He asked, 'What district is your home in?' When he heard 'Kanpur', his outburst of laughter startled even the bullocks. Hiraman lowered his head shyly as he laughed. 'That's great! Kanpur – Ear City. So there must be a Nakpur – Nose City – too'.

And when Hirabai replied that yes, there was a Nagpur, he doubled up with chuckles again.

'What a world! What incredible names! Ear City! Nose City!' Hiraman gazed intently at the flower behind Hirabai's ear. He trembled when he saw the jewel of her nose-ring glistening like a drop of blood.

(12) BIHAR

Shakeel Badayuni, *Gunga Jumna*

A film song in a village setting, performed by Hindi cinema's greatest actor Dilip Kumar to a soundtrack sung by its greatest male singer Mohammed Rafi, captures the spirit of the folk idiom which it preserves in this vital 20th century medium.

'When Our Eyes Entangle'

The fair village maiden has stolen my heart away;
In ruins lie the remnants of my livelihood.
When our eyes entangle, my heart will smart with pain;
The firework of love explodes with the sound of thunder;
When our eyes entangle, my heart will smart with pain.
If I hold your beauty in my heart, where's the harm;
If I show you my affection, where's the harm.
I too have some rights in this town of love;
Your glancing eyes have disturbed the peace and I've lost my mind.
Without seeing my sweet fair one I can find no sleep,
She's ensnared me and my heart is restless.

(13) 'BRAHMPUR' (FICTIONAL TOWN, BASED ON PATNA, BIHAR)

Vikram Seth, *A Suitable Boy*

Kedarnath Tandon, a refugee from Partition, came to live in Brahmpur. This fictional city has striking similarities to the historic city of Patna, capital of Bihar. The extract highlights the juxtaposition of Hindu and Muslim sites of worship which has been a continual source of friction between the two communities.

As they passed below the red walls of the mosque, Haresh, not being a native of Brahmpur, asked why black flags were hanging at the outer gates. Kedarnath replied in an indifferent voice that they had come up just the previous week when the ground had been broken for a temple in the neighbouring plot of land. For one who had lost his house, his land and his livelihood in Lahore, he did not appear to be embittered against Muslims so much as exhausted by religious zealots in general. His mother was very upset at his evenhandedness, even indifference.

'Some local pujari located a Siva-linga in the Ganga,' said Kedarnath. 'It is supposed to have come from the Chandrachur Temple, the great Siva temple that they say Aurangzeb destroyed. The pillars of the mosque do have bits of Hindu carving, so it must have been made out of some ruined temple, God knows how long ago. Mind your step!'

Haresh narrowly avoided stepping into some dog-shit. He was wearing a rather smart pair of maroon brogues, and was very glad to have been warned.

'Anyway,' continued Kedarnath, smiling at Haresh's agility, 'the Raja of Marh has title to the house that stands – stood, rather – beyond the western wall of the mosque. He has had it broken down and is building a temple there. A new Chandrachur Temple. He's a real lunatic. Since he can't destroy the mosque and build on the original site, he's decided to build to the immediate west and install the linga in the sanctum there. For him it's a great joke to think that the Muslims will be bowing down in the direction of his Siva-linga five times a day.'

Kedarnath, noticing an empty cycle-rickshaw, hailed it, and they got in. 'To Ravidaspur,' he said, and then continued: 'You know, for a supposedly gentle, spiritual people, we seem to delight in rubbing other people's noses in dog-shit, don't you think? Certainly I cannot understand people like the Raja of Marh. He imagines himself to be a new Ganesh whose divine mission in life is to lead the armies of Siva to victory over the demons. And yet he's besotted with half the Muslim courtesans of the city. When he laid the foundation stone of the temple two people died. Not that this meant anything to him, he's probably had twenty times that number murdered in his own time in his own state. Anyway, one of the two was a Muslim and that's when the mullahs put the black flags up on the gate of the mosque.

(14) 'CHANDRAPORE' (FICTIONAL TOWN ON THE GANGES)

E.M. Forster, A Passage to India

Forster sets the scene for the classic novel of the British in India

Except for the Marabar caves – and they are twenty miles off – the city of Chandrapore presents nothing extraordinary. Edged rather than washed by the river Ganges, it trails for a couple of miles along the bank, scarcely distinguishable from the rubbish it deposits so freely. There are no bathing-steps on the river front, as the Ganges happens not to be holy here; indeed there is no river front, and bazaars shut out the wide and shifting panorama of the stream. The streets are mean, the temples ineffective, and though a few fine houses exist they are hidden away in gardens or down alleys whose filth deters all but the invited guest. Chandrapore was never large or beautiful, but two hundred years ago it lay on the road between Upper India, then imperial, and the sea, and the fine houses date from that period. The zest for decoration stopped in the eighteenth century, nor was it ever democratic. There is no painting and scarcely any carving in the bazaars. The very wood seems made of mud, the inhabitants of mud moving. So abased, so monotonous is everything that meets the eye, that when the Ganges comes down it might be expected to wash the excrescence back into the soil. Houses do fall, people are drowned and left rotting, but the general outline of the town persists, swelling here, shrinking there, like some low but indestructible form of life.

Inland, the prospect alters. There is an oval Maidan, and a long sallow hospital. Houses belonging to Eurasians stand on the high ground by the railway station. Beyond the railway – which runs parallel to the river – the land sinks, then rises again rather steeply. On the second rise is laid out the little civil station, and viewed hence Chandrapore appears to be a totally different place. It is a city of gardens. It is no city, but a forest sparsely scattered with huts. It is a tropical pleasaunce washed by a noble river. The toddy palms and neem trees and mangoes and pepul that were hidden behind the bazaars now become visible and in their turn hide the bazaars. They rise from the gardens where ancient tanks nourish them, they burst out of stifling purlieus and unconsidered temples. Seeking light and air, and endowed with more strength than man or his works, they soar above the lower deposit to greet one another with branches and beckoning leaves, and to build a city for the birds. Especially after the rains do they screen what passes below, but at all times, even when scorched or leafless, they glorify the city to the English people who inhabit the rise, so that newcomers cannot believe it to be as meagre as it is described, and have to be driven down to acquire disillusionment. As for the civil station itself, it provokes no emotion. It charms not, neither does it repel. It is sensibly planned, with a red-brick club on its brow, and farther back a grocer's and a cemetery, and the bungalows are disposed along roads that intersect at right angles. It has nothing hideous in it, and only the view is beautiful; it shares nothing with the city except the overarching sky.

(15) 'CHHOKRAPUR' (FICTIONAL TOWN, PERHAPS BASED ON CHATTISGARH)

J.R. Ackerley, *Hindoo Holiday: An Indian Journal*

Like his better-known friend E.M. Forster, Ackerley served as private secretary and companion to an Indian maharajah. The pseudonym 'Chhokrapur' (meaning 'Laddie-town') while disguising the geographical location of Chattisgarh, reveals a sexual orientation which pervades his descriptive writing and colours his appreciation of the Indian scene.

January 15th

Over the main entrance to the palace, which leads into the marble hall of state or council chamber, there is a board on which the English word 'Welcome' is inscribed. They say that when the board was painted there was a slight misunderstanding as to its intended destination, and it was hung originally over the jail; but after a time the mistake was perceived, and it was transferred to its present position.

There is a very beautiful tank on this side lapping the white walls of the old Palace buildings. It is a large circular stretch of water, bordered on one side by an arc of steps which drop steeply down from the dusty path into the depth of the water. For some two hundred yards they curve round; where they end trees begin, enclosing in a feathery fringe the further circumference of the lake. To this tank, as to the others round the town, the people come to wash themselves and their clothes. There is only one dye, of a claret tint, made in Chhokrapur, and I grow a little tired of the uniformity of colour of the women's *saris*, the single long cloths in which they drape themselves.

But the scene this morning was very beautiful, with these red garments spread out to dry upon the steps, between the blue of the water and the blue of the sky, against a background of white cupolas and minarets and bright evergreen trees. I stood there for some time in the sunlight, idly contemplating; while the men came up out of the water, their thin brown bodies flashing and sparkling, the wet loin-cloth shaping their thighs. But what poor physiques all of them had.

The women were abundantly adorned with cheap jewellery – countless coloured glass bangles and rough silver necklaces and anklets; for the poorer people invest their small savings in this way, by converting them into silver for their womenfolk. They knelt with their red cloths in their hands, beating them with stones. I saw a woman sitting with her child between her knees, catching the lice in its hair and placing them dead on the child's palm, outstretched to receive them. I saw a boy take a handful of dirt, and descending with it to the water's edge, use it to cleanse his face and neck. I saw an old man standing immersed to his waist, facing the sun, making passes across his chest, and lifting handfuls of water to spill it out again like glittering beads between his fingers. Babaji Rao, whom I questioned later, told me he was offering oblations to the sun, the scattered water represent-ing rice, and the passes across his body meant that he was painting himself with sandal.

(16) Delhi

Khushwant Singh, *Delhi*

Musaddi Lal, born in 1265, is one of the narrators in a novel of the history of Delhi over a span of six centuries; here he describes his education in literacy and the ways of the world.

Like my Kayastha forefathers, I was trained to be a scribe. A *pandit* taught me Sanskrit and Hindi. Through my father's influence I was admitted to a *madrasa* to learn Arabic, Turki and Persian. At first I was treated roughly by the Turkish boys and the sons of Hindu converts to Islam. But when I learnt to speak Turki and dress like a Turk, they stopped bullying me. To save me being harassed, the *Maulvi* Sahib gave me a Muslim name, Abdul. The boys called me Abdullah.

I was the only child of my parents. I had been betrothed to a girl, one of a family of seven who lived in Mathura. We were married when I was nine and my wife, Ram Dulari, only seven. Four years later, when I was old enough to cohabit, my parents sent the barber who had arranged our marriage to fetch my wife from Mathura. For reasons which I will explain later, her parents refused to comply with our wishes. Then tragedy struck our home. My father died and a few days later my mother joined him. At thirteen I was left alone in the world.

The *Kotwal* Sahib was very kind to me. When he came to offer his condolence, he also offered my father's post to me.

It was at that time that my Muslim friends suggested that if I accepted conversion to Islam my prospects would be brighter; I could even aspire to become Kotwal of Mehraull. And I would have no trouble in finding a wife from amongst the new converts. If I was lucky I might even get a widow or a divorcee of pure Turkish, Persian or Afghan stock. 'If you are Muslim,' said one fellow who was full of witticisms, 'you can have any woman you like. If you are up to it, you can have four at a time.'

> *A Turk for toughness, for hands that never tire;*
> *An Indian for her rounded bosom bursting with milk;*
> *A Persian for her tight crotch and her coquetry;*
> *An Uzbeg to thrash as a lesson for the three.*

(17) Delhi

Jawaharlal Nehru, *Speeches on Independence and on the death of Gandhi*

In these two extracts of speeches which are now part of the fabric of 20th century Indian history, Nehru speaks of two momentous events: the coming of independence (in a speech delivered to the Constituent Assembly, New Delhi, 14 August 1947) and the assassination of Gandhi (in a broadcast to the nation on 30 January 1948).

Long years ago we made a tryst with destiny, and now the time comes when we shall redeem our pledge, not wholly or in full measure, but very substantially. At the stroke of the midnight hour, when the world sleeps, India will awake to life and freedom. A moment comes, which comes but rarely in history, when we step out of the old and into the new, when an age ends, and when the soul of a nation, long suppressed, finds utterance. It is fitting that at this solemn moment we take the pledge of dedication to the service of India and her people and to the still larger cause of humanity.

* * *

Friends and comrades, the light has gone out of our lives and there is darkness everywhere. I do not know what to tell you and how to say it. Our beloved leader, Bapu as we called him, the Father of the Nation, is no more. Perhaps I am wrong to say that. Nevertheless, we will not see him again as we have seen him for these many years. We will not run to him for advice and seek solace from him, and that is a terrible blow, not only to me, but to millions and millions in this country. And it is a little difficult to soften the blow by any other advice that I or anyone else can give you.

The light has gone out, I said, and yet I was wrong. For the light that shone in this country was no ordinary light. The light that has illumined this country for these many many years will illumine this country for many more years, and a thousand years later, that light will still be seen in this country and the world will see it and it will give solace to innumerable hearts. For that light represented something more than the immediate present, it represented the living, the eternal truths, reminding us of the right path, drawing us from error, taking this ancient country to freedom.

(18) Delhi

Anita Desai, *The Clear Light of Day*

In this novel of a middle-class family living in Delhi, Raja, the son of the family who has a love of Urdu poetry, pours scorn on Urdu's sister-language Hindi.

Raja had studied Urdu in school in those days before the Partition when students had a choice between Hindi and Urdu. It was a natural enough choice to make for the son of a Delhi family: Urdu had been the court language in the days of the Muslim and Mughal rulers and had persisted as the language of the learned and the cultivated. Hindi was not then considered a language of great pedigree; it had little to show for itself in its modern, clipped, workaday form, and its literature was all in ancient, extinct dialects. Raja, who read much and had a good ear, was aware of such differences.

'See,' he told his sisters when he came upon them, bent over their homework at the veranda table, laboriously writing out Hindi compositions on My Village or The Cow, 'you can't call this a language.' He made a scornful noise in his nose, holding up one of their Hindi copy-books as if it were an old sock. 'Look, its angles are all wrong. And this having to go back and cross every word as you finish writing it, it is an – an impediment. How can you think fluently when you have to keep going back and crossing? It impedes the flow of the – the composition,' he told them and they were thunderstruck by such intellectual revelations. 'Look,' he said again and wrote out a few lines in the Urdu script with a flourish that made them quiver with admiration.

(19) DELHI: DEATH OF GANDHI

Stanley Wolpert, *Nine Hours to Rama*

An eminent historian, writing as a novelist, describes the scene immediately following the assassination of Mahatma Gandhi by Hindu fundamentalists in 1948.

Swiftly they came, silently, mournfully. Singly and in droves they came, the ragged and the rich, the aged and the young, Hindu and Muslim alike, the healthy and the lame. Those who could not walk were carried, supported by others, or they hobbled there on crutches, alone. Somehow all of them managed to find the way. Somehow all of them heard, as though heaven itself had carried the report, as though it were written on dusk's fading face –

Our little father, Bapu, is dead.

From every corner of the city they came, leaving dinners untouched, leaving doors unlocked, leaving possessions unguarded, leaving the petty problems and anxieties of their own petty lives behind them, forgetting themselves entirely, forgetting jealousy and fear, forgetting hatred and falsehood, elevated, united, if but for this moment, by the enormity of their loss, the immensity of their shame.

Like pilgrims on a pilgrimage they came, emerging so it seemed from the ground itself, from the very soil of the nation he had bequeathed to them, filling each path that converged upon Gupta House with their numberless numbers, the rumble of their naked steps as lugubrious as any dirge ever chanted, as eloquent in its wordless, rhythmless song as any prayer that had ever been sung.

He had attained his liberation. He had become immortal, imperishable, one with God. No one feared for his salvation, for the destiny of his spotless soul. It was for themselves they mourned, for the loss of the best of their fellows, the wisest of their gurus, the gentlest father any nation had ever been privileged to call her own. It was the sin of their negligence that made them mourn, the burden of their guilt, the crime of their unworthiness. For no one felt entirely absolved.

(20) Delhi: End Of The Old City

Mirza Asadullah Khan Ghalib,
A Letter (April/May 1861)

*The great Urdu poet laments the destruction of his beloved Delhi
after the Mutiny of 1857 in a letter to his friend and pupil Mir
Mahdi, who had sent him a poem for correction including a verse
describing Urdu as 'the language Delhi people speak'. From
Russell and Islam, see Booklist.*

Oh, Mir Mahdi, aren't you ashamed of yourself? My good sir, 'Delhi
people' now means Hindus, or artisans, or soldiers, or Panjabis or
Englishmen. Which of these speak the language which you are
praising? It's not like Lucknow. The population of Lucknow hasn't
changed. The state has gone, but the city still has its masters of every
art.

The grass screens and the breeze from the east? Not in *this* house.
These were the advantages of the old house. Now I am in Mir Khairati's
mansion, the house faces in another direction. Anyway, I get along
alright. The trouble now is that Qari's well has been closed, and in all
the wells in Lal Diggi the water has suddenly turned brackish. Well, we
might have drunk it even so, but it comes up warm. I went out two days
ago to find out about the wells – past the Jama Masjid towards the
Rajghat Gate. I tell you without exaggeration that from the Jama
Masjid to the Rajghat Gate is a barren wilderness, and if the bricks
piled here and there were taken away it would be absolutely bare. You
must remember that on the far side of Mirza Gauhar's garden was a
hollow twenty to thirty feet deep. Now the place is level with the wall
of the garden courtyard. Even Rajghat Gate itself has been blocked up.
The parapet of the battlements has been left clear, but the rest is all
buried. You saw the Kashmiri Gate for yourself when you were here.
Now they've cleared a path for the railway from the Calcutta Gate to
the Kabuli Gate. Panjabi Katra, Dhobi Wara, Ramji Ganj, Saadat
Khan's Katra, Jarnail ki Bibi ki Haveli . . . – you won't find a trace of
any of them. In short, the city has become a desert, and now that the
wells are gone and water is something rare and precious, it will be a
desert like that of Karbala. My God! Delhi people still pride themselves
on Delhi language! What pathetic faith! My dear man, when Urdu
Bazar is no more, where is Urdu? By God, Delhi is no more a city,
but a camp, a cantonment. No Fort, no city, no bazaars, no water-
courses. . . .

(21) DELHI: OLD CITY

Mirza Farhatullah Beg, *Dihli ki Akhiri Shama*

*A visit to the house in Old Delhi of the Urdu poet Momin
(1800–52), a gentlemanly hakeem (homeopathic doctor) well
known for his cultivated interests in chess and the arts of
prediction. From Akhtar Qamber, see Booklist.*

Hakeem Momin Khan Sahib's house faces the locality known as
Hakeem Agha-Jan-ka-Chhatta. An imposing entrance leads to an
expansive, square courtyard around which the house is built. On either
side are two smaller courts, and right in front are large double halls.
There is a room on top of the rear hall. The roof of the front hall has
been turned into a balcony with a low parapet. The floors of the halls
are covered with *chandni* [white sheets]. The inner hall is furnished
with a woollen rug spread out in the centre. Here, leaning on a
gao-takiyah [bolster], sat Hakeem Sahib. Facing him and seated
respectfully on their knees were his disciples Hakeem Sukhanand,
whose *nom de plume* is Raqam, and Mirza Rahim-ud-Din Haya. It
seemed as though a durbar were being held there. No one seemed to
have the courage so much as to lift up his eyes or speak unnecessarily.
. . .

   When Maulana Sehbai and I arrived, Hakeem Sahib was playfully
rebuking Mirza Rahim-ud-Din Haya: 'My young lord, I am sick and
tired of your chess diagrams. A request for a solution once, or even a
second time, is reasonable enough, but how can I satisfy your daily
demands?'
   'Ustad,' replied the young lord, 'I cannot help it. The Resident
Bahadur keeps on receiving chess problems from England for solution.
Some of these I can work out without help and send them back to him.
Those I am unable to solve for myself if I bring to you.'
   Hakeem Momin Sahib raised his eyes towards us, took our saluta-
tions and invited us to be seated. Then he turned to the young man
again and said: 'Miyan Haya, the chess diagram you have brought this
time does not seem to me to be very intricate. You predict that the red
chess pieces will suffer defeat. I say it is the green ones that will be
vanquished. Please lay out the chess board here and I will explain
everything, but first let me have a word with Maulana Sehbai.' Then
turning to Sukhanand: 'And, Miyan Sukhanand, you had better sit and
watch the game.' He mischievously added: 'I have already given the
command that unless its mate arrives from the East this exasperating
lizard will not abandon the front wall. When it does, the solution to
the chess problem will also be found.'

(22) DELHI: THE RAINS
Ahmed Ali, *Twilight in Delhi*

The novel is a famous evocation of Muslim society in Delhi, which the author was himself forced to leave in 1947. It is set in the early 20th century, before the construction of New Delhi, which has since long extended to take in the picnic places mentioned in this passage.

The heat had been oppressive. The loo blew throughout the day, and at night the pillows were unbearable. Dust floated in the air; and in the evenings the sun hung like an aluminium disc behind the sand.

On the day previous to Asghar's departure, however, the wind changed and an easterly breeze struck up. White masses of clouds floated in the sky, and the sun rested his head on their massive backs, and the world heaved a sign of relief. At night the moon peeped from behind the sailing clouds; and the breeze remained cool.

Early in the morning the rain came suddenly pattering down. It rained for half an hour; the pleasant smell of the earth rose all around; and everything looked washed and soothing to the eyes. The sky was covered with dark collyrium black clouds. A cool easterly wind blew bringing peace and a message of beauty to the soul. The twitter of the sparrows, the screeching of the mainas, the cawing of the crows, so dull and heartrending otherwise, sounded so pleasing and intimate.

Asghar went about doing things with a light heart. It seemed to him that the whole wide world was revelling in a dream of love. The pigeon-fliers flew their pigeons with louder enthusiasm; and the vendors in the street redoubled their cries. As the day advanced women were heard singing from the nearby houses the songs of Saavan, the beautiful Indian rainy season with its associations of birth and spring:

Who has put the swing on the tree?
Come, let's swing, my friend.

Innumerable men, women and children came out of their houses and went for picnics to Okhla or Qutab Minar. Hundreds of hearts hungry for love and a little rest from the worries of life, went out of their dingy houses to enjoy the beauties of the earth just awakened by the healing touch of the rain. They carried delicacies wrapped up in cloths, in baskets, out in search of the open. The women dragged their dirty burqas [cape-like veils] like wet hens fluttering their wings. And a chatter and ceaseless babble of talk, the shouts of happy children and the noise of men shouting orders, filled the atmosphere.

(23) GANGES

Tulsi Das, *The Petition to Ram*

In a sequence of praise-poems addressed to the deities and sacred places associated with his lord Rama, the great devotional poet sings the praise of the river Ganges, holiest of all India's rivers.

River of the gods, by remembering you
  Sins and the threeefold fires are banished,
You beautify the earth like some wishing-creeper,
  Laden with pleasures and delights;
Shines your glistening flood like the moon
  Replete with elixir-water,
And your most pure wavelets yield
  Beauty as do the noble deeds of Raghuvar;
Without you, O Ganges – mother of the world,
  What would we in this Dark Age do?
And how would Tulsi cross over
  This terrible, uncrossable ocean of existence?

(24) 'KRISHNAPUR' (FICTIONAL TOWN IN UTTAR PRADESH)

J.G. Farrell, *The Siege of Krishnapur*

In an outstanding example of the many novels written about the Indian Mutiny of 1857, Farrell describes how the beleaguered Europeans, their ammunition spent, quite literally fling the remaining symbols of Western civilization in the face of the enemy.

The Collector, in a remote and academic sort of way, was musing on this question of ammunition, considering whether there was anything left which still might be fired. But surely they had thought of everything. All the metal was gone, first the round objects, then the others. Now they were on to stones. Without a doubt the most effective missiles in this matter of improvised ammunition had been the heads of his electro-metal figures, removed from their bodies with the help of Turton's indispensable file. And of the heads, perhaps not surprisingly, the most effective of all had been Shakespeare's; it had scythed its way through a whole astonished platoon of sepoys advancing in single file through the jungle. The Collector suspected that the Bard's success in this respect might have a great deal to do with the ballistic advantages stemming from his baldness. The head of Keats, for example, wildly festooned with metal locks which it had proved impossible to file smooth had flown very erratically indeed, killing only a fat money-lender and a camel standing at some distance from the field of action.

A few other metal objects had been fired, such as clocks and hair brushes . . . but they had proved quite useless. Candlesticks filed into pieces and collected in ladies' stockings had served for canister for a while, but had been swiftly exhausted. Then a find had been made. Poor Father O'Hara had contracted cholera and died shortly after the withdrawal to the banqueting hall; when his body had been heaved over the ramparts for the jackals and the pariah dogs (the only way that remained for disposing of the dead), a number of heavy metal beads, crosses, Saints and Virgins had been discovered in his effects. The Padre, consulted as to the propriety of firing them at the enemy, had given his opinion that they could perfectly well be fired and that they, or any such popish or Tractarian objects, would very likely wreak terrible havoc. However, this did not seem to be the case, particularly, except for the metal beads.

(25) NORTH INDIA

Ruth Prawer Jhabvala, *Heat and Dust*

The novel interweaves two narratives; a contemporary tells the story of her own relationships with and in India as she pieces together the enigma of a scandal in the India of the twenties, when her step-grandmother had eloped with an India prince. Olivia, the bored wife of a civil servant in a provincial town in northern India, has an affair with the Nawab, and becomes pregnant. After the ministrations of the local midwife (using a stick smeared with a secret herb) have achieved the desired abortion, Olivia encounters the face of shocked British opinion in the shape of Dr Saunders.

Although the Major was so sympathetic to India, his piece sounds like a warning. He said that one has to be very determined to withstand – to stand up to – India. And the most vulnerable, he said, are always those who love her best. There are many ways of loving India, many things to love her for – the scenery, the history, the poetry, the music, and indeed the physical beauty of the men and women – but all, said the Major, are dangerous for the European who allows himself to love India too much. India always, he said, finds out the weak spot and presses on it. Both Dr. Saunders and Major Minnies spoke of the weak spot. But whereas for Dr. Saunders it is something, or someone, rotten, for the

Major this weak spot is to be found in the most sensitive, often the finest people – and, moreover, in their finest feelings. It is there that India seeks them out and pulls them over into what the Major called the other dimension. He also referred to it as another element, one in which the European is not accustomed to live so that by immersion in it he becomes debilitated or even (like Olivia) destroyed. Yes, concluded the Major, it is all very well to love and admire India – intellectually, aesthetically, he did not mention sexually but he must have been aware of that factor too – but always, with a virile, measured, *European* feeling. One should never, he warned, allow oneself to become softened (like Indians) by an excess of feeling; because the moment that happens – the moment one exceeds one's measure – one is in danger of being dragged over to the other side. That seems to be the last word Major Minnies had to say on the subject and his final conclusion. He who loved India so much, knew her so well, chose to spend the end of his days here! But she always remained for him an opponent, even sometimes an enemy, to be guarded and if necessary fought against from without and, especially, from within: from within one's own being.

(26) NORTH INDIA

Agyeya, *Signs and Silence*

Two short lyrics from the pen of one of Hindi's foremost modern poets.

Village at Night

The cicadas' lullaby
Has put the village to sleep;
Now white cords of smoke are rocking
The homes slowly,
Like cradles.

The Mountain Does Not Tremble

The mountain does not tremble,
Nor the trees, nor the valley:
It is the small glow of the light
From the house on the hillside
Mirrored in the lake
That trembles.

(27) NORTH INDIA: LOVE SONGS

Traditional Thumris

The semi-classical love-song called thumri, popular throughout North India and Pakistan, is sometimes devotional in tone, sometimes erotic. The first of our two examples voices the agony of a young woman in separation from her beloved (who may be envisaged as Krishna, or as God in a Sufi context); the second, attributed to Wajid Ali Shah 'Akhtar', a gopi (milkmaid) feigns annoyance at the attentions of Krishna, the young lover who plays the flute. From Satrughna Shukla, see Booklist.

Whom can I tell of my sorrow, O friend?
My life ebbs away as I writhe in pain;
no peace of mind for an hour or a moment.

I know not to which country my beloved has gone,
In which rival's house he stays, my friend;
The night passes in pain, counting the stars.

* * *

Sweet friend, how can I go to fetch water?
See the mischief of the clever one wearing the crown –
this flute-player flirts on the Jumna shore;
How can I go to fetch water, friend?

Standing on tiptoe, peeping and gazing, O 'Akhtar',
As the lover at the riverbank looks longingly
How can I go for water, my friend?

(28) RAJASTHAN/UTTAR PRADESH

Biharilal, *Bihari Satsai*

The Bihari Satsai is a collection of (nominally) 'Seven hundred' independent verses, mostly on love but also touching devotional themes; though composed in Rajasthan, in terms of their Braj dialect and their general cultural reference the poems belong to the broader North Indian tradition – with Vrindaban, Krishna's playground, a special focus.

It makes no difference if my love
    lives in a distant land;
No matter where the kite may fly,
    its string lies in my hand.

Only from the almanac
we know the lunar phase
when stealing full-moon's brilliance,
my darling's face doth blaze.

What is a flower, a moonlit night,
the brightness of a glass?
The lustre of her loveliness
will all these things surpass.

(29) EASTERN UTTAR PRADESH

Shrilal Shukla, *Rag Darbari*

In a heavily satirical tone, Shukla shows how social reform is given little more than lip-service in the contemporary world of the Indian village.

'Chamarhi' was the name of a mohalla of the village where the chamars lived. 'Chamar' is the name of a caste considered to be untouchable. An untouchable is a biped whom people used not to touch in the days before the constitution came into force. The constitution is a poetic work whose seventeenth article eradicates the distinction of untoucha-bility; but because in our country people live not by poetry but by religion, and because untouchability is a religion in our country, the untouchables had separate mohallas in Shivpalganj, as in other villages [. . .]

After the constitution came into being an excellent work was done in the area separating Chamarhi from the rest of the village: a stone platform, called the 'Gandhi Platform', was built there. Gandhi, as some people recall even today, was born in India; and when his principles were consigned to the sacred waters of the Ganges along with his ashes, it was resolved that from now on all constructions built in his memory would be solid-built; and it was in the grip of this enthusiasm that the platform was erected in Shivpalganj. The platform was very useful for taking the sun on a winter's day, a facility mostly exploited by the dogs; and since no bathroom facilities had been installed for them, they would urinate on the corner while sunning themselves, and human beings soon began to follow suit in the shelter that the platform provided.

(30) UTTAR PRADESH

Premchand, *The Gift of a Cow*

The novel tells the story of a peasant-farmer, Hori, whose daily struggle revolves around his desire for an honorable life free from debt; his highest ambition, the making of a sacred 'gift of a cow' to a brahman, remains forever beyond his grasp.

The June sun was rising over the mango grove, turning the red of dawn to a brilliant silver, and the air was beginning to warm up. Farmers working in the fields beside the path greeted him respectfully and invited him to share a smoke with them. Hori had no time for such pleasantries, but they brought a glow of pride to his wrinkled face. It was only because he associated with the landlords that everyone showed him such respect. Otherwise who would pay any attention to a farmer with just three acres of land? As it was, though, even three and four-plough farmers greeted him – no small honour.

Leaving the path through the fields, he came to a hollow where so much rainwater collected during the monsoon that a little grass remained even in the height of summer. Cattle from the nearby villages came here to graze, and there was still a cool freshness in the air. Hori took several deep breaths and thought of sitting down for a while, since he'd be dying of heat in the scorching *loo* wind the rest of the day. A number of farmers were eager to lease this bit of land and had offered a good price, but the Rai Sahib – God bless him – had plainly told them it was reserved for grazing and would not be relinquished at any price. If he's been one of those selfish zamindars, he'd have said the cattle could go to hell, that there was no reason for him to miss the chance to make a little money. But the Rai Sahib still held to the old values, feeling that any landlord who didn't look after his tenants was less than human.

(31) UTTAR PRADESH: GOVARDHAN HILL

Chitsvami, *Hymn to Govardhan Hill*

Govardhan Hill (which Krishna once lifted miraculously in his hand) is described from a devotional perspective as a blissful scene from a pastoral paradise. The 'actual' hill lies in the district of Braj, near Gokul village.

On Govardhan's summit sweet
    young jasmines are in bloom;
With full-fleshed fruit and peeping buds,
    the flowers' splendour spreads afar.

Each grove's adorned with trees and vines,
    abundant flow the springs.
Says Chitsvami, 'midst a throng of Braj damsels
    Krishna, Gokul's prince, takes pleasure.

(32) Uttar Pradesh:
Kanpur To Lucknow

Lord Roberts of Kandahar, *Forty-one Years in India*

In what his preface describes as 'a plain, unvarnished tale of Indian life and adventure', Lord Roberts of Kandahar describes military operations in the area between Cawnpore (modern Kanpur) and Lucknow, scenes of some of the most dramatic events of the 1857 Mutiny.

While we were halting at this place, Watson and I had rather a curious adventure. During a morning's ride my greyhound put up a *nilghai* so close to us that Watson, aiming a blow at him with his sword, gashed his quarter. Off he started, and we after him at full speed; the chase continued for some miles without our getting much nearer, when, all at once, we beheld moving towards us from our right front a body of the enemy's Cavalry. We were in an awkward position; our horses were very nearly dead beat, and we could hardly hope to get away if pursued. We pulled up, turned round, and trotted back, very quietly at first, that our horses might recover their breath before the enemy got to closer quarters and we should have to ride for our lives. Every now and then we looked back to see whether they were gaining upon us, and at last we distinctly saw them open out and make as if to charge down upon us. We thought our last hour was come. We bade each other good-bye, agreeing that each must do his best to escape, and that neither was to wait for the other, when lo! as suddenly as they had appeared, the horsemen vanished, as though the ground had opened and swallowed them; there was nothing to be seen but the open plain, where a second before there had been a crowd of mounted men. We could hardly believe our eyes, or comprehend at first that what we had seen was simple a mirage, but so like reality that anyone must have been deceived. Our relief, on becoming convinced that we had been scared by a phantom enemy, was considerable; but the apparition had the good effect of making us realize the folly of us having allowed ourselves to be tempted so far away from our camp without escort of any kind in an enemy's country, and we determined not to risk it again.

(33) UTTAR PRADESH: LUCKNOW

V.S. Naipaul, *India: A Million Mutinies Now*

In the third travel book on the country of his ancestors, the Trinidadian writer revisits the chowk or bazaar of Lucknow, which he had earlier described in An Area of Darkness.

On the left bank of the river, directly below the hotel, there were Hindu temples. Far away, on the same bank, were the minarets of old Lucknow, reminders of the mosques and *imambaras* in which in 1962 I had looked for the glory of old Lucknow. Below, hidden by trees, were the lanes of the chowk or bazaar, which in 1962 still had a touch of the *Thousand and One Nights*, but which now, Rashid said, showed the final tragedy of the Muslim city to someone who knew how to look.

I went looking with him one morning. It was so crowded and cramped and repetitive in the lanes, the visitor might have seen the area as the expression of a single culture; and he might have missed the distinctions that Rashid saw.

The shops or stalls, as in the usual Indian bazaar, were narrow little boxes, fully open to the road or the lane, and set side by side, with hardly a gap between. The floors were a few feet above the lane. Gutters at the side received water and waste from the drains that ran between or under the stalls. This waste water didn't run off to some larger drain, Rashid said. It just stayed there, in the open gutter, and evaporated.

All the shops and stalls had metal shutters; every shop and attached house was built like a fortress, for the days of riot. From time to time, where there should have been a shop, there was a moraine of rubble, as though – out of age, fragility, or rot – the shop and the house with it had fallen inwards, a small demonstration of how the ground level of cities might rise, layer upon layer.

Had there always been a bazaar here? Was it possible to think of the time when this site was bare, a field? Rashid and I walked through a ceremonial gate, an archway, called after the great Mogul emperor Akbar. He ruled from 1556 to 1605. Perhaps the gate had been built in the late 16th century to mark a visit of the emperor's; so the outlines of the bazaar would have been then (in Shakespeare's time) what it was now.

(34) Uttar Pradesh:
Mansion Near Kanpur

Mirza Muhammad Hadi Rusva, *Umrao Jan Ada*

Umrao Jan, the heroine of this remarkable Urdu novel, is a courtesan who is brought up and trained in the great artistic centre of Lucknow, which she leaves in order to make a name for herself in the provincial town of Kanpur. She is invited to sing by a Begum at a birthday party held at her country mansion.

It is true that one only appreciates the true worth of one's home town when one is away, for now I longed to be among people of Lucknow. I had gone to hundreds of functions in Kanpur but had never looked forward to one with more eagerness. The long summer's day seemed as endless as a mountain range. At last the morning dragged into afternoon and at 5 o'clock the boy turned up. I was already dressed and made up and had got the musicians over. The boy told them the location of the house, I got into a palanquin and was on my way.

The Begum's house was an hour's distance from the city. The last bit of the road was alongside a canal which ran into a garden enclosed by a wall of cactus and thorny trees planted close together. The garden was laid out in English style. There were rows of palm trees along red gravel paths flanked by green lawns and rockeries with mountain plants sprouting out of the rocks. The garden was intersected by narrow waterways through which crystal clear water was flowing. Gardeners were sprinkling water on the plants. The leaves were washed and green. Flowers that had been scorched by the sun all day had begun to look fresh and lively.

From the garden I could hear the voices of women singing inside the house where the birthday ceremony was taking place. I stayed outside and when the musicians had arrived, I sang a song of greeting and a piece in the mode *Sham Kalyan*. Since there was no audience I did not go on. The Begum Sahiba apparently heard me from where she was and sent a gold sovereign and five silver rupees in appreciation.

In a little while it became dark. Then the moon came up and spread its silvery light over the lawn. Its reflection shimmered in the rippling water of the pool which was in the centre of the garden. The soft moonlight, the gentle murmur of water falling into the pool and the fragrance of flowers created a most bewitching atmosphere.

By the side of the pool was a wooden pavilion with painted pillars. In this pavilion arrangements had been made for the seating of guests: carpets with white sheets spread on them and cushions laid out for people to recline on.

A maidservant came out carrying two lamps with green shades and placed them in front of the carpet. The musicians were asked to retire to the servants' quarters as the function was henceforth to be exclusively for ladies. When they had left, the Begum Sahiba made her appearance. [. . .] I could not take my eyes off her face.

> They saw my eyes were dazzled by no earthly glare,
> But her beauty which only made me stand and stare.

Biographies and plot summaries

ACKERLEY, J(oseph) R(andolph) (1896–1967). Author, and from 1935 to 1959 literary editor of the BBC magazine *The Listener*, for which he solicited contributions from E.M. Forster and Christopher Isherwood. His memoir *My Father and Myself*, in which he wrote frankly about the homosexuality which underlies the tone of his better-known *Hindoo Holiday* (Extract 15), besides also revealing surprising aspects of his father's private life, was published posthumously in 1968.

AJNEYA [AGYEYA], pen-name of S.H. Vatsyayan (1911–87). Hindi poet, novelist and critic. His first work was written incognito in prison during the independence struggle, hence his pen-name of 'the Unknown One'. His novels translated into English include *To Each His Stranger* (*Apne apne ajnabi*, 1961) and *Islands in the Stream* (*Nadi ke dvip*, 1951); translated poetry collections include *Signs and Silence* (Extract 26, 1976) and *Nilambari* (1981).

ALI, Ahmed (1912–). Novelist born in Delhi, later moved to Pakis-

tan. He originally came to prominence as a writer of Urdu short stories, but subsequently turned to English. His two novels, *Twilight in Delhi* (Extract 22) and *Ocean of Night*, are nostalgic but realistic portrayals of Delhi and Lucknow respectively.

BANARSIDAS (1586–c 1643). The only real autobiographer of pre-

Ajneya

modern India. Banarsidas was a Jain, from a merchant family which migrated from Rajasthan to Jaunpur, eastern UP. He lived in various Mughal cities, eventually settling in Agra. An earnest scholar, he wrote extensively on Jain doctrine; but his autobiography *Half a Tale* (*Ardhakathanak*, 1641) shows us a man in whom the spiritual and the material are evenly balanced (Extract 1).

BEG, Mirza Farhatullah (1884–1947). Born into an old Delhi family, he grew up in Delhi but spent his working life in Hyderabad where he rose to a senior position in the state's judiciary. As a writer he is known for his very attractive essays, evocative of the old Muslim culture of Delhi, both remembered and imagined.

Bihari Satsai. Major work of 17th century Braj Hindi poetry. The *Satsai* or 'seven centuries [of couplets]' format is a traditional type of anthology of couplets of varied theme, in which the pleasures and pains of love are predominant, unified by a common poetic voice. Bihari's *Satsai* is a masterpiece of poetic compression within this genre, and reflects the cultural richness of Rajput court life with its blend of Hindu and Muslim elements.

BIHARILAL (born c 1600). Hindi poet whose biography is uncertain; he perhaps lived in Agra and Vrindaban before receiving patronage from Mirza Jai Singh at Amber (Jaipur). The couplets of his *Satsai* were probably written at the Amber court.

CHITSVAMI. Sixteenth century devotional poet and devotee of Krishna. One of the 'Astachap' group of eight

Braj Hindi hymn-writers to the sect of Vallabhacarya.

Delhi. Novel by Khushwant Singh ◊. While Indian readers of this novel will recognize autobiographical elements in the story of the present-day narrator and his recent ancestry (particularly in relation to the building of the new capital), the foreigner will find here a colourful reconstruction of episodes in the life of a city over a period of six centuries (Extract 16).

DESAI, Anita (1932–). Novelist, short-story writer and children's author writing in English; daughter of a German mother and a Bengali father. She was educated in Delhi, location of many of her narratives which tell of the lives and conflicts of middle-class urban society. Among her prize-winning novels are *Clear Light of Day* (Extract 18, 1980) and *In Custody* (1984); *Games at Twilight* (1982) is a collection of short stories.

Diary of a Tour Through Oude. W.H. Sleeman's ◊ account of his journeys in

Anita Desai

1852 and 1858 was commissioned as a basis for British strategy in dealing with 'Oudh' (Awadh), the last principality to be annexed to British India. The diary gives an unrivalled account of Indian rural society of the mid-19th century, and of the institutions of government which affected it (Extract 8).

FARRELL, J(ames) G(ordon) (1935–79). English novelist, killed in a fishing accident at the height of his literary powers. His novels include *Troubles* (1971) and *The Siege of Krishnapur* (Extract 24, 1979), both based in turbulent phases of history: Ireland during the 1920s and northern India during the Mutiny of 1857.

FORSTER, E(dward) M(organ) (1879–1970). Major English novelist, humanist and leading member of the Bloomsbury group. *The Hill of Devi* (West India and Rajasthan, Extract 13, 1953), his memoirs of a period spent as Private Secretary to the Maharajah of Dewas, records events reflected again in his great novel *A Passage to India* (Extract 14, 1924).

Forty-One Years in India (1897). Memoir of Lord Roberts of Kandahar, one of the most celebrated British soldiers of the 19th century. Roberts notes that 'my father and I spent nearly ninety years in India': the action-filled forty-one covered here are those of his own military career, 1852–1893 (Extract 32).

GHALIB, Mirza Asadullah Khan (1797–1869). Noble, poet and wit of Mughal Delhi in its twilight years until it ended in 1857, he is one of the most renowned and popular poets of Urdu and Persian ever produced by the sub-continent. He wrote poetry in both Persian and Urdu until the 1820s after which he wrote only in Persian for some 30 years. His Persian letters are regarded as models of prose and their content is full of interest. He won particular renown for his mastery of the ghazal, but his Urdu verse only received the acclaim it deserved from the beginning of this century.

Gift of a Cow, The (1936). The last novel by the Hindi author Premchand ◊. The plot weaves town and village narratives around the family of Hori, a debt-laden farmer, especially in his dealings with the village society – a favourite theme of Premchand's (Extract 30).

Gunga Jumna (1962). A Hindi/ Bhojpuri film directed by Nitin Bose with music by Naushad and lyrics by Shakeel Badayuni. A story of two brothers on opposite sides of the law – one a dacoit, the other a police officer – leads inexorably towards a tragic ending.

Half a Tale (1641). Hindi verse autobiography entitled *Ardhakathanak*, of the Jain Banarsidas. The text tells of his quest for knowledge and his irrepressible love of life, undaunted by the hard times in which he often found himself (Extract 1).

Heat and Dust (1975). A novel by Ruth Prawer Jhabvala for which she won the 1975 Booker Prize. The novel interweaves two narratives; a contemporary young English woman tells the story of her own relationships with and in India as she pieces together the enigma of a scandal from the 1920s, when her step-grandmother had eloped with an Indian prince (Extract 25).

Hindoo Holiday: An Indian Journal, (1932). Memoirs of J.R. Ackerley ◊, recounting experiences as private secretary to a Mahajarah (and hence to be compared with E.M. Forster's later *The Hill of Devi* – Western India and Rajasthan, Extract 13).

India: A Million Mutinies Now (1990). Travelogue by V.S. Naipaul ◊. Written 27 years after his first visit to India described in *An Area of Darkness* (South India, Extract 30, 1962), this book sees the lives of ordinary people in all corners of India with a novelist's eye, and describes the 'mutinies' of individuals' revolutions against the wielders of power (Extract 33).

JAHANARA. The eldest daughter of the former Mughal emperor Shah Jahan. She nursed him through the seven and a half years of his imprisonment until his death in 1666.

JHABVALA, Ruth Prawer (1927–). Novelist of Polish origin, educated in England, who has lived many years in India with her Indian husband, and writes in English. Her background gives her an original, non-British perspective on life in India. She has written extensively for the cinema,

Ruth Prawer Jhabvala

(especially in collaboration with the Ivory-Merchant team) including a screenplay for her own novel *Heat and Dust* (Extract 25, 1975).

MEHROTRA, Arvind Krishna (1947–). Poet writing in English (Extract 5). Born in Lahore, now living and teaching in Allahabad. He also translates Prakrit poetry and Hindi poetry and fiction into English.

NAIPAUL, V(idiadhar) S(urajprasad) (1932–). Trinidad-born novelist and author writing in English. His novels include *A House for Mr Biswas* (1961), which draws on his own West Indian experience. Three non-fiction books give a personal and trenchant view of the country of his ancestors: *An Area of Darkness* (1964), *A Wounded Civilization* (1977) and *India: A Million Mutinies Now* (1990) ◊.

NEHRU, Jawaharlal (1889–1964). The first Prime Minister of independent India (Extract 17). Although he favoured a socialist state built on modern sectarian principles, he inherited the political mantle of Mahatma Gandhi. Nehru was of Kashmiri Brahmin stock; his family ruled India for nearly half a century, through the successive premiership of his daughter Indira Gandhi (assassinated 1984) and her son Rajiv Gandhi (assassinated 1991).

NEWBY, Eric, (1919–). Traveller, writer and journalist. His books include *The Last Grain Race*, an account of a voyage to Australia and back in a four-masted barque; *Love and War in the Apennines*, describing his wartime escape from enemy lines; *Slowly Down the Ganges* (◊, Extract 7) describing

Eric Newby

his 1200-mile journey down the river; and his best-known work, *A Short Walk in the Hindu Kush*.

Nine Hours to Rama (1962). Novel by Stanley Wolpert on the plot to assassinate Mahatma Gandhi. The novel, largely written through dialogue and the depiction of action sequences, centres on the life and attitudes of the assassin Naturam Vinayak Godse (Extract 19).

NIRALA, pen name of Suryakant Tripathi (1899–1961). Hindi poet, novelist, and champion of the 'cause' of Hindi in a world whose élite saw proficiency in English as a measure of cultural sophistication (Extract 4).

Nirala

Nirala was part of, but also at a certain distance apart from, the 'Chayavad' poetic school which dominated the pre-Independence history of Hindi verse. Brought up in Bengal, Nirala was much influenced by the Bengali writer Tagore (◊ East India and Bangladesh).

Passage to India, A (1924). Novel by E.M. Forster ◊. The action centres on an ambiguous event during a visit of a British party to the mysterious Marabar caves: was the plain Miss Quested molested by the handsome and eager-to-please Dr Aziz, or was she not? At one level a depiction of British sensitivity (and the lack of it) towards India, the novel also weaves a complex net of interactions between characters, giving many psychological insights against the magnificently drawn backdrop of India (Extract 14, see also South India, Extract 14).

Petition to Ram, The. Seventeenth century Hindi devotional work by Tulsidas ◊ entitled *Vinay patrika*. Written in Braj Bhasa (the language of the classical Hindi *pada* or hymn), the 'petition' is a prayer of supplication seeking divine grace as a way of escape from the trials of life in the present dark age or 'Kaliyuga'. The circumstances of Tulsi's petition may include some autobiographical elements.

Pilgrimage to the Himalayas, A. Autobiographical sketches by the Hindi poet, prose-writer and feminist Mahadevi Varma ◊, originally published in Hindi as *Smrti ki rekhae* 'Lines of memory'. The sketches centre on the lives of the ordinary people of Northern India in the 1930s and 1940s, both fettered and enlivened by the richness of their traditions, beliefs and superstitions (Extract 6).

PREMCHAND, pen name of Dhanpat Rai Srivastav (1881–1936). Premchand is regarded as the 'father of modern Hindi fiction', for although not the first writer in this genre he was the first to write a substantial body of realistic novels and short stories of almost uniformly high standard. His fictional world, often marked by a Gandhian idealism, is located in the UP countryside of his birth, and is peopled with characters who struggle for a modicum of happiness and dignity while beset by debt, caste prejudice and rural poverty (Extract 30).

PURCHAS, Samuel (c 1577–1626). English travel-writer. He wrote extensive descriptions of his travels in America, Africa and Asia. The cost of publishing the five volumes of travelogue – already 'excessively rare' by the date of an 1864 Calcutta reprint – bankrupted him; but the writing, despite its archaic spelling, has a vividness of description which keeps it fresh to this day (Extract 10).

RAVIDAS (RAIDAS) (b c 1500). A poet-saint of the medieval Sant tradition. He was a member of the Chamar caste (cf Shrilal Shukla's ◊ novel *Rag Darbari*) from the Benares region. Like his older contemporary Kabir, he voiced the Sant teachings of belief in a formless God. A sect formed in his name is active in India and the diaspora.

RENU, pen-name of Phanisvar Nath (1921–77). Hindi novelist and short story writer (Extract 11). Regarded as the leading figure behind the 'regional' school of Hindi fiction of which his own great novel *The Dusty Border* (*Maila ancal*, 1954) is the exemplar.

Premchand

ROBERTS, Lord, of Kandahar (Frederick Sleigh Roberts) (1832–1914). Born at Cawnpore (now Kanpur, UP) in a military family, Lord Roberts joined the Bengal Artillery in 1852 and thus began an illustrious career which included action in the 'Mutiny' of 1857 and the second Anglo-Afghan war of 1878–80; he later served in South Africa (Extract 32).

RUSVA Muhammad Hadi (1858–1931). Regarded as the first true novelist in Urdu, his *The Courtesan of Lucknow* (*Umrao Jan Ada*, 1899) presents a vivid picture of the life of Lucknow around 1850 in the form of the autobiography of a courtesan (Extract 34). He wrote two other social novels, but they are considered inferior to his first.

Rag Darbari (1968). Hindi novel by Shrilal Shukla (Extract 29). The plot concerns a college student who returns to his village in eastern UP for a six-month stay. Local politics, petty corruption, lust, decay, humbug, exuberance, despair and the splendid sordidness of everyday life all jostle for place in a lively and richly-drawn satire on contemporary India.

SAHIR LUDHIANVI, Abdul Haye (1921–1980). Urdu poet and film lyricist. He belonged to a group of progressive writers in Urdu; edited periodicals in Lahore and Delhi. After Partition he moved to Pakistan, but soon returned to India, where the success of his poetry won him national acclaim and awards.

SETH, Vikram (1952–   ). Born in Calcutta, but brought up in Patna and Delhi, Vikram Seth was educated in élite Indian and British schools (Doon and Tonbridge) then read PPE at Oxford before going on to study in China and later to study economics at Stanford. He writes only in English, but translates from Chinese. He was best known until recently for his 'Great Californian novel', *The Golden Gate*, but his monster tome *A Suitable Boy* has become a best-seller, establishing him as one of the most important of the younger writers from India (Extract 13).

SHUKLA, Shrilal (1925–). Hindi novelist. He began writing in 1953–1954 when in a government post in Bundelkhand; he became Director of Cultural Affairs in the UP government in the 1970s. His work includes six novels, of which *Rag Darbari* (1968) ◊ was greatly acclaimed (Extract 29), and some collections of satirical essays.

Siege of Krishnapur, The. Novel by J.G. Farrell ◊, published in 1973. Set in a north Indian town during the 'Mutiny' of 1857, the novel draws on contemporary British accounts of the sepoy rebellion and of the sieges of such places as Lucknow. Farrell uses this historical flashpoint to examine the gulf of incomprehension between two cultures, and to portray the psychology of imperialism (Extract 24).

SINGH, Khushwant (1915–). Journalist, editor, translator, novelist, and historian of Sikhism. Born in Hadali in the Punjab, he originally trained as a lawyer but made his mark as the devil's advocate of Indian journalism. He was for many years editor of the widely-read *Illustrated Weekly of India*; his best-known novel, *Train to*

Pakistan (Pakistan and North-west India, Extract 28), is widely regarded as a classic, and he is probably most widely known for his acerbic observations of contemporary Indian society (Extract 16).

SLEEMAN, W.H. (1788–1856). Soldier and subsequently district officer under the East India Company. He led the campaign against the 'thugs', highway robbers who ritually murdered their victims (Extract 8). His best-known work is *Rambles and Recollections of an Indian Official* (1844).

Slowly Down the Ganges (1966). Travelogue by Eric Newby ◊, recounting a 1200-mile journey made in several stages by a variety of different means from the place where the river enters the plains (and first becomes navigable) to the Bay of Bengal. The book describes 'the river as we found it' from the perspective of a European couple both sympathetic to and uncomprehending of the lives of the people met en route (Extract 7).

Third Vow, The (1959). Short story by the Hindi author Phanisvar Nath 'Renu' ◊ (Extract 11). Set in Renu's home district of Mithila, Bihar, the story tells of the love of the simple cart-driver Hiraman for the dancer and courtesan Hirabai, and portrays the provinciality of rural Indian life against a background of folk culture.

TULSIDAS, (c 1532–1623). Hindi devotional poet. His epic work, the *Ramcaritmanas* or 'Holy Lake of Rama's Deeds', written in Benares in 1574, is a reworking in Awadhi verse of the Ramayana story, and is the

Drawing by Mahadevi Varma

single most important devotional work in the whole Hindi-speaking area. Other major works follow the Braj Bhasa tradition of hymn anthology; most are dedicated to Rama, though a collection of songs to Krishna also exists.

Twilight in Delhi (1940). Novel by Ahmed Ali ◊ (Extract 22), invoking the past splendours of Delhi as a traditional centre of Muslim culture.

VARMA, Mahadevi (1907–1978). Hindi poetess and writer. She was brought up in the literary world of Allahabad, a crucible for the conventions of modern Hindi writing which she herself influenced profoundly. She was one of the four poets of the loosely-defined school of *Chayavad* or 'Imagist' verse; the foremost Hindi poetess of this century, she was also an active propagandist for the rights of women (Extract 6). The plangency of her verse, often mystical in tone, invites comparisons with the medieval poetess Mirabai.

WAJIB ALI SHAH 'AKHTAR' (18??–1887). Ruler of the kingdom of Awadh (Oudh) when it was annexed by the British in 1856; his court had slipped into a decadent pursuit of elaborate artistic and other pleasures, and Wajid Ali was himself more interested in poetry, which he wrote under the pen-name 'Akhtar' ('Star') than with the affairs of state.

WEST INDIA
AND RAJASTHAN

Ian Raeside

Scratch a rock
and a legend springs
Arun Kolatkar, Jejuri

The huge area covered in this chapter has no real homogeneity or unity of culture but it also has no major geographical barriers, great mountain ranges or unfordable rivers, so that from the earliest times until the advent of modern roads and railways merchants have crossed it to trade between the western sea and Delhi, and conquering armies have swept across it in all directions. Working south-west from Delhi, **Rajasthan** is a mostly arid region which on the west turns into real desert that stretches across to Sind in Pakistan and on the east is roughly defined by the **Chambal** river. Running through it from north-east to south-west is the **Aravalli range**, which ends in the hill station of Mount Abu on the borders of Gujarat. East of the Chambal is **Malwa**, the plateau country which now forms the western part of the state of Madhya Pradesh and is watered by a whole string of rivers that rise in the **Vindhya** range north of the Narmada and run north to the Chambal and eventually to the Jumna and the Ganges. South and west of Rajasthan comes **Gujarat**, on the west the quasi-peninsulas of Saurashtra and Cutch and the fertile mainland on the east. This is the only part of the Deccan in which big rivers run west into the Arabian Sea, the so-called five mother goddesses of Gujarat – Banas, Sabarmati, Mahi, Narmada and Tapti – and at the mouths of the last three lie the ancient ports of **Cambay**, **Broach** and **Surat** through which India has traded with the west for a thousand years. Broach at least is so old that it is named in Ptolemy's *Geographia* in the second century AD.

South of the Tapti the mountains come back close to the western sea and run all the way down the rest of peninsular India. Usually known as

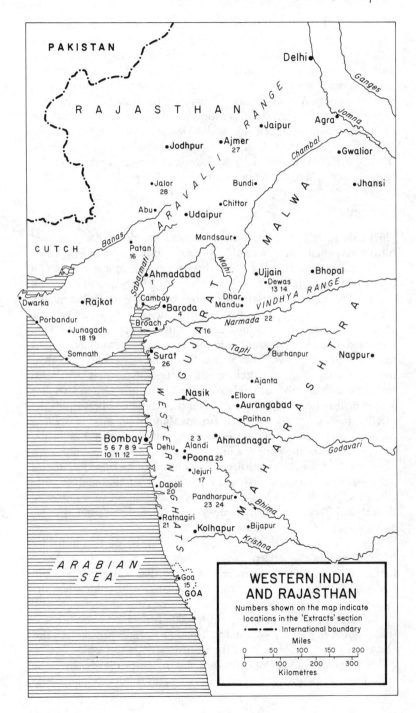

PAKISTAN

Delhi

Ganges

R A J A S T H A N

ARAVALLI RANGE

Yamna

•Jaipur

Agra

Chambal

•Gwalior

•Jodhpur

•Ajmer
27

Bundi•

•Jhansi

•Jalor
28

M A L W A

Chittor•

Abu•

•Udaipur

Mandsaur•

CUTCH

Banas

•Patan
16

Sabarmati

•Ahmadabad
1

Mahi

•Ujjain

•Bhopal

•Dewas
13 14

Cambay•

Dhar
Mandu•

VINDHYA RANGE

Dwarka•

•Rajkot

•Baroda
4

Narmada 22

•Porbandur

Broach•

•16

Tapti

•Junagadh
18 19

Burhanpur•

Nagpur•

Somnath•

•Surat
26

WESTERN GHATS

GUJARAT

M A H A R A S H T R A

•Ajanta

•Nasik

Ellora•

•Aurangabad

•Paithan

Bombay•
5 6 7 8 9
10 11 12

Dehu•

2 3
Alandi

•Ahmadnagar

Godavari

•Poona 25

•Jejuri
17

•Dapoli
20

Pandharpur
23 24

Bhima

•Ratnagiri
21

•Kolhapur

•Bijapur

Krishna

A R A B I A N
S E A

•Goa
15
GOA

WESTERN INDIA
AND RAJASTHAN

Numbers shown on the map indicate
locations in the 'Extracts' section
—•—•— International boundary

Miles

| 0 | 50 | 100 | 150 | 200 |

| 0 | 100 | 200 | 300 |

Kilometres

the **Western Ghats**, they are more like the edge of an escarpment than a true mountain range. The narrow strip between them and the sea is called the **Konkan**, lush and green with the huge rainfall of the south-west monsoon (Extracts 20 and 21), while to the east they gradually run down all the way to the east coast of India. The big rivers run the same way – Godavari, Bhima and Krishna. It is a dry land between the rivers with fingers of low hills that eventually die away in the plains of the east. All this is the **Deccan**, called in Marathi the Desh, and it forms the bulk of the state of Maharashtra, which is a great triangle stretching from its base on the coast between Bombay and Goa half way across India to a point just beyond Nagpur.

HISTORY

Obviously such a vast and varied territory has never had a unified history or a single ruler. Most of it once lay within the Empire of Ashok in the 3rd century BC, but the early period of all Indian history is a bewildering and shifting mosaic of dynasties which rose and fell, all making extravagant claims to a hegemony over lands whose boundaries we can only guess at on the basis of a few literary references and the chance preservation of stone inscriptions and of grants of land preserved on copper-plates. One is only reasonably certain about a few major centres of power. The Shakas flourished for a time from their base in **Saurashtra** and **Cutch**, rivalling the Satavahanas who ruled from Pratishthan, modern **Paithan** on the Godavari river, and who for a time at least seem to have controlled the whole middle strip of the Deccan from coast to coast. **Ujjain** in Malwa was another ancient capital – a great city from the earliest times and lying on one of the main routes from the ports of Gujarat to the Ganges basin. In the 9th century AD under the almost legendary king Bhoj it claimed to rule all the west of middle India including Rajasthan. It was during these early centuries that the Buddhists flourished and that the cave temples of **Ajanta** and **Ellora** and many more were cut out of the rocks that lay along the principal trade routes.

The 12th century is the time to get a better fix on western India, for it was then that the modern languages began to emerge as vehicles of literature instead of being merely despised dialects of Sanskrit. In Maharashtra the heartland of Marathi language and culture was the upper Godavari basin from Nasik, the holy town near its source, to well below Paithan, then east and north to take in Berar, the fertile patch that is now a rich cotton growing area, and up towards Nagpur. All this was ruled by the Yadavas from their fortress of Devgiri which is now called by its muslim name **Daulatabad** and is seen by every tourist who goes from Aurangabad to visit the caves at **Ellora**. Gujarat and

Saurashtra were ruled by a Rajput dynasty, the Solankis, from **Patan**, a city north of Ahmadabad of which only vestiges remain. It was the wealthy ministers of the kings of Patan who built the magnificent Jain temples on **Mount Abu**. To the north-east, Gujarat merges impercept-ibly into Rajasthan and Malwa and here there was no one commanding centre but a plethora of separate kingdoms (Rajasthan after all means 'land of the Rajas'). These varied from the tiny to the gigantic, and at this early period most of them were ruled by one or another branch of the Chauhans, another Rajput lineage. The greatest of them all was known as Sapadalaksha ('possessing 125,000 villages'): based on the city of **Ajmer**, it covered the greater part of present-day Rajasthan and held Delhi as a feudatory princedom.

All of this was totally overthrown by the Muslims from Afghanistan at the end of the 12th century. Mahmud of Ghazni had already made a series of lightning raids into north India aimed at the enormously rich temple towns. The sack of **Somnath** in the south-west of Saurashtra in 1026 was the most farflung and famous of these. Now Muhammad Ghuri came for good, defeating king Prithviraj of Delhi in 1192 and establishing a rule which later became the Sultanate of Delhi. It took the Muslims of Delhi another century though before they began to make serious inroads into the south of India, and it was in 1294 that Ala-ud-din Khalji got as far as Devgiri. The Yadava king was allowed to buy himself time by paying a huge tribute and the kingdom struggled on in a subjected state until 1318 when Ala-ud-din's general Malik Kafur destroyed its last flickers of revolt. Further north in Gujarat Ala-ud-din had captured Patan and destroyed the Solankis in 1299 (Extract 16) and within a few more years all the key forts of Rajasthan were taken. Thus begins a period of nearly 400 years when most of India, excluding only the far south, was ruled by Muslim Shahs who at times owed a nominal allegiance to Delhi but more often were independent and principally engaged in fighting among themselves. Mostly these dynas-ties derived from provincial governors who had revolted and gone independent once the imperial army had done its work, made its conquests and gone back to base. The Sultans of Gujarat ruled from **Ahmadabad**, built and embellished and named after the greatest of them, Ahmad Shah, who ruled from 1410 to 1442, while the ports of **Surat**, **Broach** and **Cambay** were controlled in their turn by governors who at times were almost independent. **Malwa** was another sultanate ruled from the great fort of Mandu near modern Indore. Maharashtra and beyond was under the Bahmani kingdom, but in Rajasthan many of the Hindu Rajput kingdoms still survived, especially those of Mewar (**Udaipur**) and Marwar (**Jodhpur**). The Bahmani kingdom split into five bits around 1500 and three of the resulting fragments lie within Maharashtra: **Ahmadnagar** north of Poona, **Berar** – the same Berar that formed a major part of the old Yadava kingdom – and **Bijapur** which lies outside the present Maharashtra State but which once controlled most of the south Maratha country. All these warring kingdoms were easy meat for the Mughals, the new power that was founded in Delhi with the coming of Babur – yet another Afghan invader – in 1523. His grandson the great Akbar took Gujarat in 1572 and before his death in 1605 had got Berar and the northern part of Ahmadnagar. He had also conquered or otherwise subjected all the kingdoms of Rajasthan except Udaipur. Under his successors the rest of the Muslim kingdoms of the Deccan fell, but, as usual, only to be succeeded by new independent powers who resisted control from Delhi.

By this time of course India was being subjected to new influences. Formerly most of the trade with the western ports had been conducted by Arab dhows, but in 1498 the Portuguese appeared and by 1537 they had built themselves a fort at **Diu** on the coast of Gujarat as well as killing off the Sultan Bahadur Shah. They had other small forts down the coast but their main centre was **Goa**. British, Dutch and French merchants had also established trading posts on the coast with **Surat** as their main centre (Extract 26), but when the British finally acquired **Bombay** from the Portuguese in 1667, its marvellous natural harbour soon eclipsed all other ports, in spite of its desperately unhealthy site, and the East India Company came to dominate trade with Europe. Meanwhile a new power was coming up in Maharashtra. The inspired guerrilla captain Shivaji took many key forts in the **Western Ghats** and gradually extended his lands at the expense of Bijapur to found the Maratha kingdom. In 1664 he sacked **Surat** for the first time in a lightning raid, and did it again in 1669. However after Shivaji's death in 1680 the Moghul emperor Aurangzeb brought his incompetent successors to heel. But he also destroyed **Bijapur**, the last remaining Muslim power, and after Aurangzeb himself died in 1707 everything fell apart once again. The Marathas revived under the Peshwas, a line of brahman prime-ministers who usurped power from Shivaji's descendents and established **Poona** (now spelt Pune) as their capital. From here the Peshwa and the great war-lords – Bhosle, Gaikwad, Holkar and Shinde – set out to raid and exact revenue in all directions, but especially to the north into Gujarat and Malwa. Their raids turned into occupations and huge areas fell under Maratha control. The Gaikwads based on **Baroda** possessed much of the richest land in Gujarat. The Holkars at **Indore**, the Shindes at **Ujjain** and later **Gwalior** right on the edge of the Ganges basin, the Bhosles at **Nagpur**, if only they had worked together they might easily have built a real Maratha Empire which could have successfully resisted the growing power of the British that was now creeping in on them from both sides, from Bombay and from Bengal. **Dewas**, where E.M. Forster ◊ stayed as a private secretary to the Raja and where he absorbed most of the experiences that went to make *A Passage to India*, was a small Maratha state (Extracts 13, 14). **Jhansi**, whose Rani is now celebrated as the heroine of the 1857 rebellion, was a key Maratha fort south of Gwalior. For the last 40 years of the 18th century the Marathas, through Holkar and Shinde, controlled Delhi and the Mughal emperors were their puppets. In spite of all their efforts they never subdued the tough little kingdoms of Rajasthan and most of Saurashtra and Kutch which, in the absence of any real central control were left to get on with their own lives and, as usual, to fight among themselves.

But the British were irresistible. The future Duke of Wellington won some of his earliest victories against the Marathas in 1803–04 and finally in 1817 the Peshwa was defeated outside Poona and sent into exile. All his lands fell to Britain, but the great barons of Baroda and Gwalior made their separate peaces and remained as some of the biggest estates of princely India until they were swallowed up in 1947. Meanwhile a large part of present Maharashtra, the British-owned sectors of Gujarat and from 1843 Sind in Pakistan all came under the Presidency of Bombay and **Bombay** itself became the capital city of western India. Rajasthan and Malwa remained as a confusion of inextricably entangled boundaries but with independence in 1947 most of this was sorted out. Rajasthan was demarcated, Malwa including the Holkar lands south of the Tapti went into Madhya Pradesh and the last act came in 1960 when after a series of linguistic riots over the allocation of Bombay City, the old Presidency was divided into Gujarat and Maharashtra.

LANGUAGES AND LITERATURE

Until the 11th century all India literature in the region was composed either in Sanskrit or in one of the Prakrits or Apabhramshas. Naturally the languages of the region had been maturing gradually in spoken form from long before this. Most of Rajasthan and Gujarat was occupied by a group of spoken dialects which might be called Old Gujarati, and the first works of literature in what is clearly a literary form of this were produced by the Jains who flourished in the Solanki kingdom of **Anahilwad Patan** (Extract 16). Similarly the first major body of writing in old Marathi came in the Yadava kingdom of **Devgiri** from the Mahanubhavs, another unorthodox sect with a motive to spread its religious propaganda in a language which was comprehensible to the unlettered common people. The Jain tales, which are called *rasa* or *phagu*, are often adaptations of familiar folk-tales or old stories of kings and princesses that are given a Jain twist and end in a Jain moral. The Mahanubhavas recount the words and deeds of their founder Chakradhara (mid-13th century) and also give their own versions of the traditional stories of Krishna who was almost the only deity that they recognized. Their *Lilacharitra*, the story of Chakradhara's *lila* or 'activities on earth', is especially interesting in that it is almost the only example of early prose in Marathi and because, with its detailed record of all the towns and villages through which Chakradhara passed on his proselytising mission, it tells us a lot about the extent of the Yadava kingdom to which he explicitly confined himself.

The first really major work of Marathi literature is however the *Jnaneshwari* which was composed on the banks of the **Godavari** river in 1290. It is a vivid, demotic verse commentary on the *Bhagavadgita* and most Maharashtrians hold it to be the greatest work of literature ever to have been created in Marathi (Extract 3). It has been translated several times, in spite of its length, and is supposed to have been composed by a very young brahman called Jnandev ◊ about whom many miraculous tales are told. He is said to have embraced samadhi, or voluntary death, at **Alandi** near Poona in 1296 at the age of 21.

From the time of Jnandev until the 16th century almost all the extant literature of Gujarati and Marathi is devoted to two main themes. First is a quasi-religious literature of narratives based on the age-old Hindu stories from the *Mahabharata* (◊ Classical literature), the *Ramayana* (◊ Classical literature) and the more popular puranas, especially the *Bhagavata Purana* from which most of the stories about Krishna derive. These can be paralleled in all the modern languages of India. The second theme is a totally religious literature of devotional verse in the form of short hymnlike verses addressed to God. God is for some Vishnu, or Krishna, or Ram the hero of the *Ramayana*, but for most Marathi devotional poets he is Vitthal, popularly called Vithoba, the god of **Pandharpur**. Here he stands in his temple on the banks of the Bhima, at the very edge of Marathi-speaking territory, with his hands on his hips and an enigmatic smile on his lips. Some have claimed that he was originally a Buddha figure, or a Jain image or even a form of Shiva, but for every Maharashtrian he is now firmly assimilated to Krishna. Countless poets have sung their devotion to him: Namdev ◊ the tailor who is supposed to have been a contemporary of Jnandev ◊ but who probably lived a century later; Eknath ◊ the brahman who lived at **Paithan** and was the disciple of the Hindu commander of the fort of Daulatabad, and above all Tukaram ◊, the shopkeeper from **Dehu** near Poona (Extract 24). The hymns, called *abhangas*, of these and many more 'poet saints' are sung by members of the Warkari sect on their regular pilgrimages to Pandharpur (Extract 23). Similar devotional poetry was written in Rajasthani by Mirabai ◊ and in Gujarati by Narsi Mehta ◊, but their hymns were addressed to Krishna in his temple at **Dwarka**. Narsi lived at **Junagadh** in Saurashtra where his little cell is still shown to the devout, and his poems include both erotic Krishna verse as well as more philosophical works. One of these, the description of a true Vaishnava – that is a worshipper of Vishnu/Krishna – is famous as being one of Mahatma Gandhi's favourite hymns, sung daily in the services at his ashram (Extract 18). Mirabai was a Rajasthani princess who composed in that indeterminate Old Gujarati–Rajasthani language. Her poems have come down to us in so many versions that she is claimed by both Hindi and Gujarati.

The narrative tradition referred to earlier also has innumerable practitioners but in Gujarati the most outstanding is Premananda ◊ (Extract 19) who came from **Baroda**. The verve and humour of his verse makes his versions of the old puranic stories and his tales of the life of Narsi Mehta are still enormously popular today. In Marathi, Shridhar did much the same, although with less genius and humour, and Mahipati ◊ is also noteworthy for his interminable series of 'Lives of the Saints' which are often the only source of the miraculous tales which constitute the main part of the biographies of writers like Eknath and Tukaram, and which were largely translated into English in the 1920s and 1930s by missionaries in whose hearts these devotional, superficially monotheistic Vaishnava poets struck a responsive chord.

Rajasthan, however, has a different and vigorous tradition of narrative verse. It was the practice of the Rajput rulers to maintain court-poets, often members of the Charan caste, to compose eulogies of themselves and their forefathers, and from the earliest times we find poems in praise of the heroic deeds of great princes. The earliest of these deal with the failed attempts to repel the Muslim invasions: some, such as the *Hammiramahakavya*, are composed in Sanskrit; others, including the celebrated *Kanhadadeprabandha* (Extract 28), are in Old Gujarati; yet others, like the *Hammirayana*, are written in forms of Rajasthani itself. Later, the often bloody rivalries between different Rajput states became the principal theme of poets seeking heroism to praise. Other verse narratives, more romantic than martial in character, clearly derive at no great distance from folk-poetry: the earliest known examples are the *Visaladevarasa* (Extract 27) and the *Dhola-Maru ra duha* ◊, both apparently dating from the 15th century.

The older literatures of Gujarati, Marathi and Rajasthani had no formal drama but there was always a popular tradition of travelling story-tellers whose performances could be enhanced in various ways, by musical accompaniment and by visual aids. The narrator of the story of the Rajasthan god-hero Pabuji accompanies himself on a fiddle and has behind him a long painted strip of cloth on which Pabuji's exploits are depicted and to which the singer, or his assistant, points at appropriate stages in the story (Extract 29). A more developed and relatively modern form of drama was the Rajasthani *khel* or the Marathi *tamasha* where a troupe of players toured the villages acting out traditional stories as well as up-to-date plots which were sometimes bawdy and full of topical allusions.

Finally one must realise that throughout this period there was comparatively little prose. On the whole literature meant verse until the arrival of the British and the spread of Western-style education in the 19th century. Schools were founded in Bombay, later in Poona and Ahmadabad and other provincial towns. Schools needed books from which to teach history and geography and science and to encourage their production the Bombay Native Schoolbook and School Society was set up under the patronage of the governor as early as 1820. The **University of Bombay** was founded in 1857, together with those of Calcutta and Madras, and gradually the early students of these institutions, educated in English and drilled in Shakespeare, Scott and Dickens and the English romantic poets, began to create a literature of prose and verse which reproduced all the genres of European literature: novel, short story, essay, play and lyric poem. The transformation from a traditional to a modern literature was almost complete.

As in Europe this was the great age of the periodical: the newspaper, the cultural weekly and the literary monthly; and as in Europe not only short stories and poems but most of the early novels first appeared serially in these journals. The first major novelist in Marathi, Hari Narayan Apte ◊, edited his own monthly magazine in which some 20 of his social and historical novels were published. The first great Gujarati novel, *Sarasvatichandra* by Govardhanram Tripathi ◊, came out in parts between 1887 and 1901. Narmada ◊, Gujarati poet, essayist and scourge of the orthodox, published in the first Gujarati journals. His contemporary Dalpatram ◊ who collaborated with the Scots magistrate A.K. Forbes ◊, wrote much of his verse for the Gujarati Readers which were created in mid-19th century to teach correct grammar and spelling to the rising generation. Keshavsut ◊, the first and finest Marathi lyric poet (Extract 21), was a schoolmaster heavily influenced by Keats and Shelley who published most of his work in the journal *Vividha-jnana-vistara* which means 'the spread of a variety of knowledge' – a most appropriate title for its times. It ran from 1867 to 1937.

The works of this period were often social and reformist in theme, a trend typified by the Marathi journalist Agarkar ◊ with his weekly *Sudharak* – 'The Reformer'. There were also many historical plays and novels, the latter were often in the vein of Walter Scott. In Gujarati it was the glories of ancient Patan which formed the setting. In Marathi it was inevitably Shivaji and the kingdom of the Peshwas. With the arrival of bitter opposition to the British and especially after the founding of the Congress Party and the growth of revolutionary nationalism, when in the first decade of the 20th century Lokamanya

Lokamanya Tilak

Tilak ◊ and his followers had made Poona notorious throughout India as a hotbed of anti-British agitation, one begins to find some reactionary counterblasts which praise the old ways and attack modernizing, Westernizing, christianizing trends.

Between the two world wars came the Gandhian era. Gandhi ◊ was a Gujarati, born at **Porbandar**, and after his return from South Africa in 1915 his thought and his words came to exert enormous influence upon the next generation of writers such as Dhumaketu and Munshi in Gujarati and Marathi novelists like Khandekar and Phadke. The literature of the period is full of men and women of noble soul whose love of country is expressed in their devotion to uplifting the poor and lowly. About this time Goan Konkani achieved a truly independent status. The languages of Portuguese Goa had always been slightly different from those of the neighbouring regions. There was a Marathi Konkani, a literary language from the 16th century in works of

Mahatma Gandhi

Christian propaganda printed in roman script; a Kanarese Konkani of South Goa confined to an oral literature of folk-tales and proverbs, and a Portuguese Christian Konkani in which literary works had been published in roman increasingly from the mid-19th century. As opposition to Portuguese rule grew in parallel with resistance to the British, Konkani became a revolutionary tool. Writers who came from Goa and who had previously written and published in Marathi or Kanarese, began to write and publish in Konkani in the Marathi or Kanarese script. India's seizure of Goa in 1964 did not end these divisions and the status of Konkani is still highly politicized.

Independence had come to the rest of India in 1947 and when a few months later Gandhi was murdered by a fellow Hindu, the Revolutionary and the Gandhian eras ended together. There was growing disillusion. The new short story, as written by Broker ◊ in Gujarati and pioneered in Marathi by the quarumvirate of Bhave ◊, Gadgil ◊, Gokhale ◊ and Madgulkar ◊, gives up idealism for angst: the anxiety of the city dweller in his slum tenement, the unemployed clerk, the working wife; the sufferings of the peasant, turned off his land and unable even to sell his labour because of mechanisation; the bitterness of the intellectual who sees the bright hopes of a new India submerged beneath corruption and jerrymandering. In poetry the influence of the romantics was replaced by that of the T.S. Eliot of *The Waste Land*, especially in the revolutionary verse of Umashankar Joshi ◊ in Gujarati and Mardhekar ◊ in Marathi, followed by a string of modern poets, notably Chitre ◊, Karandikar ◊ and Kolatkar ◊, whose work has been translated into English. Innovators like Suresh Joshi ◊ have acted as influential brokers of world literary movements. The strong theatre tradition in Marathi, which goes back to a cluster of major dramatists at the end of the 19th century, is still much in evidence and has attained international fame in the work of Vijay Tendulkar ◊. There has also been an increased interest in regionalism, not in what unites all Indians but on what is special to a district – to the Konkan in Pendse's ◊ novels (Extract 20), to Goa in many a Konkani writer, to north Gujarat in the novels and short stories of Pannalal Patel ◊. The most recent trend of all is the protest writing of the untouchables, still discriminated against in spite of all the safeguards in the Indian Constitution, but with enough educated men and women amongst their numbers to voice their fury, to reject Hinduism and the patronising title of Harijans that Gandhi gave them.

The most notable modern writers in Gujarati, Marathi and Rajasthani are included in the brief biographies which follow, but there is rather a shortage of good writing in English that is set expressly in Western India. The region produced no Kipling and if we had not known that Forster lived in Dewas it would have been hard to locate his novel precisely. Manohar Malgonkar ◊ has not achieved the fame of Khushwant Singh (◊ Pakistan and North-west India) or R.K. Narayan (◊ South India) and although there are a number of translations of modern Gujarati and Marathi works none has made much impression on Western readers. Yet for those who have some knowledge of the literary history of the region there will be villages and towns – such as **Dwarka, Porbandar** and **Pandharpur** – that appear in an entirely new light because of their associations with Narsi Mehta or Gandhi or the Maratha saints who sang their songs to Vithoba.

BOOKLIST

The following selection includes all titles which are extracted in this chapter as well as many of the works mentioned in the biographies. The editions cited are not necessarily the only ones available. The exact location of the extracts can be found in 'Acknowledgements and Citations' at the end of the volume. The date in square brackets is the original date of publication when known. Extract numbers are highlighted in bold for ease of reference.

Alston, A.J., *The Devotional Poems of Mirabai*, Motilal Banarsidass, New Delhi, 1980.

Arnold, Sir Edwin, *India Revisited*, Trubner, London, 1886. **Extract 25**.

Arnold, Sir Edwin, *The Light of Asia* [1879], Jaico Publishing House, Bombay, 1949.

Broker, Gulabdas, *Of Life and Love*, Bharatiya Vidya Bhavan, Bombay, 1966.

Bromfield, Louis, *Night in Bombay* [1940], Penguin, London, 1954. **Extract 5**.

Chitre, D.P., *An Anthology of Marathi Poetry 1945–65*, Nirmala Sadanand, Bombay, 1967.

Das, G.K., *E.M. Forster's India*, Macmillan, London, 1977.

Dayananda, J.Y., *Manohar Malgonkar*, Twayne, Boston, 1974.

Dé Shobha, *Starry Nights*, Penguin, New Delhi, 1989. **Extract 11**.

Deming, W.S., *Eknath, a Maratha Bhakta*, Karnatak Printing House, Bombay, 1933.

Ezekiel, Nissim, 'Island' in *Collected Poems 1952–1988*, Oxford University Press, Delhi, 1989. **Extract 10**.

Falkland, Lady, *Chow-chow: A Journal Kept in India, Egypt and Syria* [1857], H.G. Rawlinson ed,

Scholartis Press, London, 1930. **Extract 2**.

Forster, Edward Morgan, *The Hill of Devi*, Edwin Arnold, London, 1953. **Extract 13**.

Gadgil, Gangadhar G., *Shops That Bombay Hadn't Bargained For*, Popular Prakashan, Bombay, 1992. **Extract 12**.

Gadgil, Gangadhar G., *The Woman and Other Stories*, Sterling, New Delhi, 1990.

Gandhi, M.K., *Autobiography*, Mahadev Desai, trans, Phoenix Press, London, 1948. **Extract 1**.

Gokhale, Aravind V., *The Unmarried Widow*, Jaico, Bombay, 1957.

Heber, Bishop, *A Journal*, 1828, in M.A. Laird, ed, *Bishop Heber in Northern India: A Selection from Heber's Journal*, Cambridge University Press, Cambridge, 1971. **Extract 4**.

JagMohan, *Gujarati Short Stories*, Vikas, Delhi, 1982.

Kanga, Firdaus, *Trying to Grow*, Bloomsbury, London, 1989. **Extract 8**.

Karandikar, G.V., *Poems of Vinda*, Nirmala Sadanand, Bombay, 1975.

Khandekar, V.S., *Yayati*, Orient Paperbacks, New Delhi, 1978.

Kolatkar, Arun, *Jejuri* [1974], Peppercorn, London, 1978. **Extract 17**.

Kripananda, Swami, *Jnaneshwar's Gita*, SUNY Press, Albany, 1989. **Extract 3**.

Lewis, R.J., *Passages to India*, Columbia University Press, New York, 1979.

Machwe, P., *Keshavsut*, Sahitya Akademi, New Delhi, 1966.

Madgulkar, V.D., *The Village has no Walls* (*Banagarwadi*), [1955], R. Deshmukh, trans, Asia Publishing House, London, 1958.

Madgulkar, V.D., *Winds of Fire*, P. Kale, trans, Hind Pocket Books, Delhi, 1974.

Mahadevanand, Swami, *Devotional Songs of Narsi Mehta*, Motilal Banarsidas, Delhi, 1967.

Mahajan, Ashok, *Goan Vignettes and Other Poems*, Oxford University Press, Delhi, 1986. **Extract 15.**

Malgonkar, Manohar, *The Princes*, Orient Paperbacks, New Delhi, 1970. **Extract 14.**

Mehta, Gita, *A River Sutra*, Doubleday, New York, 1993. **Extract 22.**

Mistry, Rohinton, *Such a Long Journey*, Faber and Faber, London, 1991. **Extract 9.**

Mokashi, D.B., *Palkhi: An Indian Pilgrimage* [1964], Philip Engblom, trans, State University of New York Press, Albany, 1987. **Extract 23.**

Mokashi, D.B., *Farewell to the Gods (Deva calile)*, [1961], Hind Pocket Books, Delhi, 1975.

Munshi, K.M., *Gujarat and its Literature*, Bharatiya Vidya Bhavan, Bombay, 1954. **Extract 19.**

Nelson-Fraser, J., *The Poems of Tukarama*, 3 vols, Christian Literature Society, London, 1905–15.

Ovington, J., *A Voyage to Suratt, 1696*, in H.G. Rawlinson, ed, *A Voyage to Surat in the Year 1689*

by J. Ovington, Oxford University Press, London, 1989. **Extract 26.**

Padmanabh, *Kanhadade Prabandha*, V.S. Bhatnagar, trans, Aditya Prakashan, New Delhi, 1991. **Extract 28.**

Patel, Gieve, 'From Bombay Central' in *Mirrored, Mirroring*, Oxford University Press, Madras, 1991. **Extract 7.**

Pendse, S.N., *Wild Bapu of Garambi*, Ian Raeside, trans, Sahitya Akademi, New Delhi, 1969. **Extract 20.**

Raeside, I.M.P., *The Rough and the Smooth*, Asia, Bombay, 1966.

Rushdie, Salman, *Midnight's Children*, Cape, London, 1981. **Extract 6.**

Smith, J.D., *The Visaladevarasa, a Restoration of the Text*, Cambridge University Press, Cambridge, 1976. **Extract 27.**

Smith, J.D., *The Epic of Pabuji*, Cambridge University Press, Cambridge, 1991. **Extract 29.**

Tendulkar, V., *Sakharam Binder*, Hind Pocket Books, Delhi, 1973.

Tod, Lieut. Col. James, *Annals and Antiquities of Rajasthan* [two volumes 1829–1832] Oxford University Press, Oxford, 1920.

Vaudeville, Charlotte, *L'invocation: Le Haripath de Dnyander*, Ecole Francaise d'Extreme Orient, 1969.

Extracts

(1) AHMADABAD:
THE SABARMATI ASHRAM

M.K. Gandhi, *Autobiography*

Gandhi's very brief account of the founding of the ashram comes towards the end of his Autobiography, which itself stops short with the events of 1927.

The Satyagraha Ashram was founded on the 25th of May 1915. Shraddhanandji wanted me to settle in Hardvar . . . Others strongly urged me to choose Rajkot. But when I happened to pass through Ahmedabad, many friends pressed me to settle down there, and they volunteered to find the expenses of the Ashram, as well as a house for us to live in.

I had a predilection for Ahmedabad. Being a Gujarati I thought that I should be able to render the greatest service to the country through the Gujarati language. And then, as Ahmedabad was an ancient centre of handloom weaving, it was likely to be the most favourable field for the revival of the cottage industry of hand-spinning. There was also the hope that, the city being the capital of Gujarat, monetary help from its wealthy citizens would be more available here than elsewhere.

As far as the accommodation was concerned, Mr Jivanlal Desai, a barrister in Ahmedabad, was the principal man to help me. He offered to let, and we decided to hire, his Kochrab bungalow . . . [Later] plague broke out in this village and I saw evident danger to the safety of the Ashram children . . . Our ideal was to have the Ashram at a safe distance both from town and village, and yet at a manageable distance from either. And we were determined, some day, to settle on ground of our own . . . Punjabhai Hirachand, a merchant of Ahmedabad . . . volunteered to procure us suitable land. I went about with him north and south of Kochrab in search of land, and then suggested to him to find out a piece of land three or four miles to the north. He hit upon the present site. Its vicinity to the Sabarmati Central Jail was for me a special attraction. As jail-going was understood to be the normal lot of Satyagrahis, I liked this position. And I knew that the sites selected for jails have generally clean surroundings.

In about eight days the sale was executed. There was no building on the land and no tree. But its situation on the banks of the river and its solitude were great advantages. We decided to start by living under canvas, and having a tin shed for a kitchen, till permanent houses were built . . .

Our difficulties, before we had permanent living accommodation, were great. The rains were impending, and provisions had to be got from the city four miles away. The ground, which had been a waste, was infested with snakes, and it was no small risk to live with little children under such conditions. The general rule was not to kill the snakes, though I confess none of us had shed the fear of these reptiles, nor have we even now.

(2) ALANDI

Lady Falkland, *Chow-chow:*
A Journal kept in India, Egypt and Syria

*Lady Falkland seems to have been the first European woman in
Western India to take an intelligent interest in her surroundings.
She gives interesting descriptions of Poona, Satara and Wai, and
of the hill station of Mahabaleshwar at the time when it was first
developed, but here she is visiting Jnandev's Alandi.*

There is no carriage road to Alundi, so I went there in my sedan-chair, open at three sides, the head being removable when the oppressive heat was over.

The plain I traversed was in parts very rocky, and here and there small babools and *Calatropus gigantea* were spread thinly about. The distant hills which surround the plain were clear and distinct, with deeper shadows playing on them than is usually the case in India early in the day; for after the heavy rains are over, the sky does not immediately resume its cloudless aspect and wonted deep cobalt blue, but looks like a naughty child that has not quite recovered its good humour, when the least thing would bring back a flood of tears; and so the large grey clouds, tipped with white, seemed half inclined to weep.

Trees became more frequent as I approached the River Indrayani, on which the small town of Alundi is situated. Among them was the neem, the lilac-tree of India as it is called; and though the blossom is not so fragrant as *the* lilac-tree *at home*, it is very sweet and pretty: the tree is highly esteemed by the Hindoos, and it is married sometimes to a pipul! The neem I saw today was in single blessedness; but in the neighbourhood of Poona these two trees are married by being planted together, and surrounded by the low stone wall, which is so often placed round trees for which the Hindoos have a peculiar reverence . . .

Bridges, not of European construction or origin, are uncommon in the Deccan; but there is one here over the Indrayani; it is a curious one, very narrow, evidently not built for carriages, as there are at each end steps leading up to it.

The town of Alundi looks well from the bridge. Temples, neat, picturesque houses, walls in perfect order, trees in gardens, all look prosperous . . .

The little town, on nearer inspection, did not disappoint me. Among the temples are two very large, white stone ones, the ornaments carved in grotesque figures. Wittoba is worshipped here; and in one temple is buried a saint, named Naneshwar, the hero of a famous legend, which I will relate presently. The streets are very narrow, only wide enough for one bullock-cart. Little altars are dotted about on green grass, close to the water; temples stand nearly in the river, pipuls and mangos being planted on its banks.

The curiosity of the people was very great. How they ran out to look at me, wondering what I could be, and why I came there! . . . It is by making expeditions like that I made to Alundi and other places, and by taking an interest in the daily events of native life, that the monotony of an Indian existence is ameliorated.

(3) ALANDI

Jnandev, *Jnaneshwari*

The Jnaneshwari expands and clarifies every verse of the Bhagavadgita. Here Jnandev expatiates on the crucial term bhakti, devotion, on the basis of Gita IX.26. Extract from Swami Kripananda (see Booklist).

'When I am offered with devotion leaf or flower or fruit or water, I eat them, since they are given with devotion by the striving soul.'

If a devotee, with the joy of boundless devotion, brings as an offering to Me a fruit from any tree he may choose,
When he shows it to Me, however small it may be, I hold out both hands to receive it, and without even removing the stalk I taste it respectfully.
Also, if a flower is given to Me in the name of devotion, I place it in my mouth, although I should actually smell it.
But why a flower, when even a leaf would be accepted? It does not matter whether it is fresh or dry or in any other condition.
If it is offered to me with utmost love, even though it be a mere leaf, I take it with the same delight as a hungry man would rejoice at a drink of nectar.
A leaf would do, but it may happen that one cannot be found. In that case it isn't difficult to find water.
Water is found everywhere, without price, and one finds it even

without searching for it. He that offers even that to Me in the spirit of purest devotion.

Builds for Me a temple more spacious than Vaikuntha, and offers Me jewels more perfect than the Kaustubha diamond in My crown.

He makes for Me many bedrooms of milk as delightful as the Milky Ocean.

He gives Me sweetly scented delights such as camphor, sandalwood and aloe wood, and places on Me with his own hand a garland of lights like the sun.

He offers Me vehicles like Garuda, gardens filled with wish-fulfilling trees, and herds of heavenly cattle.

Tasty dishes served to Me are sweeter than nectar, and the smallest drop of water delights Me.

But why should I say more, O Arjuna? You have seen with your own eyes how, with My own hands, I untied the knot in Sudama's cloth to take out a few grains of rice.

True devotion is the only thing I recognise; I make no distinction between great and small. I am ready to be welcomed by the devotion of any person.

Truly a leaf, a flower or a fruit is for Me only a means of devotion. What I desire is complete devotion.

O Arjuna, listen to Me! Gain control over your mind and then you will never forget Me, for I dwell in the temple of your heart.

(4) BARODA/NADIAD

Bishop Heber, *Bishop Heber's Journal*

Bishop Heber in his celebrated tour of India, met the Gaikwad at Baroda in March 1825. More interestingly he met Swami Narayan a few days later at Nadiad and gives a fascinating account of the encounter between rival prelates.

About eleven o'clock I had the expected visit from Swaamee Narain, to my interview with whom I had looked forward with an anxiety and eagerness which, if he had known it, would, perhaps, have flattered him. He came in a somewhat different style from all which I had expected, having with him near 200 horsemen, mostly well-armed with matchlocks and swords, and several of them with coats of mail and spears. Besides them he had a large rabble on foot, with bows and arrows, and when I considered that I had myself an escort of more than fifty horse, and fifty musquets and bayonets, I could not help smiling, though my sensations were in some degree painful and humiliating, at the idea of two religious teachers meeting at the head of little armies, and filling the city, which was the scene of their interview, with the rattling of quivers, the clash of shields, and the tramp of the war-horse. Had our troops been opposed to each other, mine, though less numerous, would have been, doubtless, far more effective from the superiority of arms and discipline. But, in moral grandeur, what a difference was there between his troops and mine. Mine neither knew me, nor cared for me; they escorted me faithfully, and would have defended me bravely, because they were ordered by their superiors to do so, and as they would have done for any other stranger of sufficient worldly rank to make such an attendance usual. The guards of Swaamee Narain were his own disciples and enthusiastic admirers, men who had voluntarily repaired to hear his lessons, who now took a pride in doing him honour, and who would cheerfully fight to the last drop of blood rather than suffer a fringe of his garment to be handled roughly. In the parish of Hodnet there were once, perhaps, a few honest countrymen who felt something like this for me; but how long a time must elapse before any Christian Teacher in India can hope to be thus loved and honoured!

The holy man himself . . . was a middle-sized, thin, and plain-looking person, about my own age, with a mild and diffident expression of countenance, but nothing about him indicative of any extraordinary talent . . . After the usual mutual compliments, I said that I had heard much good of him, and the good doctrine which he preached among the poor people of Guzerat, and that I greatly desired his acquaintance.

(5) BOMBAY 1930s

Louis Bromfield, *Night in Bombay*

Louis Bromfield's second Indian novel is set in and around the Taj Mahal Hotel which, like his heroes and heroines, he knew at first hand as a prewar traveller.

In those days the Taj Mahal Hotel had the air of a vast and dreary county jail. Built around two or three great wells which ran the full height of the building, the stairs were of stone and the railings of iron, and around the great wells ran galleries, likewise with stone floors and iron railings. Off these the rooms opened, each one more like a cell than a hotel room, each specially furnished with an iron bed covered with netting and with a single hard mattress, a washstand, and a couple of stiff uncomfortable chairs. Overhead there was a large old-fashioned electric punkah, and outside on the cool slate floors slept the bearers. They slept there not only at night, but all through the hot days, when they were not gossiping with other bearers. The jail-like corridors were as much an exchange place of gossip as any market place. The bearers from one end to the other of the vast hotel knew everything about every guest of the hotel, his vices, his peculiarities, his meannesses or generosities. It was as if each room were walled with glass for all the world to look inside.

. . . Carol moved uncertainly along the stone balcony following the boy who was showing her to her old room – the one at the corner which overlooked the gateway to India and the whole of Bombay. Behind came Krishna with the jewel case and a small valise. As they passed each bedroom door the bearer lying there on the cool stone, rose and salaamed . . . All night they spent in bobbing up and down to stand aside or to salaam, according to the importance of the guests returning to their rooms . . . Not only was this the rule of the hotel; it was a rule imposed upon each of them by a grim and even more stony authority, the necessity of living. It was from these people going and coming all through the night that each of them earned and begged and stole enough to provide rice and meat, scraps for undernourished families in the Punjab, in Bengal, in Goa, on the coasts of Malabar and Coromandel. They wakened, rose and salaamed and dozed again, a couple of hundred times a night, without complaint, patiently because that was their lot in life. In the next life, if they salaamed enough in this one, they might perhaps be among the alcoholics and gamblers and prostitutes who came and went – the salaamed instead of the salaaming, the fortunate instead of the starving.

(6) BOMBAY 1950s

Salman Rushdie, *Midnight's Children*

Saleem, the hero of Salman Rushdie's Midnight's Children, spends part of his childhood in Bombay and witnesses the language riots which preceded the final splitting of the old Bombay Presidency in 1960. Here Saleem rides his bicycle into the middle of a march organized by the Samyukta Maharashta Samiti (United Maharashtra Party) and unwittingly helps to cause a clash with the SMS's main rival, the Maha Gujarat Parishad (Great Gujarat Party).

'Evie,' I said with quiet off-handedness, 'how'd you like to see me bicycling?' . . . 'Get out!' screams Evie . . . She's pushed me hard-as-hard, and I losing control hurtling down the slope round the end of the U-bend downdown, MY GOD THE MARCH past Band Box laundry, past Noor Ville and Laxmi Vilas. AAAAA and down into the mouth of the march, heads feet bodies, the waves of the march parting as I arrive, yelling blue murder, crashing into history on a runaway, young-girl's bike.

Hands grabbing handlebars as I slow down in the impassioned throng. Smiles filled with good teeth surround me. They are not friendly smiles. 'Look look, a little laad-sahib comes down to join us from the big rich hill!' In Marathi which I hardly understand, its my worst subject at school, and the smiles asking, 'You want to join S.M.S., little princeling?, And I, just about knowing what's being said, but dazed into telling the truth, shake my head No. And the smiles, 'Oho! The young nawab does not like our tongue! What does he like?, And another smile, 'Maybe Gujarati! You speak Gujarati, my lord?' But my Gujarati was as bad as my Marathi; I only knew one thing in the marshy tongue of Kathiawar; and the smiles, urging, and the fingers, prodding, 'Speak, little master! Speak some Gujarati!' – so I told them what I knew, a rhyme I'd learned from Glandy Keith Colaco at school, which he used when he was bullying Gujarati boys, a rhyme designed to make fun of the speech rhythms of the language:

> Soo che? Saru che!
> Danda le ke maru che!

How are you? – I am well! – I'll take a stick and thrash you to hell! A nonsense; a nothing; nine words of emptiness . . . but when I'd recited them, the smiles began to laugh; and then the voices near me and then further and further away began to take up my chant, HOW ARE YOU? I AM WELL!, and they lost interest in me, 'Go go with your bicycle, masterji,' they scoffed, I'LL TAKE A STICK AND THRASH YOU TO HELL, I fled away up the hillock as my chant rushed forward and back, up to the front and down to the back of the two-day-long procession, becoming, as it went, a song of war.

That afternoon, the head of the procession of the Samyukta Maharashtra Samiti collided at Kemp's Corner, with the head of a Maha Gujarat Parishad demonstration; S.M.S. voices chanted 'Soo che? Saru che!' and M.G.P. throats were opened in fury; under the posters of the Air-India rajah and of the Kolynos Kid, the two parties fell upon one another with no little zeal, and to the tune of my little rhyme the first of the language riots got under way, fifteen killed, over three hundred wounded.

In this way I became directly responsible for triggering off the violence which ended with the partition of the state of Bombay, as a result of which the city became the capital of Maharashtra – so at least I was on the winning side.

(7) Bombay:
Central Railway Station

Gieve Patel, 'From Bombay Central'

Bombay Central Railway Station is the point of departure for the Western Railway. Its vibrant atmosphere is captured in this poem.

The Saurastra Express waits to start
Chained patiently to the platform,
Good pet, while I clamber in
To take my reserved window seat
And settle into the half-empty compartment's
Cool; the odour of human manure
Vague and sharp drifts in
From adjoining platforms.
The station's population of porters,
Stall-keepers, toughs and vagabonds relieve themselves
Ticketless, into the bowels of these waiting pets;
Gujarat Mail, Delhi Janata, Bulsar Express,
Quiet linear beasts,
Offering unguarded toilets to a wave
Of non-passengers, Bombay Central's
In-residence population.

That odour does not offend.
The station's high and cool vault
Sucks it up and sprays down instead,
Interspersed with miraculous, heraldic
Shafts of sunlight, an eternal
Station odour, amalgam
Of diesel oil, hot steel, cool rails,
Light and shadow, human sweat,
Metallic distillations, dung, urine,
Newspaper ink, Parle's Gluco Biscuits,
And sharp noisy sprays of water from taps
With worn-out bushes, all
Hitting the nostril as one singular
Invariable atmospheric thing,
Seeping into your clothing
The way cigarette smoke and air-conditioning
Seep into you at cinema halls.
I sink back into my hard wooden
Third-class seat, buffered by

This odour, as by a divine cushion.
And do not suspect that this ride
Will be for me the beginning of a meditation
On the nature of truth and beauty.

(8) BOMBAY:
CHURCHGATE RAILWAY STATION
Firdaus Kanga, *Trying to Grow*

*Sera and Sam, the parents of the book's narrator, treat a foreign
visitor to the rush-hour crowds at Bombay's Churchgate Railway
Station.*

We had this elderly French lady, a pen-pal of Sera's, staying with us,
when Sam had the weird idea of showing her the Churchgate Railway
Station. So we went walking: this lady, Jacqui, Sera, Dolly, and Sam
wheeling me; it wasn't that far from where we lived. We'd hardly
arrived when, like her famous compatriot at the storming of the
Bastille, Jacqui screamed, 'Riot! Riot!' rolling her 'r's like Peter Sellers
playing Inspector Clouseau. And I, ever the show-off, gave Roche-
foucauld's reply, 'No, it's a revolution!' Battalions of men and women
surged towards us, faster and faster; even from a hundred yards away we
could smell their sour sweat.

'Let's go!' shouted Jacqui, quite hysterical, stamping her feet.

'Let's not!' I said. 'This is my first riot.'

'And if there's a baton-charge it will be your last,' rolled Jacqui.

'OK. Break it up,' said Sam. 'You know as well as I that this is only
the rush-hour crowd making for the trains. People come to South
Bombay to work and in the evening they hurry north where they live,'
he explained to Jacqui.

'I can't believe it!' she said. 'There cannot be so many commuting
every day.'

'Not so many,' said Sam. 'Just a couple of millions use the trains.
Another million or so go by bus.' That was when I knew what a million
must look like; there would be a million stars in the sky when you
couldn't see an inch of black.

(9) BOMBAY: CRAWFORD MARKET

Rohinton Mistry, *Such a Long Journey*

Crawford Market (Mahatma Jyotibai Phule Market) is the centre of the Bombay fruit and vegetable market. It has sculptures by Lockwood Kipling, father of Rudyard, and flooring of Caithness granite.

For Gustad, Crawford Market held no charms. It was a dirty, smelly, overcrowded place where the floors were slippery with animal ooze and vegetable waste, where the cavernous hall of meat was dark and forbidding, with huge, wicked-looking meat hooks hanging from the ceiling (some empty, some with sides of beef – the empty ones more threatening) and the butchers trying various tacks to snare a customer – now importuning or wheedling, then boasting of the excellence of their meat while issuing dire warnings about the taintedness of their rivals', and always at the top of their voices. In the dim light and smelly air abuzz with bold and bellicose flies, everything acquired a menacing edge: the butchers' voices, hoarse from their incessant bellowings; the runnels of sweat streaming down their faces and bare arms on to their sticky, crimson-stained vests and loongis; the sight and smell of blood (sometimes trickling, sometimes coagulated) and bone (gory, or stripped to whiteness); and the constant, sinister flash of a meat cleaver or butcher's knife which, more often than not, was brandished in the vendor's wild hand as he bargained and gesticulated.

Gustad knew his fear of Crawford Market had its origins in his grandmother's warnings about butchers. 'Never argue with a *goaswalla*,' she would caution. 'If he loses his temper, then bhup! he will stick you with his knife. Won't stop to even think about it.' Then, in milder tones, less terror-striking but more pedagogic, she revealed the underpinnings from whence this wise dictum rose. 'Remember, the *goaswalla*'s whole life, his training, his occupation, is about butchering. Second nature. *Bismillah*, he says, that is all, and the knife descends.'

(10) BOMBAY: THE ISLAND

Nissim Ezekiel, *'Island'*

The 'island' (ie peninsula) of Bombay has a strong, almost magical, hold on the imagination of its inhabitants.

> Unsuitable for song as well as sense
> the island flowers into slums
> and skyscrapers, reflecting

precisely the growth of my mind.
I am here to find my way in it.

Sometimes I cry for help
but mostly keep my own counsel.
I hear distorted echoes
of my own ambiguous voice
and of dragons claiming to be human.

Bright and tempting breezes
flow across the island,
separating past from future;
then the air is still again
as I sleep the sleep of ignorance.

How delight the soul with absolute
sense of salvation, how
hold to a single willed direction?
I cannot leave the island,
I was born here and belong.

Even now a host of miracles
hurries me to daily business,
minding the ways of the island
as a good native should,
taking calm and clamour in my stride.

(11) BOMBAY: JUHU

Shobha Dé, *Starry Nights*

The film star, Akshay, recalls his arrival in Juhu, the seaside suburb of Bombay favoured by rich film stars. Wealthy and glamorous people in Bombay use five-star hotels for many social events and encounters.

With Akshay's successful debut into Hindi cinema Ajay decided it was time to move out and buy a fancy car. 'Never mind the cost *yaar*,' he said. 'In this *dhanda*, appearances count. Look swanky and they'll treat you swanky. Look *sadela* and that's the treatment you'll get.' Akshay knew they couldn't really afford the bungalow at the Juhu Vile-Parle scheme, nor the sleek Honda Accord that rolled up their chawl, but he went along with Ajay's plan. He was only too anxious to get out of the dreary, two-room tenement once and for all. The neighbours gathered to wish them goodbye. They were all set to climb into their gleaming car and zoom off, when suddenly their old man dug in his heels and refused to budge. Startled by his response, they stared at him. Ajay took his arm and tried to drag him out of the dingy hovel. No way. 'This is now my house. This is where I belong. This is where I want to be,' babbled the old man. Ajay pushed Akshay towards the car and said, '*chalo bhai, chalo*, we'll deal with him later. The old *buddha's* quite senile.'

Akshay's new house was close to the Sun 'n' Sand hotel. Yet, it took him more than a year in that posh locale before he could pluck up enough courage to saunter across.

It had been one of the most thrilling moments of his life. Sun 'n' Sand symbolized showbiz. It was glamour and sin, success and sophistication. The place to be seen at. The favourite haunt of the rich and ritzy. This was where they partied and frolicked. He'd seen photographs in dozens of film magazines. He'd watched the pool-side dances in hundreds of films. He'd known all the stories that surrounded the hotel. The deals that were sealed in the coffee shop, the starlets who were bedded in the suites upstairs, the stormy story-sessions that went on behind closed doors – even the fights and knifings that erupted when the action picked up! And there he had been, standing uncertainly at the entrance, feeling gauche and stupid, wondering where to go.

(12) BOMBAY: SHOPS

Gangadhar Gadgil,
Shops that Bombay Hadn't Bargained For

This ironic history of Bombay by the major Marathi short story writer contains some truth.

If ever a proof is needed of Britain being a nation of shopkeepers one has only to see what she has done to Bombay. The city has become an anthill of shops. Every other person I run into seems to be a shopkeeper, and if he isn't that is only because he is a hawker, smuggler, bootlegger or the managing director of a corporation, which inevitably has a technical collaboration agreement with a foreign firm. Apart from ordinary commodities like sweetmeats, purgatives, contraceptives and baby foods, one can buy in Bombay such exotic merchandise as sacred threads, holy water, virtuous deeds, addresses of prospective bridegrooms, oil squeezed out of the brain of a mongoose, and eggs of crows, the eggs being used for preparing an eye-unguent for new-born babies. Bombay handles all this merchandise with expert ease and clamours for more.

Yet not long ago, before the British took it over, Bombay was a quiet retreat of bandits and pirates. It seems that the more prosperous among them had their hideouts at Malabar Hill, while the lesser thugs buried their treasure at Worli, which now houses the movie stars. The rest of the populace lived a life of happy indolence, subsisting on the simple diet of rice and fish. They washed the food down with the excellent toddy that oozed out of coconut and palm trees. As they suffered from no inhibitions or prohibitions, they allowed the toddy to ferment well, which contributed not a little to their happiness. Then they slept peacefully under banyan trees only to wake up in the evenings for prolonged bouts of drinking, dancing and music.

But one day a shipload of redfaced foreigners descended on Bombay and, instead of relaxing under banyan trees after the long and tedious journey, got very busy constructing what they called a factory and stocking it with goods. The Bombayites were astounded to learn that these grim and taciturn chappies had come all the way from their distant homeland just to set up a shop on this tropical island. Bombay ran with laughter at this egregious folly; and the pirates, who had watched with a certain amount of concern the guns on this foreign ship, were now reassured. In fact, they looked forward to a bit of innocent merriment. For chopping off the noses of obtrusive merchants was their favourite sport.

But the laughter soon faded from the Bombayites' lips. The pirates found that the redfaced foreigners were themselves highly experienced and successful pirates and had turned to shopkeeping only because they had found it to be an altogether superior form of piracy. The local pirates found themselves outgunned in battle and outwitted in business deals. Their rout was complete when the British let loose on the island a swarm of crafty banias from Surat. Soon the pirates were guarding as hired watchmen the palaces of the banias on the self-same Malabar Hill, while the rest of the gay populace was working for them as morose coolies.

Since then Bombay has learnt its lesson, and it is now the dream of every Bombayite to go into business and open at least a shop if not a managing agency firm of its own. One could not otherwise explain why the city is so crammed with shops of all descriptions. There aren't any separate and spaced out shopping areas, at least in the old Bombay city. The whole of it is one big shopping district!

(13) Dewas: The Palace – Fact

E.M. Forster, *The Hill of Devi*

E.M. Forster visited the Maratha state. of Dewas first at Christmas 1912, returning in 1929 to spend six months as Private Secretary to HH, that is His Highness Tukojirao III. There he absorbed most of the Indian background that went into A Passage to India, but here is the description of Dewas that he gives in a more factual account of his stay.

Built in the 18th century [the Old Palace] huddled in the middle of the city. It was inconvenient, dirty, dark, and a hotbed of intrigue: 'intrigue has started in the Old Palace again, I will not have it', H.H. would occasionally exclaim. Here lurked the proud ancestral servants, some of them ancestral by-blows. But here too, opening along one side of the courtyard, was the dynastic shrine, and above it lay the Durbar Hall with the sacred bed by which a lamp always burned. Here too was the ancient armoury. The place had the quality known as 'numinous': it carried one away from the bleak light into another of the Indias, and on the few occasions we slept there I had a feeling of liberation and of initiation. The royal tombs were also mysterious if seen from a boat on the Tank, and in the evening light, and unexpectedly. The Old Palace and the tombs lay in the background of our activities. We would ignore them for weeks but they were always waiting, and I expect they were in his mind when he died.

Round the Guest House no sentiments need cling. It was a dark red dump, dumped by itself by the waters of the Tank when there was any water. When there was no water it looked over cracked mud and stranded thorn bushes towards the distant town. Here the European visitors and officials stayed or were supposed to stay; here I stayed in 1912, but no one loved the Guest House.

(14) Dewas: The Palace – Fiction

Manohar Malgonkar, *The Princes*

Manohar Malgonkar's novel is about a fictional princely state a little like Dewas, of which he also wrote the history in Puars of Dewas Senior, 1963. The Dassara celebrations of many states would have been something like this.

As in all Maratha states, the Dassara was our most important festival. It was on Dassara day which comes at the end of the rains and when the harvest has been brought in, that our ancestors used to set out on their campaigns . . .

That same evening, my father and I went out in procession to the old palace in the city, riding on our state elephants. We wore jewels with our eighteenth century costumes and carried swords. The courtiers too were in costume and even the elephants were painted and caparisoned with silver bells round their necks. The procession went from the new palace to the old. In the courtyard before the old palace was the ceremony of distributing 'gold' to the populace; only, instead of gold coins, we gave away the leaves of the apta tree. After that we offered prayers in the family prayer room in the old palace, laying our swords at the feet of Ambica and seeking her blessings in the campaigns we were setting out upon.

Even as I knelt beside my father, my hands folded in prayer, I could not help feeling that it was all a great pretence, that there was no campaign of any sort for us to go on. The two bowls of incense were throwing full columns of scented smoke and the tall, many-flamed oil lamps were making weird shadows on the angry face of Ambica. She had eight hands and she was painted in red lacquer and dressed in a green sari. Seven of her hands bore weapons of combat – the mace, the wheel, the sword, the dagger, the trident, the bow and the arrow – and the eighth carried a still-bleeding human head, terrifyingly life-like, as though it had just been severed from the trunk.

I glanced sideways at my father. His eyes were tightly shut and his face looked dead white, like a bloodless mask, so that the caste mark of red sandalwood on his forehead stood out like a streak of blood. Even as I was looking at him, I saw him open his eyes wide . . . I realized that he was not looking at me, or at the goddess, or at anything at all; that he was in a trance, staring at something no one else could see.

(15) GOA

Ashok Mahajan, *'Anjuna Beach'*

Ashok Mahajan writes poetry in English which includes some vivid descriptions of Goa. This poem comes from Goan Vignettes and Other Poems (see Booklist).

Anjuna Beach

I

A noon-grey sea flashes quarrels.
I stand on rugged rock, far
Beyond the bar and sandy
Beaches of Candolim and Calangute;
Cragmartins above the spinneys of palm

Scissor wings. Pools form
Where an irregular ring
Of boulders trap the tide,
Combers through fissures there
Spout jets of foam. Sandpipers scamper

For molluscs upon the strand
Littered with chiton and volute. Robber
Crabs crawl on half-sunk
Ledges of rock in shoals
Paved with shingle and flinty

Stone. An osprey with falcate
Claw scans the wave. The littoral
Is all high ground, tangles
Of saxicolous shrubs
Black with berries or

Ragged with growths
Of crab's eye and hogweed.
Fish trawlers and ships appear
Vaporous apparitions
Over the horizon line.

II

Here and there I encounter
Stragglers in ones and twos; male,
Female; self-styled gymnosophs,
Swedes, German, French,
Nature's confreres; swimming, bathing or

Sprawled nude on the beach. Junkies
Living in frond-roofed huts
Upon the crinkled coast. Continental
Waifs, maybe. I envy their creed,
Flavoured with the aura of early man.

(16) Gujarat: Anahilwad Patan

Narasimharao Divetia, *Sahasralinga Talava*

The ruins of the ancient capital of Gujarat have inspired many Gujarati writers with reflections on vanished glory. The 'Thousand-linga lake' is now turned into a sunken field, but the Rani Wav, the great step-well, has just been re-excavated. Translated by Ian Raeside.

Here was the wide Sahasralinga lake,
Here ancient Patan lay widespread.
Here lie the bones of the queen's great well;
The tall towers there now mingled with the earth.

We name the names and then fall silent.
Old city, what are you come to now?
Standing here what child of Gujarat
Whose eyes would not be wet with tears?

There the Kuwari river with its sweet water
Like a shy young girl runs off, curves back again.
It is God's pity, shown in the river's form,
Which smilingly embraces you with loving care.

As if compassionately she said, 'O my Patan,
What if the course of time destroys the works of man?
My full flood of love flows on unendingly.
Let wealth and power be taken! My springs will never dry.

Cleaving the living rocks man swaggers in his pride
As if his deeds were immortal – yet Time engulfs them very soon.
While yet my yielding, soft and liquid body
In endless ages still remains the same.

(17) Jejuri

Arun Kolatkar, 'A Scratch'

Jejuri with its Khandoba temple has been described in a cycle of poems by the Marathi poet Arun Kolatkar, who takes a distinctly sardonic view of popular Hinduism in this poem from his collection, Jejuri.

What is god
and what is stone
the dividing line
if it exists
is very thin
at jejuri
and every other stone
is god or his cousin

there is no crop
other than god
and god is harvested here
around the year
and round the clock
out of the bad earth
and the hard rock

that giant hunk of rock
the size of a bedroom
is khandoba's wife turned to stone
the crack that runs right across
is the scar from his broadsword
he struck her down with
once in a fit of rage

scratch a rock
and a legend springs

(18) JUNAGADH

Narsi Mehta, *Hymns*

Though he is supposed to have been born in East Saurashtra, Narsi Mehta is indissolubly associated with Junagadh at the foot of the Girnar hills. First come his famous verses Vaishnava jana, Gandhi's favourite 'hymn', then an autobiographical poem which he is supposed to have written himself. Translated by Ian Raeside.

Call him a true Vaishnava who knows another's pain,
Who relieves another's sorrows, yet takes no credit for it.
He bows his head in homage to all creatures. He slanders none.
Ever firm in mind, word and deed – blessed is the mother of such a one.
Impartial, desireless – for him every woman is like his own mother.
No untruth spoken by his tongue, he lays no hand on another's goods.
In tune with the name of Ram, all the sacred places are embodied in him.
Detached and knowing no deceit, he has defeated the lusts of men.
Narsi says, the mere sight of him will redeem the sins of 71 generations.

* * *

At the foot of Girnar is the lake Damodara, there Mehtaji goes to bathe.
Among the outcastes is strong devotion to Hari; they cast themselves
    at his feet.
With joined hands they pray, asking him over and over again,
'Great man, all we ask is that you should sing a kirtan in our meeting
    place.
Thus will we gain the fruit of god's love; destroying all the ills of life.'
Seeing them thus his heart was moved. Mehtaji was a compassionate
    man.
'Where there are divisions there is no God. All are equal to the
    impartial sight.
Make all pure with cow's urine and tulsi plant!', thus did the Vaishnava
    grant their wish.
Mehtaji came at night, brought the food offerings and made festival.
Till the day dawned he sang bhajans. All the Vaishnavas were overjoyed.
He came home singing glory to Hari, sounding cymbals and conch and
    drum.
The Nagar brahmans smile and sneer, 'What a performance for a
    brahman!'
Mehtaji held his tongue. What answer can you make to feeble minds?
The people wake. Men and women ask, 'Mehtaji, why all this?
You know no caste, you know no breed. You've no idea of what is
    fitting.'
Narsi joins his hands and says, 'Vaishnavas are all the support I need.'

(19) Junagadh

Premananda, *Tales of Narsi Mehta*

In Premananda's tales of Narsi Mehta there is a humorous description of the saint's journey to visit his daughter that is known and loved by all Gujaratis. Accompanied by a band of Vaishnava friends he struggles on in a collapsing bullock cart. From K.M. Munshi, Gujarat and its Literature (see Booklist).

The body of the cart was old, the yoke was bent, the poles broken. The wooden nails belonged to some other cart, the bullocks were borrowed. A sack containing musical instruments, a bag of sacred white clay and another of tulsi wood were tied behind. The scraggy bullocks would not move and the Vaishnavas had to push them forward. When going uphill they shouted 'Victory! Victory!' all the time. Sometimes one of the bullocks, too tired to move, would lie down in the road and the other alone would be left to pull. Then they would force the first one to rise by pulling its tail. A thousand such incidents happened on the way. Every joint of the cart was loose, the axle creaked, the wheels grated. They tumbled in and out of it with the name of Ram and Krishna on their lips. In this way Mehtaji came to Una at midday and the whole village turned out to see him.

(20) The Konkan: Dapoli

S.N. Pendse, *Wild Babu of Garambi*

Pendse's 'Garambi' is not on any map, but it is an identifiable village on the road from Dapoli to Harnai.

Six miles from Harnai you come to the bridge over the Vanade river. It's a place that's famous all over the coastal strip. A mile and a half further and you are in sight of the green supari groves of Garambi. There are two roads to Dapoli from here. The locals call the place 'the new fork' and the old road goes on past Garambi village itself. If you take the turn for the village here, you start straight away on a long, stiff climb. It's a wicked hill, steep all the way, and the road beyond Garambi is extra steep. The Vanade bank, as they call this section, is so bad that even though he can see the centre of the village just below him, the bullock driver holds his life in his hands until he's safely down. Every year one or two carts go over the edge. They sacrifice hens, split coconuts before the gods, do everything they can think of, but there's no avoiding it. On the descent the bullocks are shaken up. The ground falls away like a chute, so before the lip the carter lets down the drag and makes ready. He holds the reins short and encourages his bulls with a cry. Once safely down he can at last let out his breath, stroke his bullocks lovingly and unyoke them from the cart. On one side of the bank rise the sheer rocks of the hillside and on the other are the green groves of Garambi. By night there's always a chance of a tiger lurking alongside the Vanade bank, so the carter ties a big lamp to the shaft and prepares himself. If there's the slightest whiff of a tiger he pulls up with a jerk, jumps down and turns towards Garambi. He puts his left hand to the side of his mouth and shouts, 'Ba-pu-u-u! Ho-o-o!'

Bapu's house lies close to the road and whatever time of night the call comes there will be an immediate answer from below.

'Hoay!'

And a servant will come up the bank with a lantern in his hand, clattering his staff against the stones and shouting.

This hill and the Garambi road-end where the road leads off through the village, are almost deserted now. The new road to Dapoli goes round the back by a roundabout route. It's longer, but the danger has all gone. The fame of the Garambi road-end is departed and the busy cafes that once were there are all closed up and gone.

(21) The Konkan: Ratnagiri

Keshavsut, *South-west Wind*

The 'South-west wind' of Keshavsut's poem blows from Ratna-giri District, where he was born, to Khandesh (now Jalgaon District) where he was teaching at the time. Here are the opening and closing verses. Translated by Ian Raeside.

Of all the airs that course the sky above our blessed land
It is the south-west wind that brings most inner joy.
When it blows, my mind forgets all present things;
With half-closed eyes I live a waking dream.

When it comes sweeping from the land where I was born
It blows into my heart, and all at once I stop in thought.
I bring to mind the contours of my native place.
Before my eyes I see its lofty hills and deep-set streams.

So high, where all around great rocks are spread,
Their pinnacles thrust up into the clouds
As minds of noble souls which ever climb towards heaven;
Thus do I see again, again, those mighty hills.

How glorious are the woods which clothe their flanks.
Out of the rocks the springs come tumbling
Like streams of words from some tormented poet's mouth;
Thus do I see once more those mighty hills.

Upon their high tops stand the old Maratha forts.
Once more their guardian gods speak scornfully to me,
'Where now are your brave forbears? Such feeble men you are!
Come hither. Read again this ancient crumbling page' . . .

Beyond my native land I see again the wide waters,
Rejoicing in the play of their sweet waves.
To me the dancing ripples seem as though
A transitory existence floats upon the unknowable waste.

In childhood as I went by boat upon that sea,
Those songs the water spirits sang to lull,
That very wondrous sound the wind brings now
And, hearing, how I crave eternal, healing sleep!

In this world love is but a thorny plant;
The flag of victory flutters on a pointed stake.
Then let him no more suffer joy and pain
To whom the world seems just a sorry tale.

O Goddess Sea, sing to me now those songs.
Bring with their opiate calm the fretful child
To a long sleep – sleep where never dreams will come;
Where, laid to rest, my eyes will never wet with tears.

(22) NARMADA RIVER

Gita Mehta, *A River Sutra*

*The Narmada river in Western India is a central pilgrimage site
for Hindus.*

A day seldom passes when I do not see white-robed pilgrims walking on
the riverbanks far below me. Many are like myself, quite elderly persons
who have completed the first stages of life prescribed by our Hindu
scriptures – the infant, the student, the householder – and who have
now entered the stage of the vanaprasthi, to seek personal enlightenment.

I am always astonished at their endurance, since I know the

Narmada pilgrimage to be an arduous affair that takes nearly two years to complete. At the mouth of the river on the Arabian Sea, the pilgrims must don white clothing out of respect for Shiva's asceticism before walking eight hundred kilometers to the river's source at Amarkantak. There they must cross to the opposite bank of the river and walk all the way back to the ocean, pausing only during the monsoon rains in some small temple town like Mahadeo, which has accommodated the legions of devout who have walked this route millennium upon millennium.

Then I remind myself that the purpose of the pilgrimage is endurance. Through their endurance the pilgrims hope to generate the heat, the tapas, that links men to the energy of the universe, as the Narmada River is thought to link mankind to the energy of Shiva.

It is said that Shiva, Creator and Destroyer of Worlds, was in an ascetic trance so strenuous that rivulets of perspiration began flowing from his body down the hills. The stream took on the form of a woman – the most dangerous of her kind: a beautiful virgin innocently tempting even ascetics to pursue her, inflaming their lust by appearing at one moment as a lightly dancing girl, at another as a romantic dreamer, at yet another as a seductress loose-limbed with the lassitude of desire. Her inventive variations so amused Shiva that he named her Narmada, the Delightful One, blessing her with the words 'You shall be forever holy, forever inexhaustible.' Then he gave her in marriage to the ocean, Lord of Rivers, most lustrous of all her suitors.

(23) PANDHARPUR: THE ROAD

D.B. Mokashi, *Palkhi: An Indian Pilgrimage*

There are many descriptions of the Warkari pilgrimage in the Hindu months of Ashadh and Kartik. Perhaps the most vivid is by the Marathi writer Mokashi, who joined the pilgrims ostensibly to conduct a sociological enquiry but soon threw his questionnaires away and simply recorded his experiences. Here he is at Saswad, first stop out of Poona, in the mud and rain.

I'm seated just a hand's breadth in front of Saint Tukaram's palkhi. Outside in the line, waiting for a quarter of a minute's sight of the palkhi stand all those Warkaris who have come trekking so far from so many different places. It occurs to me that if any of them had gotten the chance to see the palkhi like me from so close and in such comfort, they would have gone quite mad with joy. Each Warkari in the line comes forward in his turn. He deposits his money, and pouring all his devotion into one brief moment he closes his eyes and raises his hands before him in a namaskar. He takes his bit of the prasad and then moves on. And the person who stands waiting eagerly behind him quickly takes his place. I look at the officiating priest. His face is firmly set. He looks sharply at each Warkari. Like any other businessman in a hurry. Nothing shows on his face except the business. Others can realize the god in his possession. It strikes me as very sad that he himself is deprived of it.

There was such a pressing crowd there awaiting darshan of the palkhi that I began to feel it would be impossible to do my work. I had intended to instruct them to tell the people in their palkhi to fill out my questionnaire. But instead, I told them I would be back at a more convenient time, and I got up and went out.

The buildings surrounding the temple compound were jam-packed with Warkaris. Nine-yard saris and dhotis had been hung up together, tied to the pillars to dry. The blue smoke of the cooking fires came out in billows from the rooms and verandas. In the rain and the damp it smelled even more pungent. All about me there were great swathes of red, purple, blue, and green – all the drying saris – and the white dhotis hanging among them looked like lines cancelling out a piece of writing. All the commotion made it seem like a fair. Scattered here and there were people singing abhangas. Others were changing their clothes or tending the cooking fires, and some were in the process of putting the ritual markings on their foreheads. The children were crying and shouting shrilly.

The rain just kept on falling. All movement to and fro had to be through the covered verandas, right where all the people were lying and sitting, working or just idly standing around. I set out to make my way through them. It felt more and more like an obstacle course.

(24) PANDHARPUR: VITHOBA

Namdev and Tukaram, *Hymns*

Here are two of the countless hymns of the Maratha Saints: Namdev's Yuge atthavis, often sung during the morning worship of Vithoba, and Tukaram's Santaciya gavi, a favourite of the Warkari pilgrims on the road to Pandharpur. Note how Vitthal is given Krishna's consorts, Rukmini and Radha, one of Krishna's names Keshava, Krishna's mount and servant the eagle Garuda, and Ram's lieutenant Hanuman. Translated by Ian Raeside.

For twenty-eight years standing on the brick, on his left hand
  Rakhumai in her glorious beauty.

The supreme god-head came to visit Pundalik; at his feet flows the
  Bhima which is the world's salvation.
Glory to him, beloved of Rakhumai and Radha; O come, the darling of
  my heart.
Hands on hips, tulsi beads around his neck, he wears a silken dhoti and
  musk upon his brow.
All the gods of heaven come down each day to greet him; Garuda and
  Hanuman stand before his face.
In the months of Ashadh and Kartik the devotees arrive; they bathe
  themselves in the river Bhima.
At the first sight of you they find instant relase; Namdev worships
  Vithoba–Keshava.

In the city of the saints is profusion of love – no anxiety, no trace of
  sorrow.
There will I remain as supplicant – and they will give me charity . . .
In the city of the saints there is great treasure – Vitthal himself is all
  their wealth.
The saints' food is draughts of nectar – all day long they sing his praises.
The saints trade in the market of good doctrine – exchanging love and
  joy.
Tuka says, there's no other system there – that's why I'm a beggar at
  their door.

(25) POONA VIA THE BHOR GHAT

Edwin Arnold, *India Revisited*

*Sir Edwin Arnold returned to India in 1885–86, and later
produced a travel book. Here is his railway journey up the Bhor
Ghat to Poona – still an impressive experience for the visitor.*

By this time the vast wall of the Sahyadris – black in the sunrise and
golden in the sunset – is closely approached . . . this great barrier
which runs north and south for two hundred and twenty miles,
affording only two breaks in all the extent of the continuous ramp
where a cart road or railway could be constructed – the Bhor and the
Tal Ghauts. At Kurjat the railway boldly attacks this enormous
obstacle, beginning to climb aloft by a zigzag route of sixteen miles from
the steaming Concan up to the breezy Deccan. In that distance the
powerful engines lift the train nearly two thousand feet into the sky, by
gradients oftentimes as steep as 1 in 37, dashing over aerial viaducts,
diving into tunnels, rushing into dark cuttings, amid scenery alternate-
ly terrible and lovely, which now presents fair and far-stretching plains,

dotted with rice-grounds and villages, and now abysses of awful depth, down which the gaze plunges a thousand feet, awed yet fascinated by the combination of gloomy rock and gleaming verdure, of streams trickling or foaming through the bottom of the lonely glens, and solitary hamlets shrouded by palms. Emerging at last under the level of Khandalla . . . our train flies along under the shadows of the quick-falling night, until Poona is reached, and we descend, in clouds of dry, white, fragrant Indian dust, at the capital of the Mahrattas.

A drive next day about the cantonments and a walk through the native bazaars serve to disclose how little India changes amidst all the alterations, embellishments and ameliorations which have come with the British reign. Twenty-three years will naturally make a difference alike in men and cities, and Poona in that period has become a much larger and handsomer station . . . Maidans, which once stretched without a tree or hut to the feet of the flat hills of Kirkee and Singhur, are now covered with bungalows and gardens; a fine new bridge spans the Moota–Moola, and my ancient college of the Vishrambagh has been replaced by a magnificent new edifice beyond the Bund, where the Brahman students find lodging as well as tuition . . . The city itself, however, remains almost exactly what it was a quarter of a century – or, indeed, a century – ago. The same picturesque crowd of Brahmans, Purbhoos, Mahrattas, Koombies, Gosaeins, Banias, bright-eyed women, and naked brown babies fills the narrow lanes and the great bazaar of the Moti-chouk . . . Round the great red Lingam in the next street on the right hand used to be ranged in succession a sweetmeat shop, a dyer's shed, a tobacco stall, and a store for the sale of purple and green glass bangles. We turn, and there they are, the old-established emporiums, about as large as a piano-case, son succeeding father in the usual Hindu fashion, so that he who comes in the same way after another quarter of a century's absence will probably find the next generation of Poona dealers keeping up in the same abodes the same settled business.

(26) SURAT

J. Ovington, *A Voyage to Surat in the Year 1689*

Surat, the great port of Gujarat at the mouth of the Tapti river, was used by all the merchants of western India until it was eclipsed by Bombay. Many early travellers have left their descriptions of it, for they all started from Surat on their journey to the north and the Mughal capital at Agra. John Ovington landed in 1690 and remained there as chaplain to the English factory for two and a half years. His account of Bombay and the caves at Elephanta makes fascinating reading.

The city of Suratt . . . is situated upon a River Ten or Twelve Miles distant from the Sea. The Name of the River is Tapy, or Tindy, which rises from the Mountain of Decan, and from thence falls down through Brampore, and by Meanders from Suratt glides down gently into the Ocean. The Circumference of it, with the Suburbs, is between two and three English Miles, tending somewhat in its Position to the Form of a Semicircle or Half Moon, because of the winding of the River, to which half of it adjoyns. It is fortified with a Wall, which is flankt at certain Distances with Towers and Battlements, occasion'd by the frequent Incursions of the Enemies; but its greatest Strength is in the Castle, which commands not only the Ships and Boats in the River, but likewise guards the City by Land . . .

The Houses are many of them fair and stately, tho' unproportionable to the Wealth of the Inhabitants, who are always concern'd to conceal their Riches, and therefore never exceed in any Luxurious Furniture, lest it should prove too powerful Temptation to the Avarice of the Mogul. They are flat roof'd, or rather made a little shelving, after the manner of the Buildings in Spain and Portugal, cover'd with Tiles, and the Walls made of Brick or Stone. The Windows are without Glass, and kept open for the Convenience of the fresh Air; and the Floors both of the lower and upper Stories are all Terrass'd to make them cool. But the poorer sort, and such as inhabit the Skirts of the City, live much meaner, in Houses, whose Walls are only Bambous at a Foot distance, with the Reeds wove through them; and their Covering is only Cajan, or Palm-leaves of Trees, which gives them the common Name of Cajan-Houses.

The Streets are some too narrow, but in many places of a convenient breadth; and in an Evening, especially near the Bazar, or Market-place, are more populous than any part of London; and so much throng'd, that 'tis not very easie to pass through the multitude of Bannians and other Merchants that expose their Goods.

(27) Rajasthan: Ajmer

Narapati Nalha, *Visaladevarasa*

In this episode of the Visaladevarasa the princess Rajamati of Dhar in Malwa is married to the hero Vishaldev, prince of Ajmer. From John D. Smith, The Visaladevarasa (see Book-list).

In the land of Malwa there was festivity
as Rajamati's wedding was arranged.
The pavilion was made of sandalwood,
the marriage-dais of gold, and the garlands of pearls.
At the first circumambulation the wedding gift was
the jungle above Mandalagadh.

King Vishaldev walked around the fire in the second circumambulation.
The princess's mother was Bhanumati;
her gift was given to her son-in-law.
She gave wealth and a complete treasury;
she gave the kingdom of Sapadalaksha;
Nagaracal with the lake of Sambhar;
Toda and central Tonk,
and the country of Kudal, together with Bundi.

The king walked around the fire in the third circumambulation.
King Bhoja summoned all his womenfolk.
What was given by him as a wedding gift?
He gave spirited, swift horses;
he gave the kingdom of Mandor,
and Saurashtra and Gujarat, with the sea.

At king Bhoja's throat was the sacred thread; his garment was a dhoti;
pan in his hand and water in the cup of his palm.
The king gave as a wedding-gift
a silken bed and a quilt of *savatu*;
with the thirty-six Rajput lines watching
he bathed Vishaldev's feet and honoured his crown,
and gave the stronghold of Chittor with its twelve fortresses.

The Princess was made to sit upon a throne.
At her waist was a sari of fine spotted red cloth;
her earrings glittered;
she had a gold amulet and a tilak on her forehead.
Seeing her beauty King Vishaldev laughed for joy and said,
'This Paramar maiden has enraptured the three worlds!'

Everywhere, horses were saddled.
The King went to pay his respects to his mother-in-law;
the thirty-six lines were with him.
A coconut was filled with gems and pearls;
blessing him, his mother-in-law gave it to him and said,
'Rule in Ajmer undisturbed.'

(28) Rajasthan: Jalor

Padmanabha, *Kanhadade Prabandha*

In the Old Gujarati epic Kanhadade Prabandha *the Muslim army under Ulugh Khan is returning north after the sack of Somnath in Saurashtra, laden with booty and prisoners and the great linga from the temple of Somnath.*

Ulugh Khan now decreed, 'The temple shall remain without its idol!
Send the demon to Delhi to be crushed and turned to lime' . . .
They burned the villages and ravaged the land, destroying many towns.
They spread terror in Sorath and plundered the people's goods.
They carried off brahmans; women and children of all eighteen castes;
All lashed together with raw-hide thongs – the number beyond counting.
The army moved, the captives too; the Turks made their salaams.
With drums beating the Khan came to the borders of Sorath.
A fierce forest fire driven by the wind – what to do against these Turks?
Thus the Turks came rushing on – how to defend ourselves from them?
They took Junagad and Girnar; they seized the land of Kutch.
Kanthgehadi, Parkar and Thatta were trembling with fear.
Ulugh Khan saw all this might and was proud beyond measure.
He took the straight way through the land of Maru without a trace of fear.
Kanhadade had scorned the Emperor and denied his army passage;
So with anger in his heart the Khan says, 'Now will we seize Songiri.'
Little did Ulugh Khan know that he had incurred great sin.
In every hole he had found a lizard, but sometimes a snake comes forth.
The Turks caracol on their fierce keen horses; shout their battle-cries.
The bugles sound and the drums rumble – the very mountains tremble.
Thus the army reaching Marwar, they camped in a fair place.
Sitting in his palace the Khan took council of the great lords.
There he decided and sent his minister to Kanhadade in Jalor.
Thus did he speak, 'Now seek courage. Ulugh Khan is come to your fort.
He says, "Who dares attack me? See now what I have done.
With my army I have conquered the lands of Sorath and Gujarat.
I have made your devil-god a prisoner. Make ready then.
Be bold and block my path. Win back your precious Somnath.

Either come before me bearing gifts or show a little valour.
Or know what is good for you and preserve your house.'

(29) RAJASTHAN: KOLU

The Epic of Pabuji

*In this episode from the Epic of Pabuji his widow Phulvanti goes
to join her sister-in-law Gailovat in order that they may become
sati together. From John D. Smith, The Epic of Pabuji (see
Booklist).*

Phulvanti the virgin set out as starry midnight passed;
she came straight to Kolu.
Once or twice she halted overnight on the road;
on the fifth or fifteenth day she removed the stirrups from her feet in Kolu.
Queen Gailovat was seated in her mother-in-law's courtyard;
Phulvanti went and paid her respects.
'O mother-in-law, accept my respects!
It was written in heaven that I should have only a short time in my
    father's home and father-in-law's home.'
Phulvanti shed tears from her eyes;
She scattered tears like a frightened wild peacock.
She said, 'O mother-in-law, give me your blessing!
With your blessing I shall set off to join the satis.'
Phulvanti said, 'Queen Gailovat, Buro's queen, adorn yourself
    sixteen-fold and thirty-two-fold;
we two shall go to the steps of the Gujavo well to become sati!'
Queen Gailovat adorned herself sixteen-fold and thirty-two-fold;
now the satis came forth.
In Kolu the war-drums were beating rhythmically;
to the beat of the drums the satis came forth.
The other satis toyed with tufted coconuts,
but Gailovat toyed with a fine dagger.
The other satis mounted horses,
but the two sisters-in-law set off on foot.
At Gujavo well the war-drums were beating;
the satis assembled at Pabuji's well Gujavo.
Gailovat said, 'O midwife of the Rathors, take this fine dagger in
    your hand;
Cut open my belly and deliver my child!'
Then the midwife considered, and what did she say?
'Queen Gailovat, you have formed a foolish idea in your mind;
O sati queen, I cannot lay hands on your body!'

Gailovat said, 'O midwife of the Rathors, may your family go to the bad!
You have answered me back when the matter had been decided.
The sati queen, Buro's queen, took the fine dagger in her hand;
she cut open her belly and delivered the child.
O lord, she laid the child down on the well-head stone to sleep;
then the little boy, just born, spoke out to his mother:
'O my mother, who will rock the little boy's cradle?
Who will wash the little boy's nappies?'
Then his mother considered and what did she say?
'Little boy, I myself an going to become sati.
But little boy, the Wind-god will rock your cradle;
O son, the Rain-god will wash your nappies!'

Biographies and plot summaries

AGARKAR, Gopal Ganesh (1856–95). With Tilak and others he founded and edited the two influential Marathi newspapers *Kesari* and *Mahratta*, but later they became increasingly estranged, and in 1887 he started his own paper *Sudharak* (*The Reformer*). Sadly, he died young.

APTE, Hari Narayan (1864–1919). The first major Marathi novelist and still considered one of the greatest. Educated in **Bombay** and **Poona** he avidly absorbed the classics of English and French literature. His first novel, published when he was still a student, began as an adaptation of *The Mysteries of Old London* by G.W.M. Reynolds, a novelist now forgotten, but once valued only slightly below Dickens. In 1890, after dabbling in various publishing ventures, he founded his own magazine *Karamanuk* in which all his own writing subsequently appeared. Of his ten novels on modern social themes, several of which were left unfinished, the best are *Pan lakshat kon gheto* (*But who cares?*, 1890–3) a harrowing story of a widow which had a major effect in the campaign for Hindu reform, and *Mi* (1893–5) the autobiography of a saintly social reformer who chooses celibacy in order to be free to serve the poor.

ARNOLD, Sir Edwin (1832–1904). Educated at University College Oxford, he was made Principal of **Deccan College Poona** in 1856. Back in England on leave in 1861 he became a leader writer for the *Daily Telegraph* and its editor from 1873–89. He published a translation of the Sanskrit *Hitopadesh* in 1861 and throughout his life wrote an abundance of rather fraught romantic verse. His one bestseller was *The Light of Asia* (1879), the story of Gautama Buddha in blank verse and adapted to the sensibilities of Western readers, which went into 60 editions in England and 80 in

USA. He wrote a travel book, *India Revisited* (Extract 25) when he returned to India in 1885/86.

BHAVE, P.B. (1910–80). Marathi short-story writer, essayist and journalist. A right-winger and propagandist of traditional Hindu virtues, his published volumes run to nearly 100.

BROKER, Gulabdas (1909–). Born at **Porbandar**, a Gujarati short-story writer who was also a Bombay business man. His stories have been translated in various journals and anthologies, and there is one collection in English: *Of Life and Love*, see Booklist.

BROMFIELD, Louis (1896–1956). Journalist and novelist, he was born in Ohio. Two of his best known novels, *The Rains Came* (1937) and *Night in Bombay* (Extract 5, 1940) were set in India and both were made into popular films. Their mainly American heroes and heroines exemplify in various ways Bromfield's hostility to the snobbery and superiority of British rule, thus reinforcing the standard American view of Britain's Indian Empire.

CHITRE, Dilip Purushottam (1938–). A leading Marathi poet, he has published several collections of his own verse, as well as novels and travel writing. He is best known perhaps for his *An Anthology of Marathi Poetry 1945–65* (see Booklist) which, as well as translations of some of his own verse, contains poems by all the major post-Independence poets in Marathi.

DALPATRAM DAHYABHAI (1820–

98). Gujarati poet and co-founder of the Gujarat Vernacular Society in 1848. He was employed by A.K. Forbes to collect manuscripts of old Gujarati literature and contributed many poems to the Gujarati school texts of his time. Some of his humorous and popular verse has attained the status of nursery rhymes.

DÉ, Shobha. Model, society hostess, journalist and now author of five novels. The daughter of a district judge from small-town Maharashtra, she came to **Bombay** as a model, married into one of the wealthiest families in Bombay, divorced, had a notorious affair with a Frenchman, then married the shipping magnate, Dilip Dé, and now reigns as the queen of Bombay society and controller of several aspects of popular culture. She is famous for her great beauty, wealth and art collecting and she is feared for her sharp tongue. Her gossipy (some would say, bitchy) columns in the newspapers are read avidly, as are her novels, despite their terrible reviews, being summed up as 'filthy, semi-literate, semi-autobiographical airport-slush novelettes' (Extract 11).

DESAI, Mahadev (1892–1942). Gandhi's confidential secretary. He joined Gandhi in 1917 and died in his service, having shared in all his campaigns and tribulations. His *Diary*, written in Gujarati, was translated into English as *Day to Day with Gandhi* and published in many volumes from 1968 onwards. He himself translated much of Gandhi's writings from Gujarati into English, notably of course Gandhi's *Autobiography* (Extract 1).

Dhola Maru Ra Duha. The love-story

of Dhola and Maru is well-known throughout Rajasthan, and is the subject of several poetic versions, of which the version in *duha* (couplets) is both the oldest and the most popular. It probably dates from the 15th century AD, and is of uncertain authorship. It tells of the prince Dhola, who has been married as a child to the princess Maru; they have not met since. Maru sends a message asking Dhola to come; his other wife Malavani tries to prevent him, but he travels across the desert to claim his first bride. They then return to Dhola's home, surviving poisonous snakes and vengeful pursuers on the way.

DHUMAKETU, pen name of G.G. Joshi (1892–1965). Gujarati novelist and short story writer. A typical writer of the Gandhi era, he is associated mainly with the short story.

DIVETIA, Narsimharao B. (1859–1937). A brahman born in **Ahmadabad**, he was a civil servant (Deputy Collector) and later a lecturer in Gujarati at Elphinstone College, Bombay. The major poet of the generation after Dalpatram, his published lectures on *Gujarati Language and Literature*, (2 vols, University of Bombay, 1921, 1932) formed the first substantial account in English of Gujarati literature (Extract 16).

EKNATH (c 1533–1600). A brahman poet of Paithan who wrote many long poems in Marathi and who is especially famous for having edited a definitive text of Jnandev's *Jnaneshwari* and saved it from further corruption and modernization. Eknath wrote devotional abhangs to Vitthal of Pandharpur as well as poems such as his *Ramayana* and the

story of Krishna's marriage to Rukmini. A rare book on him by a missionary writer is W.S. Deming, *Eknath, A Maratha Bhakta*, Bombay, 1933.

EZEKIEL, Nissim (1924–   ). Born in **Bombay** of a Jewish family, Ezekiel was educated in Bombay where he later became Professor of English and American literature. He translates from Marathi, but writes only in English. He is regarded as the pioneer of new poetry in English and has been publishing poetry for over 40 years. He has had a huge influence on later poets through his writing, teaching and active role in encouraging new talent. He is also known for his active involvement in Indian PEN (Extract 10).

FALKLAND, Viscountess (1807–58). Born Amelia Fitz-Clarence, the last of ten children of William IV by the actress Mrs Jordan, she married the 10th Viscount Falkland in 1830 and accompanied him to Bombay

Nissim Ezekiel

where he was Governor from 1848 to 1853. *Chow-chow* (Extract 2), a vivid account of her time in India, was published in 1857 and, perhaps because of its unfortunate dating, was instantly forgotten.

FORBES, Alexander Kinloch (1821–64). Forbes came from a family of minor scottish gentry. In **Ahmadabad** as an Assistant Judge from 1846, he studied Gujarati and began to collect old manuscripts with the help of the poet Dalpatram ◊. They were the principal founders of the Gujarat Vernacular Society in 1848. His only book is the *Rasmala: Hindu Annals of Western India* (London 1856 and several times republished) which is a history of Gujarat and Gujarati based on the materials that he and Dalpatram had collected.

FORSTER, E(dward) M(organ) (1879–1970). Forster was introduced to Tukoji, ruler of **Dewas Senior**, by a friend during the course of an Indian tour in the winter of 1912–13. Through a similar 'old-boy' arrangement he went back as Private Secretary to the ruler in 1921. His period in Dewas gave him that sympathy with the way Indians think and behave that appears so clearly in *A Passage to India* (Central and Northern India, Extract 14; South India, Extract 14). He recounted his actual experiences in Dewas with the help of old letters home in *The Hill of Devi* (Extract 13, 1953). Forster remained to the end unfailingly helpful and supportive of Indian writers – both those who wrote in English and those who hoped to publish translations of their Indian language novels and poems. Nearly every one who came to England seems to have visited Forster in Cambridge and come away feeling cheered. See

especially G.K. Das, *E.M. Forster's India* and R.J. Lewis, *Passages to India* (both are in the Booklist). See also Central and Northern India and South India.

GADGIL, Gangadhar (1923–). Born in **Bombay**, where he has spent most of his career as a Professor of Economics. He is a major figure in Marathi literature, and is best known as a writer of the new Marathi short story, although he has written over 50 books, which include children's writing, literary criticism and plays. He actively promotes writing in Marathi. His work has appeared in translation in Raeside (see Booklist) and in a recent collection *The Woman and Other Stories* (see Booklist). See also *The Throttled Street and Other Stories* (1994). Extract 12 is from *Shops Bombay Hadn't Bargained For* (1992).

Gangadhar Gadgil

E.M. Forster

GADKARI, R.G. (1885–1919). One of the four celebrated Marathi dramatists of the turn of the century, as well as a lyric poet under the pen-name of Govindagraj. See S. Namjoshi's translation *Poems of Govindagraj*, Calcutta, 1968. Of his six most popular plays *Just One Glass* (*Ekaca* *Pyala*, 1917) on the evils of drink was frequently revived during Maharashtra's prohibition era.

GANDHI, Mohandas Karamchand (1869–1948). Mahatma Gandhi was born at **Porbandar** on the west coast of Saurashtra into an influential merchant family. After studying law in England he practised as a lawyer in South Africa between 1893 and 1915. Returning to India permanently in 1915 he soon established himself as a leader within the Congress party. His ashram, founded on the banks of the Sabarmati river near **Ahmadabad**, gave shelter to all castes and creeds and is the first of a type which has spawned ashrams and foreign devotees all over India. Gandhi was opposed to most aspects of British rule and was often imprisoned, but his reputation in Europe and America became so great that the British never dared keep him in prison too long, nor could they stand up to his occasional 'fasts unto death'. He was bitterly opposed to the partition of India and Pakistan, but by the time of the final negotiations over independence for India his political influence was small. It was a refusal to be an all-out Hindu that ended in his assassination by a rabidly right-wing Poona brahman on 30 January 1948 as he came out to lead his evening prayer meeting. Gandhi wrote copiously all his life in English, Gujarati and Hindustani, a link language now rejected but one which Gandhi favoured as combining the virtues of Hindu Hindi and Muslim Urdu. His collected works were published in English by the Government of India from 1958 onwards and have by now been completed by Volume 90. Publications in his lifetime were mostly collections of articles from his own newspapers like *Harijan* or *Young India*, or letters to certain favoured correspondents, but he also wrote his *History of Satyagraha in South Africa* in 1924 and the much better known *Autobiography or the Story of my Experiments with Truth* in 1927–29 (Extract 1). Both were published simultaneously in Gujarati and in English, and the English version

was largely the work of his secretary Mahadev Desai ◊. Gandhi's name will remain indissolubly linked with many places in Western India – with the **Sabarmati ashram**, with **Dandi** on the coast of Gujarat where he led a march to make salt illegally, with Yeravda gaol outside **Poona** where he spent many months of imprisonment and lastly with **Sevagram**, the second ashram that he set up in 1929 in the Wardha district of Maharashtra, from which his disciple Vinoba Bhave continued his work with the bhoodan and gramdan movements.

GOKHALE, Aravind V. (1919–92). Marathi writer who is unique in having confined himself almost exclusively to the short story genre of which he published over 50 collections. As well as *The Unmarried Widow* (see Booklist) there are two stories in Raeside (see Booklist).

HEBER, Reginald (1783–1826). Born into a family of country gentry and educated at Brasenose College Oxford, he made an individual and enterprising grand tour in 1805–06 through Scandinavia and Russia as far as the Sea of Azof. As a parson and later prebendary of St Asaph, he knew Coleridge, Scott and Southey and wrote over 50 hymns of which some, such as *Holy Holy Holy* and *From Greenland's Icy Mountains*, are still well-known. In 1823 he was appointed as the second Bishop of **Calcutta**, a diocese which then included Australia as well as South Africa and Ceylon. He made his northern tour of the Indian churches in 1824–25, ending at **Surat** from where he returned by sea to Bombay and then Calcutta. On a second tour to South India he died suddenly at **Trichinopoly**. His *Journal* was published in 1828 and there were two more editions that same year (Extract 4).

JNANDEV or JNANESHWAR (1275–96?). A brahman youth who wrote the seminal Marathi work called after him *Jnaneshwari* (Extract 3) at Nevasa on the banks of the Godavari in 1390 – which would mean that this immense vivid yet learned commentary on the *Bhagavadgita* was composed by a boy of 15. Jnandev is especially associated with **Alandi** near Poona, where he and his siblings were born, where he died and from where the senior Jnaneshwar palanquin now leaves on the pilgrimage to **Pandharpur**. He is also claimed by Apegaon, his father's village on the Godavari east of **Paithan**, where there is also a temple dedicated to him. There is an excellent edition and translation into French of a sequence of abhangas attributed to Jnandev in Charlotte Vaudeville (see Booklist).

JOSHI, Suresh H. (1921–86). An avant-garde poet, short story writer and critic, he co-edited a monthly journal *Kshitij* (Horizon) which played an important part in introducing the latest trends in world literature to Gujarati. A few of his short stories have been translated into English (eg in the collection by Jag Mohan, see Booklist), but he is mainly known for his immensely fertilising influence on modern Gujarati literature.

JOSHI, Umashankar J. (1911–88). The leading Gujarati poet of the 20th century. In the 1930s a Gandhian activist, he ended his career from 1966 to 1972 as Vice-Chancellor of Gujarat University in **Ahmadabad** and from 1970–76 as a member of the Rajsabha. Apart from collections of poetry, he wrote one-act plays as well as much essay and travel writing for the influential monthly magazine *Samskriti* (Culture) which he also edited. Vol IX, No 1 of the *Journal of South Asian Literature* (Michigan, 1973) is devoted to him and to selected translations of his poetry.

KANGA, Firdaus (1960–). Born in Bombay, he published his first novel in 1989. He has since written travel books and has worked in the media in the UK as a literary critic and TV writer. He is a well-known figure in Bombay, and is one of the city's few open homosexuals. His first novel contains many autobiographical elements and has been praised for being 'tenderly erotic' (Extract 8).

Kanhadade Prabandha. A *rasa* or bardic poem in Old Gujarati by Padmanabh, the hereditary bard of the Raja of Jalor, completed in 1456. It tells in vivid detail the largely imaginary tale of the resistance of the Raja's ancestor Kanhadade to the invasion of Ala-ud-din and the siege of the fortress of Jalor in 1305. The highly romantic narrative, which involves the hopeless love of Ala-ud-din's daughter for Kanhadade's son Viram, culminates in no less than three jauhars – that quintessentially Rajput self-sacrifice where, when all hope is lost, the women set fire to themselves in their inner chambers while the men sally forth from the doomed city to die in battle.

KARANDIKAR, G.V. (Vinda) (1918–). Marathi lyric poet. He has translated many of his own poems in: *Poems of Vinda* (Bombay, 1975), *Trimurti* (Calcutta 1979), *Some More Poems of Vinda* (Bombay, 1983).

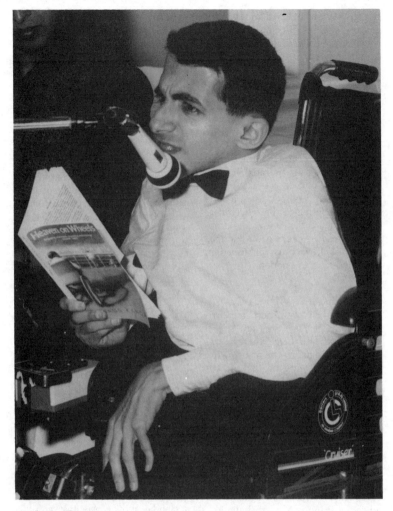

Firdaus Kanga

KESHAVSUT (1866–1905). The pen-name by which the Marathi poet K.K. Damle is always known. Born in the Konkan at **Malgund**, a village by the sea north of Ratnagiri, he spent most of his short life as a school-teacher and died at **Dharwar** of plague. The first serious modern poet in Marathi, his poems show the influ- ence of the English Romantics and some are actually translations from English. A selection is translated in P. Machwe (see Booklist) – Extract 21.

KHANDEKAR, V.S. (1898–1976). One of the two most prolific Marathi novelists of the middle decades of this century. Of his 50 odd novels and short story collections, many have been translated into other Indian languages but only *Yayati* (see Booklist) into English.

KOLATKAR, Arun (1932–). Leading modern Marathi poet who writes as much in English as in Marathi. He co-founded the poetry monthly *Shabda* and his poems have appeared in many journals and collected works; 20 are in Chitre (see Booklist). *Jejuri*, a cycle of poems relating to the village near Poona which is the centre of pilgrimage and worship of the god Khandoba (Extract 17), was first published in 1974 and later in London.

MADGULKAR, V.D. (1927–). Marathi novelist and short-story writer. Many of his works are set in **Mandesh**, the rural area where he was born. He was among the first to write dialogue consistently in dialect. His novel *Banagarwadi* (1955) was translated by Ram Deshmukh as *The Village had no Walls* (see Booklist). Also in English is *Winds of Fire*, a novel about the riots that followed Gandhi's murder.

MAHIPATI (1715–90). Marathi hagiographer. He wrote the biographies of all the poet saints of north India in a number of long poetic compilations. Most of what we know of *bhakti* poets like Jnandev ◊ and Tukaram ◊ is taken from the miraculous tales that he tells. The series *The Poet-Saints of Maharashtra* (12 vols, Poona, 1926–41) mainly consists of translations from Mahipati by Justin Abbott and other missionaries.

MALGONKAR, Manohar (1913–).

Born into an affluent brahman family of Maharashtra, he was successively professional hunter, civil servant, army officer, businessman and unsuccessful parliamentary candidate for the Swatantra Party. He began his writing career with short stories for All India Radio followed by a work of popular history in 1959. His novels include: *Distant Drum* (1960) and *Combat of Shadows* (1962) based respectively on his army and hunting experiences. *The Princes* (Extract 14, 1963) describes the impact of Independence on a small princely state, while *A Bend in the Ganges* (1964) is a story of the anti-British movement and the agonies of partition, and *The Devil's Wind* (1972) on the Mutiny of 1857. He has also written the history of the Pawars of Dewas and of the rulers of Kolhapur, a court to which he was once closely attached.

MARDHEKAR, B.S. (1909–56). The first essentially modern poet in Marathi. He was partly educated in England and published a volume of critical writing in English: *Arts and Man* (Longman, 1937). He worked for All India Radio in Bombay until his death. The collection of poems that he published in 1947 under the title *Some Poems* – a deliberate mockery of the grandiloquent titles favoured by his predecessors – caused a scandal and he was unsuccessfully prosecuted for obscenity by the Government of Maharashtra. Over 30 poems from this and later collections are published in translation in Chitre (see Booklist).

MEHTA, Gita. Best known for her study of European hippies in India, *Karma Cola*, and for her novel, *Raj*, Gita Mehta has also made a number of television programmes. Her latest novel, *A River Sutra* (Extract 22), weaves stories together on a traditional Indian model.

MIRABAI (c1500–47 or 1403–70?). There are two irreconcilable scenarios for Mira's life, but both agree that she was born in the ruling family of Merta in Rajasthan and married to a prince of Chittor. She had always been devoted to the worship of Krishna and became disgusted with the life of the court, spending her time more and more in the company of ascetics and holy men and women. As a result she was rejected and tormented by her husband (or brother-in-law) and eventually fled to Dwarka where she spent her time in the temple in prayer and devotion. Because of the removal of her virtuous presence Chittor fell on hard times and the penitent prince sent for her to return, but in an agony of indecision she threw herself down before the image and was absorbed into it. All these legends come from much later narratives or from poems attributed to Mira but unlikely to have been composed by her. The nature of the rest of her *bhakti* (devotional) verse makes the later date more probable. Her poems, which were originally composed in Old Gujarati, have been preserved in many different forms according to the bardic lineage which maintained them: some pure Hindi, some Gujarati. Mira has been much written about and often translated, the best to date being from the Rajasthani/Hindi by A.J. Alston (see Booklist).

MISTRY, Rohinton (1952–). Rohinton Mistry was born in Bombay, but has lived in Toronto since 1975. He was shortlisted for the 1991 Booker Prize and won the Commonwealth Writer's Prize for the Best

Rohinton Mistry

Book of 1992. Mistry graduated from Bombay University in mathematics and economics, then worked in a bank for ten years in Toronto, while studying part-time. He became a full-time writer in 1987, publishing mostly short stories. His first book, *Tales from Ferozsha Baag*, was published in India in 1988, but published in the West only after the success of *Such a Long Journey*. Like many writers of South Asian origin, he belongs to several traditions, and his work has been published in anthologies of Canadian writing (Extract 9).

MOKASHI, D.B. (1915–81). Marathi writer, especially of short stories (one in Raeside, see Booklist). His novel *Deva Calile* (1961) was translated as *Farewell to the Gods* and his *Palakhi* (1964), an account of the pilgrimage to Pandharpur, is well translated by P. Engblom (Extract 23).

MUNSHI, Kanaiyalal M. (1887–

1971). The most popular Gujarati novelist of the 1930s, especially for his historical series. Munshi was first a lawyer, then a Gandhian and finally a politician. Probably his greatest service to Gujarati literature was the history, *Gujarat and its Literature*, written in prison and first published in 1935. This is still the most complete and most often quoted account of Gujarati literature in English.

NAMDEV (1270–1350?). A tailor of Pandharpur who is supposed to have been a contemporary of Jnandev ◊, to have accompanied him on pilgrimage and written his biography, but who is more likely to have been two or three other people living much later. There are many devotional hymns attributed to him and his effigy stands on the main steps of the temple of **Vitthal**, at the place where he is said to be buried so that the feet of the faithful may constantly tread upon him. Some of his *abhangas* are translated in P. Machwe (see Booklist) – Extract 24.

NARMADA (1833–86). Narmadashankar Lalshankar Dave is known to all Gujaratis simply as Narmada. Slightly younger than Dalpatram ◊ and always in rivalry with him, he was the second 'only begetter' of modern Gujarati literature. He wrote essays for the first Gujarati journals and more or less created Gujarati prose. He also wrote verse, compiled the first Gujarati dictionary, called after him *Narmakosha*, and the first analysis of Gujarati metrics. His poem *Hail Proud Gujarat* is a kind of Gujarati national anthem.

NARSI MEHTA (1414–80?). As with Mira there is no agreement about his dates. According to tradition

he was a devotee and composer of devotional verse addressed to Krishna. Born in the community of Nagar brahmans at Talaja, a small town south of Bhavnagar, he outraged his caste-fellows by his readiness to sing and dance for Krishna's sake in any society no matter how low in the caste hierarchy. Some of his verses, often called *prabhatiya* or 'dawn songs', are profoundly philosophical in nature without being attached to any specific deity, while others are strongly erotic in the Vallabhite tradition where the devotee assumes the role of Radha or some other female lover of Krishna. Some of the best known stories in Gujarati are those told about Narsi, especially in the versions by Premananda ◊. At several crises in his domestic life Krishna appeared in the form of a Gujarati merchant in order to save his honour and his credit (Extract 18).

OVINGTON, John (1653–1731). Ovington sailed for Bombay as a 'casual chaplain' in an East India Co ship in 1689, arriving in 1690 and spending the next two years as chaplain to the English Factory at Surat. His account *A Voyage to Suratt* (Extract 26) came out in 1696, and he survived to be the rector of a Kentish village.

PADMANABH (fl.1450). The author of *Kanhadade Prabandha* ◊ (Extract 28).

PATEL, Gieve (1940–). A Parsi, born in Bombay, Gieve Patel is a general medical practitioner. Although he occasionally translates from Gujarati he writes only in English in which he has published three collections of verse and three plays.

He is also known as a painter and actor (Extract 7).

PATEL, Pannalal (1912–89). The major Gujarati novelist and short story writer of the post-Independence period and the first significant exponent of regionalism. He wrote especially of the peasant life of north-east Gujarat on the borders of Rajasthan where he was born. His earliest novels *Souls Entangled* (*Malela Jiv*, 1941) and *The Human Comedy* (*Manavini Bhavai*, 1947) were his biggest successes and are translated into many Indian languages. Only one or two of his stories have been translated into English.

PENDSE, S.N. (1913–). Marathi novelist, born in Ratnagiri District in the Konkan which is the setting for much of his work. After a fairly arduous upbringing and education he achieved fame with his third novel *Garambica Bapu* (1952) translated as *Wild Bapu of Garambi* (Extract 20, 1969), the story of a maverick brahman youth who makes his fortune while flouting all the conventions of caste. His seventh novel *Rathacakra* won a Sahitya Akademi prize in spite of being mildly controversial. It is the tale of a woman potentially as intelligent and enterprising as Bapu, but trapped within the orthodoxies of a Hindu family. Pendse has turned several of his novels into successful plays.

PHADKE, N.S. (1894–1978). With Khandekar ◊ the outstanding Marathi novelist of the interwar years. His romantic novels of middle-class Poona life (eg *Daulat*, 1929) were devoured by the college students of the time. By 1972 he had published over 65 novels and short-story collections of which two or three have been translated into rather Indian English (*The Whirlwind*, 1956; *Where Angels Sell Eggs*, 1957). He has also written essays and biographical pieces.

PREMANANDA (c1636–1734). Most things about him, including the tale that he lived to the age of 98, are uncertain except that he was a brahman from Baroda who composed 50 or more narrative poems on most of the traditional themes of Indian literature. Among the most popular are the story of Sudama, the poor brahman who had been a fellow student of Krishna and went to Dwarka to ask his help for his starving wife and children, and those about Narsi Mehta ◊. *Kumvarabai's Feast* is the tale of the celebration of Narsi's daughter's first pregnancy, and *Shamal's Wedding* recounts the marriage of Narsi's son. In both Krishna arrives in person to supply gifts and save the honour of the destitute Narsi (Extract 19).

RUSHDIE, Salman (1947–). Born in Bombay; educated there, at Rugby and King's College Cambridge, he first worked as an advertising copywriter. His second novel *Midnight's Children* (Extract 6, 1981) won the Booker Prize and the succeeding *Shame* (1983), *Satanic Verses* (1988) and the children's story *Haroun and the Sea of Stories* (1990) have all been enthusiastically received by the critics. Khoumeini's *fatwa* following publication of *The Satanic Verses*, by virtue of which Rushdie still must live in hiding, has greatly restricted his activities.

STEPHENS, Thomas (1549–1619).

A native of Wiltshire, he arrived in **Goa** in 1579 to spend the rest of his life there as a Jesuit priest, being known as Thomaz Estevao. He wrote in Konkani Marathi a book on Christian doctrine and an early grammar, but his fame rests on the *Krista Purana* (1616), or in its Portuguese title *Puranna da Vinda e Vida do Christo*, a life of Christ in 11 000 couplets of the Marathi ovi metre.

TENDULKAR, Vijay (1928–). Marathi playwright known throughout India. His 'modern', often experimental plays have been performed in most of the major Indian languages. *Sakharam Binder* (see Booklist) caused a great scandal for its sexual explicitness, unusual in India. *Ghashiram Kotwal* (1973), a play based on the career of a notorious police chief of 18th century Poona, had a huge success and has been performed in English in London, USA and Germany.

TILAK, Bal Gangadhar, called Lokamanya, (1856–1920). The charismatic leader who earned himself the title of 'father of Indian unrest'. His influence was exerted mainly through his oratory and his journalism in the Marathi newspaper *Kesari* which he edited from 1880 to 1908 when he was charged with sedition and deported to Mandalay for six years. Apart from his copious writing in Marathi he published two books in English: *The Orion* (1895) and *The Arctic Home in the Vedas* (1903) and in Marathi *Gitarahasya* (1915), a very individual interpretation of the *Bhagavadgita* which was translated into English in 1935. There are many biographies of Tilak, but see especially: D.V. Tahmankar, *Lokamanya*

Tilak, London, 1956; S.A. Wolpert, *Tilak and Gokhale*, Berkeley, 1962; R.I. Cashman, *The Myth of the Lokamanya*, Berkeley, University of California Press, 1975.

TOD, Lieut Col. James (1732–1835). James Tod spent many years in what is now the state of **Rajasthan**, ending as Political Agent from 1818 to 1822. He was captivated by the Rajput rulers of the region and their archaic court life, and plunged into the historical and other literature of the region. From these and his own experiences he assembled his great work *Annals and Antiquities of Rajasthan*, published in two volumes in 1829–32. Though the work of an Englishman, this is in many ways itself a part of the Rajasthani chronicle tradition (unlike most of Hindu India, the Rajputs were keen preservers of their own history). As history *Annals* is now hopelessly out of date, but it remains one of the great English works on India, and is enjoyable to read (in small doses at any rate).

TRIPATHI, Govardhanram M. (1855–1907). Always referred to simply as Govardhanram, he was a lawyer who retired early to become Gujarati's first major novelist with the serial novel *Sarasvatichandra* which came out between 1887 and 1901. Desperately romantic and with a plot which keeps the eponymous hero eternally separated from his first love, the novel has wars and battles and sieges more appropriate to the Middle Ages in an ostensibly 19th century setting. It is also full of the author's own lyric verse and, characteristic of its era, lengthy asides on the social and reformist problems of the day.

TUKARAM (1598–1649). The last great Marathi saint poet was born at **Dehu**, west of Poona, in the kunbi or farmer caste. He kept a small shop but he spent all his time in making pilgrimages to Pandharpur, in dancing and singing and composing poems to Vitthal. His *abhangs* include some of those most loved by the pilgrims of the Warkari sect as they sing along the road to Pandharpur. In all, 4 600 have been ascribed to him and many were translated into English by the missionaries who saw in him, with his single-minded, apparently monotheistic devotion, a natural christian soul. His temple at Dehu is now itself a place of pilgrimage, and the palanquin that sets out from there to Pandharpur is one that has high status in the hierarchy. Extract 24 contains his *Santaciya gavi*.

Visaladevarasa. Probably composed in the middle of the 15th century AD, the *Visaladevarasa* is an approximate contemporary of the *Dhola Maru Ra Duha* ◊, another of the earliest works of Rajasthani literature, not very sophisticated and at no great distance from folk-literature. It is said to be the work of one Narapati Nalha, about whom nothing further is known. The story tells of the great king Visaladeva's wedding to Princess Rajamati of Dhar, of a quarrel, his leaving home to travel in the East, her pangs at separation from him, and their final happy reunion.

SOUTH INDIA

Geoffrey Holden

'Looking at them from outside, one may think that they lack the amenities of modern life, but actually they have no sense of missing much; on the contrary, they give the impression of living in a state of secret enchantment. The source of enchantment is the storyteller in their midst . . .'.
R.K. Narayan, Gods, Demons and Others

'Forest, mountain, field and shore'. While the four geographic regions ennumerated by the Tamil sage Tolkappiyar ◊ (Extract 18) represent a poetic landscape wherein the human drama of love and war was enacted in south India during the first centuries of the Christian era, they remain to this day an enduring image of the geographical diversity of this unique region. From the tortuous rapids and falls of the **Kaveri**, the 'Southern Ganges', to the tropical backwaters of the **Malabar Coast**, south India is adorned with a dazzling array of natural environments despoiled only by the incursions of its populous urban centres.

Geographically, south India begins below the **Vindhya Hills** and forms a triangular shaped peninsula jutting out into the Indian Ocean. Flanked to the east by the Bay of Bengal and to the west by the Arabian Sea, the land narrows in the extreme south to an apex at **Cape Comorin**. The four modern states of Tamil Nadu, Andhra Pradesh, Karnataka and Kerala lie within these geographical boundaries.

Tamil Nadu occupies some 130 000 square kilometres in the south-eastern part of the peninsula and has a population of over 48 million. The peaks of the **Western Ghats** climb towards the south, reaching 8 760 feet where they meet the **Eastern Ghats** at Dodabetta. Below the Nilgiris lies the Palghat or Coimbatore Gap, bounded to the extreme south by the **Anaimudi Peak** at a height of 8 841 feet. The principal rivers, the Krishna, Penner, Ponnaiyar, Kaveri and Vaigai rise in the west, pass through the Eastern Ghats and drain into the Bay of Bengal.

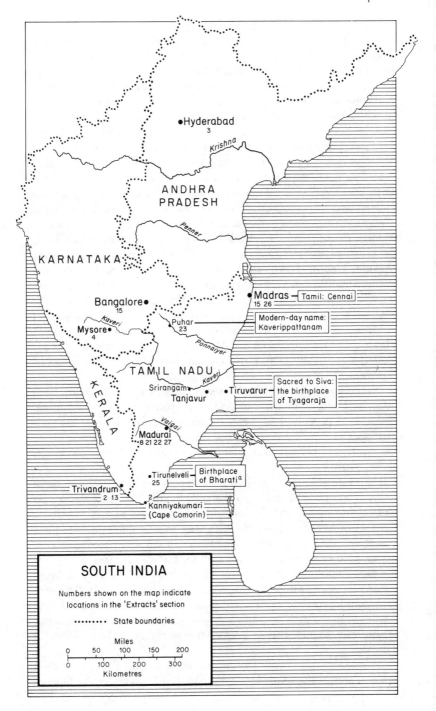

•Hyderabad
3

Krishna

ANDHRA
PRADESH

Penner

KARNATAKA

Bangalore•
15

Kaveri

Mysore•
4

Puhar
23

Ponnaiyer

TAMIL NADU

Kaveri

Srirangam•
Tanjavur•

•Tiruvarur

•Madras
15 26

Tamil: Cennai

Modern-day name:
Kaverippattanam

Sacred to Siva:
the birthplace
of Tyagaraja

K E R A L A

Vaigai

Madurai
8 21 22 27

•Tirunelveli
25

Birthplace
of Bharati[a]

Trivandrum•
2 13

Kanniyakumari
(Cape Comorin)

SOUTH INDIA

Numbers shown on the map indicate
locations in the 'Extracts' section

••••••• State boundaries

Miles
0   50   100   150   200
0   100   200   300
Kilometres

Tamil Nadu enjoys a tropical climate which is not unpleasant well away from its urban centres. The hill stations of the cool **Palni** and **Nilgiri** or 'Blue Hills' of the west offering a welcome respite from the 'hell' of Madras as the Tamil poet Mani called it (Extract 26). Lying in the path of the south-western monsoon, they have fashioned a landscape which changes from east to west. To the seaward side the rainfall is high and vegetation is luscious, dense and evergreen with an abundance of flora and fauna. Coffee, tea, teak, sandalwood, rubber and cassia are cultivated, while in the low lying deltas and drier areas rice, coconut, tobacco, sugar cane, ground nut and cotton are found.

Madras is the capital city of Tamil Nadu. It was founded in 1639 when the *Nayak* or local deputy of the Raja of Candragiri granted a tract of land to Francis Day, the chief agent of the British East India Company. Day built a fort near the shore which he named St George after the patron saint of England. Its walls still loom over Mount Road, the principal artery of the city, bounded by numerous and fascinating emporia. **George Town** which lies behind the Fort still retains the architectural flavour of its European founders. Day's settlement later became known as Madras and in 1653 the agent and council of the town were raised to the rank of presidency. A more traditional account of Madras is reported by Marco Polo, who relates how the Apostle St Thomas was martyred on a local hill in the 1st century AD. Today Madras is a cosmopolitan, populous and sprawling city with the social deprivation characteristic of all India's great urban centres.

On the seaward side of the Western Ghats are hot, humid, low lying littorals abundant in coconut and areca palms, fragrant cardamom, chillies and peppers. Rice fields extend endlessly inland up into the highlands of the Ghats, while to the south the land levels out into a wide plateau. This is **Kerala**, a land of rivers and waterfalls, rain forests and elephants.

The modern state of Kerala was established in the reorganization of Indian states in 1956 and was formed by the integration of the greater part of Travancore and Cochin with Malabar and part of the South Kanara districts of Madras state. Covering an area of just 38 863 square kilometres, but with a population of over 25 million, it is the smallest but most densely populated of all the Indian states. Legend relates how the sage Parasurama created Kerala by a throw of his *parasu* or 'axe', causing the sea to withdraw and giving the newly acquired land to some Brahmans he had brought from abroad. **Trivandrum**, the capital city, is situated in the extreme south-west of the state. It rose to prominence in the 18th century when it became the royal seat of the Maharaja of Travancore.

Bounded to the north by Maharashtra, to the East by Andhra Pradesh and to the south by Kerala and Tamil Nadu lies the modern state of **Karnataka**. Occupying an area of some 191 791 square kilometres, and counting over 30 million inhabitants, it is endowed with a salubrious climate and a wealth of natural landscapes including the fertile areas of the Kaveri and Krishna valleys and the forested Malnad or 'land of hills' which forms part of the Western Ghats, stretching from Ratnagiri in the north to Malabar in the south. Karnataka is famed far and wide for its numerous thundering waterfalls, those at Gokak, Ganganachukki, Barachukki and Jog being among the most spectacular. For a 19th century Englishman's description of the beauty of the Karnataka landscape see Extract 21.

Situated some 900 metres above sea level, **Bangalore** is the state capital of Karnataka. A modern city, it is the seat of the Indian Institute of Science and birthplace of India's atomic bomb. It is also home to the botanical garden known as Lal Bagh or 'Red Garden', a name bestowed by Hyder Ali in recognition of its abundance of red roses.

Largest of the south Indian states, with a population of some 54 million, **Andhra Pradesh** was the first linguistic state in India. As early as 1913 the Andhras had begun to agitate for a separate state and this led to the formation in 1953 of Andhra State from the northern Telugu-speaking districts of the former Madras Presidency. Subsequently the nine districts of the Nizim of Hyderabad's Dominion known as Telangana were added to form the modern state of Andhra Pradesh with **Hyderabad** as its capital.

Lying to the north of Tamil Nadu and to the east of Karnataka, Andhra Pradesh is bounded to the east by the Bay of Bengal and to the north by the states of Maharashtra, Madhya Pradesh and Orissa. Climatically **Andhra** feels rather dry in comparison to its westerly neighbours, and unbearably hot, only the Eastern Ghats with their dense forests offering some respite from summer temperatures which can soar to 40°C. Founded in the 16th century by Muhammad Quli Qutb Shah, **Hyderabad** is a sprawling city whose many mosques and graceful minarets are a constant evocation of the city's Muslim heritage.

LAND OF TEMPLES

No-one visiting south India can fail to be astonished by the number and variety of temples which adorn these southern lands. For anyone who has stood at the foot of the great temple of the goddess Minaksi at **Madurai** and gazed up at its soaring towers or *gopuram*, embellished with many exquisitely sculptured figures, the experience is unforgettable. Indeed, the Hindu temples of south India are such a remarkable feature of the southern landscape that no survey of the region would be

The Gate Tower at Maturai

complete without mentioning them. This is particularly true since they occupy such an important place in the literature of the region not only being the apocryphal location of numerous *talapuranam* or 'site-legends' (Extracts 21 and 27) and the focus of Hindu devotional hymnology

(Extracts 23 and 24), but also the dramatic setting for numerous contemporary short stories, novels and plays (such as Girish Karnad's *Naga-Mandala* in Extract 5). That the death of the poet Bharati ◊ was hastened by the unforeseen caprice of a temple elephant is perhaps symbolic of the role temples have played in the literary history of the region.

LANGUAGE AND PEOPLE

The four major languages of south India are Tamil, Telugu, Kannada and Malayalam which are spoken in the modern linguistic states of Tamil Nadu, Andhra Pradesh, Karnataka and Kerala respectively. These languages, together with several minor tongues, form an independent linguistic group which is distinct from the Indo–European family of the north, resembling in its overall logic and structure the Turkic and Finno–Ugrian tongues, though being endowed with a peculiar genius all of its own.

According to Panamparanar in his commentary to the *Tolkappiyam*, 'The good land where the Tamil language is spoken lies between the northern Venkatam [Tirupati] and the southern Kumari [Cape Comorin]'. Tamil is the oldest of the Dravidian languages, possessing a literature going back to the first centuries of the Christian era. It is rich in retroflex consonants which lend the language its characteristic musicality. Unlike the inflecting Indo–European languages, the relationship between words is indicated by suffixes and post-positions piled up one after the other, according to rigidly predetermined rules.

Kannada is spoken in the state of Karnataka and bordering areas of neighbouring states. The *Kavirajamarga*, written around 825 AD states that the region extending from the Kaveri as far as the Godavari is the region where Kannada was spoken in ancient times, and it is therefore clear that this included areas where Marathi now prevails.

Telugu was declared the official language of the modern state of Andhra Pradesh in 1966, and in the number of speakers ranks next to Hindi. Yet it is only since 1969 that the modern colloquial idiom has found a place in college and university education, English having been previously preferred. Telugu mother-tongue speakers are known as Andhras and number about 81% of the state's 43.5 million population. The largest minority language is Urdu, accounting for approximately 7% of the population with the greatest concentration in the capital city of Hyderabad at about 36%.

Four distinct regional dialects are recognized. In ancient times the Telugu country was often called Trilinga, the country which contained or was bounded by the three *linga* of Kalahasti, Srisailam and Daksharama and it is perhaps from this appellation that the word Telugu may

Girish Karnad

trace its origins. Telugu shares obvious affinities with Kannada and Tamil. Pampa and Ponna, two of the greatest Kannada poets both came from the Telugu country. Until the reign of Krishnadevaraya ◊ in the 16th century, Telugu remained very much under the spell of Sanskritic literary traditions.

Malayalam was the last of the south Indian languages to develop a separate existence and literature of its own. During the Cankam Age, so called after the literary academies or *cankam* which are said to have presided in the Tamil lands in ancient times, Kerala formed part of a larger linguistic area known as *Tamilakam* where an early form of Tamil was spoken. *Cankam* works contain many words which have survived in modern Malayalam though they have become obsolete in modern Tamil. Similarities between the two modern idioms are sufficient to make the two spoken languages mutually intelligible. Like Kannada and Telugu, Malayalam borrowed freely from Sanskrit, evolving a new script based on Tamil *Grantha* to represent the new sounds.

The lands of south India have been the meeting place of many peoples both in pre-historic and historic times, and the ethnographic make-up of the region is therefore heterogeneous. The myths which have in recent years evolved concerning the origins of the Tamils and their language should properly be regarded as a poetic reflection of the depth and richness of Tamil culture rather than historical fact.

HISTORY

It is through the poems of the *Kuruntokai* and other works composed between the 1st and 6th centuries AD that Dravidian south India first comes into historical focus (Extracts 18, 19, 20, 22). At that time it was divided into three kingdoms, the Cola, Cera, and Pantiya and a number of minor chieftaincies, several of whose rulers are mentioned as *vallal*, or patrons of bards. Allusions in poetic compositions to episodes in the *Mahabharata* and *Ramayana* (◊ 'Classical Literature'), such as Siva's destruction of the three metallic forts of the Asuras, attest to the synthesis between northern and southern traditions which was taking place. They also indicate the persistent rivalry between rulers whose epic fame was matched only by their epithets. Thus Utiyan Ceral is said to have fed sumptuously both the armies of Kurukshetra and thereby earned the epithet 'Utiyanceral of the great feeding', while his son Netunceralatan received the epithet *Imayavarampan* or 'He who had the Himalaya for his boundary' from the claim that he had conquered all of India and carved his bow emblem on the face of the Himalaya.

From around 600 AD the Deccan passed under the Calukyas while in the south, the Pallavas and the Pantiyas engaged in persistent rivalry. The period witnessed many great achievements both in literature and the arts, epitomized by the Pallava king Mahendravarman I, a kind of 7th century Renaissance Man, whose skills in painting, music, architecture and versification earned him the suitable epithet *vicitracitta* or 'wonderful mind'. A pragmatic genius, he professed Jainism for a time but discarded it in favour of Saivism when the tide of history turned against Jainism and Buddhism in the south and the two theistic Hindu sects of Saivism and Vaisnavism were in the ascendant. These latter sects found expression in a genre of devotional verse known as *bhakti* wherein the devotee is nurtured on the grace bestowed by a personal deity.

The middle of the 9th century saw the reemergence of Cola power from obscurity. Two successive rulers, Rajaraja I and his son Rajendra I now united the whole of southern India at a time when north India was divided into weak and warring states and suffering the incursions of Islamic powers. The Colas operated a highly organized administrative system noted for its encouragement of autonomous village assemblies. A credible navy was also established which helped to keep potential enemies in check. The reigns of these two kings witnessed the construction of two of South India's greatest temples, that at **Tanjore** under Rajaraja I, and the temple and surrounding town of **Gankaikon-tacolapuram** or 'the town of the Cola who took the Ganges' by his son Rajendra.

The 12th and 13th centuries were a golden age for literature, philosophy and architecture in the southern lands. While Sanskrit learning and literature found ready patronage, Kannada, Telugu and Tamil were also cultivated. The *Ramayana* and *Mahabharata* were translated into these languages by celebrated poets, while a large body of devotional, polemical, grammatical and commentarial literature also emerged. Devotional theism was harmonized with Upanisadic doctrine by a series of religious philosophers, chief of whom was Ramanuja who taught at the temple in Srirangam. Many large temples were constructed and sculptural and allied arts achieved new levels of excellence. Numerous *talapuranam* or 'site-legends' evolved, one of the more enchanting being that connected with the goddess Minaksi and her consort Siva at their temple in **Maturai**, even today an important pilgrim centre for Hindus from all over India (Extract 21). It is here that Lord Siva performed 64 *tiruvilaiyatal* or 'divine pranks', amongst which was the feeding of the gluttonous *putam* Kuntotaran who on account of his voracious appetite threatened to become the 'Destroyer of the Ages' (Extract 27).

From the beginning of the 14th century, the Delhi sultans brought a period of plundering and destruction to southern India, fortunately short-lived. Their far-flung empire could not put down the many revolts against its imperial rule; these precipitated the formation of two new kingdoms in the Deccan in the first half of the 14th century, the Muslim Bahmani kingdom of Gulbarga and the Hindu kingdom of Vijayanagar. Under constant threat from its Muslim neighbours, the Vijayanagar Kingdom became a bastion of resurgent Hindu culture with Krishnadevaraya ◊ as absolute ruler. Under his patronage Telugu scholarship attained its golden age, his court being adorned by many excellent luminaries.

In 1565 the Kingdom of Vijayanagar fell to a confederation of Muslim states. In Kerala the Portuguese occupation which had begun with Vasco da Gama's arrival at **Calicut** in 1498 continued to impoverish and demoralize the people, and precipitated a late tradition of devotional verse with the poet Eluttaccan ◊ in the vanguard (see Extract 10). After the decline of Portuguese power, south India was exposed to the successive incursions of the Danes, French, Dutch and British who fought out their domestic rivalries on Indian soil. The rise of British power owed much to the persistent squabbling of feudatory states whose rivalry made them easy prey to political and financial bribery. After 34 years of intrigue, deceit and bloodshed which culminated in the annexation of the Carnatic in 1801, British power held sway over the whole of southern India. The subsequent fight for independence formed part of the greater struggle for freedom which gripped the whole of India during the long years leading up to 1947. Yet for the Tamils the struggle for freedom from the British assumed another dimension, freedom from domination by the north, whether real or imagined. This infra-nationalism found expression in the DMK, or *Tamil Progressive Federation*, with an anti-brahman, anti-north Indian, anti-Sanskrit platform, mixing politics, religion, language, race and mythology.

Pre-modern Literature

The earliest extant literary works in any Dravidian language were composed in an early form of Tamil and belong to a period not later than the 6th century and not earlier than the 1st century AD. Legend quite naturally postulates an earlier pedigree.

Tamil tradition related in the commentary to the Iraiyanar Akapporul (c 750 AD) tells of three cankam or 'literary academies' which met at **Maturai**, lasted a total of 9 990 years and counted 8 598 poets, including several Saivite gods! While the grammar Tolkappiyam is traditionally assigned to the second cankam, it was the third cankam, presided over by Nakkirar (Extract 27) which was responsible for the Eight Anthologies, a huge body of works consisting principally of heroic poetry with much eloquent panegyric, and love poetry of an exquisite simplicity of form. One of the best known describes a King's thoughts in his garden. While the bee is ever in search of nectar, are there any flowers more fragrant than the tresses of his lady (see Extracts 21 and 22)? In another poem from the *Kuruntokai*, a collection of 400 short love poems, the lady bewails the separation from her lover as she stands on the seashore: 'Will the bright blossoms of the Neem Tree wither now I am alone?' These works, together with the *Pattupatu* or 'Ten Songs', the *Cilappatikaram* ◊ (Extract 23), *Manimekalai, Civakacin-*

tamani, Kuntalakeci and *Valaiyapati* known collectively as the 'Five Epics', and the 'Eighteen Minor Works' known in Tamil as *Patinenkilk-kanakku*, comprise the early period of Tamil literature.

Tamil grammarians from an early period developed what is tantamount to a mania for classification. Poetry was classified according to two complementary poetic concepts, *akam*, which denotes 'that which is interior', and which is concerned with the various emotional aspects of love, and *puram* or 'that which is exterior' which deals with war and the praise of kings. *Akam* was further classified into five aspects, namely union, separation, awaiting, wailing and quarrelling, each of which was associated with a *tinai* or region: *kurinci* (hills), *palai* (desert), *mullai* (forest), *neytal* (seashore) and *marutam* (fields), each being ruled over by a particular god. These regions received their names from the flowers which were to be found growing there. Similarly *puram* was divided into seven *tinai* or poetic regions six of which are the names of plants. Garlands made from these were worn at different stages of battle. Together with other classifications concerning time and seasons, melody types, birds and beasts, pastimes and occupations, these poetic conventions have produced a corpus of literature of inestimable richness which will delight all who may care to read it.

The later medieval period is characterized by Saiva and Vaisnava devotional literature to which the appellation *bhakti* has been given. The *Tevarum* or Garland of God which dates from the 7th or 8th century is a Saiva work important even today in Tamil hymnology. The *Tiruppavai* composed by the Vaisnava poetess Antal and the Saiva *Tiruvempavai* composed by Manikkavacakar are two of the best loved hymns of the Tamil poet-saints. During the Markali Festival which runs from 15 December to 15 January, they may be heard in the early mornings broadcast over the radio and via loud speakers set up for the occasion. The legend connected with the poetess represents perhaps the quintessence of the psychology of bhakti devotion. Antal's love for the deity having become excessive, she was taken in bridal procession by her father to the object of her devotion in Srirangam, where she 'merged' with the deity never to be seen again.

Of all the works of the medieval period, the *Tirukkural* by Tiruvalluvar is perhaps the best known, having been translated into several languages. Described by one scholar as 'a beacon of light for the world', it is more properly a book of maxims based on Sanskrit teaching on the *Purasarthas*, and much prized by Tamilians.

The first work in Kannada of any literary merit is Sivakoti's *Vaddaradhane*, a prose work on the lives of the older Jaina saints written around 900 AD in the oldest Kannada style called *purvahala kannada*. During the 10th century a trio of poets, Pampa, Ponna and Ranna composed further works on the Jaina saints or *Tirthankara* and versions of the Sanskrit *Mahabharata* and *Ramayana*. Although Jaina writers continued to flourish over the next centuries, particularly in the Tuluva country where two colossal Jaina statues were erected at **Karkala** in 1431 and at **Yenur** in 1603, from the 14th century onwards Jainism in the Kannada lands declined as it had elsewhere in the south at the expense of Saivism and Vaisnavism, whose flower-garlanded deities, presiding in ornamented temples extended to their devotees the possibility of spiritual union with a personal god. The new faith was expressed as elsewhere in a literature of devotion called *bhakti*, many of whose adherents were women. The poetess Mahadeviyakka ◊ was one of the more illustrious (see Extract 13).

The period up to 1650 marks some important changes in Kannada literature. Distinctive Kannada metres like the *shatpadi* and *tripadi* and lyrical poems called *ragale* came into vogue. As royal patronage declined, Kannada literature gradually freed itself from the influence of Sanskritic convention and the spoken language became a legitimate vehicle of literary expression.

The earliest extant work in Telugu is a translation of the Sanskrit *Mahabharata* in the reign of Rajaraja Narendra (c 1019 AD), by Nannaya. This was followed in the 13th and 14th centuries by translations of the Sanskrit *Ramayana*, both serving as vehicles for the propagation of Brahmanism which from the 12th century onwards was in the ascendant at the expense of Jainism and Buddhism. The poet Srinatha, a great devotee of Siva, stands somewhat apart from the Sanskritic tradition. Though he translated Sriharsha's *Naishadakavya*, he is also credited with inventing the *Kridabhiramam*, a kind of drama and of a number of *catu* or 'stray verses' on miscellaneous subjects. These are highly prized by Telugu speakers even today. From the beginning of the 16th century the practice of translating from Sanskrit originals was gradually replaced by Telugu *prabandha*. Taking their inspiration from the Sanskrit *mahakavya* or 'great poem', they were similarly embellished with superfluous ornamentation. The *prabandha* achieved its high water mark under the patronage of Krishnadevaraya, himself no mean scholar and poet. His *Amuktamalyada* or 'The Giver of the Worn Garland' which deals with the life of the *alvar* Visnucitta, and the love of his foster daughter Goda for the god Ranganatha, is counted among the five great *kavya* of Telugu literature, marking the beginning of Vaisnava influence on Telugu poetic composition. Another poet, Timmana, is known for his *Parijatapaharana*, said to have been composed to reconcile Krishnadevaraya to one of his queens, whom he fatuously believed had insulted him by sleeping with her legs stretched out towards his portrait!

In the 17th century the fall of the Vijayanagar empire and its division into a number of feudatory courts brought a decline in the fortune of the Andhras and their literature. The period up to the last decades of the 19th century is sometimes called the 'Age of Despair', though perhaps inappropriately since it also marks the appearance of a number of important prose works of which the *Valmikicaritram* of Raghunatha Nayak at Tanjore is the first. Inappropriate too, since it was at Tiruvarur in Tanjore District in the 18th century that the incomparable Tyagaraja composed the priceless gems which are today performed by all musicians following the Karnatic or southern style of Indian music.

In the 19th century Chinnaya Suri published two works, the *Niticandrika* and *Balavyakaranamu*, which upheld an archaic form of prose known as *granthika*, and were largely to blame for the fossilization of Telugu prose which remained in a kind of classical time-warp well into the 20th century. The absence of a flexible, modern idiom was a serious handicap for Telugu writers at a time when Tamil and Malayalam had already made significant strides towards a modern, literary idiom.

Malayalam illustrates more lucidly than any other in the southern family the perfect synthesis of Dravidian and Sanskritic elements within a single literary language. It is a language which must surely rank today amongst the most dynamic of all the modern Indian literary idioms. This was achieved through the interaction of three literary traditions; the Tamil *pattu* or 'song', a hybrid Malayalam–Sanskrit style known as *manipravalam*, and a tradition of folk songs and ballads sung in the colloquial language of the common folk called by some *Pacha Malayalam* or 'pure Malayalam'. These produced in the 15th century the *Krisna pattu* or *Krisna gatha*, attributed to a poet traditionally known as Cherusseri Nambudiri who adorned the court of King Udayavarman of Kolathunad.

During the 16th and 17th centuries the oppressive regime inflicted on the Malabars by the Portuguese precipitated a devotional genre known as *Kilippattu* or 'Parrot songs' which were recited through the symbolic medium of a bird or even a bee. Its outstanding exponent was Tuncattu Eluttaccan ◊ (Extract 10) who came to be regarded as the 'father' of the Malayalam language and was endowed with many wonderful legends. One of these tells how his birth was foretold in the stars, while another relates how Eluttaccan resisted the sorcery of some jealous brahmans by divine grace.

In recent years Kerala has become famous for a variety of dance-drama known as *Kathakali* which is based upon ancient stories called *purana*. The actors neither speak nor sing and meaning is conveyed through *mudra* or gestures. The colour and pattern of the make-up worn by the actors indicate the type of character which is being represented. The storyline or *attakatha* is narrated in words and songs by a small group who stand to the rear. The earliest extant *attakatha* is *The Story of Nala* dating from the 16th or 17th century.

MODERN LITERATURES

After European rule had been consolidated in India, traditional forms of literary expression became inadequate to deal with the process of confrontation which was now taking place between the two mutually antagonistic cultures. During the 18th and early 19th centuries it was above all Christianity which exerted an impact on the literatures of south India, though in Andhra it was never so great as that experienced further south. This impact was felt not only in terms of its own literary production but also in providing literary models for converts and opponents alike. European scholars such as Bishop Robert Caldwell ◊ were much impressed by the refined qualities of the Dravidian languages and, Telugu apart, reliable modern grammars and dictionaries began to appear. Classical and medieval manuscripts were collected and published on the new printing presses introduced by Christian missionaries. These texts, full of startling historical revelations, did much to encourage a Tamil renaissance in the second half of the 19th century, while the birth and growth of journalism, at first Christian-orientated, led to a proliferation of journals and periodicals written in the vernacular tongues.

The first attempts at modern prose were made in the latter half of the 19th century, guided by European models. In Tamil, Samuel Vetanayakam Pillai's ◊ *Piratapa Mutaliyar Carittiram* published in 1879 was written, so the author tells us, with a view to entertain. Yet like his contemporaries he regarded the European epic novel as the sublime expression of the 'greatness' of European nationhood: 'Thus as long as there do not appear prose-epics in our own languages, this country will definitely make no real progress.' It is a view which has not been vindicated by history. Inspired by the European Romantic tradition, a surfeit of historical compositions followed, epitomized by the tear-jerking romances of R. Krishnamurthi ◊, alias Kalki, which graced the pages of *Anantavikatan* and afterwards his own journal *Kalki* for week after week from the late 1920s to the late 1950s.

Modern verse too turned to European models for its inspiration. B.M. Shrikantaiah's *English Geethegalu* or 'English Poems', a translation of a number of recognized English Romantics into Kannada, reflected the growing frustration with the traditional forms of Kannada verse such as the *campu*, and signalled the search for a new poetic medium able to cast light on the shifting patterns of Indian society. While verse continued to look to European models for form and subject it could not help but remain imitative, though that is not to say that some outstanding works were not composed both in prose and verse during this period. The Romantic tradition in Malayalam poetry had culminated in 1909 with Kumaran Asan's *Vina Purvu*, 'The Fallen Flower', an elegiac composition of much beauty and stylistic merit. The indigenous Romantic movement, however sublime, could be valid only in the short term. The freedom struggle demanded poets of a different metal.

In the first decades of the 20th century a sharpening of tensions between the Indians and the British precipitated an intellectual and emotional call to freedom. In his poem 'My Teacher', the Malayali poet Vallathol raised Gandhi to the ethereal levels of a god, while Subramania Bharati's ◊ call of 'Freedom! Freedom! Freedom!' rang out at political rallies across the country. The cause of the minority and the individual also had its champions. Bharati himself was a fierce opponent of the caste system, while his 'Freedom for Women' speaks for itself.

The freedom struggle did not, however, favour everyone. Writers of Indian English whose literary careers had been launched by a fortuitous concatenation of historical, cultural and political circumstances were confronted with increasing antagonism as the national movement gathered pace during the 1930s. When India gained independence in 1947 this antagonism culminated in the enshrining of Hindi as the official language of the Union. It is not without some irony that a language which had been the object of such vehement detestation should be replaced by another which in the south at least was even more vigorously disliked.

The breaking free from a political yoke which had always implied a kind of domestication of the Indian spirit coincided quite understandably with a breaking free from the literary chains of the past. In the period leading up to independence a new vitality entered literary composition. Inspired by Marxist and humanist traditions, south Indian writers turned more and more to the social deprivations of everyday life. The experience of the common man and woman became their obsession. The short story became more and more a vehicle of humanist and progressive ideologies and their communication to the masses via the pages of literary journals.

Chandu Menon's ◊ *Indulekha* published in 1889 had already hinted at things to come in its portrayal of the conflict between traditional and modern social structures among the Nayar and Nambudiri communities of Kerala. Now Kesava Dev, one of the earliest Malayali writers to focus on the downtrodden of society came forth with *From the Gutter*. In this novel, the rickshaw puller Pappu, a kind of working class hero, brings up an orphan girl as his own daughter. Educated, she is attracted to a wealthy young man and marries him, while Pappu, who has by this time contracted tuberculosis, lives out the rest of his life in poverty.

Another writer from Kerala, Vaikom Muhammad Basheer, dealt with controversial issues amongst his own Muslim community, while Ponkunnam Varkey protested against the orthodoxy of the Christian Church. Putumaippittan, one of the *Manikkoti* group of Tamil writers, lamented the transitory nature of the human condition. His work is both disturbing and exhilarating, nowhere better experienced than in 'Street Lamp' (Extract 28). Among Malayalam poetry of the 1930s, N.V. Krishna Variyar's 'Rats' is a brutal affirmation of the belief held by the 'progressive' poets that poetry must serve the cause of the ordinary folk (Extract 12).

Literary production during the Freedom Struggle also reflected a growing awarness of political identity at the infra-national level. The notion of a traditional 'homeland' with real or imagined historical validity had of course always been apparent to the Tamils since the days of the *Tolkappiyam* (Extract 18). When Subraminia Bharati composed his 'Mother Tamil' he was merely echoing a national ethos which had existed for centuries (Extract 25). But infra-nationalism was not peculiar to Tamil. Telugu too had its champion in the shape of Visvanantha Satyanarayana whose passionate love of the Telugu land and people was complimented by a firm belief in the superiority of Indian culture over that of the Europeans.

The 1940s which had seen the evolution of humanist and progressive themes also witnessed their decline. Social realism was an inevitable blind alley in a world which dreamt of a golden age yet to come. Readers as well as writers became sick of simple, ugly realism devoid of imagination. Into this well of disillusionment came Thakali Sivasankara Pillai ◊. Known in his native Kerala chiefly for his short stories, Thakali had already made excursions into social realism with *Scavengers Son* and *Two Measures*, when *Shrimps* (*Chemmeen*), announced a new direction. In this novel Thakali carefully disected the dubious morality of a community of fisherfolk against the backdrop of their superstitious fear of the sea, which in its reference to the goddess Katalamma approaches the quality of fable (Extract 11).

In the 1950s and 1960s socially committed writers continued to believe their exhortations to social justice could bring about revolution. This has clearly not been the case. True, stories such as *Cyclone* by the Telugu writer Palagummi Padmaraju continued to press the socialist cause. Unemployment, dowry menace, the deprivations of the rural and urban poor continued to find expression (Extract 1).

However, by the 1960s writing in all four literary languages had moved away from the socialist platform towards an existentialist or pessimistic mode, no better illustrated than by the works of M.T. Vasudevan Nair, the most popular novelist in Malayalam of the 1960s. His youthful heroes, paralysed by a morbid fear of their elders, pierced by disillusion and alienated from society, drift aimlessly through life like ghosts. In *Dragon Seed* the author introduces us to the hero Govindankutty who has all the characteristics of a latter day Oblomov as 'Day after day he sits watching the river where the uprooted vegetation from the subsiding banks whirls round in eddies without any progression. His days too whirl around him like ghosts that have not been laid to rest'.

The 1960s also witnessed an increasing interest in the psychology of human relationships. Sexual and other formally taboo themes were tackled with enthusiasm, as attested by the pen of the Kerala poetess Kamala Das (◊, Extract 9). The publication in 1962 of *New Voices* by a group of Tamil poets was another indication that the literary status quo was crumbling. While these poets traced their descent from the likes of Bharati, Putumaippittan and Pichamurti, their work represents a break with tradition though not a negation of cultural heritage. In Kannada too the English Romantic inspired *Navodya* movement which had prevailed during the first decades of the 20th century had by the 1940s given way to progressive themes influenced by Marxist and socialist ideologies. However, post-independence writers frustrated with social-ist ideas which had brought neither political nor literary revolution now came up with *Navya Kavya* (New Poetry), whose greatest protagonists, Gopalakrishna Adiga and Ramachandra Sharma, were like their Tamil counterparts experimentalist in subject and form, frequently startling, occasionally shocking.

Since the 1970s thousands of short stories, novels, poems and plays have been written in south Indian languages. It is clearly not possible to list them all here. While some writers continue to rake the ashes of the burning ground others sparkle with the colours of imagination. Age-old tradition jostles shoulder to shoulder with the newest of the new. So broad is the spectrum of literary composition in south India today that, as Gopalakrishna Adiga says:

> One must crawl hereafter, groping along the walls;
> The blind man rides the lame:
> How the path unfolds remains to be seen.
>
> *Song of the Earth*

BOOKLIST

Atikal, Prince Ilanko, *Cilappatikar-am*, Alain Danielou, trans, George Allen & Unwin, London, 1967. **Extract 23.**

Bharati, Subramania, 'Mother Tamil' in P.S. Sundaram, ed, *Poems of Subramania Bharati*, Vikas Publishing, Delhi/Jodhpur University Press, 1982. **Extract 25.**

Das, Kamala, *The Dance of the Eunuchs* in A.N. Dwivedi, *Indian Poetry in English: A Literary History and Anthology*, Arnold Heinemann (India), 1980. **Extract 9.**

Elliot, Robert H., *The Experiences of a Planter in the Jungles of Mysore*, Chapman and Hall, London, 1891. **Extract 4.**

Eluttaccan, *Mahabharatam*, in K.M. George, trans, *A Survey of Malayalam Literature*, Asia Publishing House, 1968. **Extract 10.**

Forster, E.M., *A Passage to India*, Penguin, 1982, p 137. **Extract 14.**

Frater, Alexander, *Chasing the Monsoon*, Viking, 1990. **Extract 13.**

Karanath, K. Shivaram, *Chomas Drum*, U.R. Kalkur, trans, Indian Book Company, New Delhi. **Extract 7.**

Karnad, Girish, *Naga-Mandala*, Oxford University Press, Delhi, 1990. **Extract 5.**

'Kuruntokai', J.B. Marr, trans, *The Eight Anthologies*, Institute of Asian Studies, Tiryvanmiyur, Madras. **Extract 22.**

Mani, 'Narakam' in *The Smile of Murugan*, K. Zvelebil, trans, Leiden, 1973. **Extract 26.**

Naipaul, V.S., *An Area of Darkness*, Andre Deutsch, 1964, p 217. **Extract 30.**

Narayan, R.K., *Gods, Demons and Others*, Heinemann, 1965. **Extract 17.**

Narayan, R.K., *Malgudi Days*, Heinemann, 1977. **Extracts 15 and 16.**

Nath, Kedar, *Return to India*, Cassells, London, 1988. **Extract 2.**

Padmaraju, Palagumi, 'Cyclone', *Indian Literature*, Vol XXIX, No 5, Sahitya Akademi, Rabindra Bhavan, New Delhi, 1986. **Extract 1.**

Pillai, Thakali Sivasankara, *Chemmeen*, Narayana Menon, trans, Gollancz, London. **Extract 11.**

Putmaipittan, 'Street Lamp', in G.J. Holden, trans, *Putmaipittan Katikal*, Star, Madras, 1959. **Extract 28.**

'Mahadeviyakka', in Ramanujan, A.K., *Speaking of Siva*, Penguin, Harmondsworth, 1973. **Extract 6.**

Ramanujam A.K., 'Art and Life's Beauty', in Dhenaveera Kanavi and K. Raghavendra Rao, eds, *Modern Kannada Poetry*, K. Raghavendra Rao, trans, C.S. Kanavi, Dharwar. **Extract 8.**

Ramaswamy, Sundara, 'Window', Ashokamitran, trans, in Ka Naa Sumbramaniyam, ed, *Tamil Short Stories*, Vikas, New Delhi, 1980. **Extract 29.**

Roosevelt, Eleanor, *India and the Awakening East*, Hutchinson, London 1954. **Extract 3.**

Taylor, William, *Oriental History Manuscripts in the Tamil Language*, Vol 1. **Extract 21.**

Variyar, N.V. Krishna, 'Rats', in K.M. George, trans, *A Survey of Malayalam Literature*, Asia Publishing House, Delhi, 1968. **Extract 12.**

Extracts

(1) ANDHRA PRADESH

Palagumi Padmaraju, 'Cyclone'

In 'Cyclone' Palagumi contrasts, to use his own words, 'the reactions of two individuals, one accustomed to a secure life, the other living from moment to moment in an uncertain world, to the fury of the cyclone'.

It was very dark outside. The wind was gathering more strength. The train moved very slowly. Rao was nearing his destination. He was hoping some members of the Theists' Club would be at the station. It was going to be a problem getting his things out. The wind roared outside like an angry ocean. He could hear the crash of falling trees.

The beggar woman sat facing the young couple. She began 'There is my little mother here. And there is the little father too. Little mother! Have pity on this poor woman and ask father to spare me a coin. Why do you turn away like that? Has my little mother had a quarrel with my little father? Little father smokes too much. Little mother should not allow it. Ah! my little mother is smiling.'

'Give her something and send her away', said the young woman.

'I know my little mother is very kind-hearted. Now grandfather will also give me something. I should not have annoyed him. I know he is a very kind man.'

Everybody gave her something except Rao. They were all amused by her talk. But Rao's mind was pre-occupied. He was thinking of the storm and his approaching destination.

The train had stopped. Rao did not know it for some moments. Umbrella in hand, he got up and opened the door. The wind threw him back with such force that he almost fell down. The beggar woman offered to carry his things down. He did not stop her. He ran across the platform into the shelter of the station. The beggar woman staggered with the burden of his luggage behind him and put the things in the waiting room. There was not a single light anywhere in the station. He took some money out and offered it to the woman. She did not actually refuse it, but said something which he could not make out, and was gone the next moment.

(2) ANDHRA TO KERALA

Kedar Nath, *Return to India*

*The narrator has met Helmut, a backpacking German, on a bus
to Kerala. In the incident that follows, Kedar Nath contrasts
Indian and European attitudes to petty corruption.*

Our conversation was cut short by a commotion at the front of the bus.
Its cause, so it seemed, was a tall, powerfully built man who had got on
the bus a few minutes earlier. His air of authority came not only from
his large hypnotic eyes above his grey handlebar moustache, but also
from his stentorian voice that reflected his official position.

He was an inspector, as I found out from one of my fellow passengers.
Near him stood a medium-sized young man in khaki shirt and trousers.
He was the bus conductor. He had been cocky, even arrogant. Now he
was nervously fingering his leather pouch and looked thoroughly
scared. It turned out that he had taken the fare from a passenger at
Trivandrum, but not given him a ticket yet. The inspector was all for
penalizing him: a fine of 10 rupees would have been enough to spoil his
service record.

The driver, a wiry chap with a hatchet face, was pleading for the
conductor. Both of them were natives of Kerala.

'But he committed the same offence the day before yesterday,' the
inspector, a Tamil Nadu man, told him in English. 'My dear sir, you are
nobody, I am nobody, but it is corrupt people like this gentleman here
who have built palatial houses for themselves in big cities. At any rate,
I have caught him red-handed again. He must understand that it is a
state bus service and not his private company.'

'Forgive him, sir,' appealed the driver. 'He is new to the job; he does
not yet know the rules of service. This will be a lesson to him. He won't
do such a thing next time.'

'You deserve a bunch of roses for what you have said,' the inspector
remarked, 'but I have my duty to perform.'

An old woman called out:

'Do give him a chance, inspector. Anybody can make a mistake.
Have pity on him.'

Several other people joined in the plea for mercy.

The inspector, who was beginning to soften a little, put up his hand
and asked for silence.

'Has anyone else a complaint against this person?' he then shouted.

In reply, some people shook their heads, while others murmured: 'No
– no complaint.'

'Well, in that case . . .' came from the inspector as he was turning in
the opposite direction.

Suddenly a finger shot up into the air.

'Here!' Helmut was saying aloud. 'I have a complaint to make.'

The other swung round:

'Really? Go on, I am listening.'

'He sold me the ticket but didn't give the change owing to me, saying he had none,' Helmut reported.

'What was the amount involved?'

'A trifle – only 10 paise. I don't mind the money, but I don't like to be cheated.'

'Ah, this is serious!' the inspector turned to the conductor, who mumbled something by way of explanation. 'May I have your name and address, please?'

Helmut took out a card and passed it on to him.

The inspector looked at it in a puzzled sort of way, as if he could not make it out. 'What nationality are you?'

'German. Helmut Hühnerfuss is my name.' Hühnerfuss means chickenfoot; I repressed a smile. The inspector gave the card another look before slipping it into his brief-case.

'Well,' he told the conductor, 'you certainly are making India popular among foreigners.'

By now almost everybody was trying to placate him, so he let the culprit off with a final warning. A moment later the conductor came up to Helmut. His manner, as he handed back the amount, was rigidly formal, thinly masking his shaken confidence.

'You really want him to lose his job?' asked the driver when we arrived in Kanya Kumari.

(3) HYDERABAD

Eleanor Roosevelt, *India and the Awakening East*

In the following passage Eleanor Roosevelt, wife of Franklin D. Roosevelt, who visited India in 1954 at the invitation of Prime Minister Nehru, reveals all the innocence of the proverbial 'American in Paris'.

All through my trip I had been hearing of the dreadful famine conditions in the whole Madras area, where after six years of drought, people were experiencing indescribable hunger. The lucky ones were being kept alive on one little bowl of gruel a day; others even boiled leaves to stay the pangs of hunger. I had intended going there from Bangalore, but I had begun to feel somewhat weary; also the constant flying had affected my ears . . . Reluctantly I decided it would be wiser to travel at a more leisurely pace, so we went directly to Hyderabad.

The first day we spent in Hyderabad was the beginning of the Holi carnival, an ancient Indian festival when people gather in the streets and throw brightly coloured dyes at one another. I understand that the dyes are made of talc tinted with a colour and mixed with crushed micas; whatever their composition they are most effective: the streets, people's clothes and hair and skin are brilliantly stained for several days. This first day of Holi the fun seemed fairly mild and most of the participants were young people. Nevertheless, having no spare clothes to throw away, we took no chances and tried to stay out of the way of the revellers.

Hyderabad is a walled city with, I believe, eight gates. Towards the end of the day we visited one part of the fortifications surrounding the old capital. The light as the sun set and the moon rose on the walls gave the scene a fairyland look, and we climbed up inside and stood on top of a wall that looked over the great plains.

(4) KARNATAKA

Robert H. Elliot, *The Experiences of a Planter in the Jungles of Mysore*

An Englishman describes the beauty of the south Indian landscape as it existed still relatively undefiled in the latter half of the 19th century.

In the year 1885 I sailed for India, with a trifling capital, and with that firm belief in my own capabilities which is common to youth, and which one looks back upon in after life with mingled feelings of wonder and amusement. With my capital and belief I landed at Bombay, and a week later embarked for Mangalore in a salt-laden native craft (Patama), the use of which I hired for the sum of thirty five florins. We sailed down the palm-fringed coast, with that sublime indifference to time and progress which is the wonder, and not unfrequently the envy, of Europeans. The craft moved lazily onwards, the hubble-bubble passed from mouth to mouth, and the crew whiled away the hours with the aid of their monotonous chants. Sometimes we stopped for fishing, sometimes we ran into a little harbour to land some salt and to take in water and coconuts. At last, and after nine days' sail, we reached our destination.

After toiling up the Munzerabad ghaut we gained an elevation of about 3 500 feet above sea-level. Let us toil up some 1 500 more, and take a bird's eye of the country from one of those lofty summits which overhang the passes farther north. We choose the earliest dawn, partly to avoid the tropical sun, partly for the chance of a shot at a bear or bison, and to climb through the region of the morning mists into the purer atmosphere of the highest peaks. At last the topmost height is gained, and we look down on the misty sea which shrouds the land below. But the milky vapour soon yields to the rays of the fierce tropical sun, till peak after peak of the lesser hills appear like islets in the ocean; and presently the rising breeze and the fast-mounting sun dissolve and dissipate those aerial 'draperies' which hide the landscape from view.

(5) KARNATAKA

Girish Karnad, *Naga-Mandala*

The merging of truth and fiction in Rani's otherwise empty life is announced and symbolised in this opening scene.

PROLOGUE

(*The inner sanctum of a ruined temple. The idol is broken, so the presiding deity of the temple cannot be identified.*

It is night. Moonlight seeps in through the cracks in the roof and the walls.

A man is sitting in the temple. Long silence. Suddenly, he opens his eyes wide. Closes them. Then uses his fingers to pry open his eyelids. Then he goes back to his original morose stance.

He yawns involuntarily. Then reacts to the yawn by shaking his head violently, and turns to the audience.)

MAN: I may be dead within the next few hours.

(*Long pause.*)

I am not talking of 'acting' dead. Actually dead. I might die right in front of your eyes.

(*Pause.*)

A mendicant told me: 'You must keep awake at least one whole night this month. If you can do that, you'll live. If not, you will die on the last night of the month.' I laughed out loud when I heard him. I thought nothing would be easier than spending a night awake.

(*Pause.*)

I was wrong. Perhaps death makes one sleepy. Every night this month I have been dozing off before even being aware of it. I am convinced I am seeing something with these eyes of mine, only to wake up and find I was dreaming. Tonight is my last chance.

(*Pause.*)

For tonight is the last night of the month. Even of my life, perhaps? For how do I know sleep won't creep in on me again as it has every night so far? I may doze off right in front of you. And that will be the end of me.

(*Pause.*)

I asked the mendicant what I had done to deserve this fate. And he said: 'You have written plays. You have staged them.

(6) KARNATAKA

Mahadeviyakka

Having betrothed herself to Mallikarjuna, the presiding deity of the temple at Udutati, the poetess addresses her Lord as Cennamallikarjuna, the Beautiful Lord White as Jasmine.

> My body is dirt,
> my spirit is space:
>   which
> shall I grab, O Lord? How
> and what,
>   shall I think of you?
>   cut through
>   my illusions,
>   lord white as jasmine.

(7) KARNATAKA

K. Shivaram Karanath, *'Choma's Drum'*

As a setting for his indictment of bonded labour, the author introduces us to Bhogana Village set deep in the Karnataka jungle.

It is pitch dark.

The fearsome forest is dark which even the fireflies do not twinkle anywhere to breach. In the dead stillness not a leaf stirs, not a worm rustles under the dry leaves that lie thick on the ground, nothing. Sound? Not even a token of it.

The jungle creatures seem to have vowed silence. The panther that growls nightly from one corner of the jungle or the other, the owls that challenge the nocturnal silence, the insects that fill the air with earsplitting screech – all are hushed.

This is Bhogana village – a village in the depth of the hillside jungle, embracing about fifty houses and two hundred people. Just now there is no sign of any human beings; no light shines from any window. It is ten, maybe eleven at night.

After all these disagreeable signs you may ask. What does it matter whether such a village exists or not? As though in answer there suddenly comes a sound shattering the silence. It is difficult to say where it comes from.

In this terrain, every sound rolling back and forth from hillock to hillock, mingles with its echo and re-echo before impinging on the ears. Damadhamma, dakadhakka. It goes on for eight or ten minutes, sometimes slow like the fall of a hammer at a smithy, sometimes frantic like the pounding heart of an animal in its last gasp.

(8) KARNATAKA: MATURAI

A.K. Ramanujan, 'Art and Life's Beauty'

In characteristic enigmatic style the poet offers an alternative interpretation of the Dance of Siva.

In one of Madhurai's dirty streets,
The face of this male leper
Is splintered.
    A face without a nose,
Hands with fingers chopped off,
    And feet
Without ankles.
    Sweet pudding of pus ringing the eyes
Is infested with mosquitoes,
    The wound serves
As a snake-headed flower to peacock-hued flies.
    His wife by his side
Dons a new marriage bracelet round her neck.
    Behind him
The door-keeping heavenly courtesans
Of a centuries' old temple.
    Below the smashed nose
The thirty-second principle proclaimed in sculptural science
Through a gentle smile.
    Even in the thighs broken by the grandson
Of Khilji, Time incarnate, the display of the triple dancing pose.
    In the locket between the thighs
The Tamil rowdies'
Sanskrit.
Remembering these two,
In America, on Art and Life, I
Delivered lectures.
    They all appreciated it highly.

(9) KERALA

Kamala Das, 'The Dance of the Eunuchs'

An encounter with a band of eunuchs can be intimidating to the uninitiated. Within Indian tradition they are nevertheless regarded with considerable awe and have counted kings amongst their patrons.

It was so hot, so hot before the eunuchs came
To dance, wide skirts going round and round, cymbals
Richly clashing, and anklets jingling, jingling,
Jingling . . . Beneath the fiery gulmohur, with
Long braids flying, dark eyes flashing, they danced and they danced,
   oh, they danced til they bled . . . There were green
Tatoos on their cheeks, jasmines on their hair, some
Were dark and some were almost fair. Their voices
Were harsh, their songs melancholy; they sang of
Lovers dying and of children left unborn . . .
Some beat their drums; others beat their sorry breasts
And wailed, and writhed in vacant ecstacy. They
Were thin in limbs and dry; like half-burnt logs from
Funeral pyres, a drought and rottenness
Were in each of them. Even crows were so
Silent on trees, and the children, wide eyed, still;
All were watching these poor creatures' convulsions.
The sky crackled then, thunder came, and lightening
And rain, a meagre rain that smelt of dust in
Attics and the urine of lizards and mice . . .

(10) KERALA

Eluttaccan, *Mahabharatam*

In this extract from the Mahabharatam, Sakuntala regretfully departs Kanva's hermitage,

Heavy with the sorrow
of departure, tears fell on her breast.
Wiping them as she wept,
she went round the Sage
with her son
and said Farewell, with folded hands,
and in a broken voice.

And when Sakuntala rose to leave
the Sage took the boy on to his lap
hugged him and kissing his head many times
blessed him:
'Long be thy life and be thou good . . .'

Tenderly, with slow movements,
he caressed his daughter, and as he said:
'Be thou happy and come back',
he broke down and the tears flowed.
The ascetic lost his strength,
sighed deeply,
and became subject to
human affliction, though momentarily.

(11) KERALA

Thakali Sivasankara Pillai, *Shrimps*

*Karuthamma, the daughter of a Hindu fisherman, and Parikut-
ti, the son of a Muslim fish wholesaler meet on the seashore while
Parikutti's husband Palani is out at sea. Their defiant behaviour
angers the sea goddess Katalamma.*

Palani's cry rose above the roar of the storm. Why did he cry out for
Karuthamma? The guardian angel of the fisherman at sea is his wife at
home. He was begging her to pray for his safety. Didn't the first
fisherman come safely home in spite of the storm because of the power
of the fisherwoman's prayer? Palani too believed he could be saved. He
had a wife. She would pray for him. Hadn't she given him her word
even the night before?

The fury of the storm increased. Palani fought it. But it joined forces
with the waves. Another huge wave came rolling. By the time he could
utter 'Karu . . .' the wave had rolled on.

There was nothing to be seen. The storm and the thunder and the
lightning joined together in the destruction.

The water churned devillishly and blew up to the skies. The whole
sea became a kind of cave. The storm became an entity. The boat
reappeared on top of the waves. Palani was lying on top of it. He was
clinging to it.

Wouldn't that merciless slaughter ever end? Then, caught up in a
whirlpool, the boat sank like a stone.

A solitary star appeared and shone. It was the fisherman's
Arundhati,[1] their guiding star. But that night it seemed to lack lustre.

The next morning day dawned on the calm sea as if nothing had happened. Some of the fishermen said there had been a great storm in mid-ocean during the night. The waves had come right up to the front of some of the houses. And sea snakes had been seen on the white sands. Panchami stood on the seashore, tears running down her cheeks. The baby in her arms was crying bitterly for her father and mother. Palani, who had gone out fishing the evening before, had not come home. Karuthamma was nowhere to be found.

Panchami wept, and as she wept she tried to comfort the baby.

Two days later the bodies of a man and woman locked in embrace were washed up on the shore. They were the bodies of Parikutti and Karuthamma.

And at the Ceriyalikkil seafront, a dead shark that had been baited was also cast up on the shore.

[1] Arundhati, the symbol of chastity.

(12) KERALA

N.V. Krishna Variyar, 'Rats'

'Are you rats or men?' asks the poet in this harrowing, rat's eye view of urban famine.

The bustle has stopped.
The streets drown in the dark.
Let's get down now from this attic.
We should find ourselves something to eat,
Shouldn't we?

This ladder is old, ramshackle;
make no noise.
Did your feet get stuck in the cobwebs?
careful children.

Wait. Don't you get from out there
the stench of rotting flesh?

That's only a car: roaring, rumbling along the road;
nothing to be scared about.

Don't fall to and start biting and pulling.
Ask yourself first:
Is it fully dead, will it move?

Try it out with a lick first, then sink
your nails bit by bit,
and then, careful! put your teeth to it.

No breath, no movement. Eat quietly.
No, no, that's only the garbage
moving in breeze blowing
through the chinks in the wall.

What? Sour? Does your tongue
find it wet, dripping? Blood?
It's been dead so long: still its love
of life will not die?

No, no don't get scared. It won't get up,
it may move just a little. Go on,
those hands cannot get you.

You wonder, don't you, that this dead thing
had life a few days ago.
The breasts then were full. The hips and thighs were full.
You weren't born yet.
Your dad and I have seen lots of people here,
Coming here to sleep in this dungeon.
I have seen the pair by lamplight
and in the dark,
several pairs of lips sucking at those
you bite now.
That hair was fragrant, now it's in bits.
It was a nuisance at nights,
that laughter, those sobs!

(13) KERALA: KOVALAM

Alexander Frater, *Chasing the Monsoon*

*The narrator describes the atmosphere as the monsoon
approaches at the end of the hot season.*

Trivandrum roasted, the temperatures climbing to their annual apogee
in an eruption of volcanic heat that felt as if giant magnifying glasses
were focusing all the sun's rays directly on to the city. Soon, with a
whoosh and a muffled whump, the whole place must spontaneously
ignite.

Out at Kovalam beach the atmosphere was as close as the air in a locked room, the sea a motionless silver plain stippled with fragile pencil-thin fishing canoes. On the horizon ships slid by on rails, their smoke unravelling aft in low, lateral lines which sometimes closed and joined like hawsers on a suspension bridge. Large crows perched in the waterside coconut palms. Down on the beach a young couple bathed, the woman in a bright emerald sari, her husband in a woollen costume of a kind that had been fashionable during the Jazz Age. A small listless surf kept falling and turning soundlessly back on itself in a cloying way, like cream. The couple's black skins indicated that they were local, but the heat caused them visible distress and they soon abandoned the water for deep shade where, wearily, they anointed themselves with oil.

The monsoon hijacked every conversation. People kept seeing signs. One man told me he had observed partridge feather clouds, another sparrows bathing in the dust. Both were considered propitious. A hot wind blew fitfully. Someone said it was called the *loo*.

I hadn't known sun like this before. It penetrated the crown of the head and imploded in the brain so that you got dazzle inside as well as out. Even the smallest movement activated the sweat glands. They soaked clothes and flooded shoes; walking became a mushy business, like treading grapes. The temperature was 42 degrees Celsius but felt higher. One of the local papers warned that such heat caused severe stress and urged its readers to change their underwear – which should be made from the lightest natural fibres – several times a day.

(14) SOUTH INDIA

E.M. Forster, *A Passage to India*

A more eloquent evocation of the antiquity of the southern lands by a European author remains to be written.

The Ganges, though flowing from the foot of Vishnu and through Siva's hair, is not an ancient stream. Geology, looking further than religion, knows of a time when neither the river nor the Himalayas that nourished it existed, and an ocean flowed over the holy places of Hindustan. The mountains rose, their debris silted up the ocean, the gods took their seats on them and contrived the river, and the India we call immemorial came into being. But India is really far older. In the days of the prehistoric ocean the southern part of the peninsula already existed, and the high places of Dravidia have been land since land began, and have seen on the one side the sinking of a continent which joined them to Africa, and on the other the upheaval of the Himalayas from the sea. They are older than anything in the world. No water has ever covered them, and the sun who has watched them for countless aeons may still discern in their outlines forms that were his before our globe was torn from his bosom. If flesh of the sun's flesh is to be touched anywhere, it is here among the incredible antiquity of these hills.

(15) SOUTH INDIA

R.K. Narayan, 'The Blind Dog, Fellow Feeling'

Narayan is at his best in these matter-of-fact descriptions of the ubiquitous Indian canine, and the Madras–Bangalore express. The extract is from Malgudi Days.

It was not a very impressive or high-class dog; it was one of those commonplace dogs one sees everywhere – colour of white and dust, tail mutilated at a young age by God knows whom, born in the street, and bred on the leavings and garbage of the marketplace. He had spotty eyes and undistinguished carriage and needless pugnacity. Before he was two years old he had earned the scars of a hundred fights on his body. When he needed rest on hot afternoons he lay curled up under the culvert at the eastern gate of the market. In the evenings he set out on his daily rounds, loafed in the surrounding streets and lanes, engaged himself in skirmishes, picked up edibles on the roadside and was back at the Market Gate by nightfall.

The Madras–Bangalore Express was due to start in a few minutes. Trolleys and barrows piled with trunks and beds rattled their way through the bustle. Fruit-sellers and *beedi*-and-betel-sellers cried themselves hoarse. Latecomers pushed, shouted and perspired. The engine added to the general noise with the low monotonous hum of its boiler; the first bell rang, the guard looked at his watch. Mr. Rajam Iyer arrived on the platform at a terrific pace, with a small roll of bedding under one arm and an absurd yellow trunk under the other. He ran to the first third-class compartment that caught his eye, peered in and, since the door could not be opened on account of the congestion inside, flung himself in through the window.

(16) SOUTH INDIA

R.K. Narayan, *Malgudi Days*

This extract from his own introduction to Malgudi Days, and the map offered by his publishers may help to answer the perennial question, 'Where is Malgudi?'

I have named this volume *Malgudi Days* in order to give it a plausibly geographical status. I am often asked, 'Where is Malgudi?' All I can say is that it is imaginary and not to be found on any map (although the University of Chicago Press has published a literary atlas with a map of India indicating the location of Malgudi). If I explain that Malgudi is a small town in South India I shall only be expressing a half-truth, for the characteristics of Malgudi seem to me universal.

(17) SOUTH INDIA

R.K. Narayan, *Gods, Demons and Others*

In this introductory chapter to a volume of short stories inspired by the Ramayana, Mahabharata and other epics, Narayan portrays the idiosyncracies of the village storyteller in his rural surrounding.

Looking at [the villagers] from outside, one may think that they lack the amenities of modern life, but actually they have no sense of missing much; on the contrary, they give the impression of living in a state of secret enchantment. The source of enchantment is the storyteller in their midst, a grand old man who seldom stirs from his ancestral home on the edge of the village, the orbit of his movements being the vegetable patch at the back and a few coconut palms in his front yard, except on some very special occasions calling for his priestly services in a village home. Sitting bolt upright, cross-legged on the cool clay-washed floor of his house, he may be seen any afternoon poring over a ponderous volume in the Sanskrit language mounted on a wooded reading stand, or tilting towards the sunlight at the doorway some old palm-leaf manuscript. When people want a story, at the end of their day's labours in the fields, they silently assemble in front of his home, especially on evenings when the moon shines through the coconut palms.

On such occasions the storyteller will dress himself for the part by smearing sacred ash on his forehead and wrapping himself in a green shawl, while his helpers set up a framed picture of some god on a pedestal on the veranda, decorate it with jasmine garlands, and light incense to it. After these preparations, when the storyteller enters to seat himself in front of the lamps, he looks imperious and in complete control of the situation. He begins the session with a prayer, prolonging it until the others join and the valleys echo with the chants, drowning the cry of jackals. Time was when he narrated his stories to the accompaniment of musical instruments, but now he depends on himself. 'The films have taken away all the fiddlers and crooners, who have no time nowadays to stand at the back of an old storyteller, and fill his pauses with music,' he often comments. But he can never really be handicapped through the lack of an understudy or assistants, as he is completely self-reliant, knowing as he does by heart all the 24 000 stanzas of the Ramayana, the 100 000 stanzas of the Mahabharata, and the 18 000 stanzas of the Bhagavata. If he keeps a copy of the Sanskrit texts open before him, it is more to demonstrate to his public that the narration is backed with authority.

(18) ANCIENT TAMILAKAM

Tolkappiyar, *Tokappiyam, Porulatikaram*

In this early example of Tamil verse, the sage Tolkappiyar ennumerates the four poetic landscapes of the ancient Tamil lands.

The forest world ruled by Mayon the Dark One,
The land of mountains ruled by Ceyon the Bright One,
Ventan's domain of pleasant streams,
The world of great sands ruled by Varuna,
Are said to be in the order mentioned;
Mullai, kurinci, marutam and neytal.

(19) ANCIENT TAMILAKAM: FIELDS

Kuruntokai

The lovers have quarrelled and disdain sullies the lips of the abandoned.

From amid the flooded paddy
Carp snatch at ripe fruit
As it falls from the mango trees
On the edge of the fields.

At our place he talked big!
But now he's back home,

Every whim of his son's mother
Tugs at his arms and legs
Like a dancing puppet.

(20) Ancient Tamilakam:
Battlefield

Purananuru

The poet describes the hand-to-hand fight between the Cola Porvaikkopperunarkilli and Mallan. The latter was a common name for a king.

In the village called Amur noted for its very sweet toddy,
He shattered the unfettered strength of a mighty wrestler.
With one leg folded on his chest
And the other folded on his back
He frustrated his opponent's trickery.

For one moment, whether he will or no,
Let the brave Tittan[1] of victorious wars
Witness, how bending bamboo like a hungry elephant
He crushed and dashed from head to foot
The mightly wrestler who had entered the battle ground,
And conquered him.

[1] Tittan the Cola.

(21) Ancient Tamilakam: Maturai

William Taylor, *An Abstraction of the Fifty Second Tiruvilaiyatal of the God Siva at Maturai based on the Maturai Talapuranam*

Siva bestows a chant on the poor brahman Terami, but Nakkirar believes the chant to be defective. For the chant, see Extract 3.

While one named Terami was occupied in his usual office of preparing flowers, and putting them on the image of the god, it so happened that the king, Sudamani, went one day to one of his flower gardens, and a particular thought occurred to him while there, respecting which he resolved on a poetical contest; and hence he tied a sum of gold in a packet, and hung it suspended to the bench of the poets, saying, 'Whichsoever of you shall succeed by a chant in telling me the thought that is in my mind, he shall be rewarded with this packet of gold.' They all attempted, but failed. Terami, hearing of this circumstance, paid homage to the god, and said, 'I have long been performing this duty of preparing and robing you with flowers, without establishing myself in life: I am poor, and I cannot afford to pay the expenses of marriage; enable me to win this purse of gold.' The god condescended to his request, and put a chant into his hands, which he carried to the collegiate bench; when the poets all said, 'We find no fault with the versification; if it suit the thought in the king's mind, and he approve, you can then take the reward.' The king admitted that the chant contained his thought, and ordered the reward to be given. While Terami was just about cutting the string, Narkiren, from Kailastri, said, 'Hold! There is fault in this chant, take it back.' The god, being moved, came forth, clothed in the habiliments of a poet, and coming up to the bench inquired who found fault in his stanzas? Narkiren replied, 'I do.' 'What fault?' 'It is not in the versification, but in the subject.' On this objection being proffered, a discussion arose; and on Narkiren manifesting obstinacy, the god opened a little eye on his forehead, perceptible only to Narkiren; who being infatuated, said, 'Even if Indren were to open his thousand eyes, I would not yield': whereon the god entirely opened his fiery eye, (which burns what it fixes on); and Narkiren, perceiving the commencement of combustion, ran away as fast as possible and plunged himself in the golden lotos tank, which removes all kind of sin, and there remained to cool at leisure.

(22) ANCIENT TAMILAKAM: MOUNTAINS

Kuruntokai

This early Tamil poem is said to have been given to the poor brahman Terami by the god Siva to enable him to win a literary prize at Maturai and get married.

> O bee, fair of wing,
> Ever in search of flower-garlands,
> Tell me not what I fain would hear,
> But what you really saw.
> Among all the flowers you know
> Is any more fragrant than the tresses
> Of my lady of the close-set teeth?
> Graceful as the peacock she dwells,
> Rich in love with me.

(23) ANCIENT TAMILAKAM: CITY OF PUHAR

Prince Ilanko Atikal, *Cilappatikaram*

In this extract from Book I, 'Blessings', the author tells of the wonders of Puhar.

Blessed be the Moon!
Blessed be the Moon that wraps the Earth
in misty veils of cooling light,
and looms, a royal parasol
festooned with pollen laden flowers,
protecting us.

Blessed be the Sun!
Blessed be the Sun that, endless pilgrim,
slowly circles round the axial mountain,
image of the royal emblem
of the beloved monarch of the land
where the Kaveri flows.

Blessed be the mighty clouds!
Blessed be the mighty clouds that on the Earth
shower down rain as generous
as he who rules the land
a raging sea surrounds.

Blessed be Puhar, city of wonders!
Blessed be the city of wonders,
immortal testimony to the power
of a glorious line of kings
whose fame has spread to every land
the boundless sea surrounds.

(24) TAMIL NADU

Antal, *Tiruppavai*

*In this example of Tamil devotional verse, young maidens rise
before dawn and make their way from house to house rousing
their tardy companions to fulfil the Markali vow and so enjoy the
blessing of good marriages.*

On the good day of Markali when the moon is full
will you not go to bathe in water, you who are suitably ornamented
Happy young maidens from the village blessed by cowherds,
son of Nantakopan who wields a sharp and terrible lance,
the young lion of Yacotai with the beautiful eyes,
with his dark body, bright eyes
and his face like the rayed moon,
it is Narayan! It is to us that he will give the drum!
Oh Maiden, will the people of the world not worship you?

You who dwell in the world,
do you not hear the sacred service we perform for our Maiden?
As we hymn the foot of the Supreme Being
who softly slept on a sea of milk,
neither consuming ghee, but bathing in water at break of day
we will not paint our eyes with mai,
nor crown ourselves with flowers,
we will not do things which should not be done,
nor utter slanderous words;
Will we not rejoice oh Maiden
as we contemplate the manner of our release,
Bestowing with our hands every sort of alms and charity!

(25) TAMIL NADU

Subramania Bharati, *'Mother Tamil'*

*Tamil, cries the poet, is a language not only of legendary fame
but of the modern world.*

> Siva of old was my father
>   And Agastya the Aryan sage
> Found me attractive
>   A grammar my thoughts to engage.

Three kings of different clans
  Brought me up fondly and fair
So that the place I obtained
  Could with high Aryan compare.

Poets in the Tamil land
  Made a heady mixture in glee
Of wine, fire, wind and sky
  And passed on that potion to me.

Many skills and sciences besides
  They mastered and left behind;
My fame spread all over the world
  My children could improve their mind.

But Time the blind destroyer
  Has scattered the treasures I had,
Because he cannot distinguish
  Between the good and the bad.

Sweeping all things before him
  Like a flash flood unopposed
It is he who is to blame
  For the way he has disposed

Of the numerous sweet tunes
  That fell on my maiden ears
Whose names alas! I cannot
  Recall for all my tears.

Because of my Father's grace
  And that sage's spiritual might
The killer Time till now
  Hasn't dared to affront my sight.

But today I heard something
  A foreigner impart –
My dears, what shall I say?
  It pierced my very heart.

'Many new sciences subtle
  Elemental and profound
Are growing up in the west
  And in Tamil will never be found.

That language cannot express them –
 It does not have the tool;
Slowly it will die now –
 The western tongues will rule.'

So spoke the silly fellow;
 Oh how the very thought smarts!
Go forth in the eight directions
 And bring home all sciences and arts.

Because of my Father's grace
 And that sage's spiritual might
This great scandal will end
 And my flame ever burn bright!

(26) TAMIL NADU

Mani, 'Hell'

In metamorphosis yet reluctant to change; the poet's well-known metaphors define the historical and cultural dilemmas of post-independent Tamil Nadu.

Tamilakam is neither in the East
Nor quite in the West.
She placed the pan on the stove
But refused to cook.
Famine and loss
Are the result.
She does not move forward,
She does not go back.
The present is hanging in the middle.
Hardened tradition and
Settled belief
Locked from inside
Refuse to give a hand
To cut the knot.
What should one do?

(27) TAMIL NADU

Parancotimunivar, *Tiruvilaiyatarpuranam*

The god Siva is well known among Tamil Saivites for his wicked sense of humour. In this extract, his insatiable attendant Kuntotaran (who has been fasting) threatens to consume everything in the universe. For the god, it is just another divine amusement!

Milk pudding made from uncrushed, unpolished white rice, fried curry, baked curry, more cooked dishes, several vegetable curries, milk sweetened and mixed with curds and ghee, all drenched in a flood of honey, endless quantities of water from a huge pot, mountains of fruit and all shapes of sweet-meats, sugar cane and sweetened coconut he devoured, and as if that wasn't enough, more boiled rice and all kinds

Kuntotaran's enormous appetite (Extract 27)

of fruit, yet still he wasn't satisfied, gobbling up as much rice as he possibly could, and with his large podgy hands stuffing his cavernous stomach with further mountains of rice and cakes. Like the filling of the ghee ladle in the sacrificial oblation his burning hunger raged like an angry, boiling fire.

'Lord', said Siva's consort, 'if you let loose any more of your ravenous attendants, they will devour and keep in their bellies everything on the earth. Then you will certainly have earned your reputation as "Destroyer of the Ages".'

(28) TAMIL NADU

Putumaipittan, *'Street Lamp'*

The sublime art of one of Tamil's most enigmatic writers is revealed in this tale of an old man and a street lamp.

At the end of the road, where it turns the corner, is a municipal street lamp.

In lonely solitude it struggles to shed its feeble light.

Youth, old age, death. These are not the privilege of man alone. And for the street lamp it is the season of old age.

There it stands. Its stone body a little bent. The reflector on its head slightly broken on one side. When that playful youth cast his stone, did he worry about the suffering it would cause?

Should the wind beat against it, will life at one stroke be ended?

Should life remain, it will kill it blow by blow.

Will the wind not thank it, at least for the little light it cast?

Alas, it is no more! Now in the cold rain, who will notice its suffering?

Does the wind understand?

Henceforth no lamp is needed on that side. Uproot it!

The lamp has a friend. An old man.

Will friendship come through likeness in years? In this, what wonder.

For the lamp an old man.

For the old man a lamp.

The old man does not know it is to be uprooted.

How could he know?

Does he not need to fill his belly?

Without food will life not end?
The street lamp is his only friend. Its light, what solace it bestowed.

That evening too he came.
A gaping hole was there.
Dark! Dark!
Like a blind man whose stick is snatched away.
That day the world was void, desolate, without meaning.

Peace?
Whence will it come!

From a broken street lamp! And yet in some small way it had sustained him.
And though the light had dimmed, to touch and see the mere stone brought comfort.
The following day, in the morning, they beheld the body of an old man lying there.

Now there's a new lamp.
An electric lamp
Beneath it gleeful children play
What do they care for an old man and a lamp?
Some day they too will be like this. What of it?
Everywhere and always it is like this.
Old things pass
New things come
This is the way of the world.

(29) Tamil Nadu

Sundara Ramaswamy, 'Window'

A unique if somewhat claustrophobic ambience is created by the author in this tale of a sick child confined to a cot.

I lay on a cot by the side of a window.

Months ago I crawled into it one evening and hadn't got out of it since. I never imagined I would turn into a part and parcel of the cot for this long. Five months? The date. Also the day of the week.

I have been lying on the cot by the side of the window for a long time.

My limbs had thinned away and they looked like twigs. My body had become badly emaciated. Once my younger sister stood staring at me for a long time. I don't know what prompted her but she said, 'You look like a gecko lizard, brother', and ran away. I felt as though pulled up from the cot to a great height and then dropped suddenly.

For a long time I hadn't looked in the mirror. No one brought one to me. I did want to take a look. My mind was a maze and what I said no one could hear. They probably thought I would be upset if I saw myself in a mirror. But I did want to see my face.

My sides with the protruding ribs began to resemble a woven basket and even the mattress I lay on became uncomfortable. My collar bones jutted out of my shoulders and there was now an ugly pit underneath my neck. The pit would easily hold a small glass of water.

I couldn't fold my legs. I couldn't move them either. My entire body would burn as though in contact with a burning torch. My eyes became the source of torrents of tears. But I never made a sound. I had long got used to swallow pain in silence.

This is what happened one day.

A wasp dropped on my chest from the ceiling. Someone would always be by my side – my sisters or my father or mother. But fatefully none was around when the wasp fell. I didn't know what to do . . . It had fallen right in the middle of the chest. For a while it circled round a point. Then began moving over to my neck. I tried to catch a glimpse of it but I couldn't. The wasp was getting ready to sting. I thought.

There was not a soul in the room.

I might scream but who would be able to hear it? An inflammation had choked my throat and prevented any sound emanating from my mouth. The effort would only result in excruciating pain.

Now the wasp was up my ear. Would it get into it?

'Mother!'

No sound.

Tears flooded down my face and soaked the pillow. I had shed quantities of tears in the brief years of my life – I had grown on my tears.

Something uncanny happened. Who told my mother? She came running in. She ran as though the place was on fire. As though someone was violently dragging her to me.

The wasp had climbed up my nose and was now advancing towards the temple.

'Mother!'

The call resounded only within my head.

My mother stood at the doorstep. 'My boy!' She screamed and came rushing to me.

She fanned my face with the flowing end of her saree. She wiped my face.

What she shed that day were tears of blood.

(30) VIJAYANAGAR

V.S. Naipaul, *An Area of Darkness*

V.S. Naipaul's deeper understanding of south India and its heritage is surely questionable. His acid sharp powers of observation have, nevertheless, resulted in some startling cameos.

Mosque on temple: ruin on ruin. This is in the North. In the South there is the great city of Vijayanagar. In the early sixteenth century it was twenty-four miles round. Today, four hundred years after its total sacking, even its ruins are few and scattered, scarcely noticeable at first against the surrealist brown rock formations of which they seem to form part. The surrounding villages are broken down and dusty; the physique of the people is poor. Then, abruptly, grandeur: the road from Kampli goes straight through some of the old buildings and leads to the main street, very wide, very long, still impressive, a flight of stone steps at one end, the towering *gopuram* of the temple, alive with sculpture, at the other. The square-pillared lower storeys of the stone buildings still stand; in the doorways are carvings of dancers with raised legs. And, inside, the inheritors of this greatness: men and women and children, thin as crickets, like lizards among the stones.

A child was squatting in the mud of the street; the hairless, pink-skinned dog waited for the excrement. The child, big-bellied, rose; the dog ate. Outside the temple there were two wooden juggernauts decorated with erotic carvings: couples engaged in copulation and fellatio: passionless, stylised. They were my first glimpse of Indian erotic carving, which I had been longing to see; but after the first excitement came depression. Sex as pain, creation its own decay: Shiva, god of the phallus, performing the dance of life and the dance of death: what a concept he is, how entirely of India! The ruins were inhabited. Set among the buildings of the main street was a brand-new whitewashed temple, pennants flying; and at the end of the street the old temple was still in use, still marked with the alternating vertical stripes of white and rust. One noticeboard about six feet high gave a list of fees for various services. Another, of the same size, gave the history of Vijayanagar: once, after the Raja had prayed, there was 'rain of gold': this, in India, was history.

Biographies and plot summaries

AIYAR, U.V. Swaminatha (b 1855). Doyen of Tamilology in the second half of the 19th century, U.V. Swaminatha Aiyar enjoys fame as the scholar who unearthed, edited and printed many of the priceless compositions belonging to the earliest strata of Tamil literature. Inscribed on palm-leaf manuscripts, these had been passed down through generations, being periodically recopied to preserve their integrity from the ravages of termites. They had nevertheless fallen into virtual decay during the Medieval period owing to neglect by Saivite and Vaisnavite scholars who considered secular, Jaina and Buddhist works taboo and therefore disavowed them.

BHARATI, Subramania (1892–1921). Revolutionary, poet and patriot, Subramania Bharati was born into a middle-class family in the district of Tinnevelly, now **Tirunelveli** in Tamilnadu. A non-conformist even from his school days, Bharati imbibed the traditions of the English Romantics, proclaiming himself the *dasan* or worshipper of the poet Shelley. Having become notorious to the British authorities through his journalistic and literary activities he took refuge in the French possession of Pondichery in 1908 returning to Madras in 1920. In June 1921, while visiting the temple elephant at the **Parthasarathi Temple** in Triplicane the usually affectionate beast tossed him into the air and seriously injured him. His body already addicted to opium, Bharati died in September 1921. Bharati, who may properly be considered the animating spirit of the freedom struggle in south India is famed for his patriotic songs which rang out at political meetings across the Tamil land throughout the years leading up to Independence. In his break with traditional form and subject he may be counted as one of the founders of modern Tamil verse (Extract 25).

CALDWELL, Robert (1814–1891). Bishop Robert Caldwell was one of the first scholars to recognize unhesitatingly the existence of a Dravidian family of languages in South India, distinct from the Indo–European languages of the north. His pioneering work *A Comparative Grammar of the Dravidian or South-Indian Family of Languages* was first published in 1856.

CHELLAPPA, C.S. (1912–   ). Poet and short story writer associated with the Tamil 'New Poets', he founded the review *Eluttu* 'Writing' which published for the first time many path-breaking compositions of the late 1950s and 1960s.

Cilappatikaram. Traditionally attributed to Ilankovatikal, a grandson of the Cola king Karikalan, this epic of Tamil literature is something of a tragi-comedy in its tale of Kovalan the son of a wealthy merchant of the city of Puhar and Kannaki, the beautiful daughter of a famous shipowner. The marriage goes well for a time but then Kovalan falls for the dancer Matavi. Selling even Kannaki's jewels to indulge his infatuation, he returns penniless and repentant to his uncomplaining wife. Having relinquished her precious pair of anklets to her husband, the mis-matched couple set off to the great city of Maturai where Kovalan hopes to recover their fortune. Intending to sell one of Kannaki's anklets in the bazaar, he is spotted by the wicked goldsmith of the Pantiya king. A drunken guard sent to apprehend him hurls his sword at Kovalan, and mortally wounded he falls to the ground. Hearing the news, Kannaki at first swoons, but recovering, and blazing with anger, parades the remaining anklet through the city as proof of her husband's innocence.

DAS, Kamala (1934–). Born in Kerala, Kamala Das has written both in English and Malayalam. Much of her work is dedicated to an exploration of love and sex particularly from a woman's perspective (Extract 9).

DEV, Kesava (1902–). Born into a humble working family, Kesava Dev is famed in Kerala as a champion of the downtrodden and as a communist crusader for social change. In the foreword to the first Malayalam edition of his novel *Neighbours* he outlined his life's work with the following words: 'I have never found writing a problem. My problem has been life. I have endeavoured to interpret and analyse life, rushing into the most colourful aspects of life's struggles, learning about life through its struggles'.

ELUTTACCAN (16th century). Author of several classical works in Malayalam, he is famed for popularising the *kilipattu* or 'Parrot Song', a form of devotional verse. The title Eluttaccan is composed of two words, *eluttu* 'writing' and *accan* 'leader' or 'father'. While there is no absolute proof as to the date of the poet, he probably lived towards the end of the 16th cerntury. He has been immortalized as the father of the Malayalam language. See Extract 10.

FORSTER, E(dward) M(organ) (1879–1970). Perhaps the best known European author to have written on India, Edward Morgan Forster was educated at King's College Cambridge and elected to an honorary fellowship in 1946. *A Passage to India* (Extract 14) which first appeared in 1924, has gained much popularity in recent years due in large part to its immortalization in celluloid which has lent it epic status on a par with 'Gone with the Wind'. It is well to remember that this popularised vision of India belongs properly to the pre-independence era and is not representative of the India of the late 20th century. Forster fans will also enjoy *The Hill of Devi* based on visits to India made by the author in 1912, 1913 and 1921 (Western India, Extract 13).

FRATER, Alexander (1939–). Chief travel correspondent of the

Alexander Frater

London *Observer*. His books include *Chasing the Monsoon* (Extract 13), *Beyond the Blue Horizon* (the book of a television series which recreated the original Imperial Airways eastbound route to Australia) and *Stopping Train Britain*. He also edited *Great Rivers of the World*.

JANAKIRAMAN, T. (1921–). Born in Thevangudi near Tanjavur, Janakiraman's novels and short stories focus on the lives of everyday middle-class families in Tamil Nadu. He has written over 10 novels of which *The Thorn of Passions* (1961), *Mother Came* (1965) and *Wooden Cow* (1979) are outstanding.

KARANATH, K. Shivarama. Another champion of the underdog, K.S. Karanath's *Choma's Drum*, published in Kannada in 1978, is the grim tale of the bonded labourer Choma, whose unfulfilled longing to become a farmer leads him to drink and drum-beating as an escape from his miserable life of slavery (Extract 7).

KARNAD, Girish (1938–). Born in Matheran near Bombay, Girish Karnad is one of India's foremost playwrights in the Kannada language, employing the themes and traditions of the folk theatre to explore the psychological dimensions of contemporary, day-to-day life (Extract 5). His other plays include *Yayati*, the reinterpretation of a Hindu myth on responsibility and *Hayavadana* whose plot is borrowed from the Sanskrit *Kathasaritsagara* via Thomas Mann's *The Transposed Heads*.

KRISHNAMURTHI, R. (1899–1954). Alias 'Kalki' he was first and foremost a journalist although his fame rests on his humorous sketches and voluminous historical romances which were serialized week after week in two popular Tamil journals *Anantavikatan* and his own journal *Kalki*. These could not unjustifiably be described as 'early 20th century soaps'.

KRISHNADEVARAYA (early 16th century). The last great king of Hindu India, Krishnadevaraya acceded to the Vijayanagar throne in 1509 at the age of 25. He is famed for his munificent patronage of many great poets who adorned his court. No mean poet himself, he is remembered for his *Amuktamalayada*, one of the five great *kavya* or poems of Telugu.

MAHADEVIYAKKA (12th century). Mahadevi was born in **Udutadi**, a village in Sivamogga. The story of her initiation to Siva worship at the tender age of 10 by an unknown guru, and her subsequent wanderings, wild and god-intoxicated in search of her divine beloved follows a familiar formula. Having fallen in love with Mallikarjuna, 'Lord white as jasmine' otherwise 'Arjuna, Lord of goddess Mallika' the presiding deity at the Udutadi temple, Mahadeviyakka addressed him as 'Cennamallikarjuna' or 'Beautiful Lord white as Jasmine' and took his name for a signature. Betrothing herself to the god she longed to escape the attentions of mortal suitors, and renouncing the habiliments of sensuality and convention took herself naked to Kalyana, abode of Virasaiva saints, where in an encounter with the guru Allama she declared herself to be forever married to Cennamallikarjuna. 'But why take off clothes, as if by that gesture you could peel off illusions?' proffered the guru. Her suitable rejoinder to this probing question may be read in Extract 7.

MANI, C. (1907–). One of the 'New Poets' working in the late 1950s and early 1960s, his 'Hell', first published in C.S. Chellappa's review *Writing* was a milestone in modern Tamil poetry. According to Chellappa 'a panavision movie with stereophonic sound-track' this poem of 334 lines evokes a haunting image of Madras in the second half of the 20th century.

MENON, Chandu (1847–1900). Chandu Menon is known principally for his novel *Indulekha* published in 1889. As a comment on the social structure of Kerala society in the 19th century it was an early precursor of the social novels of the 1930s. Chandu Menon died when he had completed only the first part of a second novel *Sarad*.

MENON, Vallattol Narayana (1879–1958). 'Vallattol' was one of the most important poets in Malayalam during the decades leading up to independence. He was closely associated with the freedom struggle, during which time he wrote My *Teacher* in praise of Gandhi, and his poems on 'Mother India'. After independence Vallattol like many other writers turned to social issues. He is also remembered for his encouragement of the arts, particularly Kathakali.

NAIPAUL, V.S. (see under Northern and Central India).

NARAYAN, Rasipuram Krishnaswami (R.K.) (1906–). R.K. Narayan, who is considered by some the foremost Indo–English novelist, wrote quietly and unassumingly through the first half of the 20th century and into the 1960s, seemingly untouched by the social cataclysms which were taking place around him. Indeed if we search for moral or social conviction in his work we will not find it. His success lies elsewhere, in the familiarity and ordinariness of his creation – Malgudi, a perennial South Indian town which as more than one critic has observed is the only character that grows, changes, has a spirit and a soul. *Gods, Demons and Others* is a collection of stories most of which are based on the well known *Mahabharata* and *Ramayana*. *The Mispaired Anklet* however is taken from the less well known *Cilappatikaram*, one of the great Tamil epics of the early period (Extract 23).

NATH, Kedar. After spending 10 years in Europe, the journalist Kedar Nath returned to the spot on the Ganges where he had committed his father's ashes to the waters of the sacred river, and to make a pilgrimage to the Kanya Kumari Temple at Cape Comorin. According to legend it was here that Siva married the goddess Parvati, and the seven varieties of rice thrown at the wedding were transformed into the seven coloured sands of the Cape. *Return to India* (Extract 2) has been serialized in *Die Welt* and his work has appeared in the *Herald Tribune*, *Sunday Telegraph* magazine and the *Spectator*.

PADMARAJU, Palagummi (1915–1983). Born at **Tirupatipuram** in Andhra Pradesh, Padmaraju started his career as a lecturer in chemistry. His most celebrated work, *Cyclone*, is a collection of 18 short stories in

R.K. Narayan

which he explores the psychology of the middle and lower classes (Extract 1). In employing the living speech of the Godavari districts where he grew up Padmaraju's stories, novels and plays are lent topographical authenticity.

Tiruvilaiyatarpuranam. Parancotimunivar composed his account of the 64 *Tiruvilaiyatal* or divine pranks performed by Siva at Maturai around the beginning of the 17th century, basing his poem on earlier Sanskrit works (Extract 27).

PILLAI, Samuel Vetanayakam (1826–89). A retired district judge at Maya-varman, S.V. Pillai published his *Piratapa Mutaliyar Carittiram* in 1879. Considered one of the first modern prose works in Tamil, the book is somewhat rambling, though not un-entertaining, having been written, as the author admitted, to supply a want of prose in Tamil literature.

PILLAI, Tamotaran (1823–). A stalwart of early Tamilology whose valuable work in unearthing and edit-ing early Tamil manuscripts belong-ing to the Cankam and medieval period has been persistently oversha-dowed by his better known contem-porary U.V. Swaminathaiyar. Chief among these are editions of the gram-matical works *Viracoliyam* (1881), Irayanar's *Akapporul* (1883) and *Tol-kappiyam Porulatikaram* (1885).

PILLAI, Thakali Sivasankara (1912–). Thakali is one of Kerala's most able writers. He is best known for his novel *Shrimps* (*Chemmeen*) which has been translated into several Indian and European languages. Several hundred of his stories have been pub-lished in literary collections. Among his novels are *Son of a Scavenger*, *Two Measures*, a analysis of problems faced by the landless peasantry, and *Steps on the Ladder*, a critique of government. *Shrimps* tells of the relationship be-tween Karutama and Parikutti set against the backdrop of a superstitious fishing community living on the coast of central Kerala (Extract 11).

PUTUMAIPPITTAN, pseudonym of C. Virdhachalam (1906–48). Even if this 'Miraculous Madman', had eaten intoxicating drugs and danced with devils as his pseudonym implies, the poet, novelist, playwright, editor, translator, critic and short story writer C. Virdhachalam may properly be considered one of the most important literary figures of Tamil Nadu in the first half of the 20th century. Active in the famous *Manikkotai* group during the 1930s unfortunately he died while many of his manuscripts still lay unpublished. Putumaippitan was the supreme master of the short story, his pen flowing like the aqueous strokes of a watercolourist's brush, melting the colours, revealing a profound understanding of universal imperma-nence. In 'Street Lamp', the struggle between dark and light is a metaphor of the author's own dialectic. The lamp is uprooted. The old man dies . . . But what of it? 'Everywhere and at all times it is like this. Old things pass. New things come. This is the way of the world' (Extract 28).

RAMANUJAN, A.K. (1929–). Indian-born, Ramanujan moved to the USA where he became Professor of Linguistics and Dravidian Studies at the University of Chicago. He is recognized not only for his own com-positions in English but also for his competent translations of verses from the early Tamil anthology the *Kurun-tokai*.

RAO, Gurazada Appa (1862–1915). Poet, playwright, short-story writer and social reformer, Gurazada is wide-ly accepted as the father of the mod-ern drama and the short story in Telegu. His play *Kanyasulkam*, which may be considered the first significant social drama written in Telegu, ridi-cules the practice of selling young girls in marriage to aging husbands, while advocating widow remarriage. His short story *Diddubatu* was pub-lished in February 1910 in *Andhra*

Bharati a Telegu monthly journal, and has been hailed as the first modern short story in the Telegu language. Together with the linguist G.V. Ramamurti Pantulu, Gurazada Appa Rao is remembered for his crusade against the archaic classical style known as *granthika* which dominated Telugu prose during the 19th and early 20th centuries.

TOLKAPPIYAR (c 1–6 centuries). The traditional author of the *Tolkappiyam*, the work which represents not only the first extant grammar of the Tamil language but the sublime ex-pression of Dravidian culture in the first centuries of the Christian era (Extract 18).

TYAGARAJA (1767–1847). Born in *Tiruvarur* in Tanjore District, Tyagaraja studied Telugu and Sanskrit under his father, Rama Brahman. Tradition tells how the presiding deity of the Tiruvarur Temple appeared to his father in a dream informing him that a male child, a genius of music and letters, would be born to him and that he might therefore be named Tyagaraja.

NORTH-EAST INDIA AND BANGLADESH

William Radice

> The singer alone does not make a song, there has to be someone who hears: / One man opens his throat to sing, the other sings in his mind.
> *Rabindranath Tagore*
> *'Broken Song'*

Bengal is not the whole of the north-east region of the sub-continent covered in this chapter, but Bengal is at its core; and as Bengal is a land of great rivers – of the vast joint delta system formed by the Ganges, Brahmaputra and Meghna debouching through various channels into the Bay of Bengal – it is best, in attempting to grasp the equally many-branched literature of the region, to adopt riverine imagery. The Ganges links Bengal with upper India, and the main languages and literatures of the north-east cannot be detached from northern India's Sanskrit, Hindu roots. Those who have seen Satyajit Ray's *Apu Trilogy* will remember that Apu's father Harihar goes to the holy city of Kashi (**Benares**) to earn money by reading from the Sanskrit scriptures. Bengali Vaishnavas, whose worship of the love of Radha and Krishna inspired so much medieval literature and whose modern offshoot, the Hare Krishna Consciousness movement, has brought Bengali piety to the highstreets of Western cities, have kept distant **Vrindavan** as firmly in their sights as Catholics do Rome. But although Bengal is *Ma Ganga*'s child, she has grown up far away from her Himalayan grandparents: in geographical circumstances defined not only by the rivers but by the sea. Today, cyclones and tidal waves from the Bay of Bengal periodically put Bangladesh on the world's television screens; historically the region has been given much of its significance by those who came to it by sea. Arab traders and missionaries turned **Sylhet** in north-east Bangladesh into one of the subcontinent's few maritime cultures, the source of the *lascar* seamen who worked on British merchant ships, and of the large Sylheti community in today's East End of London. The Portuguese trading settlements gave to the developing Bengali language words such as *chabi* ('key'), *girja* ('church') and *janala* ('window'). The British came and founded, just over 300 years ago, the great city of **Calcutta**, which became the capital (until the shift to Delhi in 1912) of British India and the cultural and political seedbed of so much that characterizes India today. Bengal thus became linked to the rest of India by a movement upstream as well as down: the downstream flow of her pre-British Hindu cultural inheritance, and the upstream flow of her 19th century urban and intellectual development. Situated to the east, she became the main entry point into India for ideas and influences from the West. By flowing out of India through Bengal, the great rivers allowed the outside world to sail in.

The other main factor in the 'specialness' of Bengal has been Islam, and the way in which Islam has mixed with what was there already. The mixture has been as rich and creative – but sometimes as dangerous and volatile – as the unique combinations of rain, silt and river-flooding that make Bengal one of the most fertile (and ecologically unstable) regions of the world. The initial waves of Turki conquests in the early 13th century produced such disruption and confusion that cultural activity was almost defunct for two centuries. However, as separate Muslim kingdoms stabilized – particularly that of Husain Shah and his son Nusrat Shah in the late 15th and early 16th centuries – a hybrid literary culture developed; so that Muslim Bengali poets in the kingdom of Arakan in Lower Burma, for example, wrote Vaishnava *padas* (songs about Radha and Krishna) as well as poems on Perso-Arabic subjects. This healthy hybridism was damaged during the 19th century, when the Hindu-dominated Bengal Renaissance led to Muslim feelings of insecurity and inferiority, and to the self-asserting demand for a separate Muslim homeland after Independence. A sense of being Bengali, however, proved much more powerful than a sense of being Pakistani. Pakistan was broken up by the India-supported Bangladesh Liberation War of 1971, with the loss of up to 3 million lives. The effect of this double secession has been strange indeed: the heart of Bengal – the deltaic region – is certainly fully Bengali again, and Bangladesh is crucial to the total Bengali cultural and political scene. But it is as if the heart has been cut out and then re-inserted. The body of Bengal will never feel the same again after such a dramatic and violent experience. And the Bangladeshi culture that is now rapidly developing is decidedly distinct from Calcutta and West Bengal, even when it is not particularly Muslim.

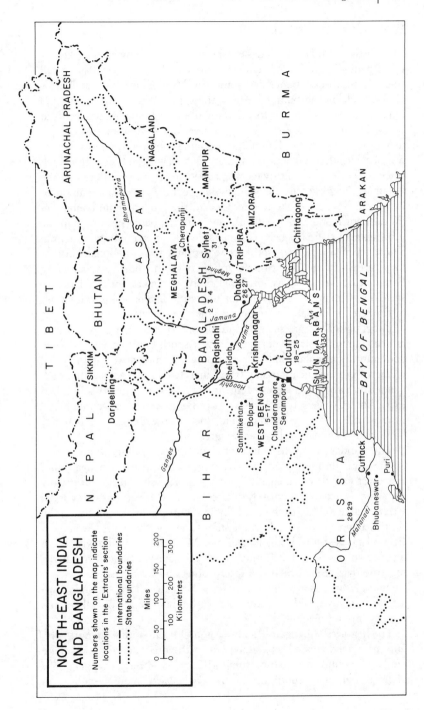

NORTH-EAST INDIA
AND BANGLADESH

Numbers shown on the map indicate
locations in the 'Extracts' section

— · — International boundaries

· · · · · · · State boundaries

Miles
0   50   100   150   200

0   100   200   300
Kilometres

TIBET

ARUNACHAL PRADESH

NAGALAND

MANIPUR

BURMA

ASSAM

Bhramaputra

MEGHALAYA

Cherapunji

Sylhet
31

Meghna

MIZORAM

TRIPURA

Chittagong

ARAKAN

BHUTAN

SIKKIM

Darjeeling

NEPAL

BANGLADESH

Dhaka
26 27

2
3 4

Rajshahi

Jamuna

Padma

Shelidah

Krishnanagar

Hooghly

Calcutta
18–25

SUNDARBANS

30

BAY OF BENGAL

BIHAR

Ganges

Santiniketan

Bolpur

WEST BENGAL
5–17

Chandernagore

Serampore

ORISSA

28 29

Mahanadi

Cuttack

Bhubaneswar

Puri

BENGALI AND ITS RELATIVES

The north-east region includes the Tibeto-Burman languages spoken by tribal people along India's eastern border and in the Chittagong hill tracts in south-east Bangladesh, and the Munda languages spoken by groups such as the Santals. All of these have their own poetic and musical traditions, and visitors to Rabindranath Tagore's ◊ university at **Santiniketan** in West Bengal may retain as one of their most evocative memories the sound of Santali girls singing robustly in chorus as they walk back to their villages at dusk. As regards written literature, which since the early 19th century means printed and published literature, the dominant languages are Bengali, Assamese and Oriya. The main areas in which these are spoken correspond to the modern state boundaries (West Bengal and Bangladesh, Assam, Orissa); but as elsewhere in the subcontinent there has been considerable migration and intermingling. There are many Bengali speakers in Assam, and communal tensions have arisen from a continuing influx over the northern border of Bangladesh. Tripura (east of Bangladesh) is almost entirely Bengali-speaking. Calcutta is a magnet for migrants: Bangladeshis, with their distinctive rural dialects (some of which, especially Sylheti and the Chittagong dialect are scarcely intelligible to other Bengalis); Oriyas; and communities from north and even south India. Some of these communities, such as the Marwaris from Rajasthan, are old-established elements in the Calcutta scene (the Calcutta Chinese are another such element). Others are more recent products of rural poverty and urban expansion. Conversely, communities of Bengali speakers can be found in most cities in north India: some, such as the Bengalis of Benares, have been there since the middle ages.

The standard (non-dialectal) forms of Bengali, Assamese and Oriya are as mutually intelligible as, say, Italian and Spanish. Bengalis and Assamese can also read each other's literature, as the script is virtually the same. Oriya has an entirely different script, with attractively curved letters that are closer to the south Indian scripts in appearance than the north Indian. The Bengali script shares some letters with Devanagari (the script used for Hindi, Nepali and Marathi), but otherwise has a distinctive elegance that is much prized. In cursive Bengali handwriting, the 'bar' from which the letter-forms hang down is less evident than in Nagari. As in so many spheres of Bengali culture, Rabindranath Tagore has provided his countrymen with a benchmark of calligraphic fluency and refinement.

The histories of Bengali, Assamese and Oriya literature are normally, and justifiably, treated separately; but in the pre-modern period there are good grounds for treating them as one. All three language groups claim as their oldest surviving text the *Charyapadas*, a unique collection of obscure Buddhist songs discovered in 1907 in Nepal. They are thought to date from the 11th century, and were brought there, perhaps, by Buddhist monks fleeing the effects of Muslim incursions into Bengal. In the medieval period (15th–18th centuries), the most regionally distinctive literary genre was the *mangal-kabya*, long narrative poems intended to be performed rather than read, describing the birth of deities indigenous to Bengal (Manasi, Chandi and others), how they consolidated their positions in the Hindu pantheon, and how human beings started to worship them. Mukundaram Chakrabarti, who wrote a celebrated *Chandimangal* at the end of the 16th century, has been accorded the title 'the Chaucer of Bengal' (reflecting a tendency among 19th century Bengalis to look for analogues to the English authors they assiduously studied). But the overriding literary inspiration in the region was Vaishnava (Krishnaite) religion and mythology. The origin for this was the *Gitagovinda* of Jaydeva (see Classical Literature), which was composed in the north-east; but the torrent of lyric songs about Radha and Krishna in all three languages was impelled by the extraordinary and messianic Chaitanya (1486–1530), who settled at **Puri** in Orissa, and won converts from all over the north-east to his highly emotional version of *bhakti*.

Chaitanya was the subject of numerous verse biographies, especially the impressively complex *Chaitanya charitamrita* of Krishnadas Kaviraj; and important disciples such as the 17th century Shrinivas Acharya, Narottam Das and Shyamananda Das (all trained by Jiva Goswami in Vrindavan) themselves became the subjects of biographies and commentaries. Chaitanyaite literature has retained its importance for scholars and Vaishnava devotees, and Vaishnava *padas* are a major influence on the great modern tradition of Bengali song. But for the non-devotee the most interesting Krishnaite work is the startlingly irreverent and racy *Shrikrishnakirtan* of Baru Chandidas ◊ (Extract 7). The existence of this long and delightfully down-to-earth series of bouts both verbal and physical between Radha and Krishna was not known until Basantaranjan Ray discovered the manuscript in 1916: almost as if *The Miller's Tale* had not been discovered by Chaucer scholars until that date.

Like north India, the north-east produced local versions of the *Mahabharata* and *Ramayana* that have remained popular to this day: Madhava Kandal's Assamese *Ramayana*; Krittibas's Bengali *Ramayana*; Sarala Dasa's Oriya *Mahabharata*; and more. When the great 19th century Bengali epic poet Michael Madhusudan Datta ◊ decided, while working as a teacher and journalist in Madras, to turn his literary energies to Bengali rather than English, it was the *Ramayana* of Krittibas and the *Mahabharata* of Kasiram Das that he asked his friends in Calcutta to send him. As the modern era approached, the literatures of the three main languages diverged. The Ahom kings of eastern Assam took to writing their chronicles in Assamese rather than in Ahom (a form of Thai), giving to the region a tradition of historical writing almost unique in the pre-modern literature of the subcontinent. In South Orissa, the Bhanja dynasty developed a uniquely virtuoso vernacular version of Sanskrit *kavya*, carrying wordplay and eroticism to a new extreme. In Bengal, the medieval tradition reached a highly sophisticated conclusion in the court poetry of Bharatchandra Ray (1705–1760), whose *Annadamangal* fused *mangal-kabya*, Sanskrit *purana*, and Moghul history.

CALCUTTA

Calcutta is to modern Bengali culture and literature what Paris is to France: indeed Bengali intellectuals have long been fascinated by Paris as the ultimate metropolis, and knowledge of French is regarded as a supreme accomplishment. There is considerable pride that **Chandernagore**, 20 miles up the Hooghly from Calcutta, lasted as a French colonial redoubt right up to 1950, and still maintains French educational traditions. Michael Madhusudan Datta ◊ is famous for (among other things) furnishing his house in French style, laying out a French garden, and habitually speaking to his mistress in French after their return from five years in Europe. But the fact that the Bengali word *antel* (derived from French *intellectuel*) means a 'pseudo-intellectual' suggests that British-influenced traditions of humour and pragmatism remain as a counter-influence to the fondness for abstraction and intellectualism for which Bengalis are noted throughout the subcontinent.

To see the culture of Calcutta solely in terms of Western influence is, of course, a travesty: Bengalis would be Bengali whoever had won the battle of Plassey, or even if there had been no battle and no colonial settlements at all. One of the fascinations of studying the leading figures of the Bengal Renaissance is to see how distinctively Bengali they are, whether they are writing in Bengali or English. Calcutta intellectuals have been 'bicultural' for generations, but that does not mean that their personalities have been split. There is a style, energy and panache in the Bengali character that goes beyond language, beyond whatever combinations of East and West have been incorporated into it. Readers of the extracts in this chapter from Madhusudan (Extract 20), Nazrul Islam ◊ (Extract 11) or Nirad C. Chaudhuri ◊ (Extract 9) will perhaps be able to sense this, whether the source language is English or Bengali.

In many ways *La Mode de Calcutta* characterized the British who lived there as well as the Bengalis. Certainly this was true up to 1857, and at the **Tollygunge** or **Calcutta Club** it is still possible to meet stalwarts of British origin who have preserved the tradition right up to the present day. In the many descriptions of 'first arrival' in The City of Palaces – by William Hickey ◊ (Extract 22), or the anonymous author of *Hartley House, Calcutta* (Extract 18), or Bishop Heber ◊ – we sense the excitement of discovering a different world; and when we look at the many beautiful drawings and paintings of Old Calcutta, by Thomas Daniell, William Baillie, James Baillie Fraser, Thomas Prinsep or Sir Charles D'Oyly, again our impression is not of an alien colonial implant but of a distinctive way of life that Bengalis and British built up together. It is summed up in Frederick Fiebig's panoramic view of Calcutta from the Ochterlony Monument, in six parts, published in 1847. The whole extraordinary city is laid out before us, and if Wordsworth could have been there at the artist's elbow he would surely have wished to repeat and amplify his feelings on Westminster Bridge that 'Earth hath not anything to show more fair . . .'.

Many figures from the early British period have a firm place in the cultural and literary history of Bengal. All of them loved Calcutta. Sir William Jones (1746–94), co-founder of the Bengal Asiatic Society and supreme pioneering Orientalist, found his *bagan-bari* ('garden-house') at **Alipur** a perfect Arcadian retreat. William Carey (1761–1843) of the Serampore Mission Press, who was also a notable teacher at the East India Company's Fort William College for the study of Oriental languages, has a firm place in the early history of Bengali printing and prose writing. David Hare (1775–1842) inspired extraordinary loyalty and affection for his philanthropic activities, and for his role in founding Hindu College in 1817 – the powerhouse of English education in 19th century Calcutta and later (renamed Presidency College) the nucleus of Calcutta University. Henry Louis Vincent Derozio (1809–31) ◊, a Eurasian teacher at Hindu College, is celebrated for his bold stand in defence of embryonic Indian nationalism; his romantic poems were much imitated (Extract 21). Captain D.L. Richardson (1801–65), a prolific poet and essayist, was another inspiring teacher at Hindu College in the 1830s and 1840s, whose classroom readings from Shakespeare made a deep impression on Macaulay. Others, such as the Scots missionary Alexander Duff (1806–78), founder of the General Assembly's Institution (now Scottish Church College), have not left behind such affectionate memories; but generally even a cursory study of the development of Calcutta's colleges, schools, hospitals, or welfare organizations tells a story not of confrontation but of cooperation between 'Nabobs' and 'Baboos'.

After the 'Mutiny' of 1857 – that tragic watershed in the history of British India – the relationship began to sour. The Imperial machine was efficient, but it lacked charm: many British became professional administrators, rather than people who gave their hearts and souls to India; so that by the time we reach the era of Rabindranath Tagore ◊ there was little possibility of creative cooperation. Tagore compared the British with the Moghuls, who 'lived and died in India' and left behind 'their human personality' in their buildings and other works of art. British rule was 'official and therefore an abstraction. It has nothing to express in the true language of art. For law, efficiency and exploitation cannot sing themselves into epic stones.' Tagore created his school and university in a spirit of rejection of the British educational machine in Calcutta: a striking contrast with his grand-father 'Prince' Dwarkanath Tagore, whose name appears on the foundation committees of most institutions in early 19th century Calcutta, including Hindu College.

Tagore acknowledges no British influence, except perhaps for the impact of English Romantic poetry on his early verse (for a while he was known as 'the Shelley of Bengal'). But it is difficult not to feel that the Imperial 'Pax Britannica' – coinciding almost exactly with the dates of Tagore's life – made it possible for a figure of his stature to emerge. Moreover, just as the relaxed, tolerant, 18th century atmosphere of the Company Days had its counterpart in the zest, the spirit of enquiry, the gaiety of the early phase of Bengali culture, so one feels that Victorian stiffness and repression, and Christian missionary earnestness, was matched by a new stuffiness amongst Bengalis. The Brahmo Samaj, the Hindu reform movement founded by Rammohan Roy (1772–1833) and greatly developed by Tagore's father Debendranath (1817–1905) ◊, was a generally admirable attempt to make sense of the Hindu spiritual inheritance in the light of modern rationalism and historical sense; but in its later schisms and posturings – especially the 'New Dispensation' of Keshabchandra Sen (1838–1884) – and in the cults that formed round the illiterate mystic Ramakrishna Paramahamsa (1836–1886) and his disciple Swami Vivekananda (1863–1902) – one finds a new uncertainty, an *angst* about how to live and what to be. This unhappiness, if one can so simply call it, so alien to the spirit of old Calcutta, fuelled nationalist agitation: first the campaign against Curzon's partition of Bengal in 1905 (rescinded in 1912 but the seeds of later divisions had been sown); the *swadeshi* boycott of British goods; terrorism in the 1930s; and finally Bengali support for the pro-Japanese ventures of Subhaschandra Bose (1897–?1945), who is revered in Calcutta to this day as *Netaji* (the *Führer*), an enthusiasm that is as difficult for outsiders to understand as the unreconstructed Stalinism which – in words if not in deeds – characterizes part of the Left Front government that has ruled West Bengal since 1977.

Social and political unhappiness was an inevitable consequence of the unplanned expansion of Calcutta into the monster that it has become today. It had its roots in the stark and pestilential contrast between 'Black Town' and 'White Town' that was noticed even by 18th century visitors to Calcutta; it grew as the city grew to Victorian proportions without the governmental will to construct services fast enough to cope with the expansion; it was given the final, calamitous *coup de grace* by Partition in 1947, when the influx of Hindu refugees from East Bengal doubled its population. The city is still reeling, but when it celebrated its tercentenary in 1990 it could justifiably take pride in the progress it has made to overcome problems that would have reduced a less civilized place to anarchy. The two magnificent volumes published by Oxford University Press in the tercentenary year (*Calcutta: The Living City* – see Booklist) tell an impressive story of defiance of adversity; and the best way for the modern visitor to appreciate this spirit of 'winning through' is to take a ride on the excellent new **Metro** – the first in South Asia.

The history of modern Bengali literature is in many ways a story of the ever-increasing intrusion of the city into all aspects of Bengali life. The great classic figures of Bengali literature – Michael Madhusudan Datta ◊, the novelist and essayist Bankimchandra Chatterjee ◊, Rabindranath Tagore ◊ – were products of Calcutta, wrote about it at times, but were not obsessed with it. But a writer such as Bibhutibhushan Banerji ◊, whose semi-autobiographical novels *Song of the Road* (*Pather Panchali*) ◊ (Extract 16) and *Aparajita* describe his own drift to the city and are the source for Satyajit Ray's *Apu Trilogy*, shows the process by which a culture rural in origin has relentlessly been urbanized. The great modern poet Jibanananda Das ◊, who moved from **Barisal** in East Bengal to the city to work as a college teacher, also typifies this process (Extract 30). Today there are Calcutta writers such as Mahasweta Devi ◊ (Extract 10) who have deliberately looked for inspiration outside the city; but on the whole, to read a Calcutta novelist or poet now is to read about Calcutta, about the agonies and absurdities that living in Calcutta imposes on anyone with any sensibility at all.

This contraction of literary horizons to the boundaries of the Calcutta Metropolitan Area has affected those who write in English too. Writers such as Abhitava Ghosh or Amit Chaudhuri ◊, both recipients of literary prizes in the West, seem to accept that Western interest in Bengal is likely to mean Western interest in Calcutta. Nirad C. Chaudhuri ◊ (Extract 9), by his migration to Delhi and finally to Oxford, implies that a Calcuttan writer will not command attention on anything other than Calcutta unless he moves away from the place. Calcuttans are infuriated, however, when a foreigner finds the negative aspects of Calcutta fascinating, rather than their heroic struggle against those aspects. True, Dominique Lapierre's *The City of Joy* ◊, the filming of which in 1991 aroused violent protests, tells a double story of triumph over poverty and adversity; but the struggles of the rickshaw puller and the Polish priest Stephan Kovalski are not exactly the struggles that the Calcutta middle-class would like foreigners to admire (Extract 23). Against huge odds, Calcuttans fight to preserve qualities of civilization that characterized the city in the past: its seats of learning, its libraries, its rich literary culture, its fine schools (among them **South Point**, the largest school in the world, just as **Calcutta University** is said to be the largest university in the world), its progressive attitude to women, the general decency in human relationships that makes it a far safer city in which to walk and live than New York, London, Berlin – or, for that matter, Bombay or Delhi.

RABINDRANATH TAGORE

Bengali writers are generally known in Bengali by their first names, so to Bengalis Rabindranath Tagore is 'Rabindranath', pronounced 'Robindronath', because in Bengali the vowel that in Hindi would be a short 'a' sound is pronounced like an 'o'. It is commonly said that to pronounce Bengali properly you must speak with a *rasagolla* in your mouth, one of those syrupy sweets which Bengalis adore. To win Bengali hearts you must express as much enthusiasm for their *mishti bhasha* ('sweet language') as for Bengali *mishti* ('sweets') themselves; it is also advisable to develop a taste for *macher jhol* ('fish curry'), *luchis* (small puffed-up chapatis), and above all *Rabindrasangit* – the songs of Tagore, the more than 2000 songs that have become the national music of Bengal.

Tagore – and it is convenient to stick to the anglicised form of his family name *Thakur* – is the only writer in a modern Indian language to have become a world figure. Admittedly his world standing has been obscured, and has sometimes virtually been eclipsed, since his death in 1941, and some will be content to accept Jorge Luis Borges's dismissal of him as 'above all, a hoaxer of good faith, or, if you prefer, a Swedish invention'. It is also tempting to accept Nirad C. Chaudhuri's view – in his fascinating chapter on Tagore in *Thy Hand, Great Anarch!* – that his reputation is never likely to be secure, because if the impossibility of translating him. Translation of a writer who was always – whether in prose or verse – fundamentally a lyric poet, and who wrote so much (26 telephone-book sized volumes) from which the hapless translator must inadequately select, is certainly a major problem; but there are other great writers (Goethe, Baudelaire, James Joyce) who present immense translation problems, who have nevertheless won full international respect of a kind that has so far eluded Tagore. Probably what is needed is a combination of literary translation, editions that make access to the

Rabindranath Tagore

original texts easier (ie annotated parallel texts), and mature biography and criticism. In my own two books of translations of Tagore, *Selected Poems* and *Selected Short Stories*, in Ketaki Kushari Dyson's selection of his poems, and in Martin Kämpchen's German translations (see Booklist), a new start has perhaps been made with the first of the three requirements above; but I suspect that not much further progress will be made until the others have been tackled. Bengali criticism of Tagore is voluminous, and now Prasanta Kumar Pal is setting new standards of detail and scholarship in his massive *Rabi-jibani* ('Life of Rabindranath'), six volumes of which have so far appeared. But Bengali critics tend to be so much in awe of Tagore that (with a few maverick exceptions) they have not yet really attempted *criticism*: the task of assessing Tagore's work, understanding what he was trying to do, defining where he succeeded and failed.

One way forward might be to see all of Tagore's endeavours as a search for balance: a balance between the aesthetic and the moral, the spiritual and the mundane, India and the West, Nature and man, and so on. Because of his diverse literary and cultural inheritance, in which so many ancient and modern, Western and Indian influences were combined; and because of the unexpected international exposure that the Nobel Prize for literature in 1913 thrust on to him; his pursuit of balance was complex and fraught with risk. Like Visva-Bharati, his school and university at Santiniketan, everything he did was experimental. All great writers are experimenters, but there is something uniquely exposed and vulnerable about the risks that Tagore took. To appreciate this riskiness and vulnerability is the way both to a critical understanding of his successes and failures, and to respect for his courage as an artist and man.

Risk-taking and the pursuit of balance were strongly present in Tagore's family background. His grandfather 'Prince' Dwarkanath Tagore (1794–1846) was the greatest Bengali entrepreneur of the early British period, famous for his wealth and hospitality, his philanthropy, and for his daring in twice defying the Hindu ban on sea-voyages by his visits to Europe (he died in London). His friendship with the great pioneering reformer Rammohan Roy (1874–1833), and his support for the foundation of the Brahmo Samaj, was risky, in terms of his standing in orthodox Hindu society, but was motivated by a desire to achieve a balance between Hindu tradition and the Westernizing tendencies unleashed by the British. His son Debendranath (1817–1905) ◊ was a different, more cautious, more introspective and religious personality (Extract 25). For much of his life he worked to pay off his father's debts – even fulfilling his father's extravagant promises to charities – and to establish the Tagore estates in East Bengal on a sound footing. By nailing his own colours to the Brahmo Samaj mast, however, he also showed daring. His policies as *Acharya* (Minister) of the Samaj were perceived as conservative by more radical elements in the movement, leading ultimately to a break-away Samaj under Keshabchandra Sen in 1866. But his willingness to shift ground on fundamentals such as the infallibility of the Vedas, and the way in which he permitted his 14 sons and daughters to develop in highly individual ways, tell a different, progressive story. Rabindranath Tagore was more mercurial and romantic than his father: he could not stomach the constrictions and pious enthusiasms of the Samaj. But his own moral earnestness, his desire to build institutions, do good in the world, his preoccupation with God, his own attempts at a synthesis of the old and the new, the Indian and Western, placed him firmly within his family's tradition. Like his grandfather and father, he lived his life at the centre of modern Bengali culture – but also, because of his radicalism, outside it. Like them he had to face considerable opposition from orthodox, conservative elements: so when a party came to Santiniketan to congratulate him on winning the Nobel Prize, he sharply reminded them of how ready they had been to denigrate him in the past.

Tagore remained an outsider in many ways. Physically he was an outsider from Calcutta by eccentrically living first on his father's estates in East Bengal, then at **Santiniketan**; and Calcutta writers of the 1930s and 1940s struggled to create a modern, mainstream literary culture separate from him (as the poet Buddhadev Bose put it, 'it was impossible not to imitate Rabindranath, and it was impossible to imitate Rabindranath'). Yet the net effect of his massive contribution to Bengali culture and literature has been unifying and steadying. The Bengali he wrote, constantly evolving throughout his career, is a central linguistic resource from which all writers must draw; his works are required reading for any Bengali who wants to consider himself literate; his songs are sung all over Bengal; **Visva-Bharati** – even if it has fallen short of his universalist ideals – has remained a Bengali cultural centre, whose annual *Paush Mela* brings Bengal together, country and city, Calcutta *literati* and the wandering Baul singers whose heterodox spirituality influenced Tagore profoundly. His sensitive

'Uttarayan', Tagore's house in Santiniketan

concern for women – so evident in his stories and novels – has surely enhanced the confidence and self-assurance of educated Bengali women today, who seem, by their graceful ability to combine traditional virtues with a progressive independence of spirit, to embody that very spirit of balance that the Tagore family cultivated. Not just the Tagore family: in most of the great figures – Rammohan Roy, Ishwarchandra Vidyasagar, Bankimchandra Chatterjee – there is the same civilized search for a balanced culture, Indian but modern. But without the Tagore family, the Bengal Renaissance would probably have been neither as steadying nor as dynamic.

Orissa, Assam and East Bengal (Bangladesh)

Orissa, Assam and East Bengal (now Bangladesh) have all had to fight for their literary and linguistic identity. In the case of Orissa and Assam, the battle was against Bengali dominance. In the early period of British Rule, Bengalis ran the administration; in 1836, Bengali was imposed on the schools and courts of Assam, and in Orissa, partition between Bengal, Central Provinces and Madras ensured an equivalent imposition of Bengali, Hindi or Telegu. In both regions, missionaries and enlightened British linguists such as John Beames (District Magistrate of Balasore), joined forces with intellectuals who, because they had been educated in Calcutta, had seen what Bengalis were achieving and wanted the same. In the early 1870s Assamese and Oriya finally achieved official recognition, and their modern literary revival began in earnest. Bengali literary influence, however, remained strong: many leading modern writers of Assam and Orissa can be compared with one or other of the great Bengali writers. So far the greatest figure in the region outside Bengal has probably been Phakirmohan Senapati (1843–1918), author of numerous novels and stories and a classic autobiography, and translator of the whole *Ramayana* and *Mahabharata* into modern Oriya. At present, Orissa seems to be making its greatest impact on Indian cultural life through the cinema, with films by Sadhu Mehra and Nirad Mohapatra to equal Satyajit Ray ◊, Mrinal Sen and Ritwi Ghatak in Bengal.

In East Bengal the struggle has been rather different. Because of the Calcutta/Hindu dominance of the Bengal Renaissance, and the relative slowness of the Bengali Muslims to seize the new educational opportunities that Calcutta offered, Bengali Muslims who sided with the goal of an independent Pakistan suppressed their Bengali in favour of their Muslim identity. Some disowned the Bengali language itself, and claimed that Urdu was their mother-tongue. After Partition, writers belonging to groups such as the East Pakistan Renaissance Society chose to write on mainly Islamic subjects, and to exaggerate the non-Sanskritic element in Bengali vocabulary by importing many Persian and Arabic words. Other (more lasting) writers such as the poet Jasimuddin or the novelist Syed Waliullah ◊ (Extract 4) chose rural Muslim subjects, but did not borrow excessively from Persian or Arabic; their approach, like that of the Muslim writers of medieval Bengal, was essentially syncretistic.

With the oppression of East Pakistan by its more powerful Western wing, and above all the attempt to impose Urdu as the national language of the whole of Pakistan, pan-Islamic feeling in East Bengal was quickly and dramatically burnt up by the flames of Bengali linguistic nationalism. The Language Movement against Urdu culminated in 'Ekushey', 21 February 1952, when demonstrators for the recognition of Bengali as the state language of East Pakistan were shot by the police. This remains a national day of remembrance in Bangladesh. As the freedom struggle developed, Tagore and other classic writers of Hindu Bengal were accepted by Bengali Muslims as *their* poets and writers. Tagore's songs became such an expression of patriotic identity that in 1967 the authorities banned them. Ultimately, after Liberation in 1971, Tagore's *Amar Sonar Bangla* ('My Golden Bengal') was adopted as the national anthem of Bangladesh. The fact that Tagore's *Jana Gana Mana* is the national anthem of India, is a neat demonstration of his ability to reflect and express both regional Bengali and pan-Indian aspirations.

Since 1971 Bangladesh has had a rough ride politically, and sometimes those in power have sought to play the Islamic card again. One does find hostility to the Hindu Bengali literary heritage in some quarters, and some Bangladeshis regard Tagore, Madhusudan or Bankim as *bideshi* ('foreign'). Some classic writers are given special prominence in Bangladesh. Nazrul Islam ◊, though born in West Bengal and essentially a Calcuttan, is widely regarded as the national poet and song-writer of Bangladesh, because of his humble Muslim origins. Nazrul's attitudes, however, were never narrowly Islamic: they were syncretistic, or revolutionary-communist. The pioneering Muslim feminist and educationalist Begum Rokeya (1880–1932) ◊ is also a respected figure in Bangladesh, whereas in West Bengal – despite her contribution to Muslim girls' education in Calcutta – she is scarcely known. The Hindu writers who are popular in Bangladesh tend to be those who give prominence to the land and villages of East Bengal: the novelist Manik Bandyopadhyay (1908–56), the poet Jibanananda Das (1899–1954) ◊, or Tagore in his East Bengal phase – particularly the beautiful stories with an East Bengal background that he wrote in the 1890s.

The leading contemporary writers of Bangladesh, such as the poet Shamsur Rahman or the short story writer Hasan Azizul Huq, steer a

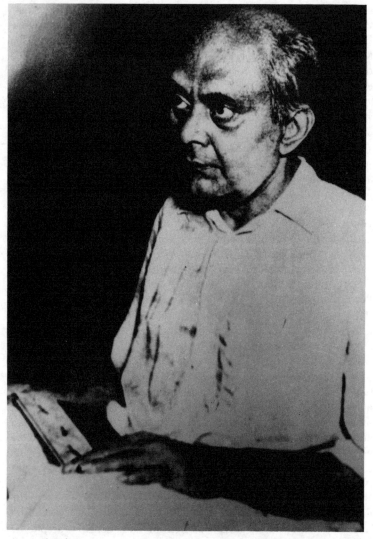

Nazrul Islam

subtle course between their East Bengal heritage, with its distinctive dialects and harrowing experience of the liberation war, and an outlook that is sometimes more open and international than that of their counterparts in Calcutta. Bengali has an advantage in Bangladesh in that it is (apart from the Tibeto-Burman languages in the south-east) the *only* language: it is less exposed to Hindi and English influences than Bengali in Calcutta. Dhaka, unlike Calcutta, has no professional theatre (Calcutta's theatrical life goes back to the 1860s); but its television plays are appreciated throughout Bengal. Even though the political and religious divide between the two Bengals remains great, television may yet bridge it – as it bridged the capitalist-communist divide in Europe.

Whatever may happen politically in the future, it seems impossible that the fascinating landscape and riverscape of East Bengal – the inspiration of so many writers through the centuries – can remain cut off from its former metropolis forever. The visitor to Bangladesh finds a refreshing integration between town and country: the middle-classes of Dhaka or Chittagong will often distinguish between their *basa* ('residence') in the city and their *bari* ('home') in the village. Many are able to speak a rural dialect as well as standard Bengali. Travellers by air from Calcutta to Dhaka can look down in bewilderment at the lack of any kind of natural border, the complete artificiality of the 1947/1971 Partition (Extract 26). Can the chief value of a literary companion such as this book be to show that literature expresses unities and connections that completely override political divisions, that Bengal is Bengal, a cultural and geographical entity that all Bengalis know in their heart of hearts to be indivisible?

Shamsur Rahman

BOOKLIST

The following selection includes all titles which are extracted in this chapter as well as other relevant works. The editions cited are not necessarily the only ones available. The exact location of the extracts can be found in 'Acknowledgements and Citations' at the end of the volume. Extract numbers are highlighted in bold for ease of reference.

Anon, *Hartley House, Calcutta*, Pluto, London/Winchester MA, 1989. **Extract 18**.

Banerji, Bibhutibhushan *Song of the Road (Pather Panchali)*, T.W. Clark and Tarapada Mukerji, trans, Allen and Unwin, London, 1968. **Extract 6**.

Bardhan, Kalpana, trans, *Of Women, Outcastes, Peasants and Rebels. A Selection of Bengali Short Stories*, University of California Press, 1990. **Extracts 2 and 10**.

Bhattacharya, Deben, trans, *Songs of the Bards of Bengal*, Grove, New York, 1969. **Extract 5**.

Bose, Buddadev, *An Acre of Green Grass*, Bombay, 1948.

Bose, Nemai, *The Indian Awakening and Bengal*, Calcutta, 1960.

Chandidas, Baru, *Singing the Glory of the Lord Krishna: The Srikrsnakirtana*, M.H. Klaiman, trans, Scholars Press, CA, USA, 1984. **Extract 7**.

Chatterjee, Bankimchandra, *The Abbey of Bliss (Anandamath)*, Nares Chandra Sen-Gupta, trans, Calcutta, 1907. **Extract 8**.

Chaudhuri, Amit, *A Strange and Sublime Address*, Heinemann, 1991. **Extract 19**.

Chaudhuri, Nirad C., *Autobiography of an Unknown Indian*, Chatto and Windus, London, 1951.

Chaudhuri, Nirad C., *Thy Hand, Great Anarch! India: 1921–1952*,

Chatto and Windus, London, 1987. **Extract 9**.

Chaudhuri, Sukanta, *Calcutta, the Living City*, 2 Vols, Oxford University Press, Delhi, 1990.

De, S.K., *Bengali Literature in the Nineteenth Century 1757–1857*, Calcutta, 1919 (new ed, 1962).

Derozio, Henry Louis Vivian, *The Fakeer of Junghera: A Metrical Tale and Other Poems*, Calcutta, 1828. **Extract 21**.

Devi, Mahesweta, 'Daini' in *Of Women, Outcastes, Peasants and Rebels. A Selection of Bengali Short Stories*, Kalpana Bardhan trans, University of California Press, 1990. **Extract 10**.

Dimock, Edward C., and Levertov, Denise, trans, *In Praise of Krishna: Songs from the Bengali*, University of Chicago Press, 1967. **Extract 13**.

Dimock, Edward C. *The Thief of Love: Bengali Tales from Court and Village*, University of Chicago Press, 1963. **Extract 14**.

Dutta, Krishna and Robinson, Andrew, *Rabindranath Tagore: The Myriad Minded Man*, Bloomsbury, London, 1995.

Gardner, Katy, *Songs at the River's Edge: Stories from a Bangladeshi Village*, Virago, 1991/Pluto, 1996. **Extract 31**.

Ghosh, Amitav, *The Shadow Lines*, Bloomsbury, London, 1988. **Extract 26**.

Gupta, Ksetra, *Kabi madhusudan o tar patrabali*, Calcutta, 1963. **Extract 20**.

Hajnóczy, Rózsa, *Fire of Bengal*, Eva Wimmer and David Grant, trans, The University Press, Dhaka, 1993. **Extract 1**.

Hartman, Betsy and James K. Boyce, *A Quiet Violence: View from a*

Bangladeshi Village, London, 1983.

Heber, Bishop Reginald, *Bishop Heber in Northern India: Selections from Heber's Journal*, M.A. Laird, ed, CUP, 1971. **Extract 27.**

Hickey, William, *The Calcutta Attorney: Memoirs of William Hickey*, Peter Quenell, ed, London, 1960. **Extract 22.**

Huq, Hasan Azizul, 'Bhushaner Ekdin' in *Of Women, Outcastes, Peasants and Rebels. A Selection of Bengali Short Stories*, Kalpana Bardhan, trans, University of California Press, 1990. **Extract 2.**

Islam, Nazrul, *Selected Poems of Nazrul Islam*, Kabir Chowdury, trans, Bangla Academy, Dhaka, 1963. **Extract 11.**

Kämpchen, Martin, *The Honey Seller and Other Stories*, William Radice, trans, Rupa, New Delhi, 1995. **Extract 12.**

Kripalani, Krishna, *Tagore: A Life*, London, 1961.

Lapierre, Dominique, *The City of Joy*, S.A. Pressinter, trans, Arrow, London, 1986. **Extract 23.**

'Literature: The North-east', *The Cambridge Encyclopaedia of India*, Cambridge University Press, 1989.

Mohanti, Prafulla, *My Village, My Life: Nanpur: A Portrait of an Indian Village*, London, 1973. **Extract 29.**

Mohanty, Gopinath, *Paraja*, Bikram K. Das, trans, Oxford University Press, 1987. **Extract 28.**

Nasrin, Taslima, *Shame*, Tutul Gupta, trans, Penguin, New Delhi, 1994.

Novak, James J., *Bangladesh: Reflections in the Water*, Indiana University Press, 1993.

Rahman, Shamsur, *Selected Poems of Shamsur Rahman: A Bilingual Edition*, Kaiser Haq, trans, Brac Prokashona, Dhaka, 1985. **Extract 3.**

Ray, Bharatchandra, *Vidya-Sundara* in *The Thief of Love: Bengali Tales from Court and Village*, Edward C. Dimock, trans, University of Chicago Press, 1963. **Extract 14.**

Ray, Sukumar, *Collected Nonsense*, Sukanata Chauduri, trans, OUP, Delhi, 1988.

Raychaudhuri, Tapan, *Europe Reconsidered: Perceptions of the West in Nineteenth Century Bengal*, OUP, Delhi, 1988.

Raychaudhuri, Upendrakishore, *The Stupid Tiger and Other Tales*, William Radice, trans, Deutsch, London, 1981.

Robinson, Andrew, *The Art of Rabindranath Tagore*, Deutsch, London, 1989.

Robinson, Andrew, *Satyajit Ray: The Inner Eye*, Deutsch, London, 1989.

Rokeya, Begum (Rokeya Sakawat Hossein), *Sultana's Dream and Selections from the Secluded Ones*, Feminist Press, New York, 1988. **Extract 24.**

Seely, Clinton B., *A Poet Apart: A Literary Biography of the Bengali Poet Jibanananda Das (1899–1954)*, University of Delaware Press, 1990. **Extract 30.**

Sen, Sukumar, *History of Bengali Literature*, Delhi, 1960.

Tagore, Debendranath, *The Autobiography of Debendranath Tagore*, Satyendranath Tagore and Indira Devi, trans, London, 1914. **Extract 25.**

Tagore, Rabindranath, *I Won't Let Go: Selected Poems*, Ketaki Kushari Dyson, trans, Bloodaxe, Newcastle, UK, 1991.

Tagore, Rabindranath, *Quartet*, Kaiser Haq, trans, Heinemann, London, 1993.

Tagore, Rabindranath, *Selected Poems*, William Radice, trans, Penguin, Harmondsworth, 1985.

Extracts 15 and 17.
Tagore, Rabindranath, *Selected Short Stories*, William Radice, trans, Penguin, Harmondsworth, 1994.
Extract 16.
Waliullah, Syed, *Tree Without Roots*, Qaisar Saeed, Anne-Marie Thi-baud, Jeffrey Gibian and Malik Khayyam, trans, Chatto and Windus, London, 1967. **Extract 4**.
Zbavitel, Dušan, *Bengali Literature*, Otto Harrassowitz, Wiesbaden, Germany, 1976.

Extracts

(1) ASSAM

Rózsa Hajnóczy, *Fire of Bengal*

This massive novel, from which Hungarians get their main image of India, was written by the wife of Gyula Germanus, an eminent Hungarian scholar of Islam whom Tagore invited to his university at Santiniketan from 1929 to 1932. A mixture of autobiography, travelogue and adulterous romance, it takes the reader to places all over India, including Cherapunji in Assam, 'the wettest place in the world'.

Gertrud is a restless soul, lacking the patience to sit at home. The eternal quest of the geographer carries her from place to place. Not even the torrential rain can cool her ardour. Indeed, it is rain which has preoccupied her most of late. She has installed a rain-gauge in front of the villa and has informed us that we are to accompany her to Cherapunji, not far away, which has the highest rainfall in the world. It is the only claim that Cherapunji has to recognition. Yet it is of exceptional importance, Gertrud assures us. The average rainfall is nearly four hundred inches, and in 1861 – a landmark in the history of rainfall! – it rose to seven hundred and eighty-seven inches. When I consider that on the plains eighteen inches of rain is enough to cause a flood, I can image the torrents that descend on the heads of people here.

I was reluctant to leave Shillong even for a day, considering little Sam's condition, yet I could not withstand Gertrud's insistent quest.

On a glorious sunny morning we set off by car for Cherapunji. Our road took us through dense forests in which the car was hopelessly out of place. Gigantic butterflies, the size of a crow or kite, fluttered among the shrubs, the sun glittering on their rainbow wings. The natives hunt them with bow and arrow, for, fried in mustard-seed oil, the butterfly is a favourite dish.

The road made a gradual ascent until, on the crest of the mountain, the forest was left behind, and we were in thick mist, which enveloped us in its cool damps, so that we were reduced to walking pace. To our left gaped a sheer drop of two thousand three hundred feet. If the driver made an error of only two feet, we would be hurled to our death. To continue on such a dangerous road in this fog was tempting fate. Gertrud was keenly disappointed not to be able, because of the fog, to see over the precipice, which is known hereabouts as the Giant's Jaws. No German geographer had ever been here before, and she would be the first to make a morphological description of this region. I myself regretted not being able to get a view of the hills stretching away to our right. Then suddenly, as if the gods had taken pity on us, there was the merest break in the clouds, and a streak of light, like a celestial beam, illuminated the whole panorama. The lush turf, with the green of perpetual moisture, lay like a carpet, mingled with brilliant flowers, among the trees. As the last shreds of mist dispersed, everything emerged into view.

(2) Bangladesh

Hasan Azizul Huq, 'A Day in Bhushan's Life'

Bangladesh's most distinguished writer of short stories here portrays with grim power a villager of limited intelligence caught up in the horrific events of 1971. This is the end of the story: Bhushan has earlier been furious with his son Haridas for failing to pull his weight in the fields.

Bhushan saw a young woman, about twenty-five, trying to reach the shelter of the tamarind tree through the bullets whizzing by all around her. She nestled a dark, chubby baby in her bosom. She had almost reached the tree when there was the sound of a sharp snap. The woman stopped, with her hand on the baby's head. Bhushan saw the bright red blood pouring through her fingers, soon mixed with the white matter of the baby's brain now emptied into her palm. The young woman turned around, looked at the baby's face, and like a lunatic she shook the baby a few times with both hands and threw it away with a scream that no human voice would have seemed capable of. And then her hands tore away her dirty blouse. Bhushan saw her round breasts swollen with milk. She pointed to her chest and shouted, 'Come on, you bastards. Shoot me here! Here!'

Next moment one of her swollen breasts burst open like a ripe cotton flower of a *shimul* tree. Her body was thrown off with a jerk. She fell under the tree and lay with her open eyes frozen in the fierce anger of her last moment.

In the midst of all this, Bhushan could also see that Haridas was standing a little away from him. He was going to grab him and pull him back, when Haridas suddenly kneeled to the ground. Bhushan turned and saw, right before him, within barely two feet, one of the men in khaki holding his stubby black gun. His huge fair-skinned face was dripping with sweat and red with anger. He was so close that Bhushan saw his eyes; he even smelled the sweat of his body. The man was shouting abuse at him.

At this point, Bhushan was seeing nothing else. The muscles of his hands tensed up his flat paws, as he considered the throat of the man. He stood looking at the man's neck, and he seemed to be undecided, till his body finally made up its mind, and sprang to the side of Haridas in a single stride of concentrated energy.

By then, Haridas was lying on the ground, his body quite still, only a bit of his fading life lingering in his eyes like a faint spark left in cooling embers. Bhushan crouched beside him, his face bent close to Haridas's face, and he talked to him with all the tenderness of a father for a son. 'Haridas, my son, my darling son'. With his rough peasant hands, Bhushan stroked the body of his dying son, and he kept singing to the boy, 'Haridas, my dear son, my darling boy!'

Then there was a single odd crack, with which Bhushan's stubby pillarlike body shook a few times and became very still, releasing him from feeling anything any more.

(3) BANGLADESH

Shamsur Rahman,
'Preferences' and 'Lines on a Cat'

The first poem shows that the leading contemporary poet of Bangladesh is capable of political rage, as well as the wry tenderness of the second.

Preferences

I love the venomous snake hidden in the green
because it is not more malignant than a deceiving friend.
I love the blind vampire bat

because it is a great deal more compassionate than the critic.
The angry scorpion's bite is dear to me
because its agony is sweeter
than the red-lipped kiss of a faithless sweetheart.
I love the graceful tiger in the dark forest
because the dictator's
calculated all-consuming viciousness is alien to it.

Lines on a Cat

For a few years we had a cat about our house,
lapping up our love, especially my youngest daughter's.
She looked after its daily needs, kept it clean
and well fed, giving up her own share of fish at meals,
and waited up for it to come back from its prowls.
One day it didn't; we searched in vain,
it had disappeared without trace.
My daughter in her sorrow lay in bed
two days without eating, keeping with me
a reproachful silence: as if I had worked
her pet's disappearance!

How could I make her realize it often happens
someone takes leave saying, 'Till we meet again',
and disappears just like this, leaving behind
a vast emptiness as a gift: we never meet again.

(4) BANGLADESH
Syed Waliullah, *Tree Without Roots*

*This famous novel tells the story of a man of humble origins
called Majeed, who claims he has found the grave of a Muslim
pir (saint) and establishes a cult around it, achieving a dominant
position in the community but failing to find inner or domestic
happiness.*

One morning, after having watched the workmen busy on the mosque,
the foundations of which were just being laid, Majeed started on his
way to the village, and as he walked along, the wild wind of the month
of Falgoon suddenly sprang up. This first explosion of spring, violent
and aggressive, always struck unexpectedly when one had almost come
to believe that the balmy days of winter, the cloudless blue skies,
golden sunshine, and early-morning mists, would be with one forever.

Startled, Majeed stopped short at the edge of the fields. Only a little distance away a whirlwind spiralled up and roared away, sweeping aside dead leaves and dust – the skin of the earth which, during the rainless months, had dried into a fine, white powder.

The first signs of the change in seasons always seemed to confuse time itself. The present year and the one that had passed, this season and the one that had gone before, the present moment and another long buried, all became tangled, enmeshed, and whirled about together in a timeless void. At such times, a painful thought that might come to mind would stretch itself over one's whole life; a happy moment would grow so vast as to obliterate all else.

Majeed felt moved. The madly dancing whirlwind and the roaring gale that swept away the dead leaves and the dust laid bare something that had long remained hidden within him, and turned his thoughts to the years that had gone by. Troubled, he remained standing there by the side of the field. He sighed and thought – how long was it now that he had been living here? Eleven years? Perhaps twelve? He recalled the day when he had first come here, a day without a breath of wind, in the summer month of Sravan.

Walking on again, he told himself: Yes, time flows by. How strange that this burst of wind should remind me of that, and should make so many things, so many insignificant little things come to mind once again. Yes, time flows, things change. Nothing remains the same. But one forgets this unless one is reminded by such things as the sudden rushing of the mad wind of Falgoon. Nature changes and thus reminds us that we must change too. We must go on from adolescence to adulthood, and then from life to death.

An indefinable sadness filled him.

(5) BENGAL

Anonymous, *Bengali Folk Poems*

The wandering Baul singers of Bengal reject orthodox religion, and often mix their universalist mataphysics with a vigorous, witty use of contemporary imagery. Taken from Deben Bhattacharya, trans, Songs of the Bards of Bengal (see Booklist).

> If you wish to board an aeroplane,
> you must travel light
> to be safe from the danger of a crash.
> You must renounce
> your errors and inhibitions
> and show your credentials in the aerodrome.

Paying your fare of devotion to God,
you must give up
your worldly wealth
to buy a ticket for the seat.
The feet of your master,
the aeroplane,
will take you to Vishnu's sphere,
even before an eyelid's wink. . . .

* * *

That astounding engine
of the train
makes the wheels move
with organized power
from the beautiful earth,
fire, water and air.

But the day comes when
the passenger goes,
and the boiler breaks down
and the engine stops
and four shoulders
bear the machinery
to the funeral ground.
And all for the astounding engine
of the train. . . .

(6) BENGAL

Bibhutibhushan Banerji, *Song of the Road*

*Bhibhutibhushan's magical autobiographical novel has become
well-known through Satyajit Ray's film. It is unequalled as an
evocation of a brother and sister growing up in a Bengali village –
in perfect happiness until poverty and tragedy overcome them.*

Durga went down a little way into the water. 'There's a lot of water fruit
here, Opu,' she shouted. 'You stand there and I'll get some.' She went
in a little further and tore several plants up by the stems and threw
them on the bank. 'Catch, Opu.'

'The water fruit's right out over the water, Didi. How are you going
to get at it?'

The water fruit was indeed far out over the water. Durga did her best to reach it with a bamboo cane, but with no success. 'The bank's very steep here,' she said. 'I shall slip down into deep water if I go further out. What can I do to reach it? Oh, yes, I know, you can help. Hold on to the end of my sari and I may be able to reach them with the pole.'

Inside the jungle a yellow bird was sitting on a twig in a *moynakanta* tree. It was singing very sweetly and making the leaves dance. Opu was fascinated. 'What bird is that, Didi?'

'Don't worry about birds! Hold on to my sari for all you're worth or I shall slip in. Hold on tight now.'

Step by step Durga went down into the water, stretching out with the cane as far as it would go. Her clothes were wet through but still she could not reach. She went a little bit further and tried again, this time holding the cane with the tips of her fingers. Opu stood behind her pulling as hard as he could, but suddenly he realized that he was not strong enough to hold her and burst out laughing. He laughed so much that he let go and Durga began to slide in, but she managed to save herself in time. Then she laughed too. 'What a wash-out you are!' she exclaimed. 'You're utterly useless! But come on, let's have another go. Hold on again.' With an enormous effort she succeeded in hooking a cluster of fruit and pulling it near. She examined it eagerly to see how much fruit there was on it, but in a minute or so she flung it on the bank. 'They're quite raw. They haven't got any milk in them yet. Let's try once more. Hold on now.' Opu held on again, but he could not counter his sister's pull as she leaned forward, and little by little he found himself slipping into the water. His clothes began to get wet, so he gave up and stood there shaking with laughter. Durga laughed too. 'Silly!' she said; and for some time the lonely bamboo grove by the side of the pond echoed with the happy laughter of brother and sister.

(7) BENGAL

Baru Chandidas, *Shrikrishnakirtan*

The earliest, liveliest and most unusual Bengali Vaishnava text, describing in a sequence of more than 400 songs Krishna's courting and seduction of Radha, with the help of the go-between Barayi ('Granny') – Radha's great-aunt.

Song 10

'Radha, in the pitcher on your hip you've taken water.
Speak to me a little with your words of liquid honey!
You've a splendid bodice on your breasts, your earrings glisten;
Brighter than the sun, they wear a halo's iridescence.

Dairymaid, slow down! You must pay heed to what I'm asking:
Banish my forlorness now and then – let me embrace you!
Radha, you are spurning me, escaping with your water.
Why do you unsettle me this way by getting angry?
What's the reason you are not responding to me, Radha?
I'm burned up all over with the flames of your aloofness.
Listen to my counsel, Radha: cast aside your fury.
Think this over fully: it disfigures you, your anger.
I am in command here at the Yamuna embankment;
I will smash your pitcher on the path if you ignore me!
Radha, think this over to yourself from start to finish.
This time you must hear out my remarks, enticing Radha!'
Radha turned to stare him in the eye upon this outburst.

Song 11

'On this pathway, many people – good and bad – are going.
One should stand apart from them before discussing business.
But since you insist on making private matters public,
It is clear to me that there's no sense in your behavior.
On the path you ought to watch your feelings, son of Nanda.
Why is it you have to spend your time creating problems?
In my house my husband's mother stays, and she's malicious.
She is not afraid to cast unspeakable aspersions.
Since you are aware yourself of all your past adventures,
Why reveal them on the bank and pathway, Chakrapani?
Krishna, you must promptly put a stop to your entreaties.
Don't you know my friends are not all friendly? Some are hostile.
If these things should be divulged by any one among them,
You will be disgraced, and I will be the butt of scandal.'
Radha reached the door of her own house while she was speaking.
Krishna did not answer; he was feeling apprehensive.
Meanwhile, each of Radha's friends departed for her household.

(8) Bengal

Bankimchandra Chatterjee, *The Abbey of Bliss*

Bankim had one of the finest intellects in 19th century Bengal, and his novels and essays had a marked influence on the growth of neo-Hindu and nationalist ideas. The Abbey of Bliss (Anandamath) tells the story of the Sannyasi rebellion that occurred in North Bengal in 1773, with the rebels transformed into anti-British patriots, inspired by the teachings of the Bhagavad Gita. The extract below includes the song Bandemataram, which became a rallying-cry for Bengali nationalists in the early 20th century.

In that smiling moonlit night, the two silently walked across the plain. Mahendra was silent, sad, careless and a little curious.

Bhavananda suddenly changed his looks. He was no more the steady and mild anchorite, nor wore any more the warlike hero's face – the face of the slayer of a captain of forces. Not even was there in his mien the proud disdain with which he had scolded Mahendra even now. It seemed as if his heart was filled with joy at the beauteous sight of the earth, lulled in peace and beaming under the silvery moon, and of the glory in her wilds and woods and hills and streams, and grew cheery like the ocean smiling with the rise of the moon. Bhavananda grew chatty, cheerful, cordial and very eager to talk. He made many an attempt to open a conversation with his companion but Mahendra would not speak. Having no option left, he then began to sing to himself:

> Hail thee mother! To her I bow,
> Who with sweetest water o'erflows
> With dainty fruits is rich endowed
> And cooling whom the south wind blows,
> Who's green with crops as on her grow;
> To such a mother down I bow.

Mahendra was a little puzzled to hear the song; he could not grasp anything. Who could be the mother, he thought.

> Who with sweetest water o'erflows
> With dainty fruits is rich endowed
> And cooling whom the south wind blows?
> Who's green with crops as on her grow.

He asked, 'Who is the mother?' Bhavananda did not answer but sang on:

With silver moonbeams smile her nights
And trees that in their bloom abound
Adorn her; and her face doth beam
With sweetest smiles; sweet's her sound!
Joy and bliss she doth bestow;
To such a mother down I bow.

'It is the country and no mortal mother' – cried Mahendra. 'We own no other mother,' retorted Bhavananda; 'they say, "the mother and the land of birth are higher than heaven." We think the land of birth to be no other than our mother herself. We have no mother, no father, no brother, no wife, no child, no hearth or home, we have only got the mother.'

Who with sweetest water o'erflows
With dainty fruits is rich endowed.

Mahendra now understood the song and asked Bhavananda to sing again.

(9) BENGAL

Nirad C. Chaudhuri, *They Hand, Great Anarch!*

The best-read, most controversial and long-lived of contemporary Bengali authors, Nirad C. Chaudhuri is internationally known for his English writings, especially The Autobiography of an Unknown Indian and his recent 963-page follow-up volume, They Hand, Great Anarch! The following extract relates to his time as Secretary to the Congress politician Sarat Chandra Bose (brother of Subhas Bose), and describes a stay by Gandhi and his entourage in Sarat Babu's house.

Putting up Gandhi did not present a difficult problem; feeding him did. Mahatma Gandhi's dietary prescriptions were not only rigid and numerous, but also odd. Since they were not identical with the well known Hindu dietary rules but somewhat esoteric, Sarat Babu asked an orthodox disciple of Gandhi in Calcutta to let him have a list of the vegetables Gandhi ate. The list I saw was formidably long and representative of the ecology of Bengal. Of course, he did not eat the full range of vegetables at one meal or even on one single day, but he or his secretary in charge might demand one or other of them on a particular day or for a particular meal in order to test the resources and loyalty of his host. Also, the secretary would not specify the herb or vegetable for that day before ten in the morning, and Mahatma Gandhi wanted his meal at about midday. Therefore, no time would be available to buy a particular vegetable if demanded, and all had to be ready in the kitchen, so that the particular one called for would be at hand. To fail in supplying and cooking the vegetable was likely to be regarded as a shame on the Bose household. However, they were able to solve this problem quite successfully. Mrs Bose had a young nephew who was the superintendent of one of the markets of the Calcutta Corporation, and therefore could rouse the greengrocers to great effort, were this necessary. I knew him very well. He had no political pretensions but was a very energetic and enterprising person. He wanted to rise to the occasion, and if he had failed to procure all the vegetables regularly, I am sure he would have killed himself like Vatel, the major domo of the Great Condé, who threw himself on his sword because, when M. le Prince was receiving Louis XIV at Chantilly, he found that only two carts of sea fish had arrived instead of the forty he had ordered.

(10) BENGAL

Mahesweta Devi, 'The Witch-Hunt'

Mahesweta Devi derives many of her stories from her study of tribal people and untouchables. In 'The Witch-Hunt' severe drought gives rise to a witch scare, exploited to their own benefit by priests and local leaders (from Of Women, Outcastes, Peasants, and Rebels, A Selection of Bengali Short Stories, see Booklist).

'Look!' he shouts.

They stop all at once and lift up their torches. The flames cast moving reflections in the dark water of Kuruda, swirling like black snakes coiling and uncoiling among the big stones scattered across its bed. On one stone stands a dark naked female; her deformed body is not clearly visible, her face smeared with blood and bits of feather. She raises her hand when she sees them, with a bird's wing in the hand.

'There's the witch!' they all shout at once.

Her eyes seem to light up with expectation. She sways and laughs silently.

'It's laughing!'

Pahan lurches forward, his body withered, but his eyes turned savage with fear. All eyes become killer eyes, wild and desperate. Pahan shouts, 'In the name of Haramdeo and all the spirits, we'll drive you away!'

Now the witch's eyes also turn savage. Raising her hands, shaking her hair, she howls. Again it sounds like the bellowing of a buffalo being branded.

'Hit it with stones!' Stones fly at her. 'Be careful not to spill its blood! If its blood touches the ground, hundreds of witches will be born of it!'

She too picks up a stone and throws it at them. It hits Pahan in the head, and blood streams down his cheek. 'We have to hit it, or it will hit us more!' Stones fly. The men shout frantically and pelt stones at her.

Suddenly she screams. It tears through their collective shouting and rises to the sky, as she steps off the stone onto the riverbed and runs toward the other side of the river.

From this side they keep pelting stones at her until her terrible howl of pain moves away. Pahan listens and says that it is going toward Hesadi village. At least they themselves are saved. He wipes the blood off his face, his eyes shining with the excitment of victory against evil.

'No one sleeps tonight. You'll drink and dance throughout the night.'

'And tomorrow?'

'Tomorrow I'll worship.'

(11) BENGAL

Nazrul Islam, 'The Rebel'

It seems impossible, in choosing one poem to represent Nazrul Islam, not to settle for his most famous outburst, which gave him the soubriquet 'The Rebel Poet'. The revolutionary ardour of many of his poems, and of the journal Dhumketu ('The Comet') which he edited, led to his being imprisoned for a year by the British for sedition. Here is the last part of the poem from Selected Poems of Nazrul Islam, see Booklist.

I am consciousness in the unconscious soul,
I am the flag of triumph at the gate of the world,
I am the glorious sign of man's victory,
Clapping my hands in exultation I rush like the hurricane,
Traversing the earth and the sky.
The mighty Borrak is the horse I ride.
It neighs impatiently, drunk with delight!
I am the burning volcano in the bosom of the earth,
I am the wild fire of the woods,
I am Hell's mad terrific sea of wrath!

I ride on the wings of the lightning with joy profound,
I scatter misery and fear all around,
I bring earth-quakes on this world!

I am Orpheus, flute,
I bring sleep to the fevered world,
I make the heaving ocean quiet.
I am the flute in the hands of Shyam!
When I rush across the sky mad with anger,
The fires of the seven hells tremble in fear and die.
I carry the message of revolt to the earth and the sky!
I am the mighty flood,
Sometimes I make the earth rich and fertile,
At other times I cause colossal damage.
I snatch from Bishnu's bosom the two girls!
I am injustice, I am the shooting star,
I am Saturn, I am the fire of the comet,
I am the poisonous asp!
I am Chandi the headless, I am the ruinous Warlord,
Sitting in the burning pit of Hell
I smile as the innocent flower!
I am the cruel axe of Parshurama,
I shall kill warriors
And bring peace and harmony to this universe!
I am the plough on the shoulders of Balarama,
I shall uproot this miserable earth effortlessly and with ease,
And create a new universe of joy and peace.
Weary of struggles, I, the great rebel,
Shall rest in quiet only when I find
The sky and the air free of the piteous groans of the oppressed.
Only when the battlefields are cleared of jingling bloody sabres
Shall I, weary of struggles, rest in quiet,
I the great rebel.

I am the rebel eternal,
I raise my head beyond this world,
High, ever erect and alone!

(12) BENGAL

Martin Kämpchen, *Madhu, the Honey-seller*

Martin Kämpchen has lived in India for nearly twenty years, settling in 1979 at Santiniketan where Tagore founded his school and university. He is the leading translator of Tagore into German, and has written a number of stories based on his life in Bengal.

I spent some days in the village recently. In the quiet of the evening, stories were exchanged. Children would listen at the start, asking eager questions, but would fall asleep before the end. They were carried to their mothers later, to finish the night beside them.

I was moved by one particular story, and I want to re-tell it here. It's the story of Madhu the Honey-seller. It was told by Arup's father; he said he had heard it for the first time in Jaypur, a neighbouring village. Was it true? Of course. Had he invented any of it? He evaded the question by saying that he'd heard several versions of the story. But it really was true, and Madhu was known and revered by humble villagers in Bengal and Orissa. His life reminds me of the life-story of Chaitanya and other saints; of old myths too. But Madhu also has contemporary significance: his life is part of each of our lives. It seems to me that the religious longings of many story-tellers have worked upon it, that certain myths are brought into focus again through Madhu, that he gives fresh form to ancient memories. If a teller of his life alters or adds, does that mean that he falsifies? He does so to make it more deeply a part of our own lives. For the life of a saint never belongs to that saint alone; it belongs to all who follow him by loving God.

Madhu, as described by Arup's father, had not always been Madhu the Honey-seller. Previously he had lived on his ancestral farm, surrounded by his family and fields. He loved them equally – cherished his family and fields like a beautiful lotus in a pond. Two dozen men came each morning from the villages nearby and worked for him, and he treated them well. His eldest son had passed out of school and now shared in supervising workers and cultivating the fields. Madhu's mother and father had gone from the world, and he felt bound to them more deeply than is possible with those who are still accessible to the senses. He relished the mystery of death, without turning from life. He loved his wife for her motherly heart and her wifely body, and he never looked at his children without being gripped by the feeling that they were the life of his life – an embodiment of the gratitude he owed for his own gift of life.

But then a terrible thing happened, the thing with which the story of Madhu the Honey-seller begins. It was summer, and heat burdened the landscape. Before the mid-day meal, Madhu went as usual with his sons to the pond to bathe. With their hair and bodies well oiled, and only a *gamcha* round their hips, they stood in the water. The youngest son planted himself amidst the creepers and cresses near the bank. Madhu saw the snake: saw how – frightened by the disturbance – it glided through the water and bit the boy sharply in the arm twice. Overcome by terror and pain, the boy's small body sank soundlessly into the water and disappeared under the plants.

He died a threefold death: poison and terror compounded by the suffocating water.

'O God', gasped Madhu, 'don't take him away – he's still too small.' But he was already gone. The night stars whirled over Madhu's head like marsh-fires. Harmony was shattered. He fell and fell through emptiness.

'O God', he cried, 'don't take him away. He is still so small.' But he was already gone. Fire had cast wood and flesh up to heaven, with its usual darting and twirling. The heat of the flames united with the summer heat, ashes with the scorched earth.

Madhu did not *decide* to leave home. His crippled spirit was incapable of that. It was his weight of suffering, spreading through the organs of his body, dragging at his limbs and settling in his heart, that told him at last that he must go.

Two nights later he stole away. His children suspected that he might leave, but they did not try to stop him. His grief frightened them. His wife's eyes opened when he got up, wound his dhoti round his hips and prepared to leave, but she did not stir. Madhu paused to listen to her light, rapid breathing, and then set out.

(13) Bengal

Govindadas Kaviraj, *Vaishnava*

> One of the most celebrated writers of Vaishnava padas (songs), Govindadas wrote mostly in Brajabuli, 'the language of Vraja (Vrindavan)' a hybrid poetic language cultivated by Vaishnava poets all over north and eastern India (from Edward C. Dimock and Denise Levertov, trans, In Praise of Krishna: Songs from the Bengali, see Booklist).

Fingering the border of her friend's sari, nervous and afraid,
sitting tensely on the edge of Krishna's couch,

as her friend left she too looked to go
but in desire Krishna blocked her way.

He was infatuated, she bewildered;
he was clever, and she naive.

He put out his hand to touch her; she quickly pushed it away.
He looked into her face, her eyes filled with tears.

He held her forcefully, she trembled violently
and hid her face from his kisses behind the edge of her sari.

Then she lay down, frightened, beautiful as a doll;
he hovered like a bee round a lotus in a painting.

Govinda-dasa says, Because of this,
drowned in the well of her beauty,
Krishna's lust was changed.

(14) BENGAL

Bharatchandra Ray, *Vidya-Sundara*

Bharatchandra brought the medieval Bengali tradition to a most
sophisticated and courtly conclusion. Vidya-Sundara, the second
part of his narrative trilogy the Annada-mangal, tells of how a
Princess is seduced by a Prince, despite her vow that only he who
can defeat her in argument can marry her. From Edward C.
Dimock, trans, The Thief of Love, Bengali Tales from Court
and Village, see Booklist.

One day the poet desired Vidya in the daytime, and entered her room.
Vidya had closed her door and lay asleep; seeing her thus sleeping,
Sundar was filled with pleasure. Because of the night's sleeplessness,
she had fallen where she had stood; her companions were asleep,
outside the door. Sundar, eager for her love, was like a honeybee,
uncertainly returned to drink more lotus-nectar. He had no patience,
even to awaken her, but began his sacrifice to passion. He was filled
with desire, and she in her deep sleep thought it was a dream; her
passion began to grow. With kisses and embraces, he worshipped her
with many kinds of love. And indeed, more happiness is sometimes
found in sleep; in a dream much more success is had in finding what is
lost, than waking. And when the play of love was finished, her sleep in
joy was broken, and she awoke. Lazily, slowly, her reddened eyes
opened. She woke up slowly, and saw the sun, and said:
'How can the day have come so soon?'
Then she saw Sundar lying there, and anger seized her mind. She
thought:

'He has seen me in the depths of sleep, and in the day. My hair is disarrayed, my clothes are all awry. Such behaviour only brings humiliation to a girl. The minds of men are hard and shameful, and do not understand the proper way of things'.

Thinking thus, annoyed, she hung her head in silence and in shame. She put aside her ornaments and jewels. And Sundar understood what was in her heart, what his offence had been. He thought:

'Why have I done this insane thing? It was for her happiness and mine, but it has turned to ashes. What I thought was nectar was really poison. What shall I do?'

Thus the poet thought. And now the sun had sunk behind the hills, and it was evening. The moon had risen. He then made love to her with words, to soothe her mind. But can entreaty conquer anger?

(15) BENGAL

Rabindranath Tagore, *'Broken Song'*

Formerly known outside Bengal through his own English translations, Tagore's poetry is now beginning to be revealed through fresh translations that strive to convey something of the depth and power of the original. This moving poem reflects many of Tagore's most deeply held feelings about life and art. From William Radice, trans, Selected Poems, see Booklist.

Kashinath the new young singer fills the hall with sound:
The seven notes dance in his throat like seven tame birds.
His voice is a sharp sword slicing and thrusting everywhere,
It darts like lightning – no knowing where it will go when.
He sets deadly traps for himself, then cuts them away:
The courtiers listen in amazement, give frequent gasps of praise.
Only the old king Pratap Ray sits like wood, unmoved.
Baraj Lal is the only singer he likes, all others leave him cold.
From childhood he has spent so long listening to him sing –
Rag Kafi during *holi*, cloud-songs during the rains,
Songs for Durga at dawn in autumn, songs to bid her farewell –
His heart swelled when he heard them and his eyes swam with tears.
And on days when friends gathered and filled the hall
There were cowherds' songs of Krshna in *rags* Bhupali and Multan.

So many nights of wedding-festivity have passed in that royal house:
Servants dressed in red, hundreds of lamps alight:
The bridegroom sitting shyly in his finery and jewels,
Young friends teasing him and whispering in his ear:

Before him, singing *rag* Sahana, sits Baraj Lal.
The king's heart is full of all those days and songs.
When he hears some other singer, he feels no chord inside,
No sudden magical awakening of memories of the past.
When Pratap Ray watches Kashinath he just sees his wagging head:
Tune after tune after tune, but none with any echo in the heart.

Kashinath asks for a rest and the singing stops for a space.
Pratap Ray smilingly turns his eyes to Baraj Lal.
He puts his mouth to his ear and says, 'Dear *ustad*,
Give us a song as songs ought to be, this is no song at all.
It's all tricks and games, like a cat hunting a bird.
We used to hear songs in the old days, today they have no idea.'

Old Baraj Lal, white-haired, white turban on his head,
Bows to the assembled courtiers and slowly takes his seat.
He takes the *tanpura* in his wasted, heavily veined hand
And with lowered head and closed eyes begins *rag* Yaman-kalyan.
His quavering voice is swallowed by the enormous hall,
It is like a tiny bird in a storm, unable to fly for all it tries.
Pratap Ray, sitting to the left, encourages him again and again:
'Superb, bravo!' he says in his ear, 'sing out loud.'

The courtiers are inattentive: some whisper amongst themselves,
Some of them yawn, some doze, some go off to their rooms;
Some of them call to servants, 'Bring the hookah, bring some *pan*.'
Some fan themselves furiously and complain of the heat.
They cannot keep still for a minute, they shuffle or walk about –
The hall was quiet before, but every sort of noise has grown.
The old man's singing is swamped, like a frail boat in a typhoon:
Only his shaky fingering of the *tanpura* shows it is there.

Music that should rise on its own joy from the depths of the heart
Is crushed by heedless clamour, like a fountain under a stone.
The song and Baraj Lal's feelings go separate ways,
But he sings for all he is worth, to keep up the honour of his king.

One of the verses of the song has somehow slipped from his mind.
He quickly goes back, tries to get it right this time.
Again he forgets, it is lost, he shakes his head at the shame;
He starts the song at the beginning – again he has to stop.
His hand trembles doubly as he prays to his teacher's name.
His voice quakes with distress, like a lamp guttering in a breeze.
He abandons the words of the song and tries to salvage the tune,

But suddenly his wide-mouthed singing breaks into loud cries.
The intricate melody goes to the winds, the rhythm is swept away –
Tears snap the thread of the song, cascade like pearls.
In shame he rests his head on the old *tanpura* in his lap –
He has failed to remember a song: he weeps as he did as a child.
With brimming eyes king Pratap Ray tenderly touches his friend:
'Come, let us go from here,' he says with kindness and love.
They leave that festive hall with its hundreds of blinding lights.
The two old friends go outside, holding each other's hands.

Baraj says with hands clasped, 'Master, our days are gone.
New men have come now, new styles and customs in the world.
The court we kept is deserted – only the two of us are left.
Don't ask anyone to listen to me now, I beg you at your feet, my lord.
The singer alone does not make a song, there has to be someone who
  hears:
One man opens his throat to sing, the other sings in his mind.
Only when waves fall on the shore do they make a harmonious sound;
Only when breezes shake the woods do we hear a rustling in the leaves.
Only from a marriage of two forces does music arise in the world.
Where there is no love, where listeners are dumb, there never can be
  song.'

(16) BENGAL

Rabindranath Tagore, *'Guest'*

> *The concluding paragraphs from one of his finest stories of the
> 1890s. Tarapada, a run-away from a rural brahman family,
> lives with Matilal Babu and his family for a while. Matilal and
> his wife decide to marry Tarapada to their only daughter,
> Charu, but Tarapada disappears the night before the wedding.
> Tagore's elaborate prose is wonderfully evocative of the East
> Bengal landscape during the monsoon. From William Radice,
> trans, Selected Short Stories, see Booklist.*

Matilal Babu fixed the wedding for the month of Shraban, and sent
word to Tarapada's mother and brothers; but he did not inform
Tarapada himself. He told his *moktar* in Calcutta to hire a military-style
band, and he ordered everything else that would be needed for the
wedding.

Early monsoon clouds formed in the sky. The village-river had been
dried up for weeks; there was water only in holes here and there; small
boats lay stuck in these pools of muddy water, and the dry river-bed was

rutted with bullock-cart tracks. But now, like Parvati returning to her parents' home, gurgling waters returned to the empty arms of the village: naked children danced and shouted on the river-bank, jumped into the water with voracious joy as if trying to embrace the river; the villagers gazed at the river like a dear friend; a huge wave of life and delight rolled through the parched village. There were boats big and small with cargoes from far and wide; in the evenings the *ghat* resounded with the songs of foreign boatmen. The villages along the river had spent the summer confined to their own small worlds: now, with the rains, the outside world had come in its vast watery chariot, carrying wondrous gifts to the villages, as if on a visit to its daughters. Rustic smallness was temporarily subsumed by pride of contact with the world; everything became more active; the bustle of distant cities came to this sleepy region, and the whole sky rang.

Meanwhile at Kurulkata, on the Nag family estate, a famous chariot-festival was due to be held. One moonlit evening Tarapada went to the *ghat* and saw, on the swift flood-tide, boats with merry-go-rounds and *yatra*-troupes, and cargo-boats rapidly making for the fair. An orchestra from Calcutta was practising loudly as it passed; the *yatra*-troupe was singing to violin accompaniment, shouting out the beats; boatmen from lands to the west split the sky with cymbals and thudding drums. Such excitement! Then clouds from the east covered the moon with their huge black sails; an east wind blew sharply; cloud after cloud rolled by; the river gushed and swelled; darkness thickened in the swaying riverside trees; frogs croaked; crickets rasped like wood-saws. To Tarapada the whole world seemed like a chariot-festival: wheels turning, flags flying, earth trembling, clouds swirling, wind rushing, river flowing, boats sailing, songs sounding! There were rumbles of thunder, and slashes of lightning in the sky: the smell of torrential rain approached from the dark distance. But Kathaliya village next to the river ignored all this: she shut her doors, turned out her lamps and went to sleep.

The following morning Tarapada's mother and brothers arrived at Kathaliya; and that same morning three large boats from Calcutta, laden with things for the wedding, moored at the zamindar's *ghat*; and very early, that same morning, Sonamani brought some mango-juice preserve in paper and some pickle wrapped in a leaf, and timidly stood outside Tarapada's room – but Tarapada was not to be seen. In a cloudy monsoon night, before love and emotional ties could encircle him completely, this Brahman boy, thief of all hearts in the village, had returned to the unconstraining, unemotional arms of his mother Earth.

(17) BENGAL

Rabindranath Tagore, 'On the Sick-bed'

Despite the achievements of Jibanananda and others, Tagore managed to remain the greatest (and most modern) Bengali poet of the 20th century as well as the 19th. Here is a poem of life and joy, written when the poet was ill and nearing his death. From William Radice, trans, Selected Poems, see Booklist.

O my day-break sparrow –
In my last moments of sleepiness,
While there is still some darkness,
Here you are tapping on my window-slats,
Asking for news
And then dancing and twittering
Just as your whim takes you.
Your pluckily bobbing tail
Cocks a snook at all restrictions.
When magpie-robins chirrup at dawn,
Poets tip them.
When a hidden *koel*-bird hoots all day
Its same unvarying fifth,
So high is its rating
It gets the applause of Kalidasa
Ahead of all other birds.
You couldn't care less –
You never keep to the scale –
To enter Kalidasa's room
And chatter
And mess up his metres
Amuses you greatly.
Whenever you perch on a pillar
At the court of King Vikramaditya
And bards spout,
What are their songs to you?
You are closer to the poet's mistress:
You happily join in her round-the-clock prattle.
You do not dance
Under contract from the Spring –
You strut
Any old how, no discipline at all.
You do not turn up politely
At woodland singing-contests;
You gossip with the light in broad vernacular –

Its meaning
Is not in the dictionary –
Only your own throbbing little chest
Knows it.
Slanting your neck to right or left,
How you play about –
So busy all day for no apparent reason,
Scrabbling at the ground,
Bathing in the dust –
You are so unkempt
The dirt doesn't show on you, worry you at all.
You build your nest in the corner of the ceiling
Of even a king's chamber,
You are so utterly brazen.

Whenever I spend painful, sleepless nights,
I always look forward
To your first tap-tap at my door.
The brave, nimble, simple
Life's message that you bring –
Give it to me,
That the sunlight by which all creatures dwell
May call me,
O my day-break sparrow.

(18) CALCUTTA

Anon, *Hartley House, Calcutta*

An anonymous epistolary novel, whose hard-to-get heroine epitomizes the flirtatious refinement and elegant dissipations of Calcutta long before the Memsahibs and missionaries exerted their deadly grip.

Watson's Works, a place for building bugeros and small sloops (the road to which lies across the esplanade, to the river, in an oblique direction) is some miles from Calcutta – and to Watson's Works, in order to see the launching of a large bugero, built on a new construction, we repaired yesterday, after taking our tea; and do but conceive the éclat of half a dozen, or more, of these Eastern barges, all freighted with elegant parties, gliding down the stream together, the oars beating time to the notes of the clarinets and oboes.

Music has charms, says the poet, to sooth a savage breast – what power must it then have over a humanified one, and especially in an elegant bugero! – the heavens the most glorious canopy I ever beheld, and the surface of the water crystalline beyond all imagination – the zephyrs! – but I will trust myself with no further description of it, for there is fascination in the recollection of the scene – nor have you any thing in England to help you to the faintest idea of it.

Doyly must, moreover, be brought into the foreground – his person is so pastoral, and his sensibility so oriental – had he the Mogul's diadem, he would place it, I am confident, upon my head, and, though entitled to all the privileges of a Mussulman, live for me alone . . .

The Works are admirable, and the launch gave universal satisfaction – and so profusely were we entertained on the occasion with loll shrub, and every desirable article, that we returned applauding the spirit and politeness of our entertainer.

An accident, however, took place, which will render water parties ineligible to me in future. The beauty of the evening drew all the company upon deck – and a gentlemen in the next bugero to ours, having drank too freely, was noisy and troublesome in his compliments, and so abundantly did he warm with his subject, that, regardless of all danger, he advanced to the unrailed part, and insisted upon the honour of kissing my fair hand. I was not inclined to comply; for though the rowers are dexterous, I could not help apprehending it would bring the bugeros too close together for our perfect safety: – the company were, however, of a different opinion; and, ashamed to persist in fears that were peculiar to myself, I leaned forward, supported by poor Doyly, to gratify him – when, to the equal surprise and offence of the whole party, he attempted to salute me. Fired at this boldness, Doyly repulsed him with indignation and in the same instant was pulled overboard – and your valiant friend most opportunely fainted away.

He fell not, however, unrevenged – for the Bacchanalian, a man of large fortune, had his arms somehow entangled, so that they went souse together, and were both fished up by the dexterous Gentoos (the water being, as it were, from their diurnal immersions, their natural element) before I was restored to life.

I looked anxiously around me, and, from my then feelings should certainly have relapsed, if I had not beheld my half-drowned champion at a distance. The company, as soon as it appeared no real harm had been done, very sensibly interposed, and a general reconciliation succeeded.

(19) CALCUTTA

Amit Chaudhuri, *A Strange and Sublime Address*

Born in Calcutta, brought up in Bombay, and educated in London, Amit Chaudhuri admirably captures the poetry as well as the absurdity of Calcutta life.

The power-cut had begun at seven in the morning. Now it was twelve. It was Saturday.

The man was standing in his underwear by the window. Two hours ago he had taken off his trousers, and half an hour later, his shirt. Still he was sweating profusely.

Thank God I'm a man, he thought, would it be possible to do this if I was a woman?

After some time, he took off his vest quite unconsciously, and then his underpants; it was a while before he noticed he was naked. He wandered around his room thus, enjoying himself. He hummed to himself tunelessly a song by Tagore:

A bee drifts into my room, murmuring.
It tells me of someone – then, disappears.

He stopped to contemplate himself in the mirror. He felt a fareway, paternal compassion for his body, with its awkwardly sloping shoulders, its two nipples like gentle eyes gazing at him, the embarrassing feminine way in which the waist curved slightly into the hips.

Beneath the light of some unknown sky
Madhavi flowers blossom in a secret forest . . .
The messenger-bee comes to me, bringing news
Of that blossoming, humming it in my ears.

He spattered talcum powder on himself till his neck and shoulders and chest and nipples and belly were white, and only the navel remained black and bottomless. His hand made an affectionate slapping noise as he tried to powder the inaccessible portions of his back. It was obvious the man loved himself and the feel of himself in his modest way. His voice shook a little as he sang. Mysterious clouds of talcum powder rose and vanished around his shoulders. All this the mirror captured in its frame in a series of transient cloud-like instants. The room smelt of lavender.

Now the man entered the bath. He turned on the cold-water tap and found the water amazingly hot. He checked to see if it was the hot water tap he had turned on; but no. Undaunted, he filled to the brim a pink plastic mug and doused himself experimentally. He blubbered in anguish. In between his blubbering he still sang tunelessly, a little loudly now so that he could hear himself above the water.

> How should I remain content in this room? My mind
> Is quicksilver, troubled. I've lost count
> Of how these days pass – days spent in counting days.

A few minutes later, he came out of the bath without drying himself. Silver drops of water ran down his walnut-coloured skin. He stood in front of the window in an easterly breeze, and his arms and elbows and knees and testicles seemed to weep.

> A deep enchantment falls on me. I lose
> All interest in my work. My hours are caught
> In a web of songs, a skein of music. The bee
> Tells me of someone, then – disappears.

He allowed his body to cool. Cool as a shade in a forest, cool as a flower in the shade of a forest. In the breeze, naked and gleaming, he shivered as if a woman had kissed him.

'Aaah,' he sang, with a hint of melody. 'Aaah.'

He was sure no one could see him.

(20) CALCUTTA

Michael Madhusudan Datta, *Letters*

The founder of modern Bengali poetry and drama habitually corresponded in English. Byron was his epistolary model, but his flamboyant, reckless personality was fully his own.

My dear Raj Narain,

You will have by this time reached the old nest. Pray, write to me about Meghanad. I am looking out with something like suspended breath for your verdict.

A few hours after we parted, I got a severe attack of fever and was laid up for six or seven days. It was a struggle whether Meghanad will finish me or I finish him. Thank Heaven. I have triumphed. He is dead, that is to say, I have finished the VI Book in about 750 lines. It cost me many a tear to kill him. However, you will have an opportunity of judging for yourself one of these days.

The poem is rising into splendid popularity. Some say it is better than Milton – but that is all bosh – nothing can be better than Milton;

many say it licks Kalidasa; I have no objection to that. I don't think it impossible to equal Virgil, Kalidasa and Tasso. Though glorious, still they are mortal poets; Milton is divine.

Do write to me what you think, old man. Your opinion is better than the loud huzzas of a million of these fellows.

Many Hindu ladies, I understand, are reading the book and crying over it. You ought to put your wife in the way of reading the verse.

Write to me, and never for a moment cease to believe I am in all sincerity, Your most affectionate.

* * *

My dear Raj Narain,

I am sure I have not the remotest idea as to why you are so confoundedly silent. What can be the matter with you, old man? Has poor Meghanad so disgusted you that you wish to cut the unfortunate author?

You will be pleased to hear that not very long ago the Bidyotsahini Sabha and the President Kali Prasanna Singh of Jorasanko, presented me with a splendid silver claret jug. There was a great meeting and an address in Bengali. Probably you have read both address and reply in the vernacular papers. Fancy! I was expected to speechify in Bengali!

I have finished the sixth and seventh Books of Meghanad and am working away at the eighth. Mr. Ram is to be conducted through Hell to his father, Dasaratha, like another Æneas.

(21) CALCUTTA
Henry Louis Vivian Derozio,
The Fakeer of Jungheera

Derozio was an inspiring young teacher at Hindu College in the 1830s. His romantic English verses and nascent patriotism inspired many imitations among his pupils. The Fakeer of Jungheera is set (vaguely) in north India, but its style typifies what young progressive Bengalis felt and wrote at that time. The following 'Song' is sung by 'a young Cashmerian girl'.

Oh! lovely is my native land
    With all its skies of cloudless light;
But there's a heart, and there's a hand
    More dear to me than sky most bright.
I prize them – yes, as though they were
    On earth the only things divine,

The only good, the only fair –
 And oh! that heart and hand are thine.

My native land hath heavenliest bowers
 Where Houris ruby-cheeked might dwell,
And they are gemmed with buds and flowers
 Sweeter than lip or lute may tell.
But there's a sigh, and there's a tear
 With passion's warmth, and glory's shine;
Than bud or flower to me more dear –
 And oh! that tear and sigh are thine.

My native home, my native home
 Hath in its groves the turtle dove,
And from her nest she will not roam –
 For it is warmed with faith and love.
But there is love, and there is faith,
 Which round a bleeding heart entwine,
To thee devoted even to death –
 And oh! that love and faith are mine!

A mosque there is in fair Cashmeer
 With all its minarets bright as day,
Where resteth now of sainted Peer
 The lifeless but unfading clay.
But there's a heart, a broken heart
 Where burns a thought as in a shrine,
And cannot, will not all depart –
 The thought's of thee, the heart is mine.

(22) CALCUTTA

William Hickey, *Memoirs (1749–1809)*

William Hickey, 'Gentleman Attorney', was the Samuel Pepys of late 18th century Calcutta. His racy descriptions exude a robust enjoyment of life, and a keen sense of the ridiculous.

A succession of large and formal dinners followed Mr. Francis's, beginning with the Governor-General, Mr. Wheler, General Stibbert, Mr. Barwell, and in fact all the *Burra Sahibs* (great men) of Calcutta. The first really pleasant party I was at, after my illness, was given by Daniel Barwell, who, as I have before observed, kept house with Pott and others. The most highly dressed and splendid hookah was prepared for me. I tried, but did not like it, which being perceived by my friend Robert, he laughed at me, recommending me to funk away and I should accomplish the matter without choking myself. As, after several trials, I still found it disagreeable, I with much gravity requested to know whether it was indispensably necessary that I should become a smoker, which was answered with equal gravity, 'Undoubtedly it is, for you might as well be out of the world as out of the fashion. Here everybody uses a hookah, and it is impossible to get on without.' Mr. Gosling, less volatile and flighty than the rest of the party, immediately said, 'Don't mind these rattling young men, Mr. Hickey, there is no sort of occasion for your doing what is unpleasant; and, although hookahs are in pretty general use, there are several gentlemen that never smoke them.' I directly dismissed the hookah, never after tasting one. Often since have I rejoiced that I did not happen to like it, as I have seen the want of it, from servants misunderstanding where they were ordered to attend their masters, or some other accident, a source of absolute misery, and have frequently heard men declare they would much rather be deprived of their dinner than their hookah.

In this party I first saw the barbarous custom of pelleting each other with little balls of bread, made like pills, across the table, which was even practised by the fair sex. Some people could discharge them with such force as to cause considerable pain when struck in the face. Mr. Daniel Barwell was such a proficient that he could, at the distance of three or four yards, snuff a candle, and that several times successively. This strange trick, fitter for savages than polished society, produced many quarrels, and at last entirely ceased from the following occurrence. A Captain Morrison had repeatedly expressed his abhorrence of pelleting, and that, if any person struck him with one, he should consider it intended as an insult and resent it accordingly. In a few minutes after he had so said, he received a smart blow in the face from one, which, although discharged from a hand below the table, he saw by the motion of the arm from whence it came, and that the pelleter was a very recent acquaintance. He therefore without the least hesitation took up a dish that stood before him and contained a leg of mutton, which he discharged with all his strength at the offender, and with such well-directed aim that it took place upon the head, knocking him off his chair and giving a severe cut upon the temple. This produced a duel in which the unfortunate pelleter was shot through the body, lay upon his bed many months, and never perfectly recovered. This put a complete stop to the absurd practice.

Having partaken of several entertainments given at the Tavern by Captain Sutton and other gentlemen, I thought it incumbent upon me to return the compliment and accordingly bespoke the handsomest dinner than could be provided, for forty, at the Harmonic Tavern. On the day appointed, thirty-nine sat down to table, all of whom did ample justice to the feast, drank freely, some of my guests remaining till three in the morning, when they staggered home well pleased with their fare, and declaring I was an admirable host.

At the time I arrived in Bengal, everybody dressed splendidly, being covered with lace, spangles and foil. I, who always had a tendency to be a beau, gave into the fashion with much goodwill, no person appearing in richer suits of velvet and lace than myself. I kept a handsome phaeton and beautiful pair of horses, and also had two noble Arabian saddle horses, my whole establishment being of the best and most expensive kind. I was soon distinguished in Calcutta by the title of 'the Gentleman Attorney,' in contra-distinction to the blackguard practitioners, of which description I am sorry to say there were several.

(23) CALCUTTA

Dominique Lapierre, *The City of Joy*

When a novel designed to elicit feelings of charity and compassion in its readers becomes a huge commercial success for its author, how can he avoid accusations that he has in some way exploited the sufferings of the Calcutta slum-dwellers? But so long as the slum and pavement dwellers are there, who would not want the spirit of Mother Teresa and Stephan Kovalski to be with them? In this extract Stephan Kovalski visits Mother Teresa to ask for her help in running a leper clinic.

Sensing a presence behind her, Mother Teresa stood up. She did not fail to notice the metal cross the visitor was wearing on his chest.

'Oh Father,' she excused herself humbly, 'what can I do for you?'

Stephan Kovalski felt awkward. He had just interrupted a conversation in which he identified something unique. The eyes of the dying man seemed to be imploring Mother Teresa to bend over him once more. It was deeply touching. The priest introduced himself.

'I think I've heard people talk about you!' she said warmly.

'Mother, I've come to ask for your help.'

'My help?' She pointed a large hand towards the ceiling. 'It's God's help you want to ask for, Father. I am nothing at all.'

At that point a young American in jeans came along carrying a bowl. Mother Teresa called him over and drew his attention to the dying man.

'Love him,' she ordered. 'Love him with all your might.' She handed the young man her tweezers and cloth and left him, steering Stephan Kovalski towards an empty area with a table and bench between the room for men and the one for women. On the wall was a board bearing a framed text of a Hindu poem which the priest read aloud.

> *If you have two pieces of bread,*
> *Give one to the poor,*
> *Sell the other,*
> *And buy hyacinths*
> *To feed your soul.*

The Pole outlined his plan for a leper clinic in the City of Joy.

'Very good, Father, very good,' commented Mother Teresa in her picturesque accent, a mixture of Slavonic and Bengali. 'You are doing God's work. All right, Father, I'll send you three Sisters who are used to caring for lepers.'

Her gaze strayed over the room full of prostrate bodies and she added, 'They give us so much more than we give them.'

A young Sister came over and spoke to her in a low voice. Her presence was needed elsewhere.

'Goodbye, Father,' she said. 'Come and say Mass for us one of these mornings.'

Stephan Kovalski was overwhelmed. 'Bless you, Calcutta, for in your wretchedness you have given birth to saints.'

(24) CALCUTTA
Begum Rokeya, *Sultana's Dream*

A pioneering Muslim feminist and educationist, Begum Rokeya was also a gifted and original imaginative writer. This amusing 'Utopia' in which women rule the roost and men are kept in purdah, was originally written in English, though most of Rokeya's writings are in Bengali. Here 'Sister Sara' describes the history of her country.

'Let me tell you a little of our past history then. Thirty years ago, when our present Queen was thirteen years old, she inherited the throne. She was Queen in name only, the Prime-minister really ruling the country.'

'Our good Queen liked science very much. She circulated an order that all the women in her country should be educated. Accordingly a number of girls' schools were founded and supported by the Government. Education was spread far and wide among women. And early marriage also was stopped. No woman was to be allowed to marry before she was twenty-one. I must tell you that, before this change we had been kept in strict-purdah.'

'How the tables are turned', I interposed with a laugh.

'But the seclusion is the same,' she said. 'In a few years we had separate Universities, where no men were admitted.'

'In the capital, where our Queen lives, there are two Universities. One of these invented a wonderful balloon, to which they attached a number of pipes. By means of this captive balloon which they managed to keep afloat above the cloud-land, they could draw as much water from the atmosphere as they pleased. As the water was incessantly being drawn by the University people no cloud gathered and the ingenious Lady Principal stopped rain and storms thereby.'

'Really! Now I understand why there is no mud here!' said I. But I could not understand how it was possible to accumulate water in the pipes. She explained to me how it was done; but I was unable to understand her, as my scientific knowledge was very limited. However, she went on, –

'When the other University came to know of this, they became exceedingly jealous and tried to do something more extraordinary still. They invented an instrument by which they could collect as much sun-heat as they wanted. And they kept the heat stored up to be distributed among others as required.'

'While the women were engaged in scientific researches, the men of this country were busy increasing their military power. When they came to know that the female Universities were able to draw water from the atmosphere and collect heat from the sun, they only laughed at the members of the Universities and called the whole thing "a sentimental nightmare" '!

'Your achievements are very wonderful indeed! But tell me how you managed to put the men of your country into the zenana. Did you entrap them first?'

'No'.

'It is not likely that they would surrender their free and open air life of their own accord and confine themselves within the four walls of the zenana! They must have been overpowered.'

'Yes, they have been!'

'By whom? – by some lady-warriors, I suppose?'

'No, not by arms.'

'Yes, it cannot be so. Men's arms are stronger then women's.'

'Then?'

'By brain.'

(25) CALCUTTA

Debendranath Tagore, *Autobiography*

*Debendranath Tagore, father of Rabindranath Tagore, led the
Brahmo Samaj, the Hindu reform movement that contributed so
much to the development of 19th century Bengali culture. His
Autobiography is a moving account of his own spiritual journey.
It shines with his honesty and nobility of character.*

Suddenly, as I thought and thought, a flash as of lightning broke
through this darkness of despondency. I saw that knowledge of the
material world is born of the senses and the objects of sight, sound,
smell, touch, and taste. But together with this knowledge, I am also
enabled to know that I am the knower. Simultaneously with the facts of
seeing, touching, smelling, and thinking, I also come to know that it is
I who see, touch, smell, and think. With the knowledge of objects
comes the knowledge of the subject; with the knowledge of the body
comes the knowledge of the spirit within. It was after a prolonged
search for truth that I found this bit of light, as if a ray of sunshine had
fallen on a place full of extreme darkness. I now realised that with the
knowledge of the outer world we come to know our inner self. After
this, the more I thought over it, the more did I recognise the sway of
wisdom operating throughout the whole world. For us the sun and
moon rise and set at regular intervals, for us the wind and rain are set in
motion in the proper seasons. All these combine to fulfil the one design
of preserving our life. Whose design is this? It cannot be the design of
matter, it must be the design of mind. Therefore this universe is
propelled by the power of an intelligent being.

I saw that the child, as soon as born, drinks at its mother's breast.
Who taught it to do this? He alone Who gave it life. Again, who put
love into the mother's heart? Who but He that put milk into her breast.
He is that God Who knows all our wants, Whose rule the universe
obeys. When my mind's eye had opened thus far, the clouds of grief
were in a great measure dispelled. I felt somewhat consoled.

One day, while thinking of these things, I suddenly recalled how,
long ago, in my early youth, I had once realised the Infinite as
manifested in the infinite heavens. Again I turned my gaze towards this
infinite sky, studded with innumerable stars and planets, and saw the
eternal God, and felt that this glory was His. He is Infinite Wisdom.
He from Whom we have derived this limited knowledge of ours, and
this body, its receptacle, is Himself without form. He is without body or
senses. He did not shape this universe with His hands. By His will
alone did He bring it into existence. He is neither the Kali of Kalighat,
nor the family Shaligram. Thus was the axe laid at the root of idolatry.

(26) Calcutta to Dhaka

Amitav Ghosh, *The Shadow Lines*

The narrator's grandmother, a migrant from Dhaka in Partition, prepares for her first aeroplane journey back to the city of her birth.

One evening when we were sitting out in the garden she wanted to know whether she would be able to see the border between India and East Pakistan from the plane. When my father laughed and said, why, did she really think the border was a long black line with green on one side and scarlet on the other, like it was in a school atlas, she was not so much offended as puzzled.

No that wasn't what I meant, she said. Of course not. But surely there's something – trenches perhaps, or soldiers, or guns pointing at each other, or even just barren strips of land. Don't they call it no-man's-land?

My father was already an experienced traveller. He burst out laughing and said: No, you won't be able to see anything except clouds and perhaps, if you're lucky, some green fields.

His laughter nettled her. Be serious, she snapped. Don't talk to me as though I were a secretary in your office.

Now it was his turn to be offended: it upset him when she spoke sharply to him within my hearing.

That's all I can tell you, he said. That's all there is.

My grandmother thought this over for a while, and then she said: But if there aren't any trenches or anything, how are people to know? I mean, where's the difference then? And if there's no difference both sides will be the same; it'll be just like it used to be before, when we used to catch a train in Dhaka and get off in Calcutta the next day without anybody stopping us. What was it all for then – partition and all the killing and everything – if there isn't something in between?

I don't know what you expect Ma, my father retorted in exasperation. It's not as though you're flying over the Himalayas into China. This is the modern world. The border isn't on the frontier: it's right inside the airport. You'll see. You'll cross it when you have to fill in all those disembarkation cards and things.

My grandmother shifted nervously in her chair. What forms? she said. What do they want to know about on those forms?

My father scratched his forehead. Let me see, he said. They want your nationality, your date of birth, place of birth, that kind of thing.

My grandmother's eyes widened and she slumped back in her chair.

What's the matter? my father said in alarm.

With an effort she sat up straight again and smoothed back her hair.

Nothing, she said, shaking her head. Nothing at all.

I could see then that she was going to end up in a hopeless mess, so I took it upon myself to ask my father for all the essential information about flying and aeroplanes that I thought she ought to have at her command – I was sure for example that she would roll her window down in mid-air unless I warned her not to.

(27) DHAKA

Bishop Reginald Heber, *Journey through India*

The author of 'From Greenland's icy mountain . . .' was, as Bishop of Calcutta, an observant and sometimes poetic explorer of much warmer climes. Here is his description of the vanished splendours of Dacca ('Dhaka' in today's more phonetic spelling).

Dacca, as Abdullah truly said, is 'much place for elephant'. The Company have a stud of from 2 to 300, numbers being caught annually in the neighbouring woods of Tiperah and Cachar, which are broken in for service here, as well as gradually inured to the habits which they must acquire in a state of captivity. Those which are intended for the Upper Provinces remain here some time, and are by degrees removed to Moorshedabad, Bogwangolah, Dinapoor, &c. since the transition of climate from this place to Meerut, or even Cawnpoor, is too great, and when sudden, destroys numbers. I drove in the evening, with Mr Master, through the city and part of the neighbourhood. The former is very like the worst part of Calcutta near Chitpoor, but has some really fine ruins intermingled with the mean huts which cover three-fourths of its space. The castle which I noticed, and which used to be the palace, is of brick, yet shewing some traces of the plaster which has covered it. The architecture is precisely that of the Kremlin of Moscow, of which city indeed, I was repeatedly reminded in my progress through the town. The Grecian houses, whose ruined condition I have noticed, were the more modern and favourite residence of the late Nawâb, and were ruined a few years since by the encroachments of the river. The obelisk, or 'Mut' which I saw, was erected as an act of piety very frequent in India, by a Hindoo, who about 25 years ago accumulated a large fortune in the service of the East India Company. Another mut of an almost similar form, was pointed out to me a little way out of the town. The pagodas, however, of Dacca, are few and small, three-fourths of the population being Mussulmans, and almost every brick building in the place having its Persian or Arabic inscription. Most of these look very old, but none are of great antiquity. Even the old palace was built only about 200 years ago, and consequently, is scarcely older than the banqueting-house at Whitehall. The European houses are mostly small and poor, compared with those of Calcutta; and such as are out of the town, are so surrounded with jungle and ruins, as to give the idea of desolation and unhealthiness. No cultivation was visible so far as we went, nor any space cleared except an area of about twenty acres for the new military lines. The drive was picturesque, however, in no common degree; several of the ruins were fine, and there are some noble peepul trees. The Nawâb's carriage passed us, an old landau, drawn by four horses, with a coachman and postillion in red liveries, and some horse-guards in red also, with high ugly caps, like those of the old grenadiers, with gilt plates in front, and very ill mounted. The great men of India evidently lose in point of effect, by an injudicious and imperfect adoption of European fashions. An Eastern cavalier with his turban and flowing robes, is a striking object; and an eastern prince on horseback, and attended by his usual train of white-staved and high-capped janizaries, a still more noble one; but an eastern prince in a shabby carriage, guarded by men dressed like an equestrian troop at a fair, is nothing more than ridiculous and melancholy. It is, however, but natural, that these unfortunate sovereigns should imitate, as far as they can, those costumes which the example of their conquerors has associated with their most recent ideas of power and splendour.

(28) ORISSA

Gopinath Mohanty, *Paraja*

This is a highly regarded novel about the aboriginal Paraja tribe, who live in the mountains and forests of Koraput in Orissa. It tells a shameful story of oppression and exploitation, and records a way of life that deforestation has now largely destroyed. In this extract Mandia tries to raise the bride-price for his beloved by distilling bootleg liquor in the jungle.

Sixty rupees is a lot of money in the jungle, and Mandia found the target receding further and further away as he worked himself to a standstill. Exhausted, he stood beside his still, looking despondently at his pots, which seemed to be failing him now. His eyes were smarting from the smoke that rose from the hearth. Would he ever have the money? He *could* have saved a little more, but he had to buy saris for those wretches Jili and Bili, and they would give him no peace until he had kept his promise to them. If only he could coax a few more pots of liquor out of his still each day! If he could brew enough liquor to fill the ravine! The little stream might turn into mahua wine. But now it all seemed so slow and tedious. And other young men had followed his example and set themselves up in competition; there were at least three stills in other parts of the jungle.

Sixty rupees. How much had he now? Ten? Fifteen? Surely it must be more. He had sold gallons of liquor on the day of the festival. And he had worked all night, while the two boys who were helping him had come running back to him for more and more. The liquor had sold so quickly. Another such festival, and Mandia would be home and dry! No need for him to go to the money-lender; to become a goti; like his father, and Tikra, and all others that he had known: oh no! But how else? Come on, let's get back to work, boys.

Mandia never even saw the group of ten or eleven men who walked into his ravine at dusk, on the day following the festival. He had his back to them, and he was busy stoking the hearth with brushwood. Then he saw the terror-stricken faces of the two boys standing in front of him, and turned round. It was the Sub-Inspector of Excise, with four Excise guards and three or four other men whom Mandia had never seen before. With them was Chamru Domb, of Mandia's own village.

There was no escape; he had been caught red-handed. It was no use cringing or begging for mercy. He had broken the law, and he must suffer for it.

(29) ORISSA

Prafulla Mohanti, *My Village, My Life*

The painter Prafulla Mohanti's portrait of his native village in Orissa is one of the clearest and most touching accounts of Indian village life that has been written in English. Here he writes about the craftsmen in his village.

The villagers look upon God as the Master Craftsman who has created this beautiful universe. They admire His skill as they look around them. When they see a beautiful woman they say, 'She is like a piece of sculpture, an image of Lakshmi.' Their response to beauty is immediate.

The craftsman's function is to add beauty to Woman. The weavers spend their lives designing *saris* to match her complexion. The jeweller invents new and imaginative ornaments to decorate her. The carpenter builds her house. She then selects everything for her household, pots, vessels, plates, baskets, mats. She likes everything to be handmade. This is why, until now, the Indian craftsmen have survived in spite of discouragement during British rule, when fine mill-made fabric came from Lancashire and cheap utensils from Birmingham.

The weavers in the village could not compete with mill-made cloth and continued to produce coarse *saris* for daily use. Since Independence, their condition has become worse. Nylon and other synthetic fabrics have reached the village market and cheap printed cottons from the mills are more attractive to the villagers. Because of this, the weavers have put their looms away in the loft and look for other work. Few have their own land, and farming has never been their trade. Some have been forced to work as day labourers. The family was the only place for training, so children can no longer learn to weave by helping their parents. As the old die, their skills die with them. Only two weavers now practise their craft and then only during the monsoon, when the bad weather prevents them working as labourers. I have been working with them during my visits to the village. They have a marvellous sense of colour and design. Their workmanship and understanding of new ideas are perfect.

The potters have been more fortunate. Although they, too, have to compete with industry, the villagers usually do not like metal pots for cooking. Moreover pots are broken ritually every month, and new sets are bought to replace them. When a stray dog entered our kitchen looking for food, my mother at once said that the pots were polluted and should be thrown away. Death, anniversaries of deaths, childbirth; all make the pots unclean. At weddings and festivals, the pots are changed, and all this means work for the potters. There are four families who make pots for my village and the others nearby. It is a pleasure to watch them throw the pots; they do it so gracefully. The simple shapes they create can seldom be improved upon. The pots, which are used for storage and for cooking, are unglazed and grey in colour. In the summer they keep the water cool and refreshing. The potters also make linings for wells and stands for the tulashi plant, as well as the clay animals offered to the village deity. They have no land of their own and cultivate other people's farms. This gives them just enough to keep body and soul together.

(30) SUNDARBANS
Jibanananda Das, 'The Hunt'

No 20th century Bengali poet has been more successful in creating a completely un-Tagorean style than Jibanananda Das. He worked as a college teacher in Calcutta (dying in 1954 after being knocked down by a tram), but many of his poems hark back to his roots in Barisal in the deltaic region of Bengal. This poem is one of several inspired by the Sundarbans, the wild mangrove swamp area preserved now by both West Bengal and Bangladesh as a nature reserve. From Clinton B. Seely, A Poet Apart: A Literary Biography of the Bengali Poet Jibanananda Das (1899–1954), see Booklist.

Dawn:
Sky, the soft blue of grasshopper's belly.
Guava and custard apple trees all around, green as parrot feathers.
A single star lingers in the sky
Like the most twilight-intoxicated girl in some village bridal chamber,
Or that pearl from her bosom the Egyptian dipped into my glass of
    Nile-blue wine
One night some thousands of years ago –
Just so, in the sky shines a single star.

To warm their bodies through the cold night, up-country menials kept
    a fire going
In the field – red fire like a cockscomb blossom,
Still burning, contorting dry *ashwattha* leaves.

Its color in the light of the sun is no longer like vermilion
But has become like wan desires of a sickly *shalik* bird's heart.
In the morning's light both sky and surrounding dewy forest sparkle like
    iridescent peacock wings.

Dawn:
All night long a sleek brown buck, bounding from *sundari* through *arjun*
    forests
In starless, mahogany darkness, avoids the cheetah's grasp.
He had been waiting for this dawn.
Down he came in its glow,
Ripping, munching fragrant grass, green as green grapefruit.
Down he came to the river's stinging, tingling ripples,
To instill his sleepless, weary, bewildered body with the current's drive,
To feel a thrill like that of dawn bursting through the cold and wizened
    womb of darkness,

To wake like gold sun-spears beneath this blue and
Dazzle doe after doe with beauty, boldness, desire.
A strange sound.

The river's water red like *machaka* flower petals.
Again the fire crackled – red venison served warm.
Many an old dew-dampened yarn, while seated on a bed of grass
   beneath the stars.
Cigarette smoke.
Several human heads, hair neatly parted.
Guns here and there. Icy, calm, guiltless sleep.

(31) SYLHET

Katy Gardner, *Songs at the River's Edge*

*Sixteen months of social anthropology field-work in a village in
Sylhet inspired Katy Gardner to write this wonderfully honest
and intelligent personal account of her experiences. Here, as she
leaves Talukpur at the end of her stay, we see how hard it still is
to bridge the enormous gulf that exists between the Western
world and life in a South Asian village.*

'You have become our blood,' Amma said one night, 'but now you must
make yourself an English beti again. Why become like a Bangladeshi
girl if you have to leave us? Why don't you marry here and stay?'

But this was not on the cards, and never had been. My transformation into a Bangladeshi woman had never been more than a surface
veneer of habits and appearances which for the most part had remained
entirely within my control. My hair was oiled, and I had learnt to walk
and talk like the villagers, but inside my Western nature had remained
intact, albeit with a few dents. I had for some time realised just how
adaptable human nature is, and how easily it moulds itself to context.
Rather like a dried-up sponge, I had soaked up behaviour and feelings
whilst in the village, which were quickly squeezed out back in Dhaka,
or amongst Western friends in Sylhet.

If strange men entered our bari I too would now leave and hide with
the women, and I felt genuinely embarrassed and naked if a man came
across me outside with my head uncovered. I loathed walking through
the tea-stall area in the village, and if the trip was unavoidable I
covered my head as much as possible with my umbrella, to shield it
from male glances. I had begun to worry that sharom was contagious,
and I had caught it. But this was hardly the case; instead, I had taken

the parts of the purdah mentality which I found useful, rather than swallowing it whole. As a Western woman, however much she had 'become our blood', I was in a position of power to manipulate the system. I could take from purdah the 'freedom from' which it gives: a Muslim woman in Bangladesh, if she's lucky and her family can protect her, is free from the stares and pestering of men, or the trials of having to manage in the tough outside world, and at one level that can sometimes be very appealing. But where purdah threatened my 'freedom to', I was always able to reject it. If I was genuinely interested in talking to a male guest or walking to a nearby village alone, my feelings of sharom were easily overcome by a more rudimentary Western assumption of personal liberty.

The village had taught me things other than how to feel sharom. To my Western friends' horror, I had learnt not only how to burp and spit with the greatest of acumen, but also how to be incredibly rude. 'Go away! No, I'm not going to give you anything, leave me alone!' was something I now said with great ease to any unfortunate child or beggar who had come to me hoping for charity. Without realising it, I had got extremely used to being served by my junior brothers and sisters in the family, and like everyone else I now ordered: 'Give me my rice' when I was hungry, and took the food with a grunt. 'Dunndo bad' (thank you) had only ever inspired laughter when I used it anyway. All in all, my polite English tact, ('Er . . . I'm rather tired now . . .') had proved quite useless, and I had become, to say the least, direct. Outside the village I found myself doing things which somehow didn't seem quite right, although I had forgotten why. 'So, are you married? Do you have children?' I asked expatriates in Dhaka, or 'That's a nice wedding ring. How much did it cost?'

Biographies and summaries

BANERJI, Bibhutibhushan (1894–1950). Bengali novelist and short story writer. His village-upbringing as the son of a penurious Brahmin priest gave him material for his most famous novel *Pather Panchali* ◊ (Extract 6). After graduating in Calcutta he earned his living mainly as a teacher.

Nirad C. Chaudhuri ◊ recalls him vividly in Book II, Chapter 2 of *Thy Hand, Great Anarch!*

CHANDIDAS, Baru. Many writers of the *padas* (songs) inspired by Bengali Vaishnavism (the cult of Radha and Krishna promoted mainly by the saint Chaitanya and his followers) took the name of Chandidas, but Baru Chandidas was a distinct individual who composed the liveliest and most original of Vaishnava texts, untouched by piety probably because it pre-dates Chaitanya.

CHATTERJEE, Bankimchandra (1838–1894). The greatest novelist, essayist and periodical editor of 19th century Bengal. He used largely historical material in his novels in his pursuit of a modern Indian identity. Influenced in his youth by French rationalism, he later promoted a form of Hindu revivalism based on a novel interpretation of the character of Krishna. His song 'Bande Mataram' from his novel *Ananda-math* (Extract 8) became a nationalist rallying-cry.

CHAUDHURI, Amit (1962–). Born in Calcutta and brought up in Bombay, Chaudhuri went to University College, London. *A Strange and Sublime Address* (Extract 19) was his first novel and won a number of awards. He has written a second novel, *Afternoon Raag*.

CHAUDHURI, Nirad C. (1897–). Controversial Bengali author, who in his *Autobiography of an Unknown Indian* (1951) and sequel autobiography *Thy Hand, Great Anarch!* (Extract 9, 1987) told the whole story of the emergence of modern India from its roots in the 19th century Bengal Renaissance. Raised in a small town in east Bengal, he was educated in Calcutta, worked as secretary to the Congress politician Sarat Chandra Bose (brother of Subhas Chandra Bose, who led the Japanese-supported Indian National Liberation Army),

moved to Delhi in 1941 to work for All India Radio as a commentator on international affairs, and from 1952 to 1966 was editor of the English Bulletin of the French Embassy in Delhi (which enabled him to perfect his knowledge of French). In 1970 he moved to Britain, and has lived in Oxford ever since. He has written biographies of Clive and Max Müller, given his trenchant interpretation of Indian religion and history in *The Continent of Circe* and *Hinduism*, and in his nineties has offered to his countrymen (in Bengali) his final thoughts on the life and works of Rabindranath Tagore.

City of Joy. Blockbuster French novel by Dominique Lapierre (1985) about the work of a Polish Catholic priest, Stephen Kovalski, in one of Calcutta's most notorious slums, counterpointed with the struggle for survival of Hasari Pal (a rickshaw puller). Made into a film in 1992 (Extract 23). Dominique Lapierre is the founder of Action Aid for Leper Children of Calcutta, 26 Avenue Kleber, 75116 Paris, France.

DAS, Jibanananda (1899–1954). Leading modern Bengali poet of the post-Tagore generation. He was brought up in Barisal, on the northern edge of the Sundarban jungle in south Bengal, where his father was a Headmaster and Brahmo preacher (◊ Tagore, Debendranath). After graduating in English, he became a college-teacher, first in Calcutta and later in his home-town, where the landscape inspired his finest poetry (Extract 30).

DATTA, Michael Madhusudan (1824–73). Founder of modern Bengali poetry and drama. He had an anglicised education at Hindu College in Calcutta, and became a Christian, largely to evade an arranged marriage. After eight years as a teacher in Madras, where he married an English woman and tried to establish himself as a poet in English, he returned to Calcutta with another English woman, Henrietta White (with whom he lived for the rest of his life), and within less than three years broke entirely new ground in comedy, tragedy, lyric and dramatic poetry, and above all his masterpiece *Meghnad-badh Kabya* (1861), a literary epic based on the Ramayana but profoundly influenced by Homer, Virgil, Dante and Milton. He then spent five years in England and France, qualifying as barrister, mastering French, and writing over a hundred sonnets. On returning to Calcutta in 1867, his attempts to practise as a barrister were overcome by extravagance and alcoholism. An example of his letter-writing style can be found in Extract 20.

DEROZIO, Henry Louis Vincent (1809–31). Charismatic teacher at Hindu College in Calcutta in the 1820s, where his promotion of radical free-thinking among the students brought him into conflict with the college authorities. His Byronic English poems had considerable influence on, among others, the young Michael Madhusudan Datta ◊. Extract 21 is an example of his poetry.

DEVI, Mahasweta (1926–). Calcutta-educated writer of short stories (Extract 10). In her youth she was an active member of Gananatya, a radical theatre group that toured villages. Her fiction is distinctive for being based on first-hand study of the lives of tribal and outcaste communities in south-west Bengal and southeast Bihar, and as a journalist too she has consistently concerned herself with exploitation and oppression.

DYSON, Ketaki Kushari (1940–). Bilingual Bengali writer, educated in Calcutta and Oxford, resident in Britain for most of her professional life. Known in Bengal for her Bengali poetry and her research into the friendship between Tagore and Victoria Ocampo, and in Britain for her translations of Tagore's poetry for Bloodaxe Books (see Booklist).

GHOSH, Amitav (1956–). He took a history degree from Delhi University and worked briefly as a journalist for the *Indian Express* newspaper during the Emergency. He then took up a scholarship to read for a doctorate in social anthropology at Oxford. He has taught in the universities of Trivandrum, Delhi and Virginia. His first novel, *Circle of Reason*, was published in 1986 followed two years later by *The Shadow Lines* (Extract 26). His latest book, *In an Antique Land* (1992), weaves together multiple narratives of history, anthropology, travel and literature. His most recently published work is on Cambodia.

Gitanjali (Song Offering). Rabindranath Tagore's own translation in 1912 into Biblical English prose of a selection of his Bengali devotional lyrics. He impressed W.B. Yeats and others with the poems when he visited Britain in 1912, and their subsequent publication by Macmillan led to the award in 1913 of the Nobel Prize for Literature to Tagore. Through countless secondary translations, it has retained a world-wide following.

Gora. Epic novel by Rabindranath Tagore published in 1910 in which the moral, religious and intellectual debates of late 19th century Bengal are summed up. Gora's fanatical revivalist Hinduism is shaken when he falls in love with a Brahmo girl (◊ Tagore, Debendranath) and collapses completely when his Indian foster-parents reveal to him his *mleccha* (outcaste) Irish origins. Out of this loss of identity, however, emerges a universal humanism close to Tagore's own outlook.

GUPTA, Sunetra (1965–). Novelist and research epidemiologist, whose English novels *Memories of Rain* and *The Glassblower's Breath* explore, with extraordinary linguistic virtuosity, the predicament of an intellectual Bengali woman seeking fulfilment in relationships in a Western context.

HAJNÓCZY, Rózsa (?–1942). Author of *Fire of Bengal*, a major Hungarian novel based on the three years that she and her husband Gyula Germanus, an eminent scholar of Islam, spent at Tagore's university at **Santiniketan** (Extract 1). Fact and fiction are the warp and woof of this blend of autobiography, travelogue and scandalous romance, compelling to some, infuriating to others.

HEBER, Reginald (1783–1826). Bishop of Calcutta from 1822 until his death in Trichinopoly. He completed the task begun by his predecessor Bishop Middleton of establishing Bishop's College, a seminary for Anglican priests. He was a poet and hymn-writer, and wrote detailed descriptions of his journeys through India (Extract 26).

HICKEY, William (1749?–1830). An attorney who practised in Calcutta and whose *Memoirs* (Extract 22) give a racy account of his hedonistic life there.

The Home and the World (*Ghare-Baire*). Novel by Rabindranath Tagore ◊ in which the Swadeshi movement against Lord Curzon's attempt to partition Bengal is memorably evoked. As original in its technique as in its subject-matter, the novel explores, through the minds of its main characters, the pressures on Bimala, a young zamindar's wife, loyal to her romantic conservative husband Nihkil, but attracted also to Sandip, a radical nationalist. The novel was filmed by Satyajit Ray in 1984.

HUQ, Hasan Azizul (1939–). Leading contemporary writer of short stories, widely read and admired in West Bengal as well as in his native Bangladesh, where he teaches philosophy at Rajshahi University. The agonies of Bangladesh's struggle for independence are conveyed with savage realism in some of his best stories (see Extract 2).

ISLAM, Kazi Nazrul (1899–1976). Bengali poet and song-writer, adopted by virtue of his humble Muslim origins and fiery political radicalism as the national poet of Bangladesh (Extract 11). He served in the Bengal Infantry during the First World War, but on his return to Bengal the fiery rebelliousness of his poetry led to a gaol sentence for sedition in 1922. Entirely non-communal in his outlook, he married a Hindu in 1924. In 1942 he was struck down by presenile dementia. The Government of Mujibur Rahman rescued him from

Prafulla Mohanti

poverty in Calcutta by bringing him to newly independent Bangladesh, where a national Institute was later created in his memory.

KÄMPCHEN, Martin (1948–). German writer and translator, resident in India since 1973 and at **Santiniketan** since 1979, where he has combined writing and scholarship with social work in a Santal village (Extract 12). He is known for his short stories based on his experience of Indian village life, as well as his translations of Tagore and Ramakrishna, and his research on Tagore's relationship with Germany.

MOHANTI, Prafulla (1936–). Born Nanpur, Orissa. Writer, painter and erstwhile architect-planner. His books include *My Village, My Life* (published in 1973 and illustrated by the author), *Indian Folk Tales* (1975), *Through Brown Eyes* (1985) and *Changing Village Changing Life* (1990).

MOHANTY, Gopinath (1914–). Oriya novelist and short-story writer, author of over twenty novels and numerous translations including *War and Peace*. Comparable to Mahasweta Devi ◊ in his social commitment and interest in tribal people (Extract 28).

NASRIN, Taslima (1962–). Bangladeshi columnist, poet and novelist. Originally trained as a doctor, her radical feminist newspaper articles and alleged comments to an Indian newspaper reporter on Islam aroused the ire of Muslim fundamentalists. The Government of Begum Khalida Zia bowed to their protests and arrested her, but then allowed her (in 1994) to flee the country. Sweden gave her asylum. Her novel *Shame* (*Lajja*) tells the story of a Hindu family terrorized by Muslim rioters avenging the destruction by Hindu fundamentalists of the Babri Masjid at Ayodhya on 6 December 1992.

RAHMAN, Shamsur (1929–). Poet, regarded throughout Bengal as the leading poet in Bengali today. He has published more than 25 collections of verse, marked by compassionate secularism, verbal and intellectual eclecticism, a courageous willingness to speak up for justice and humanity, and a complete absence of egotism. (Extract 3).

RAY, Bharatchandra (1712–60). Chief poet of 18th century Bengal. The son of a zamindar in present-day Hooghly district, his life was fraught with difficulty (including a spell in the Maharajah of Burdwan's gaol) until Maharajah Krishnachandra of Nadiya recognized his poetic talent and appointed him court poet. An ancestor of his patron was duly commemorated in his major work, the three-part narrative poem *Kalika-mangal* (also known, after its first part, as *Annadamangal*). The second part, the romantic story of Vidya and Sundara, was the most successful, and the source of numerous popular dramatic renditions (Extract 14).

RAY, Satyajit (1921–92). Celebrated film-maker, whose films based mostly on well-known Bengali literary works have made Bengali culture (or more specifically Calcutta culture) internationally known. The son of Sukumar Ray ◊ he was educated partly at Visva-Bharati, where Tagore had a profound influence on him. Showered with accolades abroad for his films, in his native city he was perhaps even more popular as a writer of light detective and science fiction, and for editing the children's magazine *Sandesh*.

RAY, Sukumar (1887–1923). Famous writer of Bengali nonsense verse. He was son of Upendrakishore Raychaud-huri (1863–1915), a pioneer of book illustration and printing, and was himself a writer for children, and the father of Satyajit Ray ◊. His classic collection of verses, *Abal-tabal*, has been most ably translated into English by Sukanta Chaudhuri (see Booklist).

ROKEYA, Begum (1880–1932). Pioneering social reformer, educationalist and writer, revered in Bangladesh as a campaigner for the advancement of Muslim Bengali women, and remembered in Calcutta for the girls' school that she founded in memory of her husband Shakhawat Hossain, a liberal-minded magistrate, considerably older than her, who encouraged her in her work. Sharp-eyed

inside descriptions of purdah are a striking feature of her essays and fiction (Extract 24).

Song of the Road (*Pather Panchali*). Classic Bengali novel written in 1929 by Bibhutibhushan Banerji ◊ in which the childhood of Apu and his sister Durga (who tragically dies) is magically evoked (Extract 6). The novel was chosen by Satyajit Ray ◊ for his celebrated first film (1955). Banerji's follow-up novel *Aparajita* was the source of the other two films in Ray's 'Apu Trilogy': *The Unvanquished* (1956) and *The World of Apu* (1959).

TAGORE, Debendranath (1817–1905). Father of the poet. His high-minded integrity and deep response to the Upanishads are recorded in his famous autobiography (Extract 25). He revived and reformed the Brahmo Samaj, the monotheistic Hindu Church founded in 1828 by the 'Father of Modern India', Rammohan Roy (1772–1883), and retained the respect even of those Brahmos who broke away to form a more radical branch of the Samaj in 1866.

TAGORE, Rabindranath (1841–1941). Bengal's great literary genius, and the moulder of her modern culture. His collected works – 29 large volumes – contain some 60 collections of verse, over 100 short stories (Extract 16), novels, plays and essays. Additional volumes, especially of letters, are still being published. His more than 2000 songs have become the national music of Bengal. The award of the Nobel Prize for Literature to Tagore in 1913 made him an international celebrity, and his lecture tours of America, Europe and the Far East made headline news. Visva-

Bharati, the 'Universal-Indian' University he founded at **Santiniketan**, attracted in its heyday eminent international scholars as guest lecturers. As a painter, and founder of the Kala Bhavan (art department) at Santi-niketan, he had a major influence on the development of modern Indian art. As a national figure, he is as inseparable from the emergence of modern independent India as Mahatma Gandhi, who called Tagore 'The

Rabindranath Tagore Skating

Great Sentinel'. Songs by Tagore have been adopted as the national anthems of India and Bangladesh.

WALIULLAH, Syed (1920–71). Bengali novelist, whose *Lal Shalu* (Extract 4, 1948) and subsequent novels of East Bengali village life paved the way for the efflorescence of novel and short-story writing in Muslim Bengal (Bangladesh) today.

NEPAL

Michael Hutt

Why did man come up here?
What pleasure, what
happiness was he seeking?
Did he come here just to eat
thorns and stand rattling in
the teeth of the wind, like a
few frost-ravaged leaves?
Lakshmiprasad Devkota,
An Essay

Nepal is the world's only Hindu kingdom, and the most mountainous country on earth. From the lowlands of the **Tarai** (Extract 13), foothills of ever-increasing altitude climb to the snowcovered crests of the Himalaya, where Sagarmatha (Everest) rises to over 29 000 feet. Much of the Tarai was once covered by dense jungle where a virulent form of malaria was endemic: most has now been cleared, and the Tarai landscape resembles that of the Indian plains to the south. The foothills rise from sub-tropical valleys to alpine pastures: tiny homesteads cling to steep slopes where terraced fields have been cut by generations of farmers. The only large urban area is in the **Kathmandu Valley** (Extracts 4–9), a fertile bowl at 4 000 feet, where the brick houses of the Newars cluster together in tightly-knit towns. Among the high mountains to the north, there are scattered settlements of pastoralists and traders.

THE PEOPLE

Nepal's 19 million people belong to a great diversity of ethnic groups and speak over 40 languages. The dominant group, numerically and politically, is the Indo-Nepalese or Parbatiya ('hillspeople'). They are decended from Khasa and Rajput immigrants who have moved steadily through Nepal over the past thousand years, bringing with them their language (now called Nepali) and their religion, Hinduism. The largest Indo-Nepalese caste is the Chhetri. Above them in the hierarchy are the Brahmans and Thakuris, below them are the 'impure' occupational castes.

329

The culture, language and religion of the Indo-Nepalese are displacing those of other ethnic groups who entered the region before them, but now constitute less than 20% of the population. Traditionally, most of these speak Tibeto-Burman languages, practise a mixture of Mahayana Buddhism and their own folk religions, and have legends of ancient origins in Tibet. They include the groups from which most Gurkha soldiers come: the Gurungs and Magars of the west-central hills, the Tamangs of central Nepal, and the Limbus and Rais of the east. Along the northern border there are small mountain villages where the people speak Tibetan dialects and practise monastic Buddhism. The Sherpas, who settled in Solu and Khumbu during the 16th century, are the best-known of these.

Unlike most other minority groups, Nepal's half-million Newars possess a developed literary, artistic and architectural tradition of their own. Although their language is Tibeto-Burman, they are of less obvious Tibetan extraction than the tribal groups of the hills, and have their own caste hierarchy. At the apex Newars split into Hindus and Buddhists, but for most the distinction has little meaning. Outside the Kathmandu Valley, where most Newars still live, many market towns have Newar traders at their hearts.

The Tarai, which within 20 years will contain more than half of the total population, is peopled mainly by immigrant groups who moved northward into Nepal as the jungles were cleared and are called 'Madhesis' (midlanders) by the hillspeople. Speaking north Indian languages such as Maithili and Bhojpuri, they are generally very similar to the people of Bihar and Uttar Pradesh. In recent years, the Government of Nepal has been resettling landless hillfarmers in the Tarai, which is causing a dramatic change in the composition of the population in some areas. The Tharu tribes of the inner Tarai, whose culture is strongly linked to ancestral forest lands, are gradually receding before the encroachment of settlers arriving from both north and south.

History

The modern state of Nepal did not exist until the late 18th century, but the Kathmandu Valley has been at the heart of Himalayan kingdoms of various dimensions for at least 1 500 years. Until quite recently, 'Nepal' meant only the Kathmandu Valley – the name 'Nepal' is clearly related to that of the valley's most ancient inhabitants, the Newars.

From the 4th century or earlier, the valley and adjoining hill regions were ruled by a Hindu dynasty called the Licchavis who had, according to local chronicles, succeeded two other dynasties – the Gopalas and the Kiratas – about whom little is known. The Licchavis founded

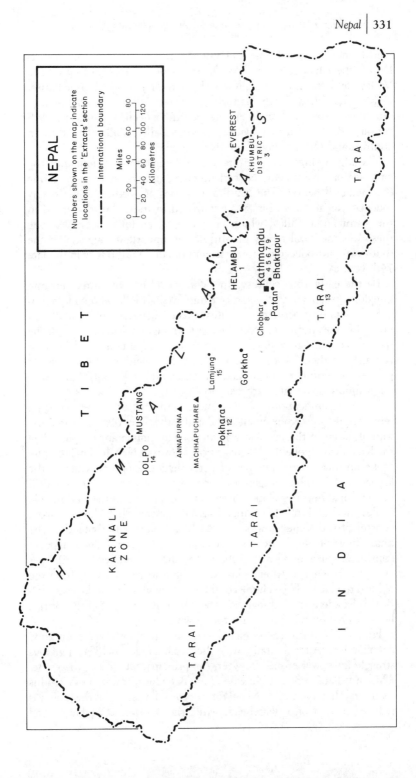

Nepal's most famous shrines and produced some of its most glorious art. During the 7th century an Indo-Tibetan trade-route opened up via the Valley, and the Licchavis grew rich in their role as intermediaries. During the 6th and 7th centuries, however, they were eclipsed by senior courtiers, and their empire began to decline during the 9th century. By 1200, a new dynasty of kings called Malla was firmly in control, and the Licchavis had disappeared.

The Malla kings were Newars, and although Sanskrit remained the language of government, Newari literature developed strongly during the medieval period. The Muslim invasions of northern India barely touched Nepal: Buddhism was eliminated in India, but flourished in the Kathmandu Valley, which became a haven for refugees. Among these was the royal family of Mithila, an important kingdom to the south, who introduced a strong element of Hindu orthodoxy in the late 14th century.

By the early 16th century, the Valley had become three separate kingdoms, each ruled by a son of King Yaksha Malla who had died in 1482. A state of perpetual hostility existed between them, and they vied with one another to erect the most ornate temples and palaces: the spectacular **Durbar Squares** of Kathmandu, **Bhaktapur** and Lalitpur **(Patan)** are their legacy. Almost all of the magnificent temples and palaces of central Kathmandu were the work of Pratap Malla, who reigned during the late 17th century.

Until the unification of Nepal, most of the rest of the region had a separate history. From about 1100 until the late 14th century, the Karnali basin in the far west was ruled by an immigrant people called the Khasa who spoke the language now known as Nepali. Their empire broke up into a large number of petty fiefdoms, one of which – the kingdom of Gorkha – began a campaign of conquest in the late 17th century. In 1744, the Gorkhalis began to encroach on the Kathmandu Valley, and in 1769 their king, Prithvi Narayan Shah, having taken control of the Valley towns, moved his capital to Kathmandu. The Shah kings of Nepal are his descendants. The Gorkhalis' campaign continued apace, and by 1814 their new empire stretched for 800 miles along the Himalaya. After a clash with the British, however, they were obliged to give up large chunks of the territory in 1816, and to accept a British Resident in Kathmandu. It was from this time that the British began to recruit 'Gurkhas' into their own army.

From 1777 until 1846, Nepal was governed by regents or army commanders. After the fall of one such commander in 1837, a vicious struggle for power ensued between the principal families of the court. This ended abruptly in 1846 when Jang Bahadur Kunwar massacred his rivals and then controlled Nepal for 31 years. The status of the king was reduced to that of a figurehead, while the position of Maharaja and prime minister became hereditary. Until 1945, every ruler of Nepal was a nephew of Jang Bahadur: the family called itself 'Rana' and ruled until 1951. The Ranas maintained Nepal's sovereignty and independence, but their conservatism and suspicion of foreign influences are now blamed for many of its woes. The regime's main concerns were to maintain law and order and collect taxes, and it sealed Nepal off from the outside world. The Ranas' huge stucco palaces, copies of Buckingham Palace and the Palace of Versailles, may still be seen all over Kathmandu.

Many Nepalis acquired an education in India after 1900, and came to identify closely with the Indian nationalist movement. Thousands more fought for the British in both world wars, and returned home with a new perspective on the world. Opposition to the Rana regime grew as a consequence, and the Ranas reacted with a mixture of repression and limited reform. Once the British had departed from India, the regime's days were numbered. In 1951 a revolution led by the Nepali Congress Party in collusion with King Tribhuvan restored the powers of the monarchy, and Nepal's first experiment with democracy began.

In 1959 general elections were held, and the Nepali Congress formed a government. This was dismissed the following year by King Mahendra, who soon replaced the 'imported' parliamentary system with the 'indigenous' system of the partyless Panchayat. Nepalis voted for representatives at the local level, but the palace made most of the major decisions. As Nepal opened up to the outside world, building roads, hospitals and national education and communications frameworks, resentment of the Panchayat system grew among the expanding educated class. (The official literacy rate leapt from 1% in 1951 to 29% in 1981, despite a doubling of the population.) In 1980 a national referendum endorsed the Panchayat system by a narrow majority, but in April 1990 it was abolished by a Congress- and Communist-led Movement for Democracy. King Birendra became a constitutional monarch, and a new government was elected in May 1991.

LITERATURE

Several literary languages are current in Nepal. Sanskrit is the language of the sacred texts of Hinduism, of ancient and medieval governance and of much medieval drama and poetry: it is the fount from which Nepal's modern literatures spring, and is still studied and written in Nepal. Tibetan is the language of the Buddhist liturgy of northern Nepal, but very little secular literature has appeared and Tibetan is, like Sanskrit, a classical language shared with other peoples. Literature has been published in very few of Nepal's many spoken languages. In the Tarai, novels, plays, poetry and stories are published in Maithili, Nepal's second most commonly-spoken language, but the majority of Maithili-speakers live across the border in India, and the Maithili writers of Nepal have not yet established a distinct Nepalese identity for themselves. One is left, therefore, with two developed literary traditions that belong originally to Nepal and Nepal alone: these are Newari and Nepali.

NEWARI LITERATURE

Newars call their language *Nepal-bhasha* (language of Nepal). Its literature began with commentaries upon and translations from classical Sanskrit texts, but the Newari-speaking Malla kings patronized scholars and poets and original works began to be composed in a classical form of the language. The earliest such text dates from the 14th century and the Newars can justly claim that, although literature in Nepali is now more extensive and prestigious, the history of Newari literature is actually much older. During the medieval period, the richest genre was poetry, although works in prose and dramas were also produced, heavily influenced by Maithili. Under the Ranas Newari literature was suppressed, but since the 1930s it has recovered significantly. Now modern genres predominate and several newspapers are current. Many Newars have made a name for themselves as Nepali writers, but also publish works in Newari: Kedar Man Vyathit, erstwhile Vice-Chancellor of the Royal Nepal Academy, is a notable example. Few translations of Newari literature exist: Lienhard's work on hymns and folksongs is revealing, though his translations are prosaic (see Booklist). Despite its tradition of richness and antiquity, Newari literature is now overshadowed by the enormous growth of literature in Nepal.

NEPALI LITERATURE

The fact that Nepali is Nepal's national language, the mother-tongue of 56% of its people, and a vital lingua-franca for the remainder, ensures that it is also the language of the bulk of the country's literature. However this literature is not ancient: in western Nepal some inscriptions have been found which date back to the 14th century, and a small number of genealogies, translations of Hindu scripture, royal pronouncements and poems survive from the 17th and 18th centuries, but the first major literary achievement dates from the mid-19th century. This was a Nepali adaptation in rhyming metrical verse of the Ramayana legend, and its author was a Brahman named Bhanubhakta Acharya ◊. Bhanubhakta's *Nepali Ramayana* remains one

Bust of Bhanubhakta Acharya

of the most important and popular works of Nepali literature: innumerable editions have been published, and it is memorized and sung at celebrations and religious feasts throughout the kingdom.

The works of Bhanubhakta Acharya were first brought to light by Motiram Bhatta ◊, who published the *Ramayana* in 1877, and a biography of its author in 1891. In the biography, Bhatta relates the popular but historically improbable tale of Bhanubhakta being inspired to write his *Ramayana* by a chance meeting with a pious grasscutter.

Because of the Rana government's censorious attitude towards literature, its development within Nepal was retarded during the early 20th century, and the most important innovations owed much to Nepalis resident in Indian towns such as Darjeeling and Benares. The most notable poet to emerge in Nepal was Lekhnath Paudyal ◊, whose poetry represented a kind of bridge between the classical traditions of Sanskrit verse and the new school of simplification (Extract 10). Most of Lekhnath's poems were devotional and philosophical, and they combined a profundity of thought with a formal clarity of expression that was unprecedented in Nepali. King Tribhuvan invested Lekhnath Paudyal with the title Kavi Shiromani, 'Crest-Jewel Poet', which is often translated as 'Poet Laureate.' But Lekhnath's inspiration sprang from time-honoured traditions, and he is not considered authentically modern. Many writers who came after him were strongly influenced by English literature, and during the 1930s the urge to modernize – to catch up with the world outside – became clearly apparent.

Balkrishna Sama ◊, a member of the ruling Shamsher family, penned rather Shakespearian plays which dealt with contemporary social issues and are still among the classics of Nepali theatre. Many of Sama's poems put forward humanistic views which were radical for their time. The short story was established by writers like Guru Prasad Mainali ◊, whose moralistic tales of Nepali village life remain popular today, and Bishweshwar Prasad Koirala ◊, Nepal's first elected Prime Minister, who drew on sources as diverse as Freud, Maupassant and Tagore to produce several superior works of fiction.

Towering over all his contemporaries was Nepal's first great modern poet, Laksmiprasad Devkota ◊. Devkota's mastery of English was excellent, and his love for the English Romantic poets – particularly Wordsworth – was a formative influence. Towards the end of his life, his egalitarian instincts made him a political exile, and his intellectual curiosity drew him into experiments with Greek mythology. Devkota was extraordinarily prolific: though chiefly renowned for dozens of volumes of poetry, he also wrote essays (Extract 1), dramas, stories and novels. His most beloved work was a 40-page poem entitled 'Muna and Madan' ◊, (Extract 5), published during the 1930s but still Nepal's best-selling book: over 7 000 copies are bought every year. Many Nepalis can recite lines from the poem which have become proverbial.

Nepal emerged with great suddenness into the wider world outside, and this is reflected by the speed at which it and its literature have changed. During the twilight years of the Rana regime, an important group of writers centred on the Kathmandu journal *Sharada*, and the *Sharada* era represents a kind of explosion into modernity, but the repercussions of the Ranas' overthrow did not become evident until the early 1960s.

With the advent of public education, the number of Nepali writers grew rapidly and poetry remained the most important and popular genre. Unfortunately, the Nepali poetry of the 1960s was often extremely obscure: as liberals and intellectuals, most poets were disturbed by His Majesty King Mahendra's dismissal of the Congress government in 1960, and felt the need for an opaque code in which to express their feelings. Nevertheless, 'Dimensionalist' poets such as Bairagi Kainla ◊ and Ishwar Ballabh ◊ – both have been members of the Royal Nepal Academy – published intricate, powerful poems which are still famous today, and the abstracted, poetic stories of Indra Bahadur Rai ◊ suggest a distinguished talent.

Other than these, the most influential poets have been Gopalprasad Rimal ◊, Mohan Koirala ◊, and Bhupi Sherchan ◊. Rimal's revolutionary poems raged against the injustices of the Rana regime and yearned for a 'new birth', employing a form of blank verse that is still popular today. Koirala's dense, symbolic poems have been appearing for over 40 years and they represent a unique view of the world as seen from the streets of Kathmandu. He can hardly be called Devkota's successor, because their poetry differs immensely, but the poetry of Mohan Koirala, if properly translated, would be Nepal's second great contribution to the world of modern literature. Bhupi Sherchan is known chiefly for a collection of poems entitled *A Blind Man in a Revolving Chair* (Extract 12) published in 1969, and his poetry is much simpler and more widely popular than Koirala's. Most poems are grand and ironic satires of contemporary Nepali society, and are justly famous.

Great advances have been made in Nepali fiction. The short story has progressed from timeworn, formulaic tales in which the honest poor are exploited by rapacious landlords to stories of well-drawn characters in urban settings encountering situations of moral uncertainty. Foreigners have begun to appear in stories and writers have addressed their perceptions of Nepal (Extract 8). After a shaky, clichéd start the novel is well-established. One of the most interesting novelists is Parijat, whose first novel *Blue Mimosa* ◊ was published some years ago in English translation. Nepali drama has suffered from the enormous popularity of Indian cinema, but plays are staged regularly and theatre is also used as a means of education in areas where low literacy levels prevail. Nevertheless, poetry remains the most important genre of Nepali literature, and recent years have seen the emergence of a new generation of talented poets who seek to write in simple language for a mass readership.

TRANSLATIONS FROM NEPALI

Very few Nepalis publish literature in English, and Nepal's writers have been poorly served by translators. Western scholarship has produced only two books: David Rubin's translations of selected poems by Devkota, and Hutt's recent book, which profiles and translates 11 poets and supplies translations of 20 short stories (both are listed in the Booklist). Many Nepalis have produced translations, but the translator's command of English is often less than perfect and the translations do not do justice to the originals, or else the translator feels obliged to adopt a Wordsworthian style when translating a poet such as Devkota, and the translation becomes incongruous. The Royal Nepal Academy's *Modern Nepali Poems* is based on a highly representative selection of 20th-century verse, but some of the translations are quaint, to say the least. Yuyutsu R.D.'s 'adaptations' of poems by Banira Giri are much sounder, but are based only loosely on the originals. A miscellany of translations ranging from the very good to the very bad may be found in newly-launched literary magazines such as *Pratik* and *Bagar*, and in privately-published booklets such as Shailendra Kumar Singh's. There are readable translations of only four novels: Shankar

Parijat

Koirala's *Khairini Ghat*, Diamond Shamsher Rama's *Wake of the White Tiger* ◊, Parijat's *Blue Mimosa* and D.C. Gautam's *Unwritten*. A volume of lyrics by the present Queen of Nepal writing as Chadani Shah, and translated by Taranath Sharma, was published recently and is still widely available.

WESTERN WRITING ON NEPAL

Before 1950, because Nepal was a remote and secret land, virtually every visitor to the kingdom recorded and published his or her experiences there. The earliest book-length account of Nepal dates from 1811. The recent growth of international tourism has inspired guides and picturebooks, accounts of exploration and mountaineering, and a body of anthropological writings that has now assumed almost epic proportions. The scene is one of comparative poverty if one looks for works of fiction by Western authors which are set in Nepal, or for travelogues that possess any literary merit. In the first category, we have only Han Suyin's ◊ *The Mountain is Young* (Extract 6), J.R. Marks's *Ayo Gurkha!* ◊ (Extract 2), and a few slender novels by Greta Rana. The second category is more extensive, though this depends on one's definition of literary merit. H.W. Tilman is distinguished from all other mountaineering writers by his literary references and eloquent, ironic prose (Extract 3), while Matthieson's *The Snow Leopard* ◊ (Extracts 11, 14), with its poetic, contemplative tone, amounts to much more than a travelogue. Coburn's ◊ book *Nepali Aama* ◊ is a uniquely accessible portrait of an elderly hillwoman, and Snellgrove's *Himalayan Pilgrimage* ◊ (Extract 4) is essential reading for all with an interest in the Buddhist culture of the high Himalaya and a taste for a well-written memoir.

BOOKLIST

The following selection includes all titles which are extracted in this chapter as well as other relevant works. The editions cited are not necessarily the only ones available. The exact location of the extracts can be found in 'Acknowledgements and Citations' at the end of the volume. Extract numbers are highlighted in bold for ease of reference.

Brown, Percy, *Picturesque Nepal*, Adam and Charles Black, London 1912. **Extract 13**.

Coburn, Broughton, *Nepali Aama. Portrait of a Nepalese Hill Woman*, Ross-Erikson, Santa Barbara, CA, 1982.

Gautam, D.C., *Unwritten*, Philip Pierce, trans, Malla Prakashan, Kathmandu, 1992.

Giri, Banira, *From the Other End*, Yuyutsu R.D. Sharma, trans, Nirala, New Delhi and Jaipur, 1987.

Han, Suyin, *The Mountain is Young*, Triad Granada, 1973. **Extract 6**.

Hutt, Michael J., *Nepali: A National Language and its Literature*, Sterling, New Delhi and London, 1988.

Hutt, Michael J., *Himalayan Voices: An Introduction to Modern Nepali Literature*, University of California Press, Berkeley, CA, 1991. **Extracts 5, 8, 10**.

Koirala, Shankar, *Khairini Ghat*, Larry Hartsell, trans, Ratna Pustak Bhandar, Kathmandu, 1984.

Lienhard, Siegfried, *Songs of Nepal*, University of Hawaii Press, 1984.

Marks, J.M. *Ayo Gurkha!*, Oxford University Press, Oxford, 1971. **Extract 2**.

Matthieson, Peter, *The Snow Leopard*, Picador, London, 1980. **Extracts 11, 14**.

Mehta, Ved, *Walking the Indian Streets*, Penguin, London, 1975. **Extracts 7, 9**.

Parijat, *Blue Mimosa*, Acharya and Zeidenstein, trans, Kathmandu, published by translators, 1972.

Pradhan, Kumar, *A History of Nepali Literature*, Sahitya Akademi, New Delhi, 1984.

Rana, Diamond Shamsher, *Wake of the White Tiger*, Greta Rana, trans, Balika Rana, Kathmandu, 1984.

Royal Nepal Academy, *Modern Nepali Poems*, Kathmandu, 1972.

Rubin, David, *Nepali Visions, Nepali Dreams. The Poetry of Laxmiprasad Devkota*, Columbia University Press, New York, 1980.

Sama, Balkrishna, *Expression after Death*, Sajha Publishers, Kathmandu, 1982.

Shah, Chadani, *Lyrical Poems of Chadani Shah*, Taranath Sharma, trans, HMG Nepal, 1986.

Singh, Shailendra Kumar, *Contemporary Nepali Poetry*, Kathmandu, 1989.

Snellgrove, David L., *Himalayan Pilgrimage*, Prajna Press, Boulder, Colorado, 1981. **Extract 4**.

Subedi, Abhi, *Nepali Literature, Background and History*, Kathmandu, Sajha, 1978.

Tilman, H.W., *Nepal Himalaya*, Cambridge University Press, Cambridge, 1951. **Extract 3**.

Whelpton, John, *Nepal* (World Bibliographical Series, No 38) Oxford, Clio Press, 1990.

Extracts

(1) CENTRAL HILLS:
HELAMBU AND GOSAINKUND

Lakshmiprasad Devkota, *An Essay*

*The Nepali poet Lakshmiprasad Devkota undertook a pilgrimage
to the sacred lake of Gosainkund (about three days' walk north
of Kathmandu) sometime during the late 1930s and wrote down
his impressions of the journey. The essay demonstrates the extent
to which the urban elite is insulated from the harsh reality of life
in the hills, and also exhibits the strong influence that the
idealistic philosophy of English Romanticism had over Devkota.*

On my journey to Gosainthan I saw mountains, but I did not see
mountain life. What I saw on the way did not reflect it: apart from a
few huts and a couple of bazaars I saw nothing but the forests, the hills
and the path I was walking on.

Men spend their lives high up here like birds, sometimes on the
pastures, sometimes in the terraced fields. In the winter there would
only be the smooth realm of snow where sheepfolds and cattlepens now
stood . . . Here, Mankind is blinded and numbed by a great frosty
regime. Life springs up from the dust: smeared with a little of the dust of
Spring time, it blooms, and then in the end it mingles once more with
the dust. There are no greater problems here than eating and scratching
a living. Here, 'home' means four posts and a roof of straw that lasts
only a couple of months, and social life rarely exceeds the coming
together of four people. Man lives a shifting, wandering life in such a
place, travelling in search of warm air and sunshine. The world is
stingy, and Nature is tightfisted: if he is lucky the earth might yield a
little maize and a few nettles.

Why did Man come up here? What pleasure, what happiness was he
seeking? Did he come here just to eat thorns and to stand rattling in the
teeth of the wind, like a few frost-ravaged leaves? Was it to display his
alienation? The children are illiterate, and their legs are bare. They
dance and play like jungle creatures, and life is just subsistence, and the
water that moulds the red clay.

(2) EASTERN HILLS
J.M. Marks, *Ayo Gurkha!*

Aitahang, a young Limbu, is absconding from his home to join up with a galla, a Gurkha recruiting party. Bhalu is his dog.

Aitahang did not sleep a wink the night before he left. Every half-hour after midnight he peered out at the moon, full and clear in the cloudless night sky, the monsoon just past. At last, when he reckoned it was two hours before dawn, he slipped down from the hayloft, still wrapped in his fur, whispered to Bhalu and entered the farmhouse. He opened the family chest, took out his new kukri and closed the lid carefully. Then he folded the fur, laid it on top of the box and laid his working kukri on top of that. This was the only way he could leave word that he had gone of his own free will. He could not have told his parents earlier; they would have forbidden him to go, and would have extracted his promise that he would not.

For a moment he stood in the darkness of the lower room, the familiar scent of pine-wood in his nostrils, hearing from outside the sounds of cattle shifting in the byre, and the clink of Bhalu's chain. Through a crack in the window boards he saw moonlight glitter on the snows of Topke, and impulsively he stretched out his hand to the lid of the chest again, tempted to replace his new kukri and steal back to the hayloft beside his brother. No one would ever know . . .

(3) EASTERN HILLS: KHUMBU
H.W. Tilman, *Nepal Himalaya*

H.W. Tilman was a member of the very first party of Western-ers ever to visit the Khumbu region, the home of the now famous Sherpas. He relates the tale of his journey with his customary sardonic humour.

Our recent access of confidence was further undermined by the appalling prospect of the next stage, from our camp on the rice stubbles of Gudel across an appallingly deep valley to Bung, and thence to another pass on the ridge beyond. Bung looked to be within spitting distance, yet the map confirmed and the eye agreed that we should have to descend some 3 000 ft. and climb a like amount to reach it. Profound emotion may find some vent in verse as well as in oaths; despair as well as joy may rouse latent, unsuspected poetical powers. Thus at Gudel, uninspired by liquor, for there was none, some memorable lines were spoken:

> For dreadfulness nought can excel
> The prospect of Bung from Gudel;
> And words die away on the tongue
> When we look back at Gudel from Bung.

The village of Bung, a name which appeals to a music-hall mind, provoked another outburst on the return journey because its abundant well of good raksi, on which we were relying, had dried up:

> Hope thirstily rested on Bung
> So richly redolent of rum;
> But when we got there
> The cupboard was bare,
> Sapristi. No raksi. No chang.

(To disarm the hypercritical I might say that the 'a' in chang, a Tibetan word for beer, is pronounced like a short 'u'.)

The neat houses and terraced fields of Bung, apparently rich in promise, covered several thousand feet of hillside. In Nether Bung they grew bananas and rice, in Upper Bung oranges and wheat. A sepoy had gone on to collect rice but on arrival the whole party scattered in search of provender like hounds drawing a cover. For ourselves we acquired nothing but a goat, worth about Rs.5, for Rs.12, having been asked Rs.20. In order to secure the rice we had to curtail the march and make a late start. Next morning the jemadar, with bloodshot eyes and husky voice, as became one who had attended an overnight harvest thanksgiving, led the rice procession up to our camp in swaying triumph.

(4) The Kathmandu Valley

David L. Snellgrove, *Himalayan Pilgrimage*

Snellgrove describes the thrill of arriving in the Kathmandu valley first on foot, and then by air.

Approaching on foot, one's arrival is the culmination of days of slow travel with ever mounting expectancy, and that feeling of calm satisfaction and happy fulfilment, which pervades one on mounting the pass and seeing the Valley at one's feet, belongs, I am sure, to the very best of human experience. These conditions of travel have changed not at all, and the many Tibetan monks and scholars, who went there in search of knowledge a thousand years ago, probably conceived of Nepal in a way which we are happily still able to appreciate nowadays.

At the beginning of 1956 I approached the Nepal Valley for the third time, travelling on this occasion by the rapid air-route from Patna. By mere speed expectation is robbed of its substance: this is now no land of promise, whose frontiers have at last been gained by one's own patience and endurance, but rather an illusive dream-country, delightful while the vision lasts, but vanishing as soon as the plane touches land, and life shows itself as prosaic as ever.

One passes through clouds and close over the tops of tree-covered mountains. Then the Valley appears suddenly below with its wooded hillocks and terraced fields, decked with the little red houses of the peasants (Khas); one sees the glistening waters of the Bagmati, the dark serried rows of houses of those inveterate town-dwellers, the Newars, and here and there a Rana palace in its pseudo-Italian style; there may just be time to glance at the great stupa of Bodhnath, as the plane completes its circling. Then the dream is over and a few minutes later one is fumbling for documents and opening cases under the watchful eyes of officials.

(5) THE KATHMANDU VALLEY

Lakshmiprasad Devkota, *Muna and Madan*

An extract from Lakshmiprasad Devkota's poem 'Muna and Madan'. Madan has been away seeking his fortune in Tibet: now he thinks nostalgically about his home.

Far away lies shining Nepal,
where cocks are crowing to summon the light
as morning opens to smile down from the mountains.
The city of Nepal wears a garland of blue hills,
with trees like earrings on the valley peaks,
the eastern ridges bear rosy clouds,
the fields are bright and dappled with shadows,
water falls like milk from distant hills.

Madan recalls the carved windows and doors,
the pipal tree loud in the rising wind,
the little house where Muna sits,
his Muna, his mother, the world of his heart.

(6) The Kathmandu Valley

Han Suyin, *The Mountain is Young*

The sight of the Himalaya in the early morning light.

Walking in the morning in the Valley of Kathmandu was a pleasure whose recollection, during the day, lifted him on a crest of remembered delight above the weariness and frustrations of his work. There was the early light, cool and frosty, delicate like a bubble, the nourishing air, heady with the smell of rising sun and the sharpness of all stirring things. It made him want to sing and run on the road still crackling with the nimble hoar of frost. Thousands of cobwebs, glistening like spun diamonds, were on the hedges and filled the cracks on top of the pink brick walls of the Rana palaces and the Newari houses. The marvellous prodigal sun threw his light about, and in the trees with their close-cupped, half-budded spring leaves, orioles and finches and sunbirds blossomed and sang their hearts out . . .

Frederic Maltby knew the bend of the road where he would suddenly see, and always with the same shock of happiness, the snow peaks, rosy in the early light, emerging above the near hills. Although from his bedroom window he could see them just as well, yet it was pleasure redoubled to meet them just at that corner, to see the lords of the snows towering incandescent pink in the early sky. I shall see them here again tomorrow, he thought, and felt himself fulfilled. He had been five years in the Valley. He would never leave it. Never would he go back to the plains. He would remain here until he died, lifting his eyes to the mountains in the morning and many times during the day. 'For the chief things of the ancient mountains, and for the precious things of the lasting hills . . .'

(7) The Kathmandu Valley

Ved Mehta, *Walking the Indian Streets*

Having graduated from Oxford in 1959, Ved Mehta and his friend, the poet Dom Moraes, spent a summer travelling in India with a sidetrip to Kathmandu. Their adventures are also recorded, with considerable embroidery, in Dom Moraes's book Gone Away.

Days in Kathmandu are, for us, days of waking. We find strange things. The strangest of all is the naturalness of the surroundings and the people. Men and women work side by side in the fields. They sing and dance with their ids but are not embarrassed. The women are beautiful and healthy, and not, like Indian women, always pulling the folds of their saris to give them more drape. The sari is the winding sheet of sex in India, but not here. And here people are not made ugly by their poverty. For the first time since we came home, it really feels as though we were on a pink cloud.

(8) THE KATHMANDU VALLEY: CHOBHAR VILLAGE

Shankar Lamichhane, *The Halfclosed Eyes of the Buddha and the Slowly Setting Sun*

This well-known short story is composed of two monologues: one from a tourist newly arrived in Nepal, the other a response from his guide. The extract takes the first passage from each of these monologues.

(*The tourist*)

'Oh guide, you do not, you cannot comprehend the joy we westerners feel when we first set foot upon the soil of your country. The Dakota crosses the Four Passes and we see this green valley, its geometric fields, its earthen houses of red and yellow and white, the scent of soil and mountains is in the air and there's an age-old peacefulness in the atmosphere . . . you were born amongst all of this and so you might feel that the embracing bosom of these blue hills confines you. But we live in the plains, or beside the sea. Our vision founders on an horizon of land or sea, and so we know the affection with which the breast of these hills forever clings to your sight. You have never had to suffer the feeling of insignificance which is engendered by a vast distance; perhaps we are always adrift in vastness, my friend, perhaps that is why this, your enclosure, appeals to us. Has it ever occurred to you that the half-closed eyes of the Buddha seem to welcome you, even at the airport? It is as if one acquires a calmness, as if one is returning once more to a resting-place.'

(*The guide speaks*):

'Come, my guest, today I am to show you some eyes.

This is Chobhar hill, where you people come to see the cleft that was made by Manjushri's sword, and the outflow of the Bagmati river. Today I'll take you up the hill where few of our guests ever go and no tourist's car can proceed. There, (in your words), the dust of time has not yet covered the culture of the past. Do you see this worn old rock? A young village artist has drawn some birds on it. Nearby, he has sketched a temple, leaving out any mention of the religion to which it belongs. Further up the hill, in the middle of the village, stands the temple of Adinath. In the temple courtyard there is a shrine of Shiva, several Buddha images and many prayer wheels, inscribed *Om Mani Padme Hum*. You say it is a living example of Nepalese tolerance and co-existence. Children play happily there, unconcerned by the variety of their gods, religions and philosophies. But, my guest, I will not take you there . . .

(9) The Kathmandu Valley: Poets

Ved Mehta, *Walking the Indian Streets*

Ved Mehta and Dom Moraes met a number of the most important Nepali poets of the day while in Kathmandu. Their meetings are described somewhat facetiously in both books, despite the fact that they had the unique privilege of visiting the poet Lakshmiprasad Devkota just before he died at the temple of Pashupatinath. Mehta's account is more sympathetic than Moraes's, nonetheless.

The assembled talent regretfully plead the deficiencies of their language, the inability to translate their thoughts and feelings, manifold and towering in Nepalese. 'To be a poet in Nepalese is to die of frustration,' one of them says. They wish they had been born in England. Our pity changes into sympathy, and the tenseness, the feeling of 'thou and I,' disappears. We are one. Dom reads a short poem about a Jesuit friend reading the river like a book of ancient wisdom, and then there is a libation, a praying for good fortune for one another, and we jeep across to the palace, silent and happy. The gods are good in Nepal. They live in Katmandu and ignore the people down south, who live in the shadow of the British raj, and with sunstroke, monsoons and flood. Katmandu's sky is clear, all the stars are visible, and a good destiny is marked out.

(10) The Himalayas

Lekhnath Paudyal, *Himalaya*

This extract from a poem by Nepal's 'Crest-Jewel Poet' expresses reverence and wonder in a description of the mountain range which dominates the Kingdom.

> A scarf of pure white snow
> Hangs down from its head to its feet,
> Cascades like strings of pearls

Glisten on its breast,
A net of drizzling cloud
Encircles its waist like a grey woollen shawl:
An astounding sight, still and bright,
Our blessed Himalaya.

(11) POKHARA

Peter Matthieson, *The Snow Leopard*

Peter Matthieson began his celebrated journey to the Crystal Mountain of Shey from Pokhara: these two extracts describe his arrival there and scenes from the first steps of the journey.

After midday, the rain eased, and the Land-Rover rode into Pokhara on a shaft of storm light. Next day there was humid sun and shifting southern skies, but to the north a deep tumult of swirling greys was all that could be seen of the Himalaya. At dusk, white egrets flapped across the sunken clouds, now black with rain; on earth, the dark had come. Then, four miles above these mud streets of the lowlands, at a point so high as to seem overhead, a luminous whiteness shone – the light of snows. Glaciers loomed and vanished in the greys, and the sky parted, and the snow cone of Machhapuchare glistened like a spire of a higher kingdom.

In the night, the stars convened, and the vast ghost of Machhapuchare radiated light, although there was no moon. In the shed where we lay down, behind a sort of inn, there were mosquitoes. My friend, dreaming, cried out in his sleep. Restless, I went out at daybreak and saw three peaks of Annapurna, soaring clear of low, soft clouds. This day we would depart for the north-west.

Grey river road, grey sky. From rock to torrent rock flits a pied wagtail.

Wayfarers: a delicate woman bears a hamper of small silver fishes, and another bends low beneath a basket of rocks that puts my own light pack to shame: her rocks will be hammered to gravel by other women of Pokhara, in the labour of the myriad brown hands that will surface a new road south to India.

Through a shaft of sun moves a band of Magar women, scarlet-shawled; they wear heavy brass ornaments in the left nostril. In the new sun, a red-combed rooster clambers quickly to the roof matting of a roadside hut, and fitfully a little girl starts singing. The light irradiates white peaks of Annapurna marching down the sky, in the great rampart that spreads east and west for eighteen hundred miles, the Himalaya – the *alaya* (abode, or home) of *hima* (snow).

(12) POKHARA
Bhupi Sherchan, *'Pokhara'*

A cynical view of the contrast between international tourism and local poverty and landlessness (from Blind Man in a Revolving Chair).

Planes are coming, planes are going,
Coming with honeymoon couples,
Going carrying soldiers
Summoned to Kutch next morning.

Planes come, carrying tourists
To see the Fishtail mountain,
Planes go carrying baskets and trunks,
Ploughs and the Fishtail's children,
Off to seek land in the plains.

Planes are coming, planes are going:
From a bench by the airfield a blind man drones,
'No milk comes from a bird,
For a sad man there's no home.'

(13) THE TARAI
Percy Brown, *Picturesque Nepal*

An account of a journey to Kathmandu before the roads were built, by one of the very few foreigners to have access to the kingdom before 1950.

Everything is conducive to drowsiness. Lying full length in palanquin or 'dooly', the gentle motion caused by the bearers, the soft patter of their feet as they shuffle along, their steady grunting chorus, the song of birds, the hum of insects, the slowly moving landscape, all combine to produce a feeling of complete rest to both mind and body which must be experienced to be appreciated. And so the miles gradually and serenely pass until a break occurs – truly a break – for one of the palanquin poles, which has evidently been rotting in idleness during the rains, shows distinct signs of giving way. In most circumstances and climates this typical act of irresponsibility might have led to 'a tide of fierce invective', but already the lotus-eating atmosphere has stealthily drawn us under its spell, and, 'lost to the hurrying world', we placidly wait while an expedition is planned and carried out to a distant clump of bamboos – waving in the wind like monster ostrich plumes – and the broken pole replaced. A few miles more through fields of shimmering crops, and then, with an almost dramatic suddenness, the road closes in, the open landscape disappears, the sky is shut out by overhanging trees, the balmy breeze changes into a hot oppressive stillness, and a strange heavy feeling comes over us all. We have entered the forest of the far-famed Terai.

(14) Western Hills: Dolpo

Peter Matthieson, *The Snow Leopard*

Matthieson's poetic account of his journey is interspersed with philosophical passages which have attracted both scorn and admiration. All a matter of taste, perhaps . . .

The secret of the mountains is that the mountains simply exist, as I do myself: the mountains exist simply, which I do not. The mountains have no 'meaning', they *are* meaning; the mountains *are*. The sun is round. I ring with life, and the mountains ring, and when I can hear it, there is a ringing that we share. I understand all this, not in my mind but in my heart, knowing how meaningless it is to try to capture what cannot be expressed, knowing that mere words will remain when I read it all again, another day.

Towards four, the sun sets fire on the Crystal Mountain. I turn my collar up and put on gloves and go down to Somdo, where my tent has stored the last sun of the day. In the tent entrance, out of the wind, I drink hot tea and watch the darkness rise out of the earth. The sunset fills the deepening blues with holy rays and turns a twilight raven into the silver bird of night as it passes into the shadow of the mountain. Then the great hush falls, and cold descends. The temperature has already dropped well below freezing, and will drop twenty degrees more before the dawn.

(15) THE WESTERN HILLS:
LAMJUNG DISTRICT

Madhav Prasad Ghimire, *Memories of Jagara*

Madhav Ghimire, a leading Romantic poet and erstwhile Vice-Chancellor of the Royal Nepal Academy, was born and grew up in the Lamjung district to the northeast of Pokhara. His nostalgia for his youth is evident in this passage.

In the middle of the night one can hear the lovely sound of the foaming Marsyangdi river from here, as it washes against its rocky shores in the valley far below. At dawn, golden sunlight falls upon the heads of the hills to the west, then descends slowly to the valleys. But it does not reach the forest on this eastern mountainside for another five hours.

I spent my childhood here, tending the cows we owned. Each year we village cowherds would work our way up to the high places, then back down to the valley again. For six months of every year I knew only two seasons: Spring and Autumn. There was really no sense of Summer: one only knew that June had begun when the Marsyangdi turned cloudy with snowmelt from the Himalayas. Down in the valley, Spring brought an indolent, drowsy feeling, but up here it brought only happiness to a youth who had never known sorrow. In the valley, the rainy season was like a visitor from abroad, but here it was a friend who played hide-and-seek with the mists as they blew through the forests and sheepfolds. On the day the rains ceased, the peaks and ridges would seem so close I would wonder why I had ever thought that they were far away. In the valley, my favourite season was Autumn: the stars seemed so distant in the clear night sky, and during the day the blue of the sky entered the brightness of the flowers. We would get up to Jagara at the end of March, when villagers were scattered throughout the forests, calling 'The kaphal is ripe! Spring has come!' By the time we reached the valley again, the ricefields were bright green and people were busy preparing for the great autumn festival, the nine nights of Durga.

I would go up to Jagara after spending six months in the wide open expanse of the valley. At that time of year the forest smelled wonderful. When one enters a virgin glade where no animals have grazed and no man has breathed, there is a green freshness in the smell of the new growth that defeats the scent of a hundred flowers, and could not even be imagined in a perfume factory.

Biographies and plot summaries

Ayo Gurkha! Novel by J.R. Marks ◊. Aitahang, a Limbu from eastern Nepal, joins the British Brigade of Gurkhas to fight in Malaya. An affectionate and quite authentic portrayal which stands out from the mass of other rather hackneyed literature on the Gurkhas (Extract 2).

BALLABH, Ishwar (1937–). Poet, member of Royal Nepal Academy 1990–94. Developed an abstract and 'impressionistic' style of Nepali poetry.

BHANUBHAKTA, Acharya (1814–68). Born western Nepal, called the *Adi Kavi*, 'founder-poet' of Nepali literature, author of *Nepali Ramayana* and many other important poems.

BHATTA, Motiram (1866–96). Born Kathmandu, educated Benares. Poet, musician and publisher. Biographer of Bhanubhakta Acharya.

Blue Mimosa. A Nepali novel by Parijat ◊, first published 1964. An alcoholic Gurkha veteran leads an aimless life until he falls in love with the enigmatic sister of a drinking companion. The woman dies soon after his sole attempt to make his feelings known to her. Has been called 'the first modern novel in Nepali': certainly one of the most unorthodox and most competently-translated.

BROWN, Percy. British civil servant employed in the Indian Educational Service during the early decades of the present century. Principal of the Government School of Art and Trustee of the Indian Museum in Calcutta. Author of several standard works on Indian art and architecture, and of *Picturesque Nepal* (Extract 13), an account of a visit to the kingdom, 1911.

COBURN, Broughton. An American Peace Corps volunteer who worked as a schoolteacher in central Nepal during the 1970s. Author of *Nepali Aama* ◊.

DEVKOTA, Lakshmiprasad (1909–59). Born in Kathmandu, Devkota was called *mahakavi*, 'great poet' and is indisputably Nepal's greatest writer to date. He worked as an English tutor and translator. He undertook voluntary exile in India during the 1940s and returned to be made a government minister. His poetry combines the influences of English romanticism, Sanskrit classicism, Greek mythology and Nepali patriotism. At least 35 volumes of verse have been published in Nepali, as well as a novel, a volume of stories and three volumes of essays. The poetry is widely translated (Extracts 1, 5).

DIXIT, Mani. Nepali author who has published several thrillers, each set in Nepal. These include *The Red Temple* (1977) and *Come Tomorrow* (1980).

GHIMIRE, Madhav Prasad (1919–). Leading Nepali Romantic poet.

Bust of Lakshmiprasad Devkota

Many of his metrical compositions celebrate the natural beauty of Nepal and invest it with religious symbolism.

GIRI, Banira (1946–). Born in Darjeeling, Giri is known mainly for her poems, which use Hindu myths to highlight contemporary social issues. She is also an accomplished novelist.

HAN Suyin (Elizabeth Cromer) (1917–). Born in China, educated in the West. Her earlier works (*A Many-Splendoured Thing*, *The Mountain is Young* ◊) are romances set in the Far East; later, she produced

accounts of modern Chinese history. She was a guest at the coronation of King Mahendra in 1955, which represented the end of Nepal's historic isolation. The experience became the setting for the latter novel. (Extract 6).

Himalayan Pilgrimage. David Snellgrove's account of a journey undertaken on foot in 1956 across the northern border regions from far western Nepal to Kathmandu. Contains vivid descriptions of the environment, art and religious culture of areas still rarely seen by foreign visitors (Extract 4).

KAINLA, Bairagi (1940–). A poet whose real name is Tilvikram Nembang. Kainla is a Limbu educated in Darjeeling. He composes complex, often abstruse poetry without precedent in Nepali.

Khairini Ghat. A popular Nepali novel by Shankar Koirala ◊. A young man returns to his village in the eastern hills after a period spent working in Calcutta, and is caught up in the social and political upheavals which accompanied the overthrow of the Rana regime.

KOIRALA, Bishweshwar Prasad (1915–82). Called 'BP', Koirala was leader of the Nepali Congress party and became Nepal's first elected Prime Minister in 1959. He made important contributions to the development of Nepali fiction, publishing several novels and a volume of short stories. He was influenced by Sartre, Freud and Maupassant, among others.

KOIRALA, Mohan (1926–). A poet who worked as clerk and schoolteacher, he was a member of Royal Nepal Academy 1974–79 and 1990–94. He has developed an innovative style of free verse, though he is sometimes criticised for obscurity. Many of his poems are extremely long. Six volumes of his poetry have been published.

KOIRALA, Shankar (1932–). Story-writer and novelist. He has had over 20 novels published, mostly dealing with rural and historical themes.

LAMICHHANE, Shankar (1928–75). Story-writer, essayist and poet. Lamichhane worked for cultural institutions in Kathmandu, and in the tourist industry. Admired for the fluency of his prose and the freshness of his outlook, he was influenced by modern American literature (Extract 8).

MAINALI, Guru Prasad (1900–71). A lawyer who was one of the first exponents of modern fiction in Nepali. Only 11 stories were published, most during the period 1935–55, but each is now considered a classic. The most famous, 'A Blaze in the Straw' describes a marital quarrel. Mainali's extensive knowledge of Nepal gave him an eye for local detail and a gift for composing authentic dialogue.

Mohan Koirala

MARKS, J.R. Ex-Gurkha officer, author of *Ayo Gurkha!* ◊ (Extract 2).

MATTHIESON, Peter (1927–). Matthieson was born in New York and educated at the Sorbonne and Yale. He is the author of travel books on South America, East Africa, Nepal (Extracts 11, 14) and elsewhere, and of novels.

MEHTA, Ved (1934–). Born in Lahore, educated at Oxford and Harvard. Mehta began as a journalist for the *New Yorker*. He has written extensively on modern India, and produced a lengthy autobiography in several volumes (Extracts 7, 9). See also North-west India and Pakistan.

The Mountain is Young. Han Suyin's ◊ romantic novel, set against the backdrop of King Mahendra's coronation in 1955, which she herself attended. Anne, a shy English girl, discovers her sexuality in sensuous Kathmandu through a liaison with an Indo–Nepali engineer. Han Suyin paints a lurid picture of Nepal and the foreign guests at the coronation, but combines this with a fine eye for scenery and a gifted pen. The novel probably introduced Nepal, then a little-known kingdom, to many ordinary readers (Extract 6).

Muna and Madan. A 40-page poem by Devkota ◊, first published in 1935, and the most popular work ever written in Nepali. A young man, Madan, resolves to travel to Lhasa in Tibet to seek his fortune. His wife, Muna, begs him not to abandon her and his aged mother, but to no avail. Madan acquires gold and musk in Lhasa but on his way home he falls ill and is nursed by a Tibetan farmer. Meanwhile, a suitor tells Muna that Madan is dead. When he reaches Kathmandu, both his mother and his wife have passed away. Composed in a singsong folk-metre, the melodrama contains many famous moral statements, and is itself a comment on the society of its time (Extract 5).

Nepal Himalaya. H.W. Tilman's ◊ account of his exploration of the mountains of central and eastern Nepal during the late 1940s, including the first-ever visit by Westerners to the Everest region. Compared with the bald diary-like style of many mountaineering books, this is a masterpiece full of laconic wit and humorous quotations from the most recondite sources (Extract 3).

Nepali Aama. Broughton Coburn's ◊ portrait of his Nepali landlady, Vishnu Maya Gurung. Black-and-white photographs are combined with Vishnu Maya's reflections and reminiscences to create a lyrical insight into village life and a profile of one of its protagonists.

PARIJAT (1937–93). Novelist and poet. A leading figure of progressive Nepali writing in all genres who first came to the fore with her novel *Blue Mimosa* ◊.

PAUDYAL, Lekhnath (1885–1966). Called *Kavi Shiromani*, 'Crestjewel Poet'. A Brahman pandit whose poetry drew on the great traditions of Sanskrit but did much to establish Nepali as a literary language. His first major work was *Reflections on the Seasons*, a poem of 600 verses published in 1916. He continued to write until his death: *The Young Ascetic* (1953, but still untranslated) is a masterly combination of autobiography, religious reflection and historical allegory (Extract 10).

RAI, Indra Bahadur (1928–). Born in Darjeeling, Rai is a novelist, story-writer and critic.

RANA, Diamond Shamsher (1919–). Historical novelist who has published four books in Nepali set in the Rana period. One of these is translated as *Wake of the White Tiger* ◊.

RANA, Greta (1943–). A Yorkshire-born poet, novelist and translator who has acquired Nepali citizenship through her marriage. She is the author of several novellas which deal with the lives of Nepali women, including *Distant Hills* and *Nothing Greener* (both 1977), and translator of *Wake of the White Tiger* ◊.

RIMAL, Gopalprasad (1918–73). Poet and dramatist who pioneered the use of non-metrical verse in Nepali, and produced stirring revolutionary poems during the struggle against the Ranas.

SAMA, Balkrishna (1903–81). A Rana who penned the most famous works of Nepali theatre, particularly *Mukunda and Indira* (1937) and *Heart's Anguish* (1929) and also made important contributions to the linguistic refinement and philosophical development of Nepali poetry.

SHERCHAN, Bhupi (1936–89). Born Tukuche, Mustang district. A hugely popular poet who developed a colloquial style of verse which satirised Nepali society from a Marxist

standpoint and reflected with considerable pathos on the human condition (Extract 12).

SNELLGROVE, David Llewellyn (1920–). A leading scholar of Buddhism who mounted eight expeditions to India and Nepal between 1953 and his retirement in 1982. Professor of Tibetan in the University of London 1974–82. A wide range of publications on Nepal, including *Four Lamas of Dolpo* (1967), *Buddhist Himalaya* ◊ (1957) and *Himalayan Pilgrimage* (Extract 4, 1959).

The Snow Leopard. Peter Matthieson's ◊ account of a journey to the remote Dolpo region to study blue sheep and snow leopards in 1973. Part memoir, part travelogue, part Zen meditation (Extracts 11, 14). 'Matthieson's philosophical ramblings are cliché-ridden' says Luree Miller, but Paul Theroux disagrees: 'A beautiful book, and worthy of those mountains he is among'.

TILMAN, Harold William (1898–1977). Explorer, mountaineer and author (Extract 3). Tilman was born in Wallasey, served on the Western Front 1915–18 and grew coffee in Kenya 1919–33. He made first ascents of many peaks in Africa and the Himalaya, including Nanda Devi in 1936 – then the highest mountain ever climbed. He made several attempts on Everest. He turned to marine exploration of the Poles in later years, and was lost at sea in the South Atlantic. Tilman's style is 'graphic, lucid and at times has an aphoristic elegance' (Jim Perrin).

VYATHIT, Kedar Man (1914–).

A poet writing in Nepali, Hindi and Newari, Vyathit has been Minister for Transport in the Nepal Government, and Vice-Chancellor of the Royal Nepal Academy. He was influenced both by the poets of the Hindi *chayavad* movement, and by a vigorous patriotism. Over 15 volumes of poetry are in print.

Wake of the White Tiger. English translation by Greta Rana ◊ of Diamond Shamsher Rana's ◊ *Seto Bagh*, the foremost historical novel in Nepali. It describes conflicts between Rana factions during the period between 1854 and the death of Jang Bahadur in 1877. According to John Welpton, the book has been 'Fairly criticized for its flagrant inconsistency with known historical fact, but it does convey something of the flavour of court life and intrigue under the Ranas'.

SRI LANKA

Christopher Reynolds

> Between five and six in the evening the broad green lawn of the esplanade, stretching southwards between the lagoon and the sea, is the rendez-vous for all the rank, beauty and fashion of Colombo . . . the world refreshes itself in the cool evening breeze after the burden of the noon-tide heat, while enjoying the gorgeous spectacle of the sunset . . .
> *Ernst Haeckel, A Visit to Ceylon*

Sri Lanka, known in English as Ceylon until 1972, is a tropical island about 300 miles by 150, lying some 40 miles off the eastern part of south India. Its northern half is flat, but mountains in the south-central portion rise to 8 000 feet. The high slopes are widely covered with tea plantations, and the lower ones with a mixture of tea and rubber. These areas were more or less uninhabited jungle before the 19th century. The climate in this southwestern corner of the island is wet, with the principal monsoon rains in May. (The average annual rainfall in Colombo, the capital, is about 90 inches.) Rice, the staple food, is grown here without artificial irrigation, in valley bottoms and on terraced slopes. This area encompasses the chief centres of population today.

The larger portion of the island – the northern two-thirds and the east coast – is much drier, with monsoon rains principally in November. Here rice needs artificial irrigation. Nevertheless these areas were the site of the first historic settlements, from about 500 BC onwards. These settlers came from India, and were composed of Sinhalese from north India, speaking an Indo-Aryan language and Tamils from south India, speaking a Dravidian language. The early kingdoms were centred at **Anuradhapura**, in the north-central plains, and developed a sophisticated system of agricultural irrigation. The Sinhalese rulers and their subjects adopted Buddhism as their national religion during the 3rd century BC, and built many Buddhist monasteries all over the dry

358

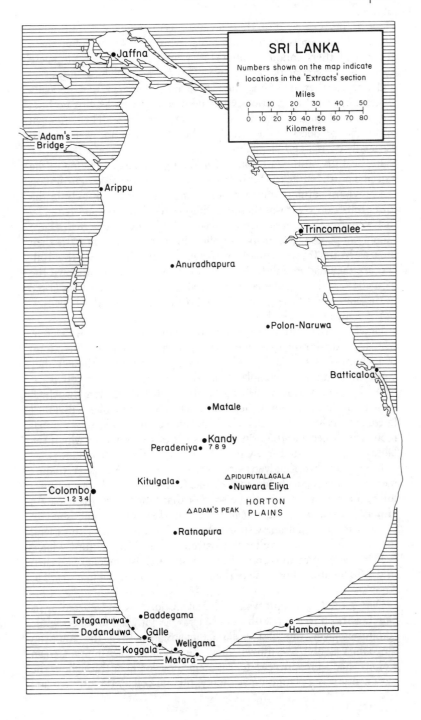

SRI LANKA

Numbers shown on the map indicate
locations in the 'Extracts' section

Miles

0   10   20   30   40   50

0 10 20 30 40 50 60 70 80

Kilometres

Jaffna

Adam's
Bridge

Arippu

Trincomalee

Anuradhapura

Polon-Naruwa

Batticaloa

Matale

Kandy
Peradeniya 7 8 9

Kitulgala   △PIDURUTALAGALA
              ●Nuwara Eliya

Colombo   HORTON
1 2 3 4   △ADAM'S PEAK   PLAINS

Ratnapura

Baddegama
Totagamuwa
Dodanduwa   Galle   Hambantota
Koggala   Weligama
Matara

zone. In the 10th century, these areas were conquered and annexed by the Chola emperors from south India, who were Hindus; but these abandoned their conquests after 150 years or so. A new Sinhalese capital was set up at **Polon-naruwa**. This did not last long, however, and after further invasions the whole northern area was gradually abandoned and the irrigation system allowed to decay, leaving nothing but malarial jungle for the next seven centuries. The principal exportable products of the island in this classical period were jewels, especially pearls, and elephants.

In the 13th century a separate Tamil kingdom arose at Jaffna in the extreme north, while the Sinhalese kingdom survived at various sites in the previously unimportant wet zone, finally settling at **Kandy** in the lower hill-country. It was then that European colonizers appeared. The first were the Portuguese, who arrived in 1505; they converted a large number of people to Roman Catholic Christianity, including the then king at **Kotte** (now a suburb of Colombo). By the end of the 16th century they had established control of the coastal areas all down the west coast, and the Christian religion which they introduced has lasted in these areas until the present day. Christians are currently about 10% of the population (which is now about 18 million).

However, the Portuguese empire was soon attacked by the Dutch, who drove the Portuguese out of Ceylon altogether by 1660. Their form of Calvinistic Christianity did not take proper root, although they controlled almost the complete coast-line of the island for 150 years. They did, however, leave behind a system of Roman-Dutch law which is still in force. Meanwhile, an independent Sinhalese Buddhist kingdom survived in a landlocked enclave centred on Kandy. Cinnamon, which became the principal product of the island in which the Dutch were interested, grew to some extent in the Kandyan areas.

It was in this Kandyan kingdom that Robert Knox, a trading merchant sailor, was held captive from 1660 to 1679. He has left us a full and detailed account of the state of that kingdom in his book *An Historical Relation of the Island of Ceylon* (Extract 8), published in London in 1681. Earlier visitors who also left mention of the island include the Muslim traveller Ibn Battuta in the 14th century, Marco Polo in the 13th century, and the Chinese Buddhist traveller Fa-Hsien in the 5th century, but none of their accounts is anything like so full as Knox's.

During the Napoleonic wars, colonial Ceylon was surrendered by its Dutch garrison to the British from Madras, and it was for a short while administered by the East India Company. In 1815 the Kandyan kingdom was also overthrown, and the whole island, now a Crown Colony, had a broadly peaceful economic development throughout the 19th century as a plantation economy, first for coffee, then for tea and rubber. The labour for the plantations was imported from India right up till the 1930s, producing a more or less settled community of 'Indian Tamils' in the hill country, who had little or no connection with the Ceylon Tamils in Jaffna.

In 1948 the island became independent again, and at first remained peaceful and prosperous. There was already a very high standard of educational and medical services, and this was maintained; but owing to the emerging problem of educated unemployment (long familiar in neighbouring India), the ever increasing population and the drop in the prices of raw material products, political discontent surfaced in 1971. Furthermore, the jungles of the dry zone, after being virtually uninhabitable through malaria for seven centuries, benefited from modern chemicals and were re-settled after 1950; and this brought the so-called Ceylon Tamils of the extreme north into conflict with the Sinhalese in the resettled zones. In particular after 1980, relationships between the two main communities deteriorated into internecine warfare.

LANGUAGES

The national languages of the country are Sinhalese, the official language, and Tamil. In addition, English is very widely spoken. Sinhalese (or Sinhala, accented on the *first* syllable – the middle vowel is short, and the word more or less rhymes with 'jingler') – is an Indo-Aryan language, of the Sanskrit family, and thus distantly related to the major languages of Europe. It is spoken only in Sri Lanka; its closest relative is Divehi, spoken in the adjacent Maldive Islands. Tamil is a Dravidian language, and widely spoken in south India as well as in northern Sri Lanka. Both languages have their own scripts (as does Divehi). The Muslim community in Sri Lanka also generally use Tamil as a home language, though as they are scattered about the island many of them speak Sinhalese also. There is also a small community of 'Burghers', of European or Eurasian origin, whose home language is English.

Though the Western capitalist economy became universal during the British period, caste survives as a social institution in both main communities. Among the Tamils it is much as in South India; among the Sinhalese it is a greatly modified system, where the 'top' caste is believed to encompass more than 50% of the population, but it is still of importance at least in the spheres of marriage and of politics.

LITERATURE

The literature of Sri Lanka appears under three main forms: works in Sinhalese or Pali, works in Tamil and works in English.

Sinhalese literature dates from ancient times. The language assumed its present written form about the year 1000, and the literary language has changed very little since then, though the spoken language differs considerably. We still have here (as also in Tamil) a 'diglossic' situation, where the forms used in writing are not the same as those used in speech, and have to be specially learnt by Sinhalese children at school. In the past, such teaching was given in the Buddhist temple, since the *sangha* (the Buddhist monks) were the custodians of literature, virtually all of which was Buddhist-inspired. Nowadays with modern secular education the gap between spoken and written language is beginning to narrow.

We hear of works of Sinhalese literature even before 1000 AD, but these have not survived, because they were written in forms of language prior to the development of the literary standard, and hence became unintelligible to later generations. Classical Sinhalese literature (roughly 1000–1600 AD) consists almost entirely (apart from technical and didactic works) of Buddhist stories, ie stories of the life of the Buddha himself, of his disciples, and especially of his previous reincarnations known as *jatakas* or 'births'. The book of 550 such *jatakas* (though actually containing only 537), already existing in Pali, was published in Sinhalese in the 14th century. Literature of this kind continued to be written down to about 1850. To this all-embracing religious bias there was a single exception in the genre called *sandesa* or 'message'. The *sandesas* are message-poems, describing the carrying of some perfunctory message from one place in Lanka to another. They are imitations of Kalidasa's famous Sanskrit poem *Meghadutam* (◊ Classical Literature), where the messenger was a cloud. Most of the messengers in Sinhalese *sandesas* were birds, and the bulk of these poems consist of elaborate poetic descriptions of the route to be followed by the messenger. Although it seems that such poems were written in Sinhalese even before 1000, when classical literature commenced, the ones we have begin in the 14th century, and they continued to be written up to the 20th century.

Prose works seem by origin to be direct translations of Pali literature, Pali being the sacred language of southern Buddhism (Northern Buddhism uses Sanskrit). Pali is a literary Prakrit, and since it was not generally intelligible to the Sinhalese villager (though he used formulae in it in his religious worship), it became common to write a *sanne*, a word-for-word translation into Sinhalese. The first prose we have (12th century) arose from the use of such translations with the intervening Pali words omitted. In recounting stories of the life of the Buddha himself and of his disciples several Pali books may be drawn on, literary skill being shown in their selection, and also in the comments added by the Sinhalese writer himself, which are frequently in the nature of similes derived from the Lankan life around him. An early prose work containing numerous such inserted similes is *Saddharma-Ratnavaliya* (Jewelled necklace of the Good Law) by Dharmasena; here the author has translated over 900 stories from the Pali *Dhammapad-atthakatha* (Commentary on the Dharmapada). Other well-known collections of stories are *Ama-vatura* and *Pujavaliya, Saddharm-alankaraya* (a translation of a Pali book of stories called *Rasa-vahini*), and the collected translations of *jataka* stories of previous births of the Buddha.

Verse is heavily dependent on the Sanskrit tradition, which is unfamiliar to Westerners. As Professor A.B. Keith says, 'the *Kavya* ('ornate poem') literature includes some of the great poetry of the world, but it can never expect to attain wide popularity in the West, for it is essentially untranslatable . . . English efforts at verse translations fall invariably below a tolerable mediocrity' (however, an exception can be made for J. Brough's poems from the Sanskrit – see Extract 13, in 'Classical Literature'). This is also the case with classical Sinhalese poetry in general. The earliest surviving poems are three of this nature, and the third, best and longest of them, *Kavsilumina* (The crest-gem of poesy), attributed to a Sinhalese king, has recently been competently translated by Ariyapala and McAlpine (see Booklist), so that the genre may be seen for what it is. These early poems are written in non-rhyming metres known as *gi*, which fell into disuse long ago, and their language was archaic and difficult even when they were written.

A new kind of poetry arose in the 14th century. This is rhymed, and confined to certain well-defined metres. The subject matter is not necessarily different, but the language is easier. The typical poem usually recounts a *jataka* story, beginning with an invocation of the Buddha, his *Dhamma* or doctrine, and his *sangha* or monks (the 'Buddhist trinity'), but will contain the expected highflown descriptions of cities and kings, and sometimes also 'clever compositions', where, after the Sanskrit manner, words may be used in diagrams or absurd alliterations. Such *jeux d'esprit* are not susceptible of translation, but some of these poems, especially as they approach the norms of everyday thought, can well appeal to Western readers – see for example Alagiyavanna's Kusa jataka poem (Extract 17).

After the colonial invasions the production of works of literary value was greatly curtailed, and comparatively little of what was written after 1600 has attained classical status, although there was a short-lived revival in the early 19th century centred on the south-coast town of Mátara.

Very few of the classical works of Sinhalese literature have been adequately translated into English, but a selection of translations can be found in *An Anthology of Sinhalese Literature up to 1815*, edited by C.H.B. Reynolds (see Booklist). The present century has seen the appearance of a quite different kind of literature, based on European traditions.

In contrast to the situation in Bengal (see 'North-east India and Bangladesh'), the 19th century in Ceylon produced no general literary revival. Christian missions and journalism were virtually the only fields for such writers as emerged in the second half of the century. Novels were frowned upon by nationalists as an immoral waste of time (as indeed they had been considered in Europe at an earlier period), and the first Sinhalese novel appeared in 1905. Early novels were didactic in tone, after the model of *Pilgrim's Progress*, which had been translated into Sinhalese in 1886. Translations of Shakespeare did encourage the development of a Sinhalese theatre – a form of art which had been quite lacking in the classical tradition – and playwrights such as John de Silva (1854–1922) had a certain success with musical plays for a time, but a modern literature only really developed after independence in 1948. The father of the new literature is undoubtedly Martin Wickramasinghe (◊ 1891–1976) who wrote the first proper novels, as well as volumes of short stories and essays, and set up his own press to publish them. He wrote constantly from 1914 up till his death, but his first major novel was written in 1944. Encouraged by his success, a number of other novelists and short-story writers followed him in developing the Sinhala literary style from an imitation classical to a modern self-subsistence. Most of these novels are concerned with the social impact of modernization on a traditional society.

Poetry has developed also, but the weight of tradition has not hastened the process, and virtually all poetry written before 1950 is heavily dependent on the classical idiom. In the last 30 years or so, however, a new and socially conscious poetry has begun to appear, together with a certain amount of satirical drama (in classical Sinhalese literature, drama is altogether absent).

A film industry also emerged after independence, the best known producer being Lester James Peries (also written Peiris, b 1920). Most modern writers in Sinhala have not been translated into English, but selections from the works of several of them can be found in English translation in *An Anthology of Sinhalese Literature of the 20th Century*, ed Christopher Reynolds (see Booklist). A few of these writers have also translated their own works, eg Sarachchandra ◊, *Curfew and a Full Moon* (1978) and *Foam upon the Stream* (Extract 16), and A.V. Suraweera, *Tread Softly*, a story of university student politics (1990). Selections of both verse and prose are available in the anthologies published by Yasmine Gooneratne (see Booklist) and by D.C.R.A. Goonetilleke (see Booklist), and in certain periodicals; some of these are in translation. In this chapter we give verse extracts from the English writings of Anne Ranasinghe ◊ (Extract 3), Patrick Fernando

Martin Wickramasinghe

(Extract 14) and Lakdasa Wikkramasinha (Extract 9), and a short story
by the Tamil writer J.S. Tissanayagam (Extract 12). Translated items
include a story from the Tamil by S. Ganeshalingham (Extract 2) and
from the Sinhalese a verse item by Monica Ruwanpathirana (Extract
11) and a prose piece by Gunasena Vithana (Extract 18).

In addition to writings in Sinhalese, there was also a flourishing
tradition among the learned in Sri Lanka of writing in Pali, the sacred
language of southern Buddhism. The best known Pali work in the
Ceylonese context is the *Mahavamsa* (Extract 10), a history of the
sangha in Sri Lanka from its beginnings in the 3rd century BC. This is

written in Pali verse, and amounts in fact to a history of the island up to 1600, though the latter part is decidedly sketchy. It was later continued down to 1815, and even later; but the main section is in the form of an epic poem, or rather two epic poems, celebrating the exploits of two great hero-kings, Duttha-gamini or Dutu-gämunu in the 2nd century BC and Parákrama-bahu the Great in the 12th century AD (the latter part is often referred to as the *Culavamsa*).

Modern Tamil literature in Sri Lanka developed under the influence of Arumuga Navalar (1822–1879), and for Muslims under that of M.C. Siddi Lebbe (1838–1898). The first noteworthy author of the modern period was C.W. Damodaram Pillai (1832–1901), but not much of significance was written before independence in 1948 (see Extracts 2 and 12 and the Booklist for references to Tamil literature in Sri Lanka).

Literature written in English by Ceylonese is a late development, but there is a good deal of earlier writing in European and other languages which retains interest today, though it is informative rather than literary.

The island is described by classical Greek and Roman writers – Pliny, Strabo, Ptolemy, Cosmas Indicopleustes, and the author of the Periplus of the Arabian Sea. Earlier Arab writers also mention it, but the fullest account is that of Ibn Battuta, the Moor from Tangier, who visited in 1344 and climbed **Adam's Peak**. Of the Chinese, the best and fullest account is by Fa-Hsien, a Buddhist traveller, who lived in **Anuradha-pura** for two years in the early 5th century. Marco Polo was in Lanka for a much shorter time about 1290. All these accounts are available in English translations.

In colonial times, accounts became fuller. Ribeiro (1685) and Queyroz (1686) in Portuguese, Baldaeus (1672) and Valentyn (1726) in Dutch, wrote substantial descriptive volumes about the Ceylon of their day. João Ribeiro was a Portuguese soldier who served his king for 40 years, both in Ceylon and in other parts of the Portuguese empire (Extract 15). His thesis was that the Portuguese crown was mistaken in trying to hold such a worldwide empire and that they should rather have devoted particular resources to the full colonization of Ceylon, 'the finest piece of land which the Creator has placed upon this earth'. Philippus Baldaeus was a Dutch predicant who spent nine years in Ceylon, mostly in the Tamil centre of Jaffna in the north.

The first recorded Englishman to arrive in Ceylon was one Ralph Fitch, a merchant, in 1589; but the most famous and important was Robert Knox, the commercial seaman, who was captured near Trinco-malee on the east coast of Sri Lanka in 1660 while ashore collecting supplies. He and several of his company were taken up-country to the Kandyan regions, and kept permanently captive there. Knox himself managed to escape in 1679, and eventually returned home and published his *An Historical Relation of the Island of Ceylon* in 1681 (Extract 8).

In the British colonial period, numerous general books about the island were written, by colonial administrators and others; the culminating encyclopaedic summary was Sir J.E. Tennent's massive *Ceylon* (see Booklist). Travellers from other countries provide lesser compilations, though some such as the famous Darwinian zoologist from Jena, Professor Ernst Haeckel, whose work was translated by Clara Bell as *A Visit to Ceylon* (see Booklist), have a particular interest. Some individual reminiscences such as those of Frederick Lewis (*Sixty-four Years in Ceylon*) are also of value and interest, and in modern times E.F.C. Ludowyk's *Footprint of the Buddha* should be mentioned (see Booklist and Galle in Literary Sites).

From a purely literary point of view the name of Leonard Woolf ◊ is the most important. His *Village in the Jungle* (Extract 6) was first published in 1913 as a result of his years in the Colonial Service in Ceylon. Next to it, in the colonial era, must be put J. Vijayatunga's charming vignettes of village life *Grass for my Feet* (Extract 20). These two works are far ahead of John Still's *The Jungle Tide* or the writings of D.J.G. Hennessy (see Booklist). With the last named should be associated Dr. R.L. Spittel's works on life among the Veddas, the vanishing aboriginal inhabitants of the eastern jungles (see Booklist).

Ceylon has long been a favourite place for holidays, and a number of well-known figures passed through it leaving a brief record. Such include Edward Lear ◊, Chekhov ◊, D.H. Lawrence ◊, Osbert Sitwell ◊, Auden and Isherwood, Evelyn Waugh (who recovered from a breakdown in Ceylon, see *The Ordeal of Gilbert Pinfold*) and from the western hemisphere Mark Twain ◊, Ella Wheeler Wilcox, Frances Parkinson Keyes and Pablo Neruda ◊.

Vijayatunga is the first name we have mentioned of a Ceylonese writing in English. Two other such began their activities in the colonial epoch, Martin Wickramasinghe ◊ and E. Sarachchandra ◊; these two are, however, primarily writers in Sinhala. There are also some who write for preference in English. Mrs Punyakante Wijenaike has written several books, novels and short stories since 1963, as have James Goonewardene and Suvimalee Gunaratna (Mrs Karunaratne), and among Tamils Raja Proctor. The Canadian Michael Ondaatje (b 1942) who is of Ceylon Tamil origin has written an amusing Sri Lankan social saga *Running in the Family* (see Booklist). The irregular periodical *Navasilu*, first published in 1976 as a journal of the English Association of Sri Lanka, is an indication of continuing activity in this sphere.

A good summary of modern literature in all three languages can be found in chapter 18 of de Silva's *Sri Lanka, A Survey* (see Booklist), and in the periodic updatings in the *Journal of Commonwealth Literature*.

SRI LANKA'S LITERARY SITES

Adam's Peak. This mountain, 7350 feet above sea level, is of an easily recognizable conical shape, standing out among the hills above Ratnapura, and it has been famous for many centuries for the 5-foot indentation in the rock on its summit, shaped like a large human foot. This has traditionally been held by Buddhists to be the footprint of the Buddha, who is said in legend to have visited Sri Lanka three times. By Muslims it is believed to be the footprint of Adam, who landed here when he was expelled from Paradise; Hindus currently believe it to be the footprint of Shiva. South Indian Christians have sometimes held it to be the footprint of St Thomas, the apostle of South India, said to be buried near Madras. All these major religions, therefore, have treated the mountain as a place of pilgrimage. Tennent says 'Around this object of common adoration the devotees of all races meet, not in furious contention like the Latins and the Greeks at the Holy Sepulchre in Jerusalem, but in pious appreciation of the one solitary object on which they can unite in peaceful worship.' Ibn Battuta, the Moorish traveller, climbed the Peak in 1344, and mentions the 'red rose as large as the palm of the hand' which grows on it. Rhododendrons still flourish on the Peak. He also mentions the chains by which the top portion of the ascent had formerly to be accomplished. Chains are still there, though no longer used. They are mentioned even earlier by Marco Polo in the 13th century.

Adam's Bridge. This name refers to a sandy embankment which stretches between Talaimannar, off the north-west coast of Sri Lanka, and Rameswaram on the south-east coast of India. The name is connected with a Muslim belief that Adam came to Sri Lanka after his explusion from Paradise, but the idea of a bridge between India and Sri Lanka is well known to Indian legend, since the story of Rama, as recounted in the Indian epic Ramáyana, tells how he crossed to Sri Lanka to recover his bride Sita from king Rávana on a bridge constructed with the help of the monkey-god Hanuman. The 'bridge' is not passable on foot.

Aluwihare. The site of an ancient temple near Mátale on the Kandy-Anuradhapura road, where traditionally the Buddhist scriptures were first written down in the 1st century BC; previously, they had been committed to memory for several centuries.

Anuradhapura. This was the first capital of the island, and remained so from the 4th century BC till the 10th century AD. The Chinese Buddhist pilgrim Fa-Hsien stayed there for two years about the year

410, while it was at its most flourishing. In describing it he says 'The people of this country say there are about 60 000 monks fed at the public expense, while the king supports five or six thousand more in the royal city . . . The Buddha's tooth is usually displayed in the middle of the third month.' (The Tooth is now kept in Kandy.) When describing the image of the Buddha in the temple, made of green jade, he speaks of a pilgrim's loneliness: 'Fa Hsien had left China for many years and associated with none but men of foreign lands . . . His companions had left him – some had remained behind, while some had died. Looking at his lonely shadow, he was often filled with sadness. So when he stood by the side of this jade image and happened to see a white silk fan from China, the offering of some merchant, tears filled his eyes and he gave way to grief.'

After the 10th century, Anuradhapura gradually fell back into jungle and became a 'buried city'. It was thus that Robert Knox passed through it in his escape from captivity in Kandy in 1679 (Extract 8). He writes the name as 'Anurodgburro', and he speaks of the ancient ruins: 'Here and there by the side of this River is a world of hewn Stone Pillars, standing upright, and other heaps of hewn Stones, which I suppose formerly were buildings. And in three or four places are the ruins of Bridges built of stone; some Remains of them yet standing upon Stone Pillars. In many places are Points built out into the River like Wharfs, all of hewn Stone.' One such ruined bridge is still to be seen today.

In the 20th century Anuradhapura, freed from its mantle of jungle, has become a tourist centre, and Rose Macaulay describes it in *The Pleasure of Ruins* (see Booklist).

Arippu. South of Mannar on the north-west coast, this former Dutch fort was built to protect the pearl fisheries off the coast, then so important. It is the spot where Robert Knox and Stephen Rutland, on their escape from Kandyan captivity, finally reached the Dutch authorities on 18 October, 1679. The ruins of the Dutch governor's house are still to be seen there, but stand at the top of a low cliff and are fast falling into the sea. The beach below consists almost entirely of crushed shells.

Baddegama. Reginald Heber (◊ 'Bangladesh and Northeast India'), Bishop of Calcutta, made one visit to Ceylon to consecrate the first Anglican church built for Sinhalese Christians. This was at Baddegama, an inland village near Galle, in 1825. The words of Bishop Heber's hymn 'From Greenland's icy mountains' are well known: the second stanza began 'What though the spicy breezes / Blow soft o'er Ceylon's isle, / Though every prospect pleases / And only man is vile'. (The English Hymnal changed 'Ceylon' to 'Java'.) Of course, the Bishop did not mean that it was only in one country that man was vile; as a Christian he would certainly have agreed that man was vile by nature. He describes the scene in his journal: 'The country then improved into great beauty, and at the end of about two miles we came within sight of a church on the summit of a hill, with the house of one of the missionaries, Mr. Mayor, immediately adjoining it, and that of Mr. Ward on another eminence close to it, forming altogether a landscape of singular and interesting beauty. We ascended by a steep road to Mr. Mayor's . . . On our right was the church, a very pretty building.' The church still stands, and was redecorated in Kandyan style in the 1950s.

Batticaloa. This town on the east coast is somewhat cut off from the mainstream of Lankan life. It has an old Dutch fort, and a large lagoon where fish are said to sing at night. It also has a village green, like an English village, on which cricket may be played. It has a very mixed population of Sinhalese, Tamil and Muslim; and is the home of the last survivals of the oriental Portuguese creole and of Portuguese-based music. Dom Moraes (whose father Frank was at the time editor of the *Times of Ceylon*) lived in Ceylon for two years as a child (see Extracts 7 and 9 in 'Nepal'). He describes the fish of Batticaloa: 'In the night full of crickets we paddled out into the bay. The rowboats moved in a chain of splashes through a sea so dark and shiny it seemed pliable, under a vast constellation of glittering stars . . . The tall naturalist let a metal pole down into the sea, and we applied our ears to the top end and presently heard, spiralled up from the warm undersea of coral and ocean flowers, a sequence of thin splintery chirps . . . "They sing best at full moon", said the naturalist in a low voice, and we rowed slowly back.'

Colombo. Originally Colombo was a small seaport (there is no natural harbour) used by Arab and Chinese traders. Its inhabitants were mostly Muslims until Portuguese times. The city became the capital of the last king of Kotte (Kotte, or Cotta, is now an inland suburb) in 1565, and was the capital under the colonial regimes, Portuguese and Dutch, which followed. The central area, the site of the original Portuguese fort and still called 'The Fort' is now the business area and no longer residential, though the President's official residence remains there.

The Fort was at first often besieged by Sinhalese or by Dutch, but after the final siege of 1656 the city was not again attacked until Japanese bombers flew over it in 1942. The Fort was surrounded by ramparts until 1870; the harbour was built after 1875.

The *Pettah* was the local residential and market area just outside the ramparts; it remains a commercial centre. As the city grew during the 19th century, it absorbed other areas.

The *Galle Face* ('Galle' is pronounced to rhyme with 'Paul') was the name given to a large grassy area facing the sea just south of the Fort. It has been a centre for evening social life (a kind of *paseo*) for many years. Professor Ernst Haeckel of Jena wrote in 1883: 'Between five and six in the evening the broad green lawn of the esplanade, stretching southwards between the lagoon and the sea, is the rendez-vous for all the rank, beauty and fashion of Colombo. Here, during the season, as in Hyde Park in London, is the spot where everyone meets everyone else; and the world refreshes itself in the cool evening breeze after the burden of the noon-tide heat, while enjoying the gorgeous spectacle of the sunset . . . The gilded youth of Colombo exhibit themselves on horseback – some of them on miserable hacks indeed – the ladies, with bouquets in their hands, recline languidly in their carriages, in the lightest and most elegant toilettes. But no sooner is the sun gone down than all hasten home; partly in order to escape the fever-laden evening air, partly to go through an elaborate process of "dressing for dinner", which is usually at half past seven, and of course in the indispensable black tail-coat and white neck-tie, as in "Old England" ' (see Booklist). The famous *Galle Face Hotel* was first built in 1856. Edward Lear ◊, an irritable traveller, stayed there in 1874. He refers to it as the 'Goldfish Hotel'. It was on the Galle Face green that D.S. Senanáyake, the first Prime Minister of independent Ceylon, used to ride in the mornings (the young Dom Moraes thought he looked like the White Knight) and died in 1953 of a fall while doing so.

Kollupitiya, or *Colpetty*, was the first residential expatriate suburb of British times, extended later into the *Cinnamon Gardens*, where originally cinnamon had been grown. In 1845 Samuel Baker was greatly disappointed by them. 'What fairylike pleasure-grounds have we fondly anticipated! What perfumes of spices, and all that our childish imaginations had pictured as the ornamental portions of a cinnamon garden! – A vast area of scrubby low jungle, composed of cinnamon bushes, is seen to the right and left, before and behind. Above is a cloudless sky and a broiling sun; below is snow-white sand of quartz, curious only in the possibility of its supporting vegetation. Such is the soil in which the cinnamon delights; such are the Cinnamon Gardens, in which I delight not'. By the time of Sir J.E. Tennent they had fallen into decay, as gardens: 'less than a century', he writes, 'has elapsed since these famous gardens were formed by the Dutch, and already they are relapsing into wilderness.' However, later the former gardens became a highly favoured residential area ('Colombo 7'), and remain so.

Further out still, to the south, is *Mount Lavinia*, a small steep hill on the sea coast where Sir Edward Barnes built himself a mansion in the 1820s. (The origin of the English name 'Mount Lavinia' is not known.) No subsequent Governor used it, and it eventually became a hotel.

All visitors to Sri Lanka passed through Colombo, and brief modern accounts of it are legion – Chekhov ◊, Mark Twain ◊, Neruda ◊, Osbert Sitwell ◊, Auden and Isherwood, for instance (see Booklist). Sitwell has surprisingly good words for the Colombo Museum (opened in 1877); it was, he says, 'fuller of interested human beings, I think, than any museum I have ever seen. All, too, were natives, crowds of jostling Cingalese, peering curiously and sadly at the bronzes made by their ancestors, and but lately discovered; works of art of great magnificence.' A convenient summary of the impressions of many of these travellers can be found in two works of H.A. Ian Goonetileke, *Images of Sri Lanka through American Eyes* and *Lanka, their Lanka* (see Booklist).

Galle. This town, 70 miles south of Colombo, was the chief port of the island in colonial times, until Colombo harbour was built in the 1870s. It is the best complete surviving walled town in the island, and one of the regular sights for visiting foreigners. Thus for instance Edward Lear was there in 1874, though he did not like the *Oriental Hotel*, and called the ramparts 'a hideously mean set-out of fortifications'. It had always been an important port, and Emerson Tennent sought to identify it with Solomon's Tarshish. An account of a childhood passed within the fort there in the early part of the 20th century is to be found in Professor E.F.C. Ludowyk's posthumous *Those Long Afternoons* (a curious title for the tropics, where all afternoons are more or less the same length – Extract 5). It was a monk from Galle who helped George Turnour, an early British Civil Servant, to procure a copy of the Mahavamsa and Commentary (the history of Buddhism in Ceylon from its beginning, written in Pali) from the rock temple Mulkirigala in · 1826. The village depicted so beautifully in Vijayatunga's *Grass for my Feet* (Extract 20) lies inland from Galle.

Hambantota. This town on the south-east coast of the island is the last place on the coast road before the jungle of Yala National Park. It is a centre of the Ceylon Malay community, but is best known for Leonard Woolf's ◊ occupation of the post of Assistant Government Agent there in 1908–11. It was during his time there that he began to plan *The Village in the Jungle* ◊ (Extract 6), his melancholy masterpiece, describing a small village in the south-eastern jungles of Ceylon.

Horton Plains. This large plateau at an elevation of 7 000 feet was in the latter part of the 19th century a centre for game hunting. One of the best known of the hunters there was Tommy Farr, subject of various contemporary rhymes, after whom the Resthouse has now been named (The Farr Inn). It was exceedingly remote until the 1950s.

Jaffna. The centre of the Ceylon Tamils, who had an independent kingdom there in the 14th-16th centuries, this town is probably best known to the literary Englishman of today as the place where Leonard Woolf had his early sexual experience, described in the second volume of his autobiography, *Growing* (1961). In those days – as late as 1905 – land access from Colombo involved an 85-mile journey by bullock cart, as the railway was not yet completed. From the early times of British settlement, however, Jaffna was a centre for American missionaries, and some of their accounts of it can be found in Ian Goonetileke's *Images of Sri Lanka through American eyes* (see Booklist).

Kandy. Nearly all travellers visited Kandy, and described especially the Perahara (procession) in the Sinhalese month of Asala (July or August), centred on the Temple of the Tooth wherein a sacred tooth relic of the Buddha himself is kept. This relic (or a facsimile) is carried round the streets of Kandy in procession; nightly processions take place for a week, but the last night is the grandest. D.H. Lawrence ◊ lived in Kandy for a few months and saw a perahara there in 1922, but this was an extra one, put on for the Prince of Wales.

Kitulgala. A resthouse on the road from Awissawella to Hatton (the continuation of the high-level road from Colombo up the Ginigat-Hena pass), Kitulgala is well known as the site of much of the filming of *Bridge on the River Kwai*, the account of the Burma-Siam railway during the second world war.

Koggala. On the south coast between Galle and Mátara, Koggala is the birthplace of Martin Wickramasinghe, the father of modern Sinhalese literature. Most of the area was cleared during the war to make way for an airfield, and little remains of the old village, but there is a Wickramasinghe museum (not always open).

Kotte. This place (called Cotta by the early missionaries) is now one of the outer suburbs of Colombo, but was the capital at the time the first colonists, the Portuguese, appeared in 1505. The Portuguese were led to it by a long and roundabout route, to disguise its nearness to the coast, thus giving rise to a proverb, 'The way the Portuguese went to Kotte'. It has again been brought back to the headlines by being the site chosen for the grand new parliament buildings of Sri Lanka, and has been dignified again with its old sobriquet of Jayawardhana-pura. Not far off is Gotami Vihara where George Keyt, Sri Lanka's most famous and successful contemporary artist (1900–93), decorated the interior of a Buddhist temple as long ago as 1940.

Nuwara Eliya. The hill station of Sri Lanka, Nuwara Eliya was virtually uninhabited before British times and was developed by Samuel Baker, who later explored widely in Africa and elsewhere. 'Baker's Farm' was occupied by him between 1848 and 1856, and his *Eight Years in Ceylon* contains many vigorous descriptions (see Booklist). In John Galsworthy's last novel *Over the River* (1933) we find a difference of opinion on the pronunciation of this name: 'Do you know a place in Ceylon called Neuralya?' 'No.' 'What?' Dinny saw a faint smile creep out among the Judge's folds and wrinkles. 'Put the question another way, Mr. Brough; we generally call it Neurālya.' 'I know Neurālya, my Lord.'

Peradeniya. A few miles on the Colombo side of Kandy, this place is famous for its extensive Botanical Gardens, the first in Asia (founded in 1822), and formerly also for its satinwood bridge over the Mahaweli River, a single 800-foot span bridge without nail or bolt, which was replaced in 1906. The Gardens have been visited by almost every traveller to Sri Lanka, and during the second world war they formed the headquarters of Lord Louis Mountbatten and South-East Asia Command.

In more recent times, Peradeniya has become known for its university campus, the first to be built outside Colombo. Neruda ◊ who had been Chilean consul in Ceylon in his youth, returned for a short visit in 1957 and was entranced by the campus. Sarachchandra's novel *Curfew and a Full Moon* (1978) is set there.

Pidurutalagala. Also referred to as 'Pedro', Pidurutalagala is Sri Lanka's highest mountain (8 200 feet). It is, or was, an easy walk from Nuwara Eliya, but is now crowned with a TV station. Hermann Hesse (1877–1962), the author of *Siddhartha*, climbed it in 1911 and described the wonderful view from the summit.

Polon-Naruwa. This second buried city, which flourished as the capital of King Parákrama-Bahu I at the end of the 12th century, was disinterred from the jungle much later than Anuradhapura, and even in the 1920s was hard to get to. Of modern travellers, Rose Macaulay and Dom Moraes have both described Polon-Naruwa, which is distinctly more interesting than Anuradhapura to the average Western traveller. The half-American poet Thomas Merton, who was there in the last month of his life in 1968, was particularly moved by the huge open-air rock figures at Gal Vihara.

Ratnapura. The city of gems, Ratnapura was visited by Edward Lear ◊ in November 1874, when he stayed with Hugh Nevill, a literary minded civil servant who formed a large collection of Sinhalese manuscripts, now in the British Library. As usual, Lear did not like it. Though he found 'beautiful bamboo and palmy scenery', he disliked Nevill's house, and 'loathe the climate generally, and Ratnapura especially.'

Serendip. Also written as Sarandib, Serendip is the Arabic form of *Sinhala-dipa* ('Sinhalese island'). The medieval story of *Three Princes of Serendip*, who were always making happy discoveries, caused Horace Walpole in the 1750s to coin the word 'serendipity', the art of making such happy discoveries.

Taprobane. The Greek name for Ceylon was still four syllables to Milton ('utmost Indian isle Taprobané'), but as the name given to the former Grand Oriental Hotel in the centre of Colombo it was only three syllables. The hotel has now reverted to its former name. Taprobane is also the name given by Count Eric de Mauny, a Frenchman, to the small island off Weligama on the south coast where he set up a house and garden and resided for much of the 1930s. Later, it was bought by Paul Bowles, the American writer, who used it during the 1950s.

Totagamuwa. This small village on the south-west coast north of Galle was the place where the monk Sri Rahula, perhaps the greatest of classical Sinhalese poets, had his temple in the 15th century. It can still be visited.

Trincomalee. This magnificent harbour on the east coast has always been, like neighbouring Batticaloa, rather apart from the mainstreams of Sri Lankan life, but it was near here that Robert Knox and the crew of the frigate *Ann* were captured while ashore in 1660, taken up to Kandy and kept prisoner for many years. Until the recent civil disturbances it was a centre for tourist deepsea fishing.

Weligama. Formerly written Belligam, Weligama is a town on the south coast between Galle and Mátara. It was visited by Edward Lear in 1874, and the resthouse there found favour in his eyes: 'A clean resthouse in a compound where vast breadfruit trees congregate, one of which I drew. Breakfast was highly decent: mulligatawny soup, fish and rice, chicken and cutlets, fish and banana curry and bananas, cum four glasses of feeble brandy and soda water.' (This is what we now call lunch.) 'The great charm of these places is their calm and quiet, for here one is only conscious of the blue sea and the wonderful shore vegetation. But the heat!' Later, this place acquired considerable fame because of the small rocky offshore island where a Frenchman, the Comte de Mauny, built a house and formed a garden for himself in the 1930s, christening the islet 'Taprobane' (see above).

Note: The quotations from Dom Moraes (under Batticaloa) and Edward Lear (under Ratnapura and Weligama) are from *Lanka Their Lanka* by Ian Goonetileke – see Booklist).

BOOKLIST

The following selection includes all titles which are extracted in this chapter as well as other relevant works. The editions cited are not necessarily the only ones available. The exact location of the extracts can be found in 'Acknowledgements and Citations' at the end of the volume. Extract numbers are highlighted in bold for ease of reference.

Adam International Review, Nos 367–369, 1972.

Alagiyavanna, *Kusa Jatakaya*, T. Steele, trans, Trübner, 1871. **Extract 17**.

Auden, W.H., and Christopher Isherwood, *Journey to a War*, Faber, London, 1973.

Baker, Samuel, *Eight Years in Ceylon*, Longmans, 1855 (reprinted Colombo, 1966).

Baldaeus, Philippus, *True and Exact Description of the Great Island of Ceylon*, Peter Brohier, trans, *Ceylon Historical Journal*, VIII (1958–59). **Extract 7**.

Fa-Hsien, *A record of the Buddhist countries*, Li Yung-hsi, trans, Peking, 1957.

Fernando, Patrick, 'Boat Song', in D.C.R.A. Goonetilleke, *Modern Sri Lankan Poetry*, Delhi, 1987. **Extract 14**.

Gooneratne, Yasmine, *Poems from India, Sri Lanka, Malaysia and Singapore*, Heinemann, Singapore, 1979. **Extract 9**.

Gooneratne, Yasmine, *Relative Merits*, Hurst, London, 1986. **Extract 1**.

Gooneratne, Yasmine, ed, *Stories from Sri Lanka*, Heinemann, Singapore, 1979. **Extract 13**.

Goonetileke, H.A. Ian, *Images of Sri Lanka through American Eyes*, US IS, Colombo, 1976.

Goonetileke, H.A. Ian, *Lanka, their Lanka*, Navrang, New Delhi, 1984.

Goonetilleke, D.C.R.A., ed, *Modern Sri Lankan Drama*, Delhi, 1991.

Goonetilleke, D.C.R.A., ed, *Modern Sri Lankan Poetry*, Sri Satguru, Delhi, 1987. **Extracts 9 and 14**.

Goonetilleke, D.C.R.A., ed, *Modern Sri Lankan Stories*, Sri Satguru, Delhi, 1986. **Extracts 12 and 13**.

Gunaratna, Suvimalee (later Karunaratne), 'The Golden Oriole' in *Bili Pooja*, Hansa, Colombo, 1973 and D.C.R.A. Goonetilleke, *Modern Sri Lankan Stories*, Sri Satguru, Delhi, 1986. **Extract 13**.

Haeckel, Ernst, *A Visit to Ceylon*, Clara Bell, trans, Kegan Paul, 1883.

Heber, Reginald, in J.W. Balding, *One Hundred Years in Ceylon*, Centenary Volume of the Church Missionary Society, Madras, 1922.

Hennessy, D.J.G., *Green Aisles*, Colombo Book Centre, Colombo, 1949.

Hensman, ed, *Community 6 Ceylonese Writing: Some Perspectives 2*, Colombo, 1963.

Journal of South Asian Literature, Vol 12, Nos 1 and 2, 1976 (special issue on the poetry of Sri Lanka); Vol 22, No 1, 1987 (special issue on Sinhala and Tamil writing from Sri Lanka); Vol 23, No 1, 1988.

Kanesalinkam, C. (S. Ganeshalingham), 'Solidarity', K.N. Arooran, trans, from *Adam International Review*, Nos 367–369, London, 1972. **Extract 2.**

Knox, Robert, *An Historical Relation of the Island of Ceylon*, London, 1681 (reprinted Glasgow, 1911), Colombo, 1989. **Extract 8.**

Lewis, Frederick, *Sixty-four Years in Ceylon*, Colombo Apothecaries, Colombo, 1926.

Ludowyk, Evelyn F.C., *Footprint of the Buddha*, Allen and Unwin, London, 1958.

Ludowyk, Evelyn F.C., *Those Long Afternoons*, Lake House Bookshop, Colombo, 1989. **Extract 5.**

Macaulay, Rose, *The Pleasure of Ruins*, Weidenfeld, 1953.

McAlpine, W.R. and M.B. Ariyapala, trans, *The Crest-Gem of Poetry (Kavsilumina)*, Royal Asiatic Society of Sri Lanka, Colombo, 1990.

Mahanama, Ven, *Mahavamsa*, W. Geiger and Mabel H. Bode, trans, Government of Ceylon, 1950, pp 167–168. **Extract 10.**

Obeyesekere, R. and C. Fernando, *Anthology of Modern Writing from Sri Lanka*, University of Arizona Press, Tucson, 1981. **Extract 11.**

Ondaatje, Michael, *Running in the Family*, Gollancz, London, 1983.

Queyroz, Fernão de, *Temporal and Spiritual Conquest of Ceylon*, S.G. Perera, trans, Colombo, 1930.

Ranasinghe, Anne, 'In our lane' from *Against Eternity and Darkness*, Samanala, Colombo, 1985. **Extract 3.**

Reynolds, C.H.B., ed, *An Anthology of Sinhalese Literature up to 1815*, Allen and Unwin/Unesco, 1970.

Reynolds, C.H.B., ed, *An Anthology of Sinhalese Literature of the 20th Century*, Paul Norbury, Unesco, 1987.

Ribeiro, João, *Historic Tragedy of the Island of Ceylon*, P.E. Pieris, trans, 4 ed, Colombo, 1948. **Extract 15.**

Ruwanpathirana, Monica, 'Your Friend She is Woman', in R. Obeyesekere and C. Fernando, *Anthology of Modern Writings from Sri Lanka*, University of Arizona Press, Tucson, Arizona, 1981. **Extract 11.**

Sarachchandra, Ediriwira *Foam Upon the Stream – A Japanese Elegy*, Heinemann Asia, Singapore, 1987. **Extract 16.**

de Silva, K.M., *Sri Lanka: A Survey*, Hurst, London, 1977.

Sivakumaran, K.S., *Contemporary Tamil Writing in Sri Lanka*, Vijeyaluckshmi Book Depot, Colombo, 1974.

Sivathamby, K., *Tamil Literature in Sri Lanka*, Madras, 1978.

Spittel, R.L., *Wild Ceylon*, Colombo Apothecaries, Colombo, 1924.

Still, John, *The Jungle Tide*, Blackwood, London, 1930.

Suraweera, A.V., *Tread Softly*, Colombo, 1990.

Tennent, Sir J.E., *Ceylon*, Longman, London, 1859.

Tissanayagam, J.S., 'Misunderstanding' in D.C.R.A. Goonetilleke, *Modern Sri Lankan Stories*, Sri Satguru, Delhi, 1986. **Extract 12.**

Toronto South Asian Review, Fall 1984. **Extract 18**.

Valentyn, François, *Description of Ceylon*, Andrew Armour, trans, S. Arasaratnam, ed, Hakluyt Society, 1978.

Vijayatunga, Jinadasa, *Grass for My Feet*, Arnold, London, 1935 (reprinted 1970 and 1974). **Extract 20**.

Vithana, Gunasena, 'The prisoner', Cyril Perera, trans, *Toronto South Asian Review*, Vol 3, No 2, 1984. **Extract 18**.

Wickramasinghe, Martin, *Lay Bare the Roots*, Lakshmi de Silva, trans, M.D. Gunasena, Colombo, 1968.

Wickramasinghe, Martin, *Viragaya, the Way of the Lotus*, Ashley Halpe, trans, Tisara Press, Colombo, 1985. **Extract 19**.

Wijenaike, Punyakante, *A Way of Life*, Deepani, Colombo, 1987. **Extract 4**.

Wikkramasinha, Lakdasa, 'To My Friend Aldred' in D.C.R.A. Goonetilleke, *Modern Sri Lankan Poetry*, Delhi, 1987 and Yasmine Gooneratne, *Poems from India, Sri Lanka, Malaysia and Singapore*, 1979. **Extract 9**.

Woolf, Leonard, *Growing*, London, 1961.

Woolf, Leonard, *The Village in the Jungle*, Oxford University Press, 1981. **Extract 6**.

Yatawara, T.B., trans, *The Story of the Tunnel (Ummagga Jatakaya)*, Luzac, 1898.

Extracts

(1) Colombo

Yasmine Gooneratne, *Relative Merits*

An extremely lively and well-written account of a prominent family in the uppermost reaches of Ceylon colonial society. Yasmine Gooneratne, née Bandaranaike, now lives in Australia.

On learning of Auntie Aggie's arrival at Colombo airport, my mother had taken instantly to her bed. She had seemed in perfectly good health when I had last met her a fortnight earlier, but now she lay weak and helpless in her bedroom upstairs with Gwen keeping vigil on one side of her sick-bed and Auntie Aggie on the other. A deep and unaccustomed hush lay upon 'No. 11', as the servants talked with lowered voices in the kitchen, Gwen's two young sons and her step-daughter Hayanthi tiptoed about the house, and Gwen's *ayah*

Punchi Hami trotted up the stairs at regular intervals with cups of restorative coriander and malted milk, and placed handkerchiefs soaked in iced water and *eau de cologne* on my mother's tortured forehead.

Exactly what was wrong with her I was never to find out. And I wasn't given a chance to ask because as soon as Auntie Aggie set eyes on me she patted my mother's arm lightly with the words, 'Don't worry about a *thing*, Ess, I'll be right back,' and tiptoed out of the sickroom with me into the passage outside, where she proceeded to give me her view of the situation. My mother, said Auntie Aggie, was very ill indeed, delayed shock following Daddy's death, complicated by the fact, said Auntie Aggie indignantly, that she was just not taking care of her health. And how could she? It was a case of worry, worry, worry all the time. If it wasn't worry about the estates, with wretched superintendents asking what was to be done about fencing this piece of land and re-planting that ('I went out, and just shooed them away,' Auntie Aggie said triumphantly. 'I said, "Go away, don't you know my sister is ill? Go away *at once!*" And they went'), it was worry about the house. These servants, said Auntie Aggie, and even dear Gwennie, didn't seem to be able to do a single thing without worrying poor little Ess about it: whether it was a matter of ordering the meals, or checking the laundry list, or directing the gardener, they all had to worry poor Ess. And then there were Gwen's children, a constant source of worry to Ess, said Auntie Aggie, with their arguments, and their quarrels, and their unremitting *noise*. What little Ess needed, said Auntie Aggie, was a sister's tender care, and now at last, after all these years, she would see that she got it. She had told Gwen that she could go right back to Galle with her children, and with those servants of hers who only made more *worry* for poor little Ess: she was here now, she had told Gwen, and she would take care of everything.

When she allowed me back – very, very *quietly* – into my mother's room, I found my mother's eyes open, with an expression in them that was impossible to read. With Auntie Aggie sitting there beside her I couldn't very well ask her if she were shamming; but, in spite of the drawn blinds, the shaded light, and the tiptoeing servants and children, she didn't look ill to me. Especially when, on the afternoon of our return to Kandy, she reacted with quite unexpected energy to one of Auntie Aggie's efforts at nursing her. Following what appeared to be a practice of Trinidad sickrooms, my aunt had been tenderly patting my mother's elbows and wrists with a pad of cotton-wool she kept dipping in a saucer she had placed on the table beside my mother's bed. The patient, who had been talking seemingly at random, in a vein of self-pity so uncharacteristic of her that for a moment I had wondered whether she was not in fact really delirious, suddenly sprang, as it were, to vigorous life. 'What the *hell* do you think you're doing, Aggie?' she said. 'That isn't bay rum, that's my best brandy. Gwen, get it away from her, and put it away at once.' She then sank back upon her pillow, and resumed her delirium.

'Your Auntie Aggie's not going to last long in Colombo,' Brendon said as we drove back to Kandy that night. 'Yes, I know she's here on your mother's invitation, I know she's sold all her property in Trinidad and has nothing to return to, I know she's come prepared to spend the remainder of her life with your mother, but I don't give her visit six months. Don't ask me how your mother and Gwen propose to get rid of her, but they will. You'll see.'

(2) Colombo

C. Kanesalinkam (S. Ganeshalingam), *'Solidarity'*

This short story depicts the closed shop of Tamil boys seeking to earn pennies at a Colombo bus stop.

A small crowd at the Purakkottai bus stop. Young porters, boys between ten and twenty, bring down the luggage from the tops of the country buses. They are wearing sarongs, sometimes tucked up to the knee, and dirty sleeveless vests. Their hair is matted and dusty. Some are wearing scarves girdled around their throats, others wear a towel twisted about their heads. They are beating a boy as crows would attack an Indian cuckoo expelled from the nest.

'Tell the truth, you brat; how many cents did you take for carrying that suitcase to the station?'

'Twenty-five cents.'

'You better hand it over to us.'

'It's my hard-earned money!'

'Who asked you to come here anyway?'

'Give us that money.'

'No, I won't.'

'You rascal.'

'How dare you?'

'Hit him on the face.'

One boy slapped him. Another grabbed his hands and snatched the twenty-five cents. One tore his vest, another pushed him forward. Another scratched his back with sharp nails.

'Ma! Ma!' cried the boy in agony. The other boys laughed.

The next day, a loaded bus from Badula arrived. The same boys watched another new strange face going up the ladder and bringing down a suitcase.

'Who is this fellow climbing up before we could? How dare he?' They were all ready to lay hands on him.

'You fellows, wait! Let's see where he will go with his tip,' said Nettaiyan and all the others kept quiet.

The new boy carried the heavy luggage of a fat man to the Fort Railway Station in Colombo, via Norris Road. The boys watched angrily. As soon as the stranger came back the drama was re-enacted.

(3) COLOMBO
Anne Ranasinghe, *'In our lane'*

The German-born poet observes a street scene in a suburb of Colombo.

> She lays a piece of corrugated paper
> Under the yellow temple tree,
> And there they sit – aged seven, four and three,
> The small one barely two – a solemn row
> With hungry eyes, their backs against the drain
> While their mother does the washing
> In the house across the lane.
>
> They never move, nor do they shout or fight.
> Only occasionally the baby softly wails,
> And Maramma – that's what she calls herself –
> (She is the one who's seven) takes him on
> Her little lap; and with mosquito-bitten arms
> She cradles him against her. Her black hair
> All cut uneven falls and hides her eyes
> While in a thin yet sweet and childish voice
> She sings him Tamil lullabies.

(4) COLOMBO
Punyakante Wijenaike, *A Way of Life*

Mrs Wijenaike writes of her childhood in Colombo in the 1930s.

In those days the intended bride and groom did not see each other until the marriage broker finished negotiating. The first time grandfather came calling I was all excited, dressed in a lace dress which fell way below the knees. My legs were covered in black stocking like the legs of the girls in an English fashion magazine and my hair piled up according to fashion again. My father dressed in his Mudliyar costume complete with gold buttons and sword. My mother wore a long sleeved blouse and long skirt and my younger sister, who had been bidden to play the piano at the correct time, was hiding behind the great curtain, giggling.

When I first saw your grandfather I decided I would not marry him! When he sat beside me on the couch mother had prepared, his legs swung to and fro, way up beyond the reach of the red carpet! How could I marry a short man? And he did not speak much either. He only sat and swung his legs, back and forth, like the pendulum of a clock.

But of course my mother was determined that I make up my mind that very day. She had gone through great trouble laying out the silver tea-pot and the silver tray. Silver dishes piled with cucumber sandwiches and stuffed-eggs mingled with ease among kavuns, kokis and milk rice. Rich cake was ready in round dishes. How could I say 'no' in the face of all this? And what about the marriage broker's fees?

So we got married in a month's time and drove away in a horse and carriage after that picture was taken.

(5) GALLE

Evelyn F.C. Ludowyk, *Those Long Afternoons*

Lyn Ludowyk (1906–1985) was brought up in a Burgher family in the fort at Galle, and these are reminiscences of his childhood, published posthumously. He became Professor of English at the University of Ceylon, and was known especially as a theatrical producer. Eventually he retired to England with his Hungarian wife.

My aunt Sylvie eventually 'put her hair up', wore long dresses and, shortly afterwards, was confirmed. My brother and I were taken to the service. My aunt sat in the front pew, with a small group of other girls in white. There were candles alight in the church and when she knelt before the bishop, he placed his hands upon her head. As he walked back to the top of the chancel steps to give the congregation his blessing I noticed that his teeth seemed to be black.

It was this detail that nagged at me after the service long after it had ended and we were at home with my aunts, uncle Dick and various friends. My aunt had received a prayer book with white bone covers and a cross stamped in red on them. This took my mind away from the bishop's teeth for a while, but at last in a pause in the conversation I asked my aunt if she had noticed that the bishop's teeth were black. She was not allowed to reply. My aunt Gertie rounded on me with:

'What kind of child are you? You go to church and this is all that comes to your head.' My uncle was gentler: 'He is a very clever man and the head of the church for the whole island. If you were like him, you wouldn't bother if your teeth weren't white.'

This was clearly unfair. I was consoled later by the newly confirmed who confessed that she hadn't seen the bishop's teeth because she had to bow her head, but that there was a peculiar smell of 'starch or something' coming from him. I knew I had been right. This made me antipathetic to the bishop, on whose account I had been put in my place by the adults. Later, when I sang in the choir, I did observe that his teeth were a dirty black. My early prejudice was reinforced by his needless severity towards the inoffensive Tamil catechist. It gave me the feeling that I had been right to draw attention to the colour of his teeth.

(6) HAMBANTOTA

Leonard Woolf, *The Village in the Jungle*

Leonard Woolf set his best known work in the jungle around Hambantota, where he was posted from 1908 to 1911. The scene is set at the very beginning of this story, in a pitiless dry-zone jungle where means of livelihood are very scarce, and human beings in a way very close to animals. It is already clear that tragedy will come.

There are people who will tell you that they have no fear of the jungle, that they know it as well as the streets of Maha Nuwara or their own compounds. Such people are either liars and boasters, or they are fools, without understanding or feeling for things as they really are. I knew such a man once, a hunter and tracker of game, a little man with hunched-up shoulders and peering, cunning little eyes, and a small dark face all pinched and lined, for he spent his life crouching, slinking, and peering through the undergrowth and the trees. He was more silent than the leopard and more cunning than the jackal: he knew the tracks better than the doe who leads the herd. He would boast that he could see a buck down wind before it could scent him, and a leopard through the thick undergrowth before it could see him. 'Why should I fear the jungle?' he would say. 'I know it better than my own compound. A few trees and bushes and leaves, and some foolish beasts. There is nothing to fear there.' One day he took his axe in his hand, and the sandals of deer-hide to wear in thorny places, and he went out to search for the shed horns of deer, which he used to sell to traders from the towns. He never returned to the village again, and months afterwards in thick jungle I found his bones scattered upon the ground, beneath some thorn-bushes, gnawed by the wild pig and the jackal, and crushed and broken by the trampling of elephants. And among his bones lay a bunch of peacock feathers that he had collected and tied together with a piece of creeper, and his betel-case, and the key of his house, and the tattered fragments of his red cloth. In the fork of one of the thorn-bushes hung his axe: the massive wooden handle had been snapped in two. I do not know how he died; but I know that he had boasted that there was no fear in the jungle, and in the end the jungle took him.

(7) KANDY

Philippus Baldaeus, *True and Exact Description of the Great Island of Ceylon*

The Reverend P. Baldaeus (1632–71) arrived in Ceylon in 1656, but the events of forty years earlier were still recent in the minds of his informants. He describes the death of the queen of Kandy.

In July 1613, the Empress *Dona Catharina* who was then pregnant became seriously ill with high fever, and finding herself worse daily she sent for the princes of *Migonne* and *Ove* to whom she unburdened herself and in all secrecy spoke of her affairs, and with the consent of the Emperor appointed the princes guardians over her children. She was greatly affected at the thought of her eldest son the prince *Mahastanne*, ever since whose death she could hardly have been prevailed upon to take any food. She expressed her regret that she could not live to see the total expulsion of the *Portugezen* nation and longed for the promised aid of the *Hollanders* thereto, and on account of this could not rest. And since the death of her son she was never happy but full of anxieties and sad memories, unable to rest or to sleep, and was troubled about her other children's future after her death. She arranged for annual payments to her servants, freed her slaves, male and female, and gave her children costly trinkets and other valuables which she had for a long time safe-guarded.

Her disorder being found to become more and more alarming every day she was removed from *Welmantotte* Palace to *Modeni*, whilst there she in the presence and within hearing of the Emperor enjoined the prince to avenge the death of her son by destroying in the first instance his medical attendant to whom she chiefly ascribed her son's death. The injunction was listened to by the prince with much delicacy as the

Empress was at times found not in a sane state of mind. With all this sadness the palace became now the scene of much bustle and confusion, and by the Emperor's order double guards were posted on all the frontiers of the realm in order to arrest any outbreak or disturbance which might ensue on the decease of the Empress. In one of her lucid intervals she desired that her five children might be brought to her, namely the crown prince *Comaro Singastanne, Janiere Astanne,* and *Lamait* and the princesses *Mahadascyn* and *Hantan Adascyn.* She embraced and fervently kissed them all shedding tears 'My beloved flesh and blood' she said, 'behold your mother who gave you birth. She can now be only spared to you for a very short time' and then calling to her the two princes she gave them charge of these children exclaiming 'Behold these my dearest possessions (your masters and mistresses). Guard them as the apple of your eyes and thereby evince your gratitude for the kindness you have received at our hands' and then looking at the Emperor she said 'You are the cause of my death', which remark ultimately affected his health, for he entertained the most affectionate attachment for the Empress.

(8) KANDY

Robert Knox, *An Historical Relation of Ceylon*

Robert Knox (1641–1720) describes King Rajasinha II of Kandy, by whose orders he was held prisoner in Ceylon for 19 years. At this time the Dutch controlled the sea coast, and Knox eventually managed to escape to them in 1679.

As to the Person of the present King. He is not tall, but very well set, nor of the clearest colour of their complexion, but somewhat of the blackest; great rowling Eyes, turning them and looking every way, always moving them: a brisk bold look, a great swelling Belly, and very lively in his actions and behaviour, somewhat bald, not having much hair upon his head, and that gray, a large comely Beard, with great Whiskers; in conclusion, a very comely man. He bears his years well, being between Seventy and Eighty years of age; and tho an Old man, yet appears not to be like one, neither in countenance nor action. His Apparel is very strange and wonderful, not after his own Countrey-fashion, or any other, being made after his own invention. On his head he wears a Cap with four corners like a Jesuits three teer high, and a Feather standing upright before, like that in the head of a fore-horse in a Team, a long band hanging down his back after the Portuguez fashion, his Doublet after so strange a shape, that I cannot well describe it, the body of one, and the sleeves of another colour; He wears long

Breeches to his Anckles, Shoes and Stockings. He doth not always keep to one fashion, but changes as his fancy leads him: but always when he comes abroad, his Sword hangs by his side in a belt over his shoulder: which no Chingulays dare wear, only white men may: a Gold Hilt, a Scabberd most of beaten Gold. Commonly he holdeth in his hand a small Cane, painted of divers colours, and towards the lower end set round about with such stones, as he hath, and pleaseth, with a head of Gold.

His right and lawful Queen, who was a Malabar, brought from the Coast, is still living, but hath not been with him, as is known, this Twenty years, remaining in the City of Cande, where he left her; She wants indeed neither maintenance nor attendance, but never comes out of the Palace. Several Noble-mens Daughters hold Land for this Service, viz. to come to her Court in their turns to wait upon her Majesty. She bare him a Prince, but what became of him, shall hereafter be shewn. He had also a Daughter by Her, she came also in her Youth to a piteous and unfortunate death, as I shall relate in its place.

(9) KANDY

Lakdasa Wikkramasinha, 'To my Friend Aldred'

A delightful translation and adaptation of Horace's Ode (ii.4 – Ne sit ancillae tibi amor pudori). Keyt is a painter who delights in shapely women (the poem appears in Yasmine Gooneratne, Poems from India, Sri Lanka, Malaysia and Singapore and D.C.R.A. Goonetilleke, Modern Sri Lankan stories – see Booklist).

My dear chap,

In this Kandyan weather there is
no shame in having in your bed
a servant maid –
The same passion moved others too famous in time –
when there were servant maids about

    Achilles for one – who gave his heart to
Briseis, a milky slave,
and Tecmessa: enemy blood, as Horace has it;
and Agamemnon fired Troy and burnt his heart to a
    cinder, hot
for a virgin there;

and though we do not get so Greek here
we are not to such titillations immune
– being classical in our traditions.
And so it is
with you and your Jose
with such long lashes
to whom you have lost your heart.

And no fear, she is not engendered by the low
at all. Dismiss the mere thought; I envisage indeed
such an ancestry
as leading in its heyday
to some king of these parts, or some
noble lord, or at the least

some lonely Scotsman in these hills. Else
she would not have such a loyal, unmercenary mind,
or cook such yams, steaming purple
and pots of jak, steaming yellow
or have a figure

Straight out of the old poetry books:
Breasts like gourds, and ripe and Oh
nodding like geese, Thighs
like plantain trunks, and Haunches as a King could ride on,
or Keyt

And lastly
in this matter of praise, in your fortune –
Thick, black coils of hair on her head, and Elsewhere –
I mean, all's well
that ends there

And all roads lead to Rome!

(10) MAHAGAMA

Ven Mahanama, *Mahavamsa*

The national hero king Dutu-gämunu or Dutthagamini (2nd century BC) began his military career by quarrelling with his brother Tissa about the succession. Tissa was vanquished, but his life was protected by Buddhist monks.

Arrived in Mahagama he assembled again a host of sixty thousand men and marching into the field began the war with his brother. The king riding on his mare and Tissa on the elephant Kandula, thus did the two brothers now come at once together, opposing each other in battle. Taking the elephant in the middle the king made the mare circle round him. When he, notwithstanding, found no unguarded place he resolved to leap over him. Leaping with the mare over the elephant he shot his dart over his brother, so that he wounded only the skin on his back.

Many thousands of the prince's men fell there, fighting in battle, and his great host was scattered. 'By reason of the weakness of my rider one of the female sex has used me contemptuously'; so thought the elephant, and in wrath he rushed upon a tree in order to throw him (Tissa). The prince climbed upon the tree; the elephant went to his master (Dutthagamani). And he mounted him and pursued the fleeing prince. The prince came to a vihara and fleeing to the cell of the chief thera, he lay down, in fear of his brother, under the bed. The chief thera spread a cloak over the bed, and the king, who followed immediately, asked: 'Where is Tissa?' 'He is not in the bed, great king'; answered the thera. Then the king perceived that he was under the bed, and when he had gone forth he placed sentinels round about the vihara; but they laid the prince upon the bed and covered him over with a yellow robe and four young ascetics, grasping the bed-posts, bore him out as if (they were carrying) a dead bhikkhu. But the king, who perceived that he was being carried forth, said: 'Tissa, upon the head of the guardian genii of our house art thou carried forth; to tear away anything with violence from the guardian genii of our house is not my custom. Mayst thou evermore remember the virtue of the guardian genii of our house!' Hereupon the king went to Mahagama, and thither did he bring his mother, whom he greatly reverenced. Sixty-eight years did the king live, whose heart stood firm in the faith, and he built sixty-eight Viharas.

(11) Sri Lanka: Far From Home

Monica Ruwanpathirana, 'Your Friend She Is Woman'

A common theme in modern literature is that of a son or daughter who leaves the island and goes far away to earn money for the family at home (from R. Obeyesekere and C. Fernando, Anthology of Modern Writings from Sri Lanka – see Booklist).

Do you remember mother
you called me 'little daughter'
when I lived at home?
That was before I left
to ease the burden on the family
as you said.

Alone, in a far place, among strangers,
They all call me 'Lissie' now.

When I walk along the street
carrying loads in both my hands
and on my head:
people call me 'serving maid'.

When I hold the little child by the hand
and walk to school
they say – 'the baby's nanny – there she goes.'

When I cook and serve the meals,
draw water, chop the wood;
they call me 'cook'.

But mother,
when the day's work is done
and I stretch out on my mat, in my dreams you come and whisper,
'Little daughter'.

(12) SRI LANKA: LANGUAGE DIFFICULTIES

J.S. Tissanayagam, *'Misunderstanding'*

This university story concerns the gulf between the English-educated (those in the English Medium) and the vernacular-educated. Kaduwa (literally, sword) means the English language (from D.C.R.A. Goonetilleke, Modern Sri Lankan Stories – see Booklist).

Bandula saw her coming and instinctively smoothed down his well-oiled hair and pulled up his collar. He looked at her with the corner of his eye, and, assuming a nonchalant expression, started kicking the grass by the wayside and stared across the river. But he did not see the flowing river or the banks mantled with little yellow flowers on the other side. Instead he saw the image of the girl reflected on the dark waters. She was above the average height, broad – almost fat; but she did not move with the slow, indolent movement of fat people; her steps were firm and her strides elegant. Her hair was cut short and her nose and mouth small. She wore large, 'mod' wire-rimmed glasses which gave a strange light to her big, beautiful eyes. She had an air of calmness and restraint about her; but with it, there seemed a touch of haughtiness and independence of spirit. The duality fascinated Bandula. Altogether, she looked a young, self-possessed mother, rather than an eighteen year old university student.

The girl arrived at the bus-stand, and after giving him an uninterested look stared at the direction from which the bus would come. He had always wanted to rub shoulders with the girls of The English Medium; but there had always been constraints. His greatest fear was that he could not manage perfect English. He could speak in Sinhala easily, but, after all, it was not like using *Kaduwa* was it? He could manage expressing himself in English with some difficulty, but felt very awkward when doing so. Should he speak to her? After all, she was only a fresher, he a senior. Perhaps through respect for one in the second year she might not cut him dead. Bandula was not habitually shy; but these were extraordinary circumstances – addressing a girl in English. At last he drew a deep breath – it was now or never – and screwing up his courage, asked in a muffled voice, somewhat louder than needed, 'Bus service – bad no?'

Sherine started at that; a sudden loud baritone from so close. His accent was coarse, like one unused to speaking English. Sherine was confused at first, but answered, 'I don't know. I've only been here a little while.'

'Uh?' asked Bandula. She spoke very fast and he found it hard to follow.

She glanced at him briefly, and Bandula thought that though she was not strictly beautiful, she had a charming air about her.

'I said I've been waiting only a very short time.'

'Yes, yes', said Bandula, and grinned.

There was a pause. He walked about trying to think of another topic of conversation.

(13) SRI LANKA: LOVE STIRS

Suvimalee Gunaratna (later Karunaratne), *The Golden Oriole*

The short story of which this is the opening was selected as the best Sri Lankan short story of 1973. It is concerned with the stirrings of love in an unmarried schoolmistress (from Yasmine Gooneratne, Stories from Sri Lanka – see Booklist).

When Miss Vitharne walked into the classroom that morning, like the other mornings during that month, it was apparent to all that something strange and wonderful had happened in her life. It was in the way she carried herself – as if she had been elevated suddenly to a unique position of dignity. She seemed afire too, like a small sun bestowing a scintillating radiance around and about her.

'I want you to know', she told the girls in a low authoritative voice so different from the shrill tone she normally used '. . . that love is a very special magical sort of thing. I wish each and every one of you may experience it one day.' Having made this enigmatic statement she beamed on them like one who had been favoured by a particularly bountiful goddess and was magnanimously invoking the same good fortune on them. She was more than content to see the young upturned faces register surprise, and when a few giggled and exchanged covert remarks behind handkerchiefs, she beamed still more. Miss Vitharne obviously was above such petty inconsequentials that day. She turned and busied herself with writing complex and compound sentences on the blackboard for analysis.

That the girls showed surprise at Miss Vitharne's remark was not a wonder for it was not the type of remark one would expect her to make. Everyone knew Miss Vitharne to be studious and timorous, motivated to a great extent by religious impulses. It was well known that she spent her free time poring over Buddhist scriptures, participating in temple rituals and going on pilgrimages with her mother. She had even taken part in one or two Buddhist symposiums on radio and these had been major occasions in her life.

The class began to copy the sentences in their exercise books and to silently work them out. Having finished writing, Miss Vitharne went up to the window and for a short space of time lost herself freely and sensuously in the verdant greenery of flapping banana leaves, coconut palms and the hibiscus hedge. A bird swooped down from a shady tamarind tree, spreading out brilliant yellow wings. It flew low over the grass and then up and away into the sky. Miss Vitharne watched fascinated. It was not every day one saw a golden oriole – which the Sinhalese call a 'Yellow robe-thief'. With such splendidly hued wings it must certainly be a bird of good omen, she thought, for yellow was an auspicious colour. It was the colour of gold, of ripe grain, of sunshine. It was also the colour of the robes worn by Buddhist monks; but that was rather odd, she pondered. Why had such a stoically celibate clergy chosen yellow for their robes? Yellow had so many connotations of fertility, of ripeness, of material fulfilment. Perhaps that was why the hermit monks who shunned society and meditated in the solitude of forests preferred robes of a browner russet hue . . .

(14) SRI LANKA: LOVE DIES

Patrick Fernando, *'Boat Song'*

The special issue of Journal of South Asian Literature on the Poetry of Sri Lanka contains this poem and an interview with the poet by the guest editor, Yasmine Gooneratne. The poem also appears in D.C.R.A. Goonetilleke's anthology (see Booklist).

When I was a boy and did not mind the weather,
I loved to watch my paper boat,
Launched with love and prayer, sail like the royal cutter
In our vast tempestuous drain;
And I the architect followed while lightning smote,
Thunder threatened and my mother called in vain.

Now seated calmly ageing in this room,
I find this image germinate
And grow to illustrate love's unexpected doom
Regretted still, however late.

So then while rain returns to mock and thunder jeers,
Can I convince a broken soul
When it sums up its scars and all its failures,
That the love we launched together
Could have never played a more illustrious role
Being but a paper twisted for youth's dull weather?

(15) SRI LANKA: PEOPLE

João Ribeiro,
Historic Tragedy of the Island of Ceylon

*Captain Ribeiro (1622–1693), who served in Ceylon for 19
years, had a great love of the island and its people.*

It is not possible for them, wherever they are, to conceal their caste, as
this is always evident from their clothes; for they may not wear their
cloth below their knees, while those of high caste have it down to the
middle of the leg.

The Modeliars, Apuames, Adigars and other great folk among them
wear a shirt and a doublet, which those of a low caste may not do. All
of them are of the colour of the quince, some being browner than
others; they wear their hair *a la* Nazarene, with their beards full in the
ancient Portuguese fashion. In features they are well shaped and in no
way different from the Spaniards. Their bodies are well proportioned
and very strong; an ugly woman is very rare among them, because all
have beautiful eyes. They are very clean and tidy, their cooking is tasty,
and they pay much attention to their hair. The dress of their ladies is
superior to that of our women in India; they too wear a jacket and a
cloth which reaches down to the point of the foot, in a very dignified
and stately fashion.

They have a language different from the one in common use, just as
Latin among us; only their chief men learn it, and they are of subtle
intellect. Whenever they have any business with an official, before
broaching the subject they relate to him two or three pleasant things so
that it may not be possible for him to refuse their request. In their own
fashion they are good poets, and their singing is very soft, and gives
pleasure; though we did not understand what they said, yet we used to
leave off any occupation in which we were engaged, to listen to them,
for their verses were sonorous and the syllables well rounded. Their
handicraftsmen take a great pride in their work, and use very few
implements.

(16) Sri Lanka: Separation

Ediriwira Sarachchandra,
Foam upon the Stream: A Japanese Elegy

This extract, translated by the author, describes the plight of the protagonist's wife Ramya, who is left behind in Ceylon when Dharmasena goes to Tokyo.

As the days went by, the feeling grew within Ramya, and it became stronger and stronger, that her husband was going to leave her. In the beginning she did not believe that this could be possible. She had known him at times to have nursed secret likings, and to have been under the spell of some woman for a period of time, and she had watched him and even tried to humour him by inviting such a person home, or by arranging trips so that he could enjoy her company. And she had seen how his interest soon faded and he came back to her.

When he went on his second visit to Japan she believed it would happen the same way, that he would tire of his new woman and get back sobered. But it came as a shock to her when he wrote to say that he intended 'separating' from her and 'carving out a new life of his own'. He hadn't told her how she ought to act in the circumstances, or revealed what he meant by saying that he wished to 'carve out a new life of his own'. But she guessed, and a real fear began creeping upon her. What would she do if he deserted her and her daughter at this stage of her life? Would he even continue to support them, now that there was going to be another woman in his life?

She knew that once her husband left her there would be no one to befriend her, because they would all abandon her alike, although they now came seeking her. She saw her future as dark and lonely, and despised as well, because people would in the end say that it was her fault that her husband couldn't live with her. And the coming on of years would push her further away from the pale of society, and make her more and more helpless and alone.

But she was not a woman who became dispirited too easily or gave herself up over much to self-pity. She was a woman of action. So she went to her sister and told her the story. But she got very little sympathy from that quarter, because her sister feared she would become a burden on her and her husband, and reminded her of how they had objected to the marriage at the beginning, seeing that he was a man who didn't believe in the next world, and was therefore, up to no good. The sister also blamed her for leaving her husband in Japan and coming back alone instead of staying behind with him or bringing him back, because Japanese women were well known 'not to have any morals'. 'You mustn't allow your husband to gad about alone, because you know what happens when you do that,' she said.

(17) SRI LANKA: SPYING ON THE BRIDE

Alagiyavanna, *Kusa Jatakaya*

*The Pali form of the jataka stories is of less literary interest than
the adaptations made by local authors. In this extract from a
popular 17th-century Sinhalese poem, the bodhisattva (Buddha-
to-be) is born as the ugly king Kusa, and being considered too
much of a fright to be seen by his wife he connives with his
mother to pose as an elephant-keeper and as a groom, in which
capacities he indulges in horseplay with his unsuspecting bride.*

Yet, though the high Queen-Mother thus unto her son had said,
The wish to see the Princess on him incessant preyed
Unchangingly and ceaseless; and, since it thus befel,
Again the Mother spoke to him, and these fair words did tell:

'Go, hide your royal visage now, quick, cover it with care,
And where the elephant-keepers stand, straight in the midst repair:
And as among the grooms you stand, then thither will I come,
And bring fair Prabavati forth, the Bride of rarest bloom.'

Then with her radiant daughter, the Queen with joy went down
Unto the royal stables, and – beasts of high renown –
The great procession-elephants [on which, on festal day,
The King is borne] with joy they saw, and turned to go away.

With pleasure of the rarest sort, King Kusa saw his Bride,
As thus within the stable stalls he stood the grooms beside.
Some dirt lay there upon the floor, he stooped and gathered it,
And throwing it with violence, the Princess' back he hit.

That lady so assaulted sore, no sooner felt the blow,
Than round she turned, while in her face right royal wrath did glow:
'Wretch! to my royal husband shall I, this very day,
Straight shall I speak, that he may wreak the punishment he may!'

(18) Sri Lanka:
Student Revolt

Gunasena Vithana, 'The Prisoner'

This story is concerned with the aftermath of the youth insurrection of 1971, when for several weeks the government appeared in danger.

The C.I.D. interrogated Wanigasekera for a number of weeks. They accused him of destroying the science laboratory by instigating his two students Saranapala and Leelawathie. For a few days Wanigasekera was treated with the respect due to a teacher. Later they gave that up and treated him like a common criminal.

'When you were a student at Peradeniya University, were you a member of the Communist Party?'

'I was a member of the Communist Students' Union, but not a member of the Communist Party.'

'After you left the university did you join the Communist Party?'

'Yes, but after some time I left the Party.'

'You left the Communist Party saying that it was not revolutionary enough. Isn't that so?'

'No.'

'We'll give you three more days to think over carefully and tell us the truth. If you tell us the truth you can go home; or else we'll send you to the place where we propose to send Maru Sira. Do you understand?'

Wanigasekera recalled how a fat policeman held him and pushed him by the stomach, and threatened to beat him.

Jailer Jayasinghe held the common belief that teachers were responsible for the revolt. 'Their students attacked the police stations with hand grenades and shot the infants in the barracks,' he said. 'When the students overthrow the government the teachers will become ministers . . . Perhaps you too thought of becoming a minister. Your wife would then be called 'madam' . . . '

Jayasinghe's ideas about the insurrection were, of course, untrue, but Wanigasekera dared not correct him and remained silent. He felt pleased somewhat that there were people like Jayasinghe even in prisons.

'As Sir Ivor Jennings said, it was university education that ruined our country. The products of this university swallowed our educational system and the administration as well. It is these university-qualified teachers who are responsible for producing a short-sighted generation in this country.'

Wanigasekera even thought of building up a close friendship with Jayasinghe. How could he manage it? He could share his ideas with him. But he suspected that Jayasinghe spoke thus on the instructions of the C.I.D.

(19) SRI LANKA: WEDDING

Martin Wickramasinghe,
Viragaya, The Way of the Lotus

The father of Aravinda had quietly transferred some property to his son-in-law Dharmadasa, in return for a cash loan to provide a slap-up wedding for his daughter Menaka. This only came to light after his death.

What had father needed the money for? He used to earn quite enough for all our needs. He didn't drink or gamble with his friends except when the New Year came round. He was so absorbed in his profession that it was his recreation as well.

He had spent lavishly on Menaka's wedding. At least four or five hundred rupees went on a temporary pavilion that looked like one of those beautiful turreted structures put up for pirith ceremonies. The arch of welcome didn't cost him anything, of course: the people built it for him. The local personages who came to the wedding were feasted sumptuously – this was just the sort of thing he took delight in doing. Later, he would preen himself proudly when he told some friend or relation, 'Ratnajeeva Vasala Mudali and District Judge Yatisena did me the honour of coming to the wedding.' We regarded Ratnajeeva Mudali and the District Judge with almost as much respect as if they were royal visitors.

For four or five days before the wedding father threw himself into an orgy of spending. The house rang with orders for building materials, vegetables, curd, honey; we were always on the move carting off tables, chairs, cauldrons and crockery from our reluctant friends and relations (we had quite a bit of persuading to do at some places). And then, after the wedding, we had to take everything back again. At least twenty people had to be fed at every meal during those hectic days.

Menaka's wedding dress was made by the Ilangaranges – a middle-aged spinster and her sister who were the sole relics of a once important family. This family had bankrupted itself by generations of wasteful imitation of European ways. "They wouldn't take payment for making the dress," said father wagging his head and rapping one palm with the other to emphasise his admiration. "What a beautiful wedding dress – quite a new style," said our female guests, looking at father with new respect. Father's bearing then would have suited a triumphant general on his gallant steed surveying the field of battle.

After Dharmadasa and his party had left with the bride, father crowned everything with a tremendous banquet for his own family, and friends.

I could see it now. Father could not have paid for all this except by borrowing money. Although the wedding gifts usually include a tidy sum of money this, too, must have been swallowed up. Later, he must have asked Dharmadasa for three thousand rupees in order to settle these debts. And he was too honest to take all that money without furnishing some security. I felt sure that was how the deed came to be written.

(20) URALA

Jinadasa Vijayatunga, *Grass for my Feet*

A description of a remote village which lies inland from Galle in the early years of the 20th century.

The topics range from seed-grain and possible drought to the Governor of the Island and to the war, warships, and even the Kaiser and the Germans. For some inexplicable reason there is from some quarter or other a spirited defence of the prowess of the 'Gerrmun' people. Time and again the topic veers homewards and there is a discussion of the Governor (whom they call Rajjuruvo), of the various Supreme Court Judges, their fabulous salaries – each 'know-all' adding an extra thousand rupees to each salary – of the excellence of the various well-known Advocates of the Bar (on the criminal side) which leads to the subject of the latest stabbing murder, and how 'I heard when I was in Galle, a man in the market-place reciting a ballad of this murder, and oh, wasn't it gruesome?' This evokes unanimous agreement that drink is the root of all evil. Which leads to a comparing of the best-known preachers among the Bhikkus. Which brings about a reminiscence of how such-and-such a Bhikku utterly routed in a public debate a Convert Clergyman. The various Buddhist evangelists in vogue next come in for review. This by its own circuitous route leads to the subject of the miracles of *Pirith* (Buddhist chanting) and what phenomena there were when the *Yakkhas* (devils) started a stampede in their final surrender to the powers of *Pirith* on such an occasion at such a place. At this point Astrology steps in. The various planets are passed in review, and there is complete agreement among all that the world is very sinful to-day, that this *Kali Yuga* (Kali's Cycle of Time) must see terrible catastrophes, that some of the plagues, pestilences, and national disasters are the result of the wrath of Shiva at the increase among people of beef-eating. Gradually the topic comes still nearer home to food. Kandé Mama boasts: 'I was in Galle yesterday. At my nephew the Advocate's place, you know. They have a grand house, servants and cutlery all in English style. You should see. Why, even their tea-trays are run on wheels.'

'Indeed!' exclaims my stone-mason uncle.

'Indeed, yes', asserts Kandé Mama with greater emphasis. 'And at dinner, do you know what I ate – a *Bistake*?' (Beef-steak). At this there is a surreptitious passing of tongue over lips among the audience, for the '*Bistake*' being by report the White Man's favourite food has always had a fascination for them. 'And after the meal they gave me some red stuff to drink. I hesitated, but my nephew and his wife – you know he married the eldest daughter of the Kuccheri Muhandiram of *Batala Oya*: fifty thousand in jewellery and land, yes, sir – well, my nephew and my niece, his wife, they said: "*Mamandi* ('Uncle, Sir') it is only wine, drink it." Well, dash it, I drank it off then. He-he-he . . . '

Biographies and major works

ALAGIYAVANNA. He held the office of *mohottala* (secretary) at the time of King Rajasimha I at Sitavaka in the late 16th century. His principal work is the *Kusa jataka kavya*, a lengthy versified setting of the story of the Kusa Birth, when the *bodhisattva* (the Buddha-to-be) was born as a prince named Kusa, who was so ugly that he felt obliged to hide himself from his wife by pretending to be a cook or an elephant-keeper. This work is dated 1610, and is still popular.

CHEKHOV, Anton (1860–1904). Chekhov was born at Taganrog in south Russia. He is known above all as a playwright of late 19th-century Russian provincial life, but he made a trip halfway round the world in 1890 which included a few days in Ceylon. See H.A.I. Goonetileke, *Lanka, their Lanka* for interesting gossip about a

possible affair of the heart (see Booklist).

Foam upon the Stream. This is a revised conflation of two Sinhalese novels by E. Sarachchandra: *The Dead* (1959) and *Commemoration of the Dead* (1965). The subject is the relationship between a Sinhalese on leave in Japan and a Japanese girl, Noriko. The second book was originally written as if by Noriko herself. In the English version the subject is a University teacher called Dharmasena. He is greatly attracted by Noriko, who is unmarried, but he himself has a wife and a family in Ceylon. Noriko returns his affections in a restrained way. Dharmasena goes back to Peradeniya, but after a year or so he returns to Japan. After more or less persuading Noriko to come to Ceylon as his wife, he gets cold feet and goes home. After much unhappiness, both for his wife in Ceylon and for Noriko in Tokyo, he returns once more to Tokyo only to commit suicide (Extract 16).

Gam Peraliya (*Changing Village*). Martin Wickramasinghe's seminal novel has not been translated into English, but it has been filmed by Lester James Peries. It describes a village in the south of Lanka, where the old village gentry are no longer financially able to keep up their position. The elder daughter is told not to marry the up and coming young man of inferior status, and is instead married to a pleasantly unambitious man of satisfactory origins, who eventually sets off to make his fortune and is not seen again. Finally the daughter is permitted to marry the up and coming Piyal, though in fact the former husband does turn up again on his deathbed. The characters of this story appear in two further novels.

GOONERATNE, Yasmine (nee Bandaranaike) (1935–). Her background is beautifully described in her autobiographical history *Relative Merits* (1986, Extract 1). She has devoted her academic career to English literature, of which she is currently professor at Macquarie University, New South Wales. With her husband she founded the journal *New Ceylon Writing* in 1970; she edited the issue of *Journal of South Asian Literature* devoted to the poetry of Sri Lanka (Michigan, 1976), and a volume *Stories from Sri Lanka*, and has published collections of her own poems.

LAWRENCE, D.H. (1885–1930). Lawrence was born near Nottingham.

His fame rests upon his novels and poetry, but also upon his second marriage to Frieda von Richthofen with whom he travelled widely in the hopes of recovery from tuberculosis. He stayed in Kandy in March and April 1922, but did not like it much. He died in Nice.

LEAR, Edward (1812–88). Born in London. Lear felt himself to be primarily a painter, though nowadays he is known chiefly as an author of Nonsense Rhymes. He published several illustrated books of European travel, and eventually in 1873 he came to India, with his Greek servant Giorgio, where he remained for over a year, fitting in a visit to Ceylon in November/December 1874. He died at San Remo in 1888. Some of his Indian Journal was published by R. Murphy in 1953.

NERUDA, Pablo (1904–73). Chilean poet, whose original name was Neftalí Ricardo Reyes. Neruda became a communist and friend of Allende, but when he was young he spent two years as Chilean consul in Colombo in 1928–30, where he moved in artistic circles, becoming friends with the critic Lionel Wendt and the artist George Keyt. However, he suffered from pursuit by his Eurasian mistress from Burma. He revisited Sri Lanka in 1957. See H.A.I. Goonetileke, *Lanka, their Lanka* (see Booklist).

RAHULA, SRI. Probably the most famous of classical poets, Sri Rahula lived at Totagamuva on the south-west coast, where he was head of a *pirivena* or theological college, and flourished in the 14th century. His principal works are the *Säla-lihini san-*

desa (*Starling's Message*) and *Kavya-sekharaya* (*The Poetic Garland*) which is a *mahakavya* or ornate poem in the Sanskrit tradition, telling the story of the *Sattubhasta jataka*, the Grain-bag Birth. He was connected to the royal family of Kotte, then the capital, and was made *sangharaja* or head of all Ceylonese monks by king Parákrama-bahu VI. The *Gira sandesa* poem (*The Parrot's Message*) is devoted to his honour.

RANASINGHE, Anne (1926–). Born Anneliese Katz at Essen in 1926, she was sent to England as a Jewish refugee in 1939, while her parents remained to perish in the Holocaust. After the war she married a Sinhalese professor of Gynaecology (now dead), and has lived in Sri Lanka ever since, though it is clear from her poetry that she misses the climatic changes of Europe. See the thoughtful account by Norman Simms in *Journal of South Asian Literature* 23.1 (1988), pp 94–107.

SARACHCHANDRA, Edirivira (also written Sarathchandra, and earlier known as E.R. de Silva, 1914–). Born near Dodanduwa on the south coast, Sarachchandra learnt Sanskrit and Pali, and went to Santiniketan in 1939 to study Indian philosophy under Tagore. He taught Pali at University College, Colombo, and after postgraduate work on Buddhist philosophy he became Professor of Pali in the University of Ceylon. He developed an interest in drama, and wrote a number of Sinhala dramas in which he modernized and gave literary acceptability to an outdated mode of 19th-century folk drama. The first of these dramas, *Maname*, is translated by Lakshmi de Silva in the *Toronto South Asian Review* (1984), and

another play, *Pemato jayati soko*, by D.M. de Silva (Salzburg, 1976). He has also written a number of novels and short stories, and has published two versions of his own novels in English, *Curfew and a Full Moon* (see Booklist), a story of the Insurrection of 1971 as it affected the universities, and *Foam upon the Stream* ◊ (a conflation of two originals dated 1959 and 1965) which is a unique study of a Sinhalese in Japan (Extract 16). In addition, he has written *With the Begging Bowl* in English, a skit suggested by his own time as Sri Lankan Ambassador in Paris. He is the most distinguished living Sinhalese author, and received a festschrift in 1988 through the Sri Lanka National Commission for UNESCO.

SITWELL, Osbert (1892–69). Born in London, Sitwell succeeded his father as baronet in 1943. He is best known for his autobiography *Right Hand, Left Hand* and its sequels, but his remarks on Colombo come from *Escape with Me* (1939), an account of a trip he made to Angkor and Peking in 1933–34.

TWAIN, Mark (1835–1910). Twain's real name was Samuel Clemens. He was born in Missouri in 1835. His reputation as a writer, founded on *Innocents Abroad*, published in 1869, was consolidated by *Tom Sawyer* in 1876. He travelled round the world on a lecture tour in 1895–96 and was in Ceylon for just a few days in January and March 1896. He died in 1910.

VATTAVE ('A monk from Vattava village'). Vattave wrote one of the most famous of 15th century poems, the *Guttila kavya*, the story of the

Edirivira Sarachchandra

Guttila Birth, wherein the *bodhisattva* was born as a musician called Guttila. He has trouble with his teacher, a Beckmesser figure called Musila, whom he eventually discomfits.

VIJAYATUNGA, Jinadasa (1902–89). Born in the inland village of Urala, near Galle. From early days he spent much time in India, including a period teaching English at Shanti-

niketan; but he lived in New York for three years, and in England 1931–40. Thereafter he split his time between India (of which he became a citizen) and London. His first and best work was *Grass for my Feet* (London, 1935; reprinted Colombo, 1974), and although he published a number of other works in English, none of them reached the same level of inspiration (Extract 20). In old age when he became desolate in London, the Government of Sri Lanka brought him home and gave him a house in Colombo at their own expense in 1989, but he died within a few weeks of returning.

Village in the Jungle. Leonard Woolf's novel is the melancholy story of a dying village in the dry-zone jungle of the south-east of Ceylon, where Silindu, a poor and eccentric villager, is in the financial power (like most of the village) of the Headman and of a low-country trader. His daughter is demanded as the price of any security. Eventually, after much goading, he shoots them both, and is sent to prison for life. The story ends with the total disappearance of the village beneath the jungle (Extract 6).

WICKRAMASINGHE, Martin (1891–1976). Born in the southern coastal village of Koggala, the early death of his father left him, as the only son, a potential breadwinner for nine sisters. He therefore lacked an advanced formal education, which in fact allowed him to develop literary writing in his own way. He became a newspaper editor at the age of 40, but he had been publishing his own writings since 1914 and continued to write till he was over 80. His early writings are all in Sinhala, but after 1950 he also published in English. The works he wrote in English are generally essays; but English translations exist of his book of childhood reminiscences under the title *Lay Bare the Roots*, excellently translated by Lakshmi de Silva (1968), and of two of his novels, *Madol Doova* (the name of a small island), published in 1947, and *Viragaya*, published in 1957 and translated under the title *The Way of the Lotus* (Extract 19). Both these

translations are by Ashley Halpe, dated 1976 and 1985 respectively. Two of Wickramasinghe's short stories are also to be found in translation by Halpe, *Daughter-in-law*, written in 1946 and translated for the Asian PEN anthology (New York, 1966), and *Slaves*, written in 1951 and translated for the *Adam* issue on the Arts in Sri Lanka (1972). His *Gamperaliya* (*Changing Village*), published in 1944, is recognized as the first full-fledged modern Sinhalese novel, and was filmed by Lester James Peries.

WOOLF, Leonard (1880–1969). Born in London, after St Paul's School and Trinity College, Cambridge, where he became one of what was later called the Bloomsbury Group, he did poorly in the examinations for the home Civil Service, applied for an Eastern Cadetship in Ceylon, and 'found myself to my astonishment, and, it must be admitted, dismay, in the Ceylon Civil Service'. He was posted first to Jaffna in 1905, to Kandy in 1907 (where his sister came out to join him), and from 1908 to 1911 as Assistant Government Agent at Hambantota. It was thereabouts that he set his best known work *A Village in the Jungle* ◊. He resigned while on leave in 1912 and subsequently married Virginia Stephen, with whom he founded the Hogarth Press. Virginia Woolf committed suicide in 1941. Leonard Woolf returned to Ceylon for a short visit in 1960, and died in 1969. The second volume of his autobiography, called *Growing* (1961), describes his years in Ceylon, and his diaries as an A.G.A. in 1908–11, which were published after his visit in 1960, contain three short stories by him, set in Ceylon and originally published in 1924.

ACKNOWLEDGMENTS AND CITATIONS

The authors and publishers are very grateful to the many literary agents, publishers, translators, authors and other individuals who have given their permission for the use of extracts and photographs, supplied photographs or helped in the location of copyright holders. Every effort has been made to identify and contact the copyright owners or their representatives. The publishers would welcome any further information.

CLASSICAL LITERATURE: (1) Michael Coulson, trans, *Three Sanskrit Plays*, Penguin, London, 1981, p 220. © The Estate of Michael Coulson 1981. By permission of Penguin Books Ltd. (2) Michael Coulson, trans, *Three Sanskrit Plays*, Penguin, London, 1981, pp 357–358. © The Estate of Michael Coulson 1981. By permission of Penguin Books Ltd. (3) Arthur W. Ryder, trans, *The Ten Princes*, Phoenix Books, University of Chicago Press, Chicago, 1960, pp 149–150. By permission of University of Chicago Press. (4) Michael Coulson, trans, *Three Sanskrit Plays*, Penguin, London, 1981, pp 91–92. © The Estate of Michael Coulson 1981. By permission of Penguin Books Ltd. (5) J.A.B. van Buitenen, trans, in *The Mahabarata: 2. The Book of the Assembly Hall, 3. The Book of the Forest*, University of Chicago Press, Chicago, 1975, pp 173–174. By permission of University of Chicago Press. (6) Wendy Doniger O'Flaherty, trans, *The Rig Veda: An Anthology*, Penguin, London, 1981, pp 240–241. © Wendy Doniger O'Flaherty 1981. By permission of Penguin Books Ltd. (7) E.B. Cowell, F.W. Thomas, trans, *The Hasha-carita of Bana*, Motilal Banarsidass, Delhi, 1968, pp 37–38. (8) Leonard Nathan, trans, *The Transport of Love: The Meghaduta of Kalidasa*, University of California Press, Berkeley, 1976, pp 27–33. Reprinted by permission of University of California Press. (9) Barbara Stoler Miller, trans, *Love Song of the Dark Lord: Jayadeva's Gitagovinda*, Columbia University Press, New York, 1977, pp 101–102. © Columbia University Press, New York. Reprinted by permission of the publishers. (10) Daniel H.H. Ingalls, trans, *An Anthology of Sanskrit Court Poetry: Vidyakar-*

a's *'Subhashitaratnakosha'*, Harvard University Press, Cambridge, MA, 1965, pp 129–131. Reprinted by permission. (11) J.A.B. van Buitenen, trans, *The Mahabarata: 1. The Book of the Beginning*, University of Chicago Press, Chicago, 1973, pp 348–349. By permission of University of Chicago Press. (12) Peter Khoroche, trans, *Once the Buddha was a Monkey: Arya Shura's Jatakamala*, University of Chicago Press, Chicago, IL, 1989, pp 97–98. By permission of University of Chicago Press. (13) John Brough, trans, *Poems from the Sanskrit*, Penguin, 1968, pp 108–109. © John Brough 1968. By permission of Penguin Books Ltd. (14) Daniel H. H. Ingalls, trans, *An Anthology of Sanskrit Court Poetry: Vidyakara's 'Subhashitaratnakosha'*, Harvard University Press, Cambridge, MA, 1965, pp 265–266. Reprinted by permission. (15) Robert P. Goldman, ed, *The Ramayana of Valmiki: An Epic of Ancient India*, Vol 3, *Aranyakanda*, Sheldon I Pollock, trans, Princeton University Press, Princeton 1991, pp 120–121. Reprinted by permission **PAKISTAN AND NORTH-WEST INDIA:** (1) Versified by C. Shackle from M. Longworth Dames, *Popular Poetry of the Baloches*, Vol 1, Royal Asiatic Society, London, 1907, p 103. (2) M. Longworth Dames, *Popular Poetry of the Baloches*, Vol 1, Royal Asiatic Society, London, 1907, p 24. (3) Versified by C. Shackle from James Darmestereter, *Chants Populaires des Afghans*, Paris, 1888–90, p 31. (4) Evelyn Howell and Olaf Caroe, trans, *The Poems of Khushhal Khan Khatak*, University of Peshawar, Pashto Academy, 1963, p 45. © Peshawar University Press 1963. (5) T.S. Eliot, ed, *A Collection of Kipling's Verse*,

Faber and Faber, London, 1941, pp 111–112. (6) Baidar Bakht and K.G. Jaeger, eds and trans, *An Anthology of Modern Urdu Poetry*, Vol 1, Educational Publishing House, Delhi, 1984, pp 18–20. (7) Vir Singh, Ruins at Avantipur. C. Shackle, trans. (8) Sir Muhammad Iqubal, *Javid-nama*, A.J. Arberry, trans, George Allen and Unwin, London, 1966, p 121. (9) Habba Kho-tun, *Deka petha guma chim mokta zan haran*, trans Christopher Shackle. Texts in J.L. Kaul, *Kash-miri Lyrics*, Rinemisray, Srinigar, 1945, p 42. (10) Lawrence Hope, *The Garden of Kama and other Love Lyrics from India*, Heinemann, 1901, p 93. (11) Rumer Godden, *Kingfishers Catch Fire*, Pan, London, 1966, pp 18–19. © Rumer God-den 1953. By permission of Curtis Brown on behalf of Rumer Godden. (12) Jahangir, *Tuzuk*, 1620. H. Beveridge, ed, *The Tuzuk-i-Janangiri or Memoirs of Janangir*, Vol 2, A. Rogers, trans, Low Price Publications, Delhi, 1989, pp 143–144. (Reprint of Royal Asiatic Society, London, 1914.) By permission of the Royal Asiatic Socie-ty. (13) Trilokinath Raina, ed and trans, *An Anthology of Modern Kashmiri Verse (1930–1960)*, Suresh Raina, Poona, 1972. © Triloki-nath Raina. (14) Mulk Raj Anand, *The Big Heart*, Hutchinson, London, 1945, pp 8–9. By permission of Random House. (15) C. Shackle, trans, *Fifty Poems of Khaaja Farid*, Bazm-e Sa-quafat, Multan, 1983, pp 130–132. (16) Balraj Khanna, *Nation of Fools*, Penguin, London, 1985, pp 135–136. By permission of Yvonne McFarlane. (17) Trans by © C. Shackle. Mazhar ul Islam, *Selected Stories*, Sang-e-Meel, Lahore. (18) Varis Shah, *Hir*, 1766, C. Shackle, trans. (19) Taufiq Rafat, trans, *Bullhe Shah: A Selection*, Vanguard, Lahore, 1982, p 102. © Vanguard Publications. By permission of Van-guard Books. (20) Rudyard Kipling, *Kim*, Mac-millan, 1961, pp 73–74. (21) Trans Khushwant Singh, *A History of the Sikhs*, Vol 1, 2 ed, OUP Delhi, 1977, pp 352–353. © 1963 Princeton University Press. Reprinted by permission. (22) J.C.E. Bowen, *The Golden Pomegranate: A Selec-tion from the Poetry of the Mughal Empire in India 1526–1858*, Thacker & Co, 1957, p 32. (23) Ved Mehta, *Daddyji*, Secker and Warburg, Lon-don, 1972, pp 35–36. Copyright 1971 by Ved Mehta from Daddyji (W.W. Norton & Co) reprinted with the permission of Wylie, Aitken & Stone, Inc. (24) Faiz Ahamd Faiz, *Ai Raush-niyon ke Shahr*, V.G. Kiernan, trans, *Poems by Faiz*, George Allen and Unwin, London, 1971, p 201. (25) Amir Hasan Sijzi, *Favaid ul Fuad* (1309–22), II9, Bruce B. Lawrence, trans (un-published typescript). (26) *Salok Farid 28, 74, 64, 85*, C. Shackle, trans. (27) V.G. Kiernan, trans, *Poems from Iqbal*, John Murray, 1955, p 58. By permission of John Murray (Publishers)

Ltd. (28) Khushwant Singh, *Train to Pakistan*, Pearl Publications, Bombay, 1967, pp 38–39. © Chatto and Windus 1956. By permission of Random House and Grove/Atlantic Inc. (29) Trans Tahira Naqvi, *The Life and Works of Saadat Hassan Manto*, Vanguard Books, Lahore, 1985, pp 286–287. © Vanguard Books. By permission of Vanguard Books. (30) Hasham Shah, *Sassi Punnun*, C. Shackle, trans, Van-guard, Lahore, 1985, pp 115, 117. By permission of Vanguard Books. (31) Richard F. Burton, *Scinde: or the Unhappy Valley*, Richard Bentley, London, 1851, Vol 1, pp 34–36. (32) Adam Zameenzad, *The Thirteenth House*, New Estate, London, 1987, pp 61–62. (33) Taufiq Rafat, *The Arrival of the Monsoon*, Collected Poems 1947–78, Vanguard, Lahore, 1985, p 56. By permis-sion of Vanguard Books. (34) H.T. Lambrick, ed and trans, *The Terrorist*, Ernest Benn, 1972, p 42. (35) H.T. Sorley, *Shah Abdul Latif of Bhit: His Poetry, Life and Times*, OUP, Karachi, 1966. (36) Paul Scott, *A Division of the Spoils*, Pan, London, 1975, pp 140–141. **CENTRAL AND NORTHERN INDIA:** (1) Banarsidas, *Half a Tale*, Mukhund Lath, trans, Rajasthan Prakrit Bharati Santhan, Jaipur, 1981, pp 92–95. (2) J.C.E. Bowen, *The Golden Pomegranate: A Selec-tion from the Poetry of the Mughal Empire in India 1526–1858*, Thacker & Co, 1957, p 36. (3) Carlo Coppola and M.H.K. Quereshi, 'A note on and poems by Sahir Ludhivani', in *Literature East and West*, 10, State University College, New Paltz, New York, 1966, p 88. (4) Trans R. Snell. Nirala, *Anamika*, Bharati Bhandar, Alla-habad, 1963. (5) Arvind Krishna Mehrotra, *Middle Earth*, OUP, Delhi, 1984, p 46. By permission of Oxford University Press. (6) Mahadevi Varma, 'Bibia' in *A Pilgrimage to the Himalyas*, Radhika Prasad and Srivastav and Lillian Srivastav, trans, Clarion Books, Delhi, nd, p 87. By permission of Hind Pocket Books. (7) Eric Newby, *Slowly Down the Ganges*, Pica-dor, London 1983, p 229. (8) P.D. Reeves, ed, *Sleeman in Oudh: An Abridgement of W.H. Slee-man's 'A Journey through the Kingdom of Oude in 1849–50'*, Cambridge University Press, Cam-bridge, 1971, p 83. (9) J.S. Hawley and Mark Juergensmeyer, *Songs of the Saints of India*, OUP, New York, 1988, p 25. Reprinted by permission. (10) Samuel Purchas, *Early Travels in India. First series, comprising 'Purchas's Piilgrimage and 'The Travels of Van Linschoten'*, R. Lepage, Calcutta, 1864, pp 6–7. (11) Phanishwar Nath Renu, *The Third Vow and Other Stories*, Kathryn G. Han-sen, trans, Chanakya Publications, Delhi, 1986, pp 56–57. (12) Nitin Bose (director), *Gunga Jumna*, Mehboob Studios, Bombay, 1962. (13) Vikram Seth, *A Suitable Boy*, Orion, London, pp 197–199. © 1993. By permission of Sheil Land

Associates. (14) E.M. Forster, *A Passage to India*, Penguin, Harmondsworth, 1967, pp 9–10. By permission of The Society of Authors. (15) J.R. Ackerley, *Hindoo Holiday: An Indian Journal*, Chatto & Windus, London, 1932, pp 78–79. By permission of David Higham Associates. (16) Khushwant Singh, *Delhi*, Penguin, 1990, pp 51–52. Reproduced courtesy of Penguin Books India Pvt Ltd and the author. (17) Jawaharlal Nehru, *Jawaharlal Nehru's Speeches*, Vol 1, Government of India, 1949, pp 25 and 42. (18) Anita Desai, *The Clear Light of Day*, Penguin, London, 1980, p 47. Reproduced by permission of the author and Rogers, Coleridge and White Ltd. (19) Stanley Wolpert, *Nine Hours to Rama*, Hamish Hamilton, London, 1962, pp 318–319. (20) R. Russell and Khurshidul Islam, *Ghalib 1797–1869, Vol 1, Life and Letters*, George Allen and Unwin, London, 1969, p 252. (21) Akhtar Qamber, ed and trans, *The Last Mushai'irah of Delhi*, Orient Longman, New Delhi, 1979, pp 52–53. By permission of Orient Longman. (22) Ahmed Ali, *Twilight in Delhi*, OUP, Bombay, 1966, pp 84–85. By permission of Oxford University Press. (23) Tulsi Das, *The Petition to Ram*, F. R. Allchin, trans, Allen & Unwin, London p 94. (24) J.G. Farrell, *The Siege of Krishnapur*, Weidenfeld and Nicolson, London, 1973, pp 333–334. By permission of Weidenfeld and Nicholson. (25) Ruth Prawer Jhabvala, *Heat and Dust*, Futura, London, 1976, pp 170–171. By permission of John Murray. (26) Top: Agyeya, *Signs and Silence*, trans the author and Leonard E. Nathan, Simant, New Delhi, 1976, p 107. Bottom: Agyeya (here Ajneya), *Nilambari*, trans the author, Clarion Books, Delhi, 1981, p 22. By permission of the Vatsal Foundation. (27) Rupert Snell, trans, Hindi Texts from Satrughna Sukla, Thumri ki utpatti, vikas aur sailiya, Delhi University, Delhi, 1983, pp 211, 206. (28) Biharilal, *Bihari Ratnakar*, ed Jagannathdas 'Ratnakar', 5 ed, Granthkar, Varanasi, 1969, pp 30, 36, 211. Trans Rupert Snell. (29) Srilal Shukla, *Rag Darbari*, 2 ed, Rupert Snell, trans, Rajkamal, Delhi, 1985, pp 123–124. (30) Premchand, *The Gift of a Cow*, Lokamaya Press, London, 1968, pp 356–357. (31) Rupert Snell, trans. From an original Braj Hindi text song sung by Pandit Jasraj on a CD recording, *The Inimitable Pandit Jasraj: Echoes of Temple Music*, Magnasound, Bombay (CD C4HV0082). (32) Field-Marshal Lord Roberts of Kandahar, *Forty-one Years in India from Subaltern to Commander-in-Chief*, Vol 1, Richard Bentley, London 1897, pp 393–394. (33) V.S. Naipaul, *India: A Million Mutinies Now*, Heinemann, London, 1990, p 356. By permission of Aitken Stone & Wylie. (34) Mirza Ruswa, *The Courtesan of Lucknow: Umrao Jan Ada*, Khwant Singh and M. A.

Husaini, trans, Hind Pocket Books, Delhi, pp 150–151. **WESTERN INDIA AND RAJAS-THAN:** (1) M.K. Gandhi, *Autobiography*, I. Raeside, ed, Penguin, Harmondsworth, 1985, pp 357, 386–387. (2) Lady Falkland, *Chow-chow: A Journal Kept in India, Egypt and Syria*, H.G. Rawlinson, ed, Scholartis Press, 1930, pp 160–162, 165. (3) Swami Kripananda, *Jnaneshwar's Gita*, SUNY Press, Albany, 1989, p 125. By permission of State University of New York Press. (4) M.A. Laird, ed, *Bishop Heber in Northern India: Selections from Heber's Journal*, Cambridge University Press, Cambridge, 1971, pp 305–307. (5) Louis Bromfield, *Night in Bombay*, Penguin, Harmondsworth, 1954, pp 57–61. By permission of the Estate of Louis Bromfield. (6) Salman Rushdie, *Midnight's Children*, Cape, London, 1981, pp 186–189. By permission of Random House. (7) Gieve Patel, 'From Bombay Central' in *Mirrored, Mirroring*, OUP, Madras, pp 3–4. By permission of Oxford University Press. (8) Firdaus Kanga, *Trying to Grow*, Bloomsbury, London, 1989, pp 18–19. By permission of A.P. Watt. (9) Rohinton Mistry, *Such a Long Journey*, Faber and Faber, London, 1991. By permission of Faber and Faber Ltd. (10) Nissim Ezekiel, 'Island' in *Collected Poems*, OUP, Delhi, 1989. By permission of Oxford University Press. (11) Shobha De, *Starry Nights*, Penguin, New Delhi, pp 36–37. Reproduced courtesy of Penguin Books India Ltd and the author. (12) Gangadhar Gadgil, *Shops that Bombay Hadn't Bargained For*, Popular Prakashan, Bombay, pp 50–51. Reproduced by permission of the author. (13) E.M. Forster, *The Hill of Devi*, Edwin Arnold, London, 1953, pp 49–52. By permission of The Society of Authors and Harcourt Brace and Company. (14) Manohar Malgonkar, *The Princes*, Orient, New Delhi, 1970, pp 28–29. By permission of the author. (15) Ashok Mahajan, *Goan Vignettes and Other Poems*, Oxford University Press, Delhi, 1986, pp 40–41. By permission of Oxford University Press. (16) Narsimharao Divetia, *Sabasralinga talava*, Ian Raeside, trans. (17) Arun Kolatkar, *Jejuri*, Peppercorn, London, 1978, p 28. (18) Narsi Mehta, *Hymns*, Ian Raeside, trans. (19) K.M. Munshi, *Gujarat and its Literature*, Bharatiya Vidya Bhavan, Bombay, 1954, p 244. (20) S.N. Pendse, *Wild Bapu of Garambi*, I Raeside, trans, Sahitya Akademi, New Delhi, 1969, pp 5–6 (slightly adapted). (21) Keshavsut, *South-west Wind*, 1898. I. Raeside, trans. (22) Gita Mehta, *A River Sutra*, Doubleday, New York, 1993, pp 7–9. By permission of Doubleday, a division of Bantam Doubleday Dell Publishing Group. (23) D.B. Mokashi, *Palkhi: An Indian Pilgrimage*, Philip C. Engblom, trans, SUNY Press, Albany, NY, 1987, pp 81–83. By permission of State University of New

York Press. (24) Namdev and Tukaram, *Hymns*. I. Raeside, trans. (25) Edwin Arnold, *India Revisited*, Trubner, London, 1886, pp 71–74. (26) H.G. Rawlinson, ed, *A Voyage to Surat in the Year 1689 by J. Ovington*, Oxford University Press, Oxford, 1989, pp 129–130. (27) John D. Smith, *The Visaladevarasa: A Restoration of the Text*, Cambridge University Press, 1976, pp 89–99. By permission of John D. Smith. (28) Padmanabha, *Kanhadade Prabandha*, Part I, vv 98, 103–116, I. Raeside, trans. (29) John D. Smith, *The Epic of Pabuji*, Cambridge University Press, Cambridge, 1991, pp 456–460. By permission of John D. Smith. **SOUTH INDIA:** (1) Palagumi Padmaraju, *Cyclone*, Indian Literature, Sahitya Akademi, Rabindra Bhavan, New Delhi, Vol XXIX, No 5, 1986. By permission of Sahitya Akademi. (2) Kedar Nath, *Return to India*, Cassells, London, 1988. (3) Eleanor Roosevelt, *India and the Awakening East*, Hutchinson, London 1954, pp 113–123. By permission of Lawrence Pollinger Ltd on behalf of the Estate of Eleanor Roosevelt. (4) Robert H. Elliot, *The Experiences of a Planter in the Jungles of Mysore*, Chapman and Hall, London, 1891. (5) Girish Karnad, *Naga-Mandala*, Oxford University Press, Delhi, 1990, pp 41–43. By permission of Oxford University Press. (6) A.K. Ramanujan, *Speaking of Siva*, Penguin, Harmondsworth, 1973, pp 116–117. By permission of Penguin Books Ltd. (7) K. Shivaram Karanath, *Chomas Drum*, U.R. Kalkur, Indian Book Company, New Delhi. (8) A.K. Ramanujam, 'Art and Life's Beauty', in Dhenaveera Kanavi and K. Raghavendra Rao, eds, *Modern Kannada Poetry*, K. Raghavendra Rao, trans, C.S. Kanavi, Dharwar, p 92. By permission of Karnatak University. (9) Kamala Das, *The Dance of the Eunuchs* in A.N. Dwivedi, *Indian Poetry in English: A Literary History and Anthology*, Arnold Heinemann (India), 1980. (10) Eluttachan, *Mahabharatam*, in K.M. George, trans, *A Survey of Malayalam Literature*, Asia Publishing House, 1968. (11) Thakali Sivasankara Pillai, *Chemmeen*, Narayana Menon, trans, Gollancz, London. By permission of Mark Paterson on behalf of the author. (12) N.V. Krishna Variyar, *Rats*, in K.M. George, trans, *A Survey of Malayalam Literature*, Asia Publishing House, 1968. (13) Alexander Frater, *Chasing the Monsoon*, Viking, London, 1990, pp 34–35. By permission of Penguin Books Ltd. (14) E.M. Forster, *A Passage to India*, Penguin, 1982, p 137. By permission of The Society of Authors. (15) R.K. Narayan, 'The Blind Dog, Fellow Feeling' in R. K. Narayan, *Malgudi Days*, Heinemann, 1977. By permission of Reed Consumer Books and Sheil Land Associates Ltd. (16) R.K. Narayan, *Malgudi Days*, Heinemann, 1977. By permission of

Reed Consumer Books and Sheil Land Associates Ltd. (17) R.K. Narayan, *Gods, Demons and Others*, Heinemann, 1965. By permisison of Reed Consumer Books and Shiel Land Associates Ltd. (18) Tolkappiyar, *Tokappiyam*, G.J. Holden, trans, Porulatikaram. (19) *Kuruntokai*, G.J. Holden, trans. (20) *Purananuru*, G.J. Holden, trans. (21) William Taylor, *Oriental History Manuscripts in the Tamil Language*, Vol 1. (22) J.B. Marr, trans, *The Eight Anthologies*, Institute of Asian Studies, Tiryvanmiyur, Madras. By permission of J.B. Marr. (23) Prince Ilanko Atikal, *Cilappatikaram*, Alain Danielou, trans, George Allen & Unwin, London, 1967. (24) Antal, *Tiruppavai*, verses 1,2, G.J. Holden, trans. (25) Subramania Bharati, *Mother Tamil*, P.S. Sundaram, *Poems of Subramania Bharati*, Vikas Publishing, Delhi/Jodhpur University Press, 1982. By permission of Vikas Publishing House, Pvt Ltd. (26) Mani, *Narakam in The Smile of Murugan*, K. Zvelebil, trans, Leiden, 1973. (27) Parancotimunivar, *Tiruvilaiyatarpuranam*, G.J. Holden, trans. (28) Putmaipittan, *Street Lamp*, in G.J. Holden, trans, *Putmaipittan Katikal*, Star, Madras, 1959. (29) Sundara Ramaswamy, *Window*, Ashokamitran, in Ka Naa Sumbramaniyam, ed, *Tamil Short Stories*, Vikas, New Delhi, 1980. By permission of Vikas Publishing House Pvt Ltd. (30) V.S. Naipal, *An Area of Darkness*, Andre Deutsch, 1964, p 217. By permission of Aitken, Stone and Wylie. **EASTERN INDIA AND BANGLADESH:** (1) Rozsa Hajnoczy, *Fire of Bengal*, Eva Wimmer and David Grant, trans, The University Press, Dhaka, 1993. By permission of the University Press. (2) Hasan Azizul Haq, 'Bhushaner Ekdin' in *Of Women, Outcastes, Peasants and Rebels. A Selection of Bengali Short Stories*, Kalpana Bardhan trans, University of California Press, 1990, pp 329–330. Copyright © The Regents of the University of California. By permission of University of California Press. (3) *Selected Poems of Shamsur Rahman: A Bilingual Edition*, Kaiser Haq, trans, Brac Prokashona, 1985, pp 20, 57. By permission of Kaiser Haq. (4) Syed Waliullah, *Tree Without Roots*, Qaisar Saeed, Anne-Marie Thibaud, Jeffrey Gibian and Malik Khayyam, Chatto and Windus, 1967, pp 127–129. By permission of Mark Patterson. (5) *Songs of the Bards of Bengal*, Deben Bhattacharya, trans, Grove, New York, 1969, pp 50–51. By permission of Grove Atlantic Inc. (6) Bibhutibhushan Banerji, *Pather Panchali*, T.W. Clark and Tarapada Mukherji, Allen and Unwin, London, 1968, pp 80–82. (7) Baru Chandidasa, *Singing the Glory of the Lord Krishna: The Srikrsnakirtana*, M.H. Klaiman, trans, Scholars Press, 1984, pp 204–205. By permission of Scholars Press. (8) *The Abbey of Bliss* (A Translation of

Bankimchandra Chatterjee's *Anandamath*), Nares, Chandra Sen-Gupta, Calcutta, 1907, pp 30–31. (9) Nirad C. Chaudhuri, *Thy Hand, Great Anarch! India: 1921–1952*, Chatto and Windus, 1987, pp 435–436. By permission of Random House. (10) Mahesweta Devi, 'Daini' in *Of Women, Outcastes, Peasants and Rebels. A Selection of Bengali Short Stories*, Kalpana Bardhan trans, University of California Press, 1990, pp 253–254. Copyright © The Regents of the University of California. By permission of University of California Press. (11) *Selected Poems of Nazrul Islam*, Kabir Chowdury, trans, Bangla Academy, Dhaka, pp 4–6. (12) Martin Kampchen, *Mit den Armen heute Leben: Erzahlungen und Erfahrungen aus Indien* (Living with the Poor Today: Tales and Experiences from India), William Radice, trans, Benno Verlag, 1991. (13) *In Praise of Krishna: Songs from the Bengali*, Edward C. Dimock and Denise Levertov, trans, University of Chicago Press, Chicago, IL, p 11. By permission of Doubleday, a division of Bantam Doubleday Dell Publishing Group Inc. (14) Bharatchandra Ray, *Vidya-Sundara* in *The Thief of Love: Bengali Tales from Court and Village*, Edward C. Dimock, trans, University of Chicago Press, Chicago, IL, 1963, pp 84–85. By permission of University of Chicago Press. (15) Rabindranath Tagore, *Selected Poems*, William Radice, trans, Penguin, Harmondsworth, 1985, pp 53–55. (16) Rabindranath Tagore, *Selected Short Stories*, William Radice, trans, Penguin, Harmondsworth, 1991, pp 213–214. (17) Rabindranath Tagore, *Selected Poems*, William Radice, trans, Penguin, Harmondsworth, 1985, pp 119–120. (18) Anon, *Hartley House, Calcutta*, Pluto, London/Winchester MA, 1989, pp 158–161. (19) Amit Chaudhuri, *A Strange and Sublime Address*, Heinemann, 1991, pp 207–209. By permission of William Heinemann Ltd and A.P. Watt Ltd. (20) Ksetra Gupta, *Kabi madhusudan o tar patrabali*, Premmay Majumdar, Calcutta, 1963, pp 146–147. (21) Henry Louis Vivian Derozio, *The Fakeer of Junghera: A Metrical Tale and Other Poems*, Samuel Smith, 1828, pp 63–65. (22) William Hickey, *Memoirs of William Hickey*, Peter Quenell, ed, pp 283–284. (23) Dominique Lapierre, *The City of Joy*, S.A. Pressinter, trans, Arrow, London, 1986, pp 255–256. By permission of Dominique Lapierre. (24) Begum Rokeya, *Rokeya-racanabali*, Bangla Academy, 1973, pp 580–582. (25) Debendranath Tagore, *The Autobiography of Debendranath Tagore*, Satyendranath Tagore and Indira Devi, Macmillan, London, 1914, pp 49–51. (26) Amitav Ghosh, *The Shadow Lines*, Bloomsbury, London, 1988, pp 152–153. By permission of Aitken, Stone & Wylie. (27) Bishop Reginald Heber, *Bishop Heber in Northern India: Selections from Heber's Journal*, M.A. Laird, ed, Cambridge University Press, 1971, pp 82–86. (28) Gopinath Mohanty, *Paraja*, Bikram K. Das, trans, Oxford University Press, 1987, pp 98–100. By permission of Oxford University Press. (29) Prafulla Mohanti, *My Village, My Life: Nanpur: A Portrait of an Indian Village*, Davis Poynter, 1973, pp 163–164. (30) Clinton B. Seely, *A Poet Apart: A Literary Biography of the Bengali Poet Jibanananda Das (1899–1954)*, University of Delaware Press, 1990, p 129. By the permission of Associated University Presses. (31) Katy Gardner, *Songs at the River's Edge: Stories from a Bangladeshi Village*, Virago, 1991, pp 153–154. By permission of Katy Gardner. **NEPAL:** (1) Lakshmiprasad Devkota, 'An essay', in *Lakshmi-Nibandha-Sangraha*, Michael Hutt, trans. (2) J.M. Marks, *Ayo Gurkha!*, Oxford University Press, pp 59–60. By permission of Oxford University Press. (3) H.W. Tilman, *Nepal Himalaya*, Cambridge University Press, 1951 (extract taken from *The Seven Mountain Travel Books, The Mountaineers*, Seattle, 1983, pp 874–875). (4) David L. Snellgrove, *Himalayan Pilgrimage*, Prajna Press, Boulder, CO, 1981, pp 1–2. (5) Lakshmiprasad Devota, 'Muna and Madan', in Michael Hutt, *Himalayan Voices: An Introduction to Modern Nepali Literature*, University of California Press, 1991, pp 49. (6) Han Suyin, *The Mountain is Young*, Triad Granada, 1973, pp 51–52. By permission of Han Suyin (7) Ved Mehta, *Walking the Indian Streets*, Penguin, London, 1975, p 93. Copyright 1971 by Ved Mehta from *Walking the Indian Streets* (first published by Penguin Books 1963) reprinted with the permission of Wylie, Aitken & Stone, Inc. (8) Shankar Lamichhane, 'The halfclosed eyes of the Buddha and the slowly setting sun', in Michael Hutt, *Himalayan Voices: An Introduction to Modern Nepali Literature*, University of California Press, 1991, pp 253, 256. (9) Ved Mehta, *Walking the Indian Streets*, Penguin, London, 1975, p 97. Copyright 1971 by Ved Mehta from *Walking the Indian Streets* (first published by Penguin Books 1963) reprinted with the permission of Wylie, Aitken & Stone, Inc. (10) Lekhnath Paudyal, 'Himalaya', in Michael Hutt, *Himalayan Voices: An Introduction to Modern Nepali Literature*, University of California Press, 1991, pp 253, 256. (11) Peter Matthieson, *The Snow Leopard*, Picador, London, 1980, pp 15–16, 23. By permission of the Harvill Press. (12) Bhupi Sherchan, 'Pokhara', *A Blind Man in a Revolving Chair* (in Nepali), Sajha Publications, Katmandu, 1969. Michael Hutt, trans. (13) Percy Brown, *Picturesque Nepal*, A&C Black, London, 1912, pp 46–47. (14) Peter Matthieson, *The Snow Leopard*, Picador, London, 1980, pp 195–196. By permission of the Harvill

Press. (15) Madhav Prasad Ghimire, 'Memories of Jagara' (in Nepali), first published in *Ruparekha* magazine, 1965, Michael Hutt, trans. **SRI LANKA:** (1) Yasmine Gooneratne, *Relative Merits*, Hurst, London, 1986, pp 122–123. By permission of C. Hurst & Co.(2) C. Kanesalinkam (S. Ganeshalingam), *Solidarity*, from *Adam International Review*, Nos 367–369, London, 1972. By permission of Adam International Review. (3) Anne Ranasinghe, 'In our lane' from *Against Eternity and Darkness*, Samanala, Colombo, 1985. (4) Punyakante Wijenaike, *A Way of Life*, Deepani, Lake House, Colombo, 1987, pp 7–8. (5) Evelyn F.C. Ludowyk, *Those Long Afternoons*, Lake House, Colombo, 1989, pp 30–31. By permission of Lake House Bookshop. (6) Leonard Woolf, *The Village in the Jungle*, Oxford University press, 1981, pp 3–4. By permisison of the Estate of the author and Chatto & Windus. (7) Philippus Baldaeus, *True and Exact Description of the Great Island of Ceylon*, Peter Brohier, trans, *Ceylon Historical Journal*, VIII (1958–59), pp 66–67. (8) Robert Knox, *An Historical Relation of Ceylon*, London, 1681 (reprinted Glasgow, 1911, Colombo, 1989). (9) Lakdasa Wikkramasinha, 'To My Friend Aldred' in D.C.R.A. Goonetilleke, *Modern Sri Lankan Poetry*, Delhi, 1987. (10) Ven Mahanama, *Mahavamsa*, W. Giger and Mabel H. Bode, trans, Government of Ceylon, 1950, pp 167–168. (11) Monica Ruwanpathirana, " Ranjini Obeyesekere, trans, in R. Obeyesekere and C. Fernando, *Anthology of Modern Writings from Sri Lanka*, University of Arizona Press, 1981. (12) J.S. Tissanayagam, 'Misunderstanding' in *Kaduwa I* (1983). Also in D.C.R.A. Goonetilleke, *Modern Sri Lankan Stories*, Delhi, 1986. (13) Suvimalee Gunaratna (later Karunaratne), *The Golden Oriole* in *Bili Pooja*, Hansa, Colombo, 1973. Also in Y. Gooneratne, *Stories from Srii Lanka*, Heinemann Asia, 1979 and D.C.R.A. Goonetilleke, *Modern Sri Lankan Stories*, Delhi, 1986. (14) Patrick Fernando, 'Boat Song', in D.C.R.A. Goonetilleke, *Modern Sri Lankan Poetry*, Delhi, 1987. (15) Joao Ribeiro, *Histroric Tragedy of the Island of Ceylon*, P.E. Pieris, 4 ed, Colombo, 1948, pp 51–52. (16) Ediriwira Sarachchandra, *Foam Upon the Stream* – A *Japanese Elegy*, Heinemann Asia, 1987, pp 129–130. By permission of Heinemann Asia. (17) Alagiyavanna, *Kusa Jatakaya*, T. Steele, Trubner, 1971, pp 74–77. (18) Gunasena Vithana, 'The prisoner', *Toronto South Asia Review*, 3, 2 1984, Cyril Perera, trans (19) Martin Wickramasinghe, *Viragaya, the Way of the Lotus*, Ashley Halpe, Colombo, 1985, pp 70–71. (20) Jinadasa Vijayatunga, *Grass for My Feet*, Arnold 1935, pp 55–57.

PICTURES: p 4 – courtesy of the BBC; p 33 – courtesy of the BBC; p 52 – from the cover of Harbans Singh, *Bhai Vir Singh*; p 88 – courtesy of Pan Books; p 90 – photograph by James Bidwell courtesy of Yvonne McFarlane; p 91 – from the cover of Charles Carrington, *Rudyard Kipling*, Macmillan; p 104 – courtesy of the Indian High Commission, London; p 112 – courtesy of Hyphen Films; p 114 – courtesy of Orion; p 145 – O.P Sharma, Modern School, New Delhi; p 148 – photograph by James Ivory courtesy John Murray; p 149 courtesy Picador; pp 150, 151 and 163 courtesy of the Nehru Centre, London; p 164 courtesy of the Indian High Commission, London; p 200 courtesy of OUP India; p 201 courtesy of Gangadhar Gadgil; p 202 – courtesy of King's College Library; p 205 – courtesy of the Nehru Centre, London; p 207 – courtesy of Faber & Faber; p 218 – courtesy of the Nehru Centre, London; p 257 – courtesy of the author; p 260 – courtesy of William Heinemann; p 273 – courtesy of Bloomsbury; p 275 – courtesy of William Raddice; p 278 and 279 – courtesy of the British Council, Dhaka; p 325 – courtesy of Prafulla Mohanti; p 327 – from the cover of Martin Kampchen, *Rabindranath Tagore and Germany*; pp 335, 338, 353 and 354 – courtesy of Michael Hutt; p 365 – from *Martin Wickramasinghe: The Sage of Koggala*; p 402 – from *Ediriwira Sarachchandra: Festschrift 1988*. Front cover and spine courtesy of the Indian High Commission, London. Back cover courtesy of King's College Library.

INDEX

This is an index of authors. **(E)** = *extract. Bold type =
biographical entry.*

Ackerley, J.R., 115, 128–129(E). **145**, 148

Aidga, Gopalakrishna, 228

Agarkar, Gopal Ganesh, 162, **198**

Aiyar, U.V. Swaminatha, **256**

Ajneya (Agyeya), 115, 138(E), **145**

Alagiyavanna, 363,376, 395(E), **399**

Ali, Ahmed, 115, 135(E), **145**

Amaru, 11

Anand, Mulk Raj, 53, 56, 58, 69–70(E), 87

Antal, 222, 248(E)

Apte, Hari Narayan, 162, **198**

Arnold, Sir Edwin, 166, 192–193(E), **198–199**

Arya Shura, 9, 11, 12, 25(E), **28**, 30

Asan, Kumaran, 226

Ashvaghosha, 8, **28**, 31

Atikal, Prince Ilanko, 229, 247(E)

Auden, W.H., 367, 372, 376

Badayuni, 125(E)

Baker, Samuel, 371, 374, 376

Baldaeus, Philippus, 366, 376, 384–385(E)

Ballabh, Ishwar, 336, **352**

Banarsidas, 115, 117–118(E), **145–146**

Bandyopadhyay, Manik, 277

Banerji, Bibhutibhushan, 271, 280, 287–288(E), **321**, 328

Bana, Banabhatta, 11–12, 18(E), 30, **28**

Battuta, Ibn, 360, 368, **366**

Basheer, Vaikom Muhammad, 227

Beg, Mirza Farhatullah, 134(E), **146**

Bhanubhakta, Acharya, 334–335, **352**

Bharati, Subramania, 226, 227, 228, 229, 248–250, **256**

Bharavi, 9, 12, **29**, 31, 32, 35

Bhartrihari, 9, 11, **29**

Bhasa, 9, **29**, 34

Bhatta, Motiram, 335, **352**

Bhatti, 9, 12, **29**, 35

Bhavabhuti, 12, 14(E), **29**, 32

Bhave, P.B., 165, **199**

Biharilal, 94, 107–108, 115, 139–140(E), **146**

Bilhana, 9, 11, **29**

Borges, Jorge Luis, 272

Bose, Buddhadev, 275, **280**

Bowles, Paul, 375

Broker, Gulabdas, 165, 166, **199**

Bromfield, Louis, 166, 172–173(E), **199**

Brown, Percy, 349–350(E), **352**

Bullhe Shah, 48, 57, 74(E), **87**

Burton, Sir Richard, 49, 56, 83–84(E), **87**

Caldwell, Bishop Robert, 225, **256**

Carey, William, 269

Chandidas, Baru, 267, 280, 288–289(E), **321**

Chakrabati, Mukundaram, 267

Chatterjee, Bankimchandra, 271, 280, **322**

Chatterjee, Upamanyu, xvii

Chaudhuri, Amit, 280, 305–306(E), **322**

Chaudhuri, Nirad C., xvii, 268, 271, 272, 280, 291(E), 321, **322**

Chekhov, Anton, 367, 372, **399**

Chellappa, C.S., **256**, 259

Chitre, Dilip Purushottam, 165, 166, **199**

Chitsvami, 107, 141–142(E), **146**

Coburn, Broughton, 339, 340, **352**, 355

Dalpatram Dahyabhai, 162, **199**, 201, 208

Dandin, 11, 15(E), 30

Das, Jibanananda, 271, 277, 281, 302, 319–320(E), **322**

Das, Kamala, 228, 229, 237, **257**
Das, Kasiram, 267
Dassa, Sarala, 267
Datta, Michael Madhusudan, 267, 268, 271, 277, 306–307, **323**
De, Shoba, 166, 178–179(E), **199**
Derozio, Henry Louis Vincent, 269, 280, 307, **323**
Desai, Anita, 115, 131(E), **146**
Desai, Mahadev, **199**
Dev, Kesava, 226, **257**
Devi, Mahasweta, 271, 280, 292–293(E), **323**, 325
Devkota, Lakshmiprasad, 329, 336, 337, 341(E), 344(E), **352**, 355
Dharmasena, 363
Dhumaketu, 163, **200**
Narsimharao B., 184(E), **200**
Dixit, Mani, **352**
Dyson, Ketaki Kushari, 273, **323**

Eknath, 160, 161, 166, **200**
Elliot, Robert H., 229, 233(E)
Eluttaccan, 221, 224, 229, 237–238(E), **257**
Ezekiel, Nissim, ix, xvii, xviii, 166, 177–178 (E), **200**

Fa-Hsien, 360, 366, 368, 376
Faiz, Faiz Ahmad, 54, 57, 62(E), 77(E), **87–88**
Falkland, Viscountess, 166, 169–170(E), **200–201**
Farid, Khwaja Ghulam, 49, 58, 70–71(E), **88**
Farid, Shaikh, 46, 78–79(E), **88**
Farrell, J.G., 115, 136–137(E), **147**, 152
Fernando, Patrick, 364, 376, 392(E)
Forbes, Alexander Kinloch, 162, 199, **201**
Forster, E.M., xvii, 114, 115, 127–128(E), **147**, 150, 158–159, 165, 166, 181(E), **201**, 229, 241–242(E), **257**
Frater, Alexander, 229, 240–241(E), **257**

Gadgil, Gangadhar, 165, 166, 179–180(E), **201**
Gadkari, R.G., **202**
Galsworthy, John, 374
Gandhi, Mohandas Karamchand (Mahatma), 102, 103, 111, 130–131, 149, 163–165, 166, 168–169(E), **202–203**, 226, 291–292, 328

Ganeshalingham, S., 365
Gardner, Katy, 280, 320–321(E)
Gautam, D.C., 339, **340**
Ghalib, Mirza Asadullah Khan, 110, 116, 133(E), **147**
Ghimire, Madhav Prasad, 351(E), **352**
Ghosh, Abhitava, 271
Ghosh, Amitav, xvii, 280, 314–315(E), **323**
Giri, Banira, 337, 340, **353**
Godden, Margaret Rumer, 53, 57, 65–66(E), **88**
Gokhale, Aravind, 165, 166, **203**
Gooneratne, Yasmine, 364, 376, 378–380(E), **400**
Goonetileke, H.A. Ian, 372, 373, 376, 399, 400
Goonetillike, D.C.R.A., 364, 376
Goonewardene, 367
Gunaratna, Suvimalee, 367, 376, 391–392(E)
Gupta, Ksetra, 280
Gupta, Sunetra, **324**

Habba Khotun, 47, 64(E), **89**
Haeckel, Ernst, 358, 367, 371, 376
Han Suyin, 339, 340, 345(E), **353**, 355
Hasham Shah, 48, 57, 82–83(E), **89**
Hajnoczy, Rozsa, 280, 282–283(E), **324**
Heber, Reginald, 166, 171–172(E), **203–204**, 269, 281, 315–316(E), **324**, 369, 377
Hennessy, D.J.G., 367, 377
Hesse, Herman, 374
Hickey, William, 269, 281, 308–310(E), **324**
'Hope, Laurence', 50, 57, 65(E), **89**
Huq, Hasan Azizul, 277, 281, 283–284(E), **324**

Iqbal, Sir Muhammad, 50, 57, 58, 63–64(E), 79(E), **88**
Indicopleustes, Cosmas, 366
Islam, Kasi Nazrul, 268, 277, 278, 281, 293–294(E), **325**
Isherwood, Christopher, 367

Jahanara, Princess, 118(E), **148**
Jahangir, 46, 56, 66–67(E), **89**
Janakiraman, T., **258**
Jasimuddin, 277
Jayadeva, 12, 13, 20(E), 30, **31**, 267
Jhabvala, Ruth Prawer, 115, 137–138(E),

147, **148–149**
Jnandev, 160, 170–171(E), **204**, 206, 207
Joshi, Suresh H., 165, **204**
Joshi, Umashankar J., 165, **204**

Kainla, Bairagi, 336, **354**
Kalidasa, 1, 8, 10–11, 13, 15(E), 19(E), 26(E), 29, **31**, 34, 35, 362
Kandal, Madhava, 267
Kampchen, Martin, 273, 281, 295, **325**
Kanesalingam, C. (S. Ganeshalingham), 377, 380–381(E)
Kanga, Firdaus, 166, 176(E), **204**
Karanath, K. Shivarama, 229, 235(E), **258**
Karandikar, G.V., 165, 166, **204**
Karnad, Girish, 217, 229, 234, **258**
Kaviraj, Govindadas, 296–297
Keshavsut, 162, 188–189(E), **205**
Keyes, Frances Parkinson, 367
Khandekar, V.S., 166, **205**, 209
Khanna, Balraj, 55, 57, 71–72(E), **89**
Khatak, Khushhal Khan, 47–48, 57, 60(E), **89**
Kipling, Rudyard, xvii, 50–51, 57, 61(E), 74–75(E), **90**
Knox, Robert, 360, 366, 369, 375, 377, 385–386(E)
Koirala, Bishweshwar Prasad, 336, **354**
Koirala, Mohan, 336, **354**
Koirala, Shankar, 338–339, 340
Kolatkar, Arun, 154, 165, 166, 185(E), **206**
Krishnadevaraya, 220, 223, **258**
Krishnamurthi, R., 225, **258**
Krittibas, 267

Lambrick, Hugh Trevor, 57, 85–86(E), **90**
Lamichhane, Shankar, 346–347(E), **354**
Lapierre, Dominique, 271–272, 281, 310–311(E), 322
Latif, Shah Abdul, 48, 58, **92**
Lawrence, D.H., 367, 373, **400**
Lear, Edward, 367, 371, 372, 374, 375, **400**
Lebbe, M.C. Siddi, 366
Lewis, Frederick, 367, 377
Ludowyk, E.F.C., 367, 372, 377, 382–383(E)

Macaulay, Rose, 369, 374, 377
Madgulkar, V.D., 165, 166, **206**

Magha, 9, 12, 31, **32**, 35
Mahadeviyakka, 223, **258**
Mahajan, Ashok, 167, 182–183(E)
Mahanama, Ven, 377, 388(E)
Mahipati, 161, **206**
Mainali, Guru Prasad, 336, **354**
Malgonkar, Manohar, 166–167, 181–182(E), **206**
Mani, C., 214, 229, 250(E), **259**
Manikkavacakar, 222
Manto, Saadat Hasan, 54, 57, 81–82(E)
Mardhekar, B.S., 165, **206**
Marks, J.R., 339, 340, 342(E), 352, **354**
Matthieson, Peter, 339, 340, 348(E), 350(E), **355**, 356
Mazhar ul Islam, 55, 57, 72–73(E), **92**
Mehrotra, A.K., 116, 120–121(E), **149**
Mehta, Gita, 167, 189–190(E), **206–207**
Mehta, Ved, 54, 57, 76–77(E), **92**, 340, 345–346(E), 347(E), **355**
Menon, Chandu, 226, **259**
Menon, Vallattol Narayana, **259**
Merton, Thomas, 374
Milton, John, 375
Mirabai, 160, 166, **207**
Mistry, Rohinton, 167, 177–178(E), **207**
Mohanti, Prafulla, 281, 317–318(E), **325**
Mohanty, Gopinath, 281, 316–317(E), **325**
Mokashi, D.B., 167, 190(E), **207**
Moraes, Dom, 345, 347, 371, 374
Munshi, Kanaiyalal M., 163, 167, **207–208**

Nadim, Dinna Nath, 54, 68–69(E), **92**
Naipaul, V.S., 116, 143(E), 148, **149**, 229, 255(E)
Nalha, Narapati, 195–196(E)
Nambudiri, Cherusseri, 224
Namdev, 160, 191–192(E), **208**
Nanddas, 107
Nannak, 47, 75–76(E), 92
Narayan, R.K., xvii, 165, 212, 242(E), 243(E), 243–244 (244 (E), **259**, 229
Narmada, 162, **208**
Narsi Mehta, 160, 161, 167, 186(E), **208**, 209
Nasrin, Taslima, 281, **325**
Nath, Kedar, 229, 231(E), **259**
Navalar, Arumuga, 366
Nayak, Raghunatha, 224
Nehru, Jawaharlal, xvii, 103, 104, 111, 116, 130–131(E), **149**

Neruda, Pablo, 367, 372, 374, **400**
Newby, Eric, 116, 121–122(E), **149**, 152
Nichols, Beverley, 113
Nirala, 116, 119–120(E), **149–150**
Nur Jahan, 76(E), **92**

Ondaatje, Michael, 367, 377
Ovington, John, 167, 194(E), **208**

Padmanabh, 167, 196–197(E), **208**
Padmaraju, Palagummi, 227, 229, 230(E), **259**
Pampa, 222
Panini, 2, 3
Parancotimunivar, 251(E)
Parijat, 337, 339, 340, 352, **355**
Patel, Gieve, 167, 175–176(E), **208–209**
Patel, Pannalal, 165, **209**
Paudyal, Lekhnath, 335, 347–348(E), **355–356**
Pendse, S.N., 165, 167, 187–188, **209**
Phadke, N.S., **209**
Pichamurti, 228
Pillai, C.W. Damodaram, 366
Pillai, Samuel Vetanayakam, 225, **261**
Pillai, Tamotaran, **261**
Pillai, Thakali Sivasankara, 227, 229, 238(E), **261**
Pliny, 366
Polo, Marco, 214, 360, 366
Ponna, 222
Premananda, 161, 187(E), 208, **209**
Premchand, 111, 116, 141(E), 147, **150**
Proctor, Raja, 367
Ptolemy, 154, 366
Purchas, Samuel, 116, 123–124(E), **150–151**
Putumaippittan, 227, 228, 229, 252–253(E), **261**

Rafat, Taufiq, 54, 57, 33(E), **92**
Rahman, Shamsur, 279, 281, 284–285(E), **326**
Rahula, Sri, **400–401**
Rai, Indra Bahadur, 336, **356**
Ramanujan, A.K., 229, 236(E), **261**
Ramaswamy, Sundara, 253–254(E)
Rana, Diamond Shamsher, 339, 340, **356**, 357
Rana, Greta, **356**, 357
Ranasinghe, Anne, 364, 377, 381, **401**
Ranna, 222

Rao, Gurazada Appa, **261**
Ravidas, 123(E), **151**
Ray, Bharatchandra, 281, 297–298(E), **326**
Ray, Satyajit, 263, 271, 276, 281, **326**
Ray, Sukumar, 281, **326**
Renu, P.N., 112, 116, 124–125(E), **151**, 152
Reynolds, G.W.M., 198
Ribeiro, Joao, 366, 377, 393(E)
Richardson, Captain D.L., 269
Rimal, Gopalprasad, 336, **356**
Roberts, Lord of Kandahar, 116, 142(E), 147, **151**
Rokeya, Begum, 277, 281, 311–312(E), **326–327**
Roosevelt, Eleanor, 229, 232(E)
Rushdie, Salman, 55, 167, 173–174(E), **209**
Rusva, Muhammad Hadi, 116, 144–145(E), **151**
Ruwanpathirana, Monica, 365, 377, 389(E)

Sahir Ludhianvi, Abdul Haye, 115, 118–119(E), **151**
Sama, Balakrishna, 335–336, 340, **356**
Sarachchandra, Edirivira, 364, 367, 374, 377, 394, 399, **401**, 402
Satyanarayana, Vishvanatha, 227
Scott, Paul, xvii, 37, 58, 86–87(E), **92**
Senapati, Phakirmohan, 276
Seth, Vikram, xvii, 114, 115, 116, 126–127(E), **151–152**
Shah, Chadani, 339, **340**
Sharma, Ramachandra, 228
Sherchan, Bhupi, 336, 349(E), **356**
Shridhar, 161
Shudraka, 29, 34
Shukla, Shrilal, 116, 140(E), 151, **152**
Shriharsha, 9, 12
Shrikantaiah, B.M., 225
de Silva, John, 364
Sijzi, Amir Hasan, 78(E), **92**
Singh, Khushwant, 54, 58, 28(E), **89**, 129–130(E), 116, 146, **152**, 165
Sitwell, Osbert, 367, 372, **401**
Sivakoti, 222
Sleeman, W.H., 116, 122–123(E), 146–147, **152**
Snellgrove, David Llewellyn, 339, 340, 343–344(E), 353, **356**
Spittel, R.L., 367, 377

Sriharsha, 223
Srinatha, 223
Stephens, Tomas, 209–210
Still, John, 367, 377
Strabo, 366
Subandhu, 11
Suraweera, A.V., 364, 377
Suri, Chinnaya, 224

Tagore, Debendranath, 270, 274, 281, 313(E), **328**
Tagore, Rabindranath, 263, 266, 270, 271, 272–276, 277, 281, 282, 298–300(E), 300–301(E), 302–303(E), 322, 324, **328**
Taylor, William, 229, 245–246
Tendulkar, Vijay, 165, **210**
Tennent, Sir J.E., 367, 371, 372, 377
Tilak, Bal Gangadhar (Lokamanya), 198, **210**
Tilman, Harold William, 339, 340, 342–343(E), 355, **356**
Timmana, 223
Tiruvalluvar, 222
Tissanayagam, J.S., 365, 377, 390–391(E)
Tod, Lieut Col James, 167, **210**
Tolkappiyar, 212, 244, **262**
Tripathi, Govardhanram, 162, **210**
Tukaram, 160, 161, 167, 191–192(E), 206, **210–211**
Tulsidas (Tulsi Das), 107, 116, 136(E), 150, **152–153**
Twain, Mark, 367, 372, **401**
Tyagaraja, **262**

Vallathol, 226
Valmiki, 5–8, 12, 27(E), 31, **35**
Varis Shah, 48, 73(E), **93**
Variyar, N.V. Krishna, 227, 229, 239–240(E)
Varkey, Ponkunnam, 227
Varma, Mahadevi, 116, 121(E), **153**
Vasudevan Nair, M.T., 227
Vattave, **401–402**
Vidyakara, 12
Vijayatunga, Jinadasa, 367, 372, 378, 398(E), **402–403**
Vir Singh, 52, 58, 62–63(E), **93**
Vishakhadatta, 13(E), 34
Vithana, Gunasena, 365, 378, 396(E)
Vyathit, Kedar Man, **356**

Wajib Ali Shah 'Akhtar', **153**
Waliullah, Syed, 277, 282, 285–286(E), **328**
Walpole, Horace, 375
Waugh, Evelyn, 367
Wickramasinghe, Martin, 364, 365, 367, 373, 378, 397–398(E), 400, **403**
Wijenaike, Punyakante, 367, 378, 381–382(E)
Wikkramasinha, Lakdasa, 365, 378, 386–387(E)
Wilcox, Ella Wheeler, 367
Wolpert, Stanley, 116, 132(E), 149
Woolf, Leonard, 367, 372, 373, 378, 383–384(E), **403**
Woolf, Virginia, 403

Zameenzad, Adam, 55, 58, 84(E), **93**